η_2	Number of unique operands
η	Vocabulary metric ($\eta = \eta_1 + \eta_2$)
n	Nodes
N_1	Total number of operators
N_2	Total number of operands
N	Program size metric ($N = N_1 + N_2$)
NL	Nesting level
$NWSC$	Normalized weighted score
O	Observation
ω	Standard deviation
P	Number of programmers on a team
$\bar{P}$	Average number of programmers on a team
(P, R)	Segment-global usage pair
(P, R, Q)	Valid data binding triple
$PRED(l)$	Prediction at Level l
r	Pearson correlation coefficient
r_s	Spearman rank correlation coefficient
r^2	Coefficient of determination
R	Release, Random, Reachability
RE	Relative error
$\overline{RE}$	Mean relative error
ρ	Population
RMS	Root mean square error
$\overline{RMS}$	Relative root mean square error
S	Program size in thousands of lines of code (KLOC)
S_c	Composite measure
S_n	Newly-written code
S_u	Re-used code
S_S	Program size in lines of code (LOC)
$\overline{SE}$	Mean Squared Error
SP	Span of statements between successive variable references
t	Test
T	Time for development
$\hat{T}$	Predicted time for development
T_p	Physical module model
t_D	Age of the system in days
TSC	Total score
$TWSC$	Total weighted score
$v(G)$	Cyclomatic number
V	Volume metric
V^*	Potential volume
$\hat{V}$	Estimated volume
$VARS$	Number of unique program variables
X	eXposure
x	Independent variable
y	Dependent variable

SOFTWARE ENGINEERING METRICS AND MODELS

Benjamin/Cummings Series in Software Engineering

Booch, *Software Engineering with Ada* (Revised Printing 1984)

Booch, *Software Components with Ada* (1988)

Conte et al, *Software Engineering Metrics and Models* (1986)

DeMillo et al, *Software Testing and Evaluation: A Report* (1987)

Other Titles of Interest

Kelley/Pohl, *A Book on C*

Savitch, *An Introduction to the Art and Science of Programming:*
Turbo Pascal Edition

Sobell, *A Practical Guide to UNIX*

Sobell, *A Practical Guide to UNIX System V*

Berger, *Computer Graphics with Pascal*

Helman/Veroff, *Intermediate Problem Solving and Data Structures:*
Walls and Mirrors

Skvarcius/Robinson, *Discrete Mathematics with Computer Science Applications*

Kerschberg, *Expert Database Systems: Proceedings*
From the First International Workshop

SOFTWARE ENGINEERING METRICS AND MODELS

S.D. Conte

H.E. Dunsmore
Purdue University

V.Y. Shen
Microelectronics and Computer Technology Corporation

The Benjamin/Cummings Publishing Company, Inc.
Menlo Park, California • Reading, Massachusetts • Don Mills,
Ontario • Wokingham, U.K. • Amsterdam • Sydney • Singapore •
Tokyo • Mexico City • Bogota • Santiago • San Juan

Sponsoring Editor: Alan Apt

Production Editor: Mary Picklum

Copy Editor: Lorraine Aochi

Cover and Consulting Designer: Gary Head

Composition: Unicomp

The basic text of this book was designed using the Modular Design System, as developed by Wendy Earl and Design Office Bruce Kortebein.

Library of Congress Cataloging-in Publication Data

Conte, Samuel Daniel
Software engineering metrics and models.
Bibliography: p. 366
Includes index.
1. Computer software—Development. I. Dunsmore, H.E.
II. Shen, V.Y. III. Title.
QA76.76.D47C66 1986   005.1   85-26856
ISBN 0−8053−2162−4
BCDEFGHIJ−HA−8 9876

The Benjamin/Cummings Publishing Company, Inc.
2727 Sand Hill Road
Menlo Park, California 94025

Foreword

If you ask an academic what Software Engineering is, you will soon find out that it is a branch of Computer Sciences — a large dose of programming methodology, specification languages, and verification techniques. Some academics wish that reliability theory applied to software were also included. Some say that Software Engineering is simply the practice of the engineering of software. But, differences between researchers and practitioners are more profound. Their two camps really do not talk much to each other. Perhaps this is due to mutual arrogance or mistrust, but I think the real reason is technical. The experimental component in software engineering as it is practiced today is entirely missing.

Experiments traditionally play an important role in engineering. For instance, experimentation generates facts about raw ideas as they come from the research community in the form of technical reports or papers. Based on experimental evidence, some of the ideas become accepted as candidates for future products, while many are rejected either completely or just for further modifications. This is all right, because in most engineering disciplines today there are many more ideas than can be converted to useful products.

What experimentation could do for software engineering is, first of all, to offer the means to demonstrate the value of research results on close-to-full-scale models. Secondly, experimental activities could pull together into the same team academics and industry personnel to work on the same experimental object. By this they would learn about each other's problems and gradually start speaking the same language. It is doubtful that without laboratories accommodating experimentation the two camps will ever work together.

However, experimentation needs a language of its own - *metrics*. In the physical sciences most observables are measured and results are presented in agreed-upon units. This is not yet the case in software and there is a lot to be done at least to approach the precision with which alternate ideas can be quantitatively compared as in engineering. Consider the complexity of modifying software. It would greatly improve the quality of a large scale program if we could predict the impact of program structure upon the ease of altering and of enhancing the program.

For the last several years there have been many promising efforts related to the quantification of program properties and of the programming process. The time has become ripe to collect in a volume the surprisingly-large variety of approaches to measure software. Professors Conte, Dunsmore, and Shen, grabbing this opportunity, have done a remarkable job. Their book is almost an encyclopedia of what is known today about measurements and experimentation in the young field of software engineering. Although academics themselves, the authors have taken special care with the practical aspects of the approaches presented, so as to end up with a reference book useful not only for their fellow researchers, but also for the serious practicing software engineer. I can foresee the widespread use of this volume as a textbook as well as a handbook for a long time to come. In particular, I hope it will further promote experimental methodology in software engineering.

L.A. Belady

Microelectronics and Computer
Technology Corporation
Austin, Texas November, 1985.

Preface

The growing cost of software has focused the attention of the computing community as never before on the software development process. This cost is growing both in absolute terms and as a percentage of the total data processing budget. The techniques of software engineering have been introduced in an attempt to counteract these cost trends. As a discipline, engineering has always relied heavily on metrics, measurement, and models to help it arrive at quantitative assessments of the cost and quality of products. However, until recently, computer software has been perceived to be impervious to these engineering approaches, with software development viewed more as an art than a science. Cost overruns, project delays, and poor reliability, which have characterized software (especially large-scale software), have in the past been accepted as the norm.

There is a growing realization among managers at all levels that we must adopt a disciplined approach to software development. Recent research and conferences on such topics as software configuration management, structural design, structured programming, testing strategies, and software metrics have all served to focus attention on the need for discipline in software development and for the quantification of software attributes. This quantification rests heavily on a better understanding of the factors that affect software production and on our ability to measure these factors. Thus, we are inevitably led to a need to develop *models* of the software development process so that we can acquire a deeper understanding of these processes, to *measure* software attributes so that we can quantify software, and to develop *metrics* that can be used to compare and predict software performance.

The need for metrics in software development was given added impetus in a recently published book, *Software Metrics: An Analysis and Evaluation* (Perlis, Sayward, and Shaw, eds.. Cambridge, MA: MIT Press, 1981), commissioned by the Office of Naval Research. According to the editors of this book, the central issues in software metrics revolve around the question, "Is it possible to identify or define indices of merit that can support quantitative comparisons and evaluations of software and of the processes associated with its design, development, use, maintenance, and evolution?" The answer to this question by experts is apparently *yes*, as the use of measurement technology to control software development activities has been identified as one of the seven task areas in the Department of Defense's Program on Software Technology for Adaptable, Reliable Systems (STARS).

We believe that the development of adequate measures of both the software itself and the software development process is essential to the production of cost-effective, timely, and reliable software. We believe that the proper development and use of software metrics will require both a concentrated effort on research, and an expanded educational effort to disseminate knowledge about the role and use of metrics. This book is an attempt to meet both of these objectives. It presents in unified form what is currently known about software metrics, with recommendations about directions for future research. It also discusses how currently known metrics can be useful to managers, analysts, and programmers. We believe it extremely important that students of computer science be made aware of the important contributions that a study of software metrics and models can make to the proper development of software.

It is important that we delimit the scope of the *software metrics* which are presented and discussed in this book. There are a number of metrics of interest to software engineers and managers related to the performance and storage requirements of computer software. However, we have chosen not to discuss them in this book since there is already a well-established body of knowledge on these metrics in the public domain.[1]

This book is intended to be used by both practitioners and students who are or who expect to be involved in managing or producing software. It is our firm belief that software engineering in general and software metrics in particular should be a part of the curriculum of all computer science programs.

As a text, this book is suitable for graduate students in computer science or in management information systems. It assumes that students have had a reasonable exposure to programming in several languages, which includes at least one major project, and have had at least one introductory course in statistics. Each chapter contains several suggested exercises or projects. Many of the exercises will require the use of a statistical package such as SPSS for data analysis.

As a reference, this book is suitable for all programmers, designers and project managers. Specific metrics for various life-cycle functions are reviewed, methodologies for applying these metrics to a local environment are presented, and specific suggestions are made about how these metrics can be used.

Our goal is that, through this book, many readers will be introduced to the world of software metrics and models. We also believe that this material will

---

1. See, for example, a description of metrics related to performance, queueing models, and memory usage in E. D. Lazowska, J. Zahorjan, G. S. Graham, and K. C. Sevcik, *Quantitative System Performance*. Prentice-Hall, Inc., Englewood Cliffs, NJ (1984).

serve as an impetus to researchers in software engineering and software developers to derive new metrics and models, and to gather data to help confirm the utility of new and existing metrics and models. Our ultimate goal is that our knowledge will be expanded so that we are better able to understand, estimate the cost of, and control the software development process.

Acknowledgments

Writing a book of this type is a long, arduous endeavor. It involves collecting and evaluating a good deal of information even before the first word is put on paper. We are indebted to a large number of people who helped to encourage and nurture this book from its inception through to the completed work you see in front of you. At the risk of overlooking some very valuable contributions, we attempt below to thank many of those who have helped us.

Many of our Ph.D. students have contributed significantly to the body of information contained herein and are now involved in their own successful careers: Steve Thebaut (University of Florida), Andrew Wang (Bell Laboratories), Scott Woodfield (Brigham Young University), and Jim Yu (Bell Laboratories). The computer-generated figures in this book were produced by APL functions originally designed by Steve Thebaut. A number of other graduate and undergraduate students have helped us including Carl Burch, Dennis Cok, Curtis Holmes, Brian Nejmeh, Vickie Owens, Mark Pasch, Prudence Zacarias, and Delores Zage.

Many of our fellow faculty at Purdue University have provided valuable insights and suggestions. Particularly, we want to recognize the ideas and criticisms of Wayne Zage (Department of Computer Science) and Richard Schweikert (Department of Psychology).

From outside Purdue University has come valuable access to data and ideas. Specifically, we thank Les Belady (MCC), Barry Boehm (TRW), Bill Curtis (MCC), Ken Christensen (IBM), Steve Davis (AIRMICS), Lorri Paulsen (IBM), and Stu Zweben (Ohio State).

Research funds for our work have been very helpful in allowing us to investigate the topics discussed in this book. Such support has come to us from the National Science Foundation (NSF), the IBM Corporation, the U.S. Army Institute for Research in Management Information and Computer Science (AIRMICS), AT&T Information Systems, the Purdue University Department of Computer Science, and the Purdue University Computing Center.

We are deeply indebted to Miss Julie Hanover, who laboriously entered much of the original text that has become this book and who made voluminous changes to bring this project to its conclusion. Julie also hand-constructed many of the figures that were not computer-generated.

We thank all those *not* named above: colleagues, researchers, managers, and students who have made direct or indirect contributions to our research and to the research area of Software Engineering Metrics and Models.

A special word of thanks to our wives Peggy, Susan, and Margaret, and to our families who have endured our time commitment to this book as well as to this area of research.

This book is dedicated to the memory of the late Professor Maurice Halstead. He developed the set of software metrics known as "Software Science" metrics and started many of us thinking about the need and use for such measurement devices. He was a friend and colleague whose presence is deeply missed.

S.D. Conte, H.E. Dunsmore, V.Y. Shen

November, 1985

Contents

4 Small Scale Experiments, Micro-models of Effort, and Programming Techniques 183

The Role of Metrics and Models in Software Development

1

Some programs are elegant, some are exquisite, some are sparkling. My claim is that it is possible to write grand *programs,* noble *programs, truly* magnificent *ones!*

> Donald Knuth, 1974 Turing Award Lecture, *Communications of the ACM* (17, 12), December 1974, p. 670.

1.1 Introduction

The promises of the computer revolution, which began in the 1950s, are coming to fruition at an accelerating pace. Those promises are being fueled primarily by a dynamic hardware technology, which seems capable of delivering computers with increasingly attractive price performance characteristics.

At one extreme, we have home and business micro-computers which open up vast new application domains, since they make economically feasible the automation of routine human functions. At the other extreme, we have new supercomputers that now make it possible for us to solve problems once considered too difficult or too costly even to attempt.

The full realization of the potential of computers, however, depends critically on our ability to produce reliable software at a reasonable cost. Despite the claims of being able to produce "elegant," "exquisite," or "truly magnificent" programs by software experts, there is great national concern that software technology lags so far behind hardware technology that this potential will never be fully realized, and that we as a country could lose our technological lead in computers to other nations. This concern has been labeled by some as a "software crisis."

Numerous reports document the observation that, while the cost of hardware to perform a given function continues to decrease dramatically, the cost of software required for that function has continued to increase.[1] Barry Boehm, a leading software expert, asserted more than 10 years ago that, in the military applications area, the cost of software was expected to reach about 80% of the total computer systems budget by the year 1985 [BOEH73]. His assertion now

---

1. Note that the *cost* of software referred to in this book is the cost of constructing and maintaining software. This is not necessarily the cost to the consumer, which depends upon market factors.

seems valid [BOEH83a]. Furthermore, it appears that up to 60% of the total software budget for all organizations using computers is being devoted to maintenance. The inexorable rise in the cost of software is due to several factors including:

- A shortage of computer specialists and an attendant increase in the salaries of these specialists. Our universities seem unable to meet the increasing demand for computer specialists, which is estimated to be growing at a rate of 12% per year [MART83]. Estimates of the current shortage in software personnel exceed 100,000 [BOEH83b]. In other areas (e.g., teachers) shortages have been short-lived, followed by a glut on the market. There is no indication that the computer personnel shortage is easing or even leveling off.

- The very low rate of gain in productivity. One study [MART83] indicates that programming productivity gains over the past 10 years have averaged less than 4% annually. The programming process has resisted automation and remains highly labor-intensive.

- The demand for more reliable, easier-to-use and more humanely engineered software. (The popular term is *user friendly* software). In society at large, this demand is dictated by the increased use of computers by unsophisticated users. In the military, the demand comes from the increasingly complex weapon systems, which depend critically on so-called embedded (i.e., mission critical) computer systems.

- The critical nature of software in all information-based systems. Hardware systems are usually delivered first, while the software needed to make them function properly comes later. This results in computer systems that cannot be operational until much later than planned and at usually a greater cost.

In addition to the higher cost of software, schedule slippage is the rule rather than the exception. Software managers appear unable to predict accurately how long it will take to develop software and how to control the software development process in order to assure timely delivery. Once a project falls behind schedule, recovery becomes difficult because of the sequential nature of the development process. The time-honored technique of trying to recover by adding more manpower[2] only seems to make things worse [BROO75]. And, of course, delays inevitably add to the cost of the delivered product.

Of increasing concern, too, is the recognition that maintenance of software is absorbing a growing fraction of the software budget. Maintenance is seldom

---

2. Throughout this book, whenever we use an ostensibly sex-identifying term such as *manpower* or *man-hours* we mean it as a generic term. We are aware that much of the manpower and man-hours in software development are being expended by female analysts and programmers. In fact, the software industry has been quicker to break down sex barriers than almost any other field.

planned properly by software managers. The word *maintenance,* narrowly interpreted, implies the effort required to eliminate post-delivery errors. In its broadest sense, however, maintenance is used to describe any post-delivery changes that are made in software to enhance its abilities including, for example, correcting defects, improving run-time efficiency, adding new features, and even documenting software [GREM84]. In general, software is not developed for ease of maintenance, and the situation is further exacerbated by the tendency of some managers to assign their least-experienced personnel to this function.

There is now a growing recognition that managers must focus on the entire software development process from requirements through maintenance in order to control the spiraling cost of software. We contend that the proper use of *software metrics, measurement, and models* is essential in the successful management of software development and maintenance. Generally, software *metrics* are used to characterize the essential features of software quantitatively, so that classification, comparison, and mathematical analysis can be applied. After a number of useful metrics is identified, it is then important to *measure* software in an algorithmic and objective fashion, so that the values of the selected metrics are consistent among different software products, and are independent of the measurer. In order to control the software development and maintenance processes, it is important to *model*[3] certain interesting factors (metrics), such as effort and defects, based on other metrics that are available. Appropriate management decisions can be made to influence these factors so that management goals can be met. In other words, the proper use of software metrics, measurement, and models has the potential of allowing us to recognize the development of "truly magnificent" software *objectively,* and to estimate the added cost of producing such software (or the reduced cost in maintaining the same) *accurately.*

1.2 The Software Development Process

The software crisis discussed earlier is at least in part the result of poor management of the software development process. The difficulty in managing software development arises out of the complexity of the application, the ability of the personnel involved, and the characteristics of the computer system on which the software is to be installed. It is difficult to assess complexity objectively and accurately; management is made even more difficult due to the rapid change of hardware technology, which affects the performance of the computer system. Therefore, it is important to understand the development process and its unique

---

3. In this context, a *model* is a mathematical relationship among software metrics.

characteristics described in this section before formulating management strategies.

1.2.1 The Software Life Cycle

It is customary to consider the software life cycle as consisting of several
phases, each phase having a defined starting point and ending point. While in
practice the phases tend to overlap, it is important to define each phase and the
activities in each phase as accurately as possible in order to define precisely
those metrics that are phase-dependent. For example, we cannot produce a
model for effort or schedule of a particular phase unless the phases are carefully
described. One commonly accepted model of the software life cycle is the
waterfall model, shown in Figure 1.1. One waterfall model is described in
[BOEH81]. The essential phases of this software life cycle, assuming a decision
has been made as to the feasibility of the project, are the following:

Requirements and Specifications — This phase should produce a complete specification of the required functions and performance characteristics of the software. It should also address the question of resource needs and preliminary
budget estimates.

Product Design — This phase should specify the overall system configuration,
the implementation language, major modules and their interfaces, configuration
control and data structures, and a testing plan.

Detailed Design — This phase should produce more detailed module specifications including their expected size, the necessary communication among modules, algorithms to be used, interface data structures, and internal control structures. It should highlight important constraints relative to timing or storage,
and include a plan for testing the individual modules.

Programming/Coding — This phase should produce an implementation of the
modules in the chosen language together with unit testing and (perhaps) subsys-
tem testing.

System Integration — This phase, usually completed by a group independent of
the original analysts and programmers, should subject the integrated modules to
extensive testing to ensure that all functional requirements are met. Errors are,
of course, corrected as discovered.

Installation/Acceptance — This phase should deliver the product to the user
organization for final acceptance tests within the operational environment for
which it is intended. Documentation and user manuals are delivered, training is
conducted, problem reports are recorded, and corrections made until the customer accepts the product.

Maintenance — This is a continuing phase in which additional discovered errors
are corrected, changes in code and manuals are made, new functions are added,
and old functions deleted.

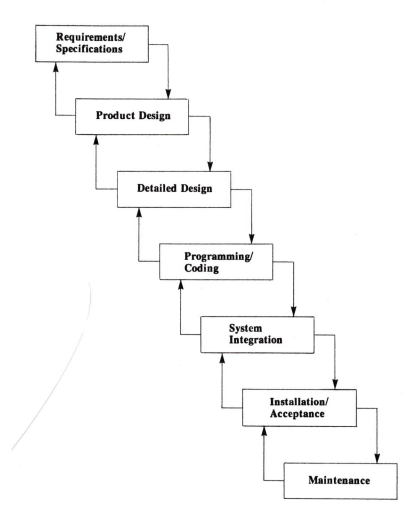

Figure 1.1   The waterfall model of the software life cycle.

These seven phases, although generally sequential, are very interdependent since changes made in one phase significantly affect activities in another. Most software managers today advocate a Systems Configuration Management approach to software development [BERS84]. This approach proposes that each phase be subjected to extensive verification and validation to ensure that the implementation satisfies the specifications, and that the specifications satisfy the requirements. It also advocates *baselining*, (i.e., temporarily freezing) definitive versions of the product at various milestones. Changes in these baseline versions are not permitted without the agreement of all parties involved.

Of particular interest in this book are the four phases beginning with Product Design and ending with System Integration. These are generally called the *software development phases.* They encompass all those activities that contribute to the software *development* effort, which usually omits activities associated with Requirements/Specifications, Installation/Acceptance, and Maintenance. The allocation of total development effort among the four phases varies somewhat from one installation to another, and may also vary with the size and type of product. However, as a rule, a reasonable distribution of effort among these phases would be as follows:

Development Phase	Allocation of Total Development Effort (%)
Product Design	15
Detailed Design	25
Programming/Coding	40
System Integration	20

(For example, see Table 5-2 of [BOEH81]).

We will also group all life-cycle phases into four categories, each of which contains some related activities. This is motivated by the fact that most data collections we use later do not categorize data in such fine detail as the seven phases listed earlier. The four phases are

Design — This phase contains the Requirements/Specifications, Product Design, and Detailed Design phases. All preliminary work before actual coding is done in this phase.

Coding — This phase is the same as the Programming/Coding phase. Actual code is developed in this phase.

Testing — This phase contains the System Integration and Installation/Acceptance phases. Internal testing with sample or "live" test data is performed in this phase.

Maintenance — This phase is the same as the Maintenance phase. Software is now in operation.

Justification for a disciplined approach to software development is based largely on studies of software error histories from completed projects. These studies show that while most errors occur during the Design phase (Requirements/Specifications, Product Design, and Detailed Design), these errors are not discovered until late in the life cycle. Furthermore, these studies indicate that errors discovered late in the cycle cost much more to repair than errors discovered and corrected when they occurred. Indeed based on a study of several large projects produced at IBM, GTE, TRW, and elsewhere, Boehm [BOEH81] estimates that the relative cost of fixing an error introduced during the requirements phase, but not discovered until maintenance, can be as much as 100 times more than that of fixing the error during the early development phases.

1.2.2 The Quality of Software

It is apparent that we cannot address the issue of development effort without addressing the *quality* of the software at the same time. A poorly designed system, although it can be put together quickly to process an acceptance test correctly, may cost more in the long run because of the additional cost of repairs. Thus, improving the quality of delivered software is a major goal of research in software engineering. This goal will be difficult to achieve unless we can define and measure the components of software quality. In a restricted sense, quality is often considered synonymous with reliability (i.e., with the presence or absence of errors).[4] However, most users do not consider error-free code that is difficult to understand, use, and modify to be of high quality. In an important paper by Boehm [BOEH76], an attempt is made to define software quality in terms of some high-level software characteristics. These characteristics are

- Reliability

- Portability

- Efficiency

- Human Engineering

- Testability

- Understandability

- Modifiability

If we can define and measure these characteristics of quality with some degree of precision,[5] then managers and customers can use such quality metrics either to set goals to be achieved by a software product, or as the basis for rejection or acceptance of a completed project. Ideally we would like to maximize the presence of each of these characteristics. For many reasons, this goal is very difficult to achieve. First, some of the characteristics are potentially contradictory. For example, improvements in portability and understandability usually result in decreased efficiency. Second, there are significant cost/benefit tradeoffs that must be considered in attempting to maximize any particular characteristic. It is well known, for example, that the cost of producing highly reliable code may be several times that for low reliability code. In general, we can

---

4. For a more complete discussion of defects and reliability, see Section 2.8.

5. Note that precise definitions of these subjective characteristics are very difficult. The remainder of Section 1.2.2 should be read with this in mind.

expect that very high quality can be achieved only at a substantial incremental cost.

Third, it seems difficult to define a single metric that can be used to measure a particular characteristic, and even more difficult to define a metric that can be used as an overall indicator of the quality of a product. In [BOEH76], each high-level characteristic is decomposed into primitive characteristics. Some primitive characteristics corresponding to *reliability*, for example, might be

- Accuracy

- Robustness

- Completeness

- Consistency

- Self-containedness

If a metric can be defined for each primitive, then measurements of these primitives can be combined to produce a single metric for reliability. However, there are significant difficulties even in defining precise measures of these primitive characteristics—especially since each primitive may itself require several submetrics for proper definition.

Even if the term *software quality* is used in a broad sense, there are currently no well-established software quality metrics, because many of the important characteristics are difficult, if not impossible, to quantify. However, if we limit the definition of quality to code error-proneness, for example, then it may be possible to compute automatically a measure of quality using metrics that will be described in Section 2.8.

Continued research on software quality is a pressing priority. Ideally we would like to define metrics for each primitive and combine these metrics in some way to produce a single figure of merit for the overall product. Assuming that metrics can be computed or estimated for each primitive, a figure of merit can be produced as follows:

Let each H_i ($i = 1, \cdots, n$) be a high-level characteristic. Let m_i be the number of primitive characteristics associated with each H_i. Let s_{ij} be a score for the ith high-level characteristic and j^{th} primitive characteristic associated with H_i. The score might range from 0 to 5, with 5 indicating a maximum score for that primitive.

Then the score SC_i for the ith high-level characteristic is

$$SC_i = \sum_{j=1}^{m_i} s_{ij} \tag{1.1}$$

and the *total score* would be

$$TSC = \sum_{i=1}^{n} \sum_{j=1}^{m_i} s_{ij} \tag{1.2}$$

This formula can be made more flexible by introducing weights w_i such that $\sum w_i = n$. Thus we arrive at a *total weighted score*

$$TWSC = \sum_{i=1}^{n} w_i \sum_{j=1}^{m_i} s_{ij} \qquad (1.3)$$

The use of weights allows a customer to select the quality characteristics that he feels are most important for his application. Finally we can compute a *normalized weighted score* using

$$NWSC = \frac{TWSC}{TSC_{max}} \qquad (1.4)$$

where TSC_{max} is the maximum possible score over all primitive characteristics allowing for repetitions. Hence, we can find this maximum possible score

$$TSC_{max} = 5 \sum_{i=1}^{n} m_i \qquad (1.5)$$

The normalized score has the property

$$0 \le NWSC \le 1$$

The closer this score is to 1, the higher the overall quality of the software. By computing $NWSC$ for programs of known quality, an acceptable range of values for $NWSC$ can be established. This type of metric would be of great value to both software managers *and* customers.

1.2.3 Characteristics of Large-scale Systems

Many researchers have concentrated on the problems involved in designing, producing, and maintaining large-scale systems. The assumption is that largeness itself affects our ability to produce and understand a product. Some examples of large-scale systems are an airline reservation system, a banking system, an electronic switching system, most operating systems, and many military command and control systems. Some characteristics that distinguish large systems from smaller ones include the following:[6]

- A large, organized team of people, including specialists, is required to design, implement, and maintain the system.

- The system is large, generally employing many thousands of lines of code, hundreds of modules, many functions performed, and so on.

- The system reflects a variety of abilities and techniques, and is difficult for any one person to understand fully.

---

6. These do not always apply to every large system, but are a typical list.

- There are strong dependencies among system components (as opposed to a collection of independent subroutines).

- The system's users typically did not design or write the system, yet must rely on it for accurate information.

- The system must be updated often and, perhaps, several versions must be maintained simultaneously.

A system exhibiting all of these characteristics is IBM's OS/360 and its successors [PADE81]. This system has evolved over many years in order to adapt to machines of different sizes, speeds, and peripherals. Thousands of installations are using one or more versions of this system, updates are released periodically, and many different versions must be maintained by IBM.

Belady and Lehman [BELA76, BELA79] collected data on several projects over some 10 years, and attempted to formulate some general laws of program evolution by analyzing this data. Generally, software systems grow in unpredictable ways as a reaction to unforeseen needs and management decisions on resource allocation. However, Belady and Lehman concluded from their study that the life cycle of large software systems possesses deterministic, measurable regularities and trends, which are more or less independent of management decisions or environmental changes. This important observation, if true, implies that we should be able to develop quantitative models to measure these trends. Their study of eight large systems led them to formulate three laws of *software evolution dynamics:*

(1) *Law of Continuing Change*
A large program that is being used undergoes continuing change until it is judged more cost-effective to rewrite it.

(2) *Law of Increasing Entropy*
The entropy[7] of a system increases with time unless specific work is done to maintain it or to reduce it.

(3) *Law of Statistically-Smooth Change*
Measures of global system attributes and project attributes may appear quite irregular for a particular system, but are cyclically self-regulating with statistically identifiable invariances and well-defined long-range trends.

Law 1 is almost self-evident. Software over time must be changed not only to repair errors that are discovered, but also to incorporate enhancements, to adapt to new hardware systems, and to adapt to a changing environment.

Law 2 is intuitive. Continuous changes made to a system tend to destroy the integrity of the system, thus increasing entropy. As a system ages, changes

---

7. *Entropy* refers to disarray. Systems that are initially well-organized tend to get disorganized as they are altered. Children's bedrooms are good examples of entropy in action.

in one module tend to affect more and more components, and hence to increase complexity. While it is possible for management to recognize this growing entropy and to attempt to control it, this is seldom done. Instead, in order to minimize cost, quick fixes are made and modules are added or modified with little attention to their effect on the total system. Furthermore, as systems age, the original designers and analysts are no longer available, and maintenance is often assigned to inexperienced personnel. This simply accelerates the deterioration in integrity.

Law 3 is less obvious and, indeed, may appear counter-intuitive. Measurements of software characteristics, in fact, often appear to be random numbers. Belady and Lehman contend, however, that even though measurements may vary at any one point in time, these measurements will exhibit a long-term trend when observed over a longer period using moving averages. They contend that feedback forces will sooner or later compel the measurements back to the basic trend.

To support these laws, Belady and Lehman analyzed data on several large systems, including the two operating systems OS/360 and DOS/360, a banking system OMEGA, and some electronic switching systems. For example, the data on the size of OS/360 gathered over 10 years exhibits the growth in modules shown in Figure 1.2. Other systems show similar growth characteristics in size, whatever the method used to measure size, although perhaps at different rates. The evidence is very strong in support of Law 1 and, in fact, supports a stronger law that can be stated as, "Systems grow in size over their useful life."

Law 2 is more difficult to substantiate since measures of software complexity are not easily defined. Belady and Lehman suggest as a definition of system complexity

$$C_R = \frac{MH_R}{M_R} \tag{1.6}$$

where C_R is the complexity of the system at release R, MH_R is the number of modules handled (changed) during release R, and M_R is the size of the system in modules at release R. Thus, C_R is the fraction of modules handled during release R. We can assume that as complexity increases, C_R increases. From 1966 to 1974, OS/360 went through 21 releases and grew from 1152 modules to 5300 modules. Figure 1.3 is a plot taken from [BELA76] of C_R versus age of OS/360 in days. The plot shows that, while the actual value of C_R fluctuates considerably, it does seem to follow a positive trend line as the age of the system increases. This supports Law 2; that is, system complexity grows with age. However, this conclusion is disputed by Lawrence [LAWR82], who examined a number of systems for which sufficient data was available. He applied the Kendall rank-order correlation statistic to test the hypothesis that the fraction of modules handled increases with age. For the 5 systems he studied, this hypothesis was rejected in 3 of them, while it was accepted for only 2 of them (OS/360 and OMEGA).

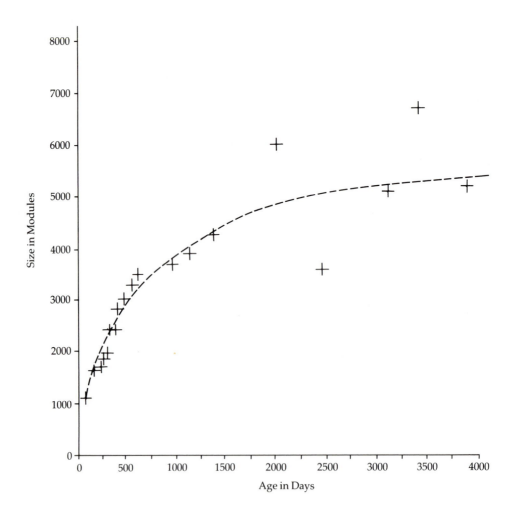

Figure 1.2   Growth of OS/360.

Law 3 is perhaps the most controversial of the three. According to Belady and Lehman, one manifestation of this law is exhibited by the invariance of the work rate. They claim that the *work input*, or the *effort expended per unit time*, remained constant over the lifetime of the system. This surprisingly strong statement implies a constant work rate over a period of many years during which technologies, languages, machines, and personnel all changed significantly. Belady and Lehman claim that, for several systems, the cumulative number of modules handled (*CMH*) could be modeled by the formula

$$CMH = a_0 + a_1 t_D \tag{1.7}$$

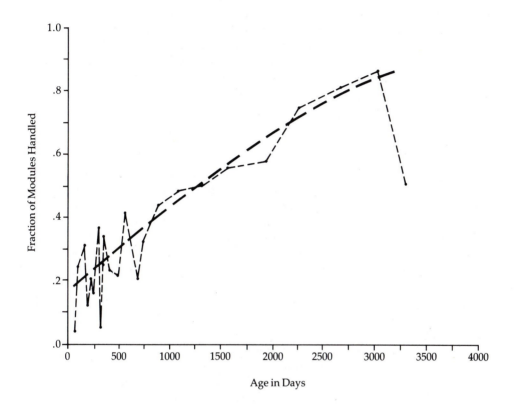

Figure 1.3   Fraction of modules handled in OS/360.

where t_D is the age of the system in days and a_0 and a_1 are regression-derived[8] constants. For OS/360, they found with proper smoothing that Equation (1.7) led to

$$CMH = 1100 + 11 t_D \tag{1.8}$$

Thus Equation (1.8) implies that on the average about 11 modules per day were handled. The value of a_1, the constant work rate, would be expected to vary from one system to another. Lawrence concluded, however, that the concept of

---

8. Regression will be discussed in Chapter 3.

an invariant work rate could not be confirmed either on OS/360 or on any of the other systems that he examined [LAWR82]. Indeed Lawrence rejects the hypotheses of statistically smooth change and invariances. He suggests instead that the dynamics of the growth process are essentially discontinuous and irregular, and that growth is subject to more effective control by managers.

If the hypotheses of Belady and Lehman can be confirmed, their pioneering work has tremendous significance for managers who, given the knowledge of quantitative long-term trends, can more confidently conduct long-range planning and resource assignment. In order to develop quantitative models of software life cycle evolution, we need to collect data about software systems systematically over a long period.

1.2.4 The Need for Software Engineering

The problems associated with the development of software, especially with large-scale software, have emphasized the need for a more disciplined approach. The term *software engineering* was coined in the late 1960s as a rubric for a variety of techniques and tools designed to allow the production of cost-effective, reliable software within specified time constraints. Originally the term was applied primarily to the generation of computer programs. But, in recent years, as Boehm [BOEH81] details, its definition has been broadened to apply to human, social, and economic considerations as well. This broadened definition requires that the software design address such questions as: Will the implementation of the proposed system result in an unacceptable loss of jobs or in a deterioration of morale among employees? Is the system designed to be easy to use and hard to misuse by the intended customers? Is the cost of using the system within the reach of the intended users?

A software engineer is potentially different from a programmer or a computer scientist. In addition to being responsible for specification and design, the software engineer must also be knowledgeable about managerial, economic, and human interfacing issues. In general, our academic institutions are not producing graduates who qualify as software engineers, although there are efforts currently underway to introduce curricula to meet this objective (see, for example, [OGLE83]).

A driving force behind the use of software engineering in system development is the Department of Defense (DoD) which is relying increasingly on computer and software technology. DoD is concerned with the availability of qualified personnel in software technology. Demand for computer specialists for military needs is projected to grow over the next decade at the rate of 12% per year, while the personnel pool of computer specialists and the productivity of programmers are projected to grow at a rate of approximately only 4% per year [BOEH83b]. Assuming that these rates are relevant to the country as a whole, the significant gap between supply and demand over the next decade implies that the country will be unable to meet its software development needs unless programmer productivity is significantly increased.

In recognition of the severity of the perceived problems in software technology, DoD has launched several programs to overcome or ameliorate these problems. One of these initiatives supported the development of the Ada[9] language (for example, see [WEGN80]). Ada and its supporting environment protocols were originally designed for mission-critical computer systems. A second initiative by DoD is known as the STARS program (Software Technology for Adaptable, Reliable Systems), which is described in the November 1983 issue of *IEEE Computer*. The STARS program is intended to encourage the use of software engineering techniques in all phases of the software life cycle. Specific objectives include[10]

- Encouraging the use of better management practices

- Improving underlying software technologies

- Increasing personnel skill levels and encouraging educational institutions to emphasize software engineering principles

- Creating more powerful development and maintenance tools

- Encouraging the use of advanced tools by industrial subcontractors

- Encouraging research in software system methodology

A third DoD initiative, actually conceived as part of the STARS program, is the formation of a Software Engineering Institute (SEI), to be located in Pittsburgh, Pennsylvania. The Institute will be responsible for creating and operating an advanced software environment. It will encourage the development of improved software practices and methodologies, provide an environment for testing these methodologies, ensure the rapid transfer of proven technologies to military contractors, and encourage educational institutions to develop courses and curricula in software engineering to improve the quality of our computer graduates.

The scope of the STARS-SEI initiatives are set forth in the various task areas that have been identified in seven papers published in the November 1983 issue of *IEEE Computer*. These areas are

- Measurement Task Area

- Project Management Task Area

- Human Resources Task Area

---

9. Ada is a trademark of the United States of America Department of Defense.

10. Note that the STARS program is still evolving at the time of writing this book. It is likely that this objective list will be revised.

- Systems Task Area

- Application-Specific Task Area

- Human Engineering Task Area

- Support Systems Task Area

The material in this book properly applies to the Measurement Task area, which is considered important since the ability to measure objectively is a foundation for all scientific and engineering disciplines [DUNH83]. The maturity of software engineering as a discipline may be reflected in the degree to which the use of metrics becomes a normal part of the software development and maintenance process.

The goal of software engineering is to produce timely software that is efficient, reliable, adaptable, maintainable, and easily usable. It is interesting to note that these goals do not imply or ensure that Knuth's goal of producing "truly magnificent" software (as quoted from 1974 Turing Award lecture) will be met. But, of course, magnificence is an art form, not a scientific form.

1.3   Software Metrics and Models

The field of software metrics is not really a new phenomenon.[11] Software metrics have been developed and used for some time.[12] Many metrics and methods to measure software complexity have been proposed and explored. This activity has led to and been fueled by interest in software development *models*. Many of the proposed metrics can be measured objectively (algorithmically), but some can only be determined subjectively (for example, the quality metrics proposed by Boehm whose components were discussed in Section 1.2.2). Many models of the programming process have been constructed using various supposedly relevant factors that pertain to software size and complexity, programmer experience, and the program development procedure.

---

11. Note that we have already mentioned in the Preface of this book that there are a number of metrics related to the performance and storage requirements of computer software that are not included in this book. We include only those metrics related to the logical complexity of software since these are the metrics most often used in software size, error, and cost models.

12. The earliest paper on metrics that we could find is by R. J. Rubey and R. D. Hartwick, "Quantitative measurement of program quality," *Proceedings of the ACM National Conference* (1968), 671-677. It has no citations for earlier work.

1.3.1 Software Complexity Metrics

The term *complexity* appears so often and in so many different contexts in software research that it may be useful to discuss its various connotations. In theoretical circles, it is common to classify algorithms as to their *computational complexity*, which means the efficiency of the algorithm in its use of machine resources. On the other hand, the perceived complexity of software is often called *psychological complexity* because it is concerned with characteristics of the software that affect programmer performance in composing, comprehending, and modifying the software. Curtis [CURT80] has suggested a definition that encompasses both types of complexity:

> *Complexity is a characteristic of the software interface which influences the resources another system will expend or commit while interacting with the software.*

This definition implies that complexity is a function of both the software itself and its interactions with other systems. The word *system* in this context includes machines, people, and other software. This abstract definition of complexity can be made operational by defining and quantifying specific software metrics that are relevant to the phenomenon under study. When these operational metrics are further combined according to some hypothesis or theory, we arrive at a software complexity model.

Specific types of complexity that have been considered include *problem complexity*, *design complexity*, as well as *program* or *product complexity*. For each of these complexity types, an appropriate metric accurately reflects the "difficulty" that a programmer or analyst encounters in performing such tasks as designing, coding, testing, or maintaining the software system. It is intuitive to assume that if one task is more difficult than another, it demands more skills or more effort to perform. We are interested in those complexity metrics that can be obtained *objectively* and that can serve as *essential* factors in models that relate to important program development metrics, such as effort.

1.3.2 Objective and Algorithmic Measurements

It is possible to define software metrics that are measured subjectively, such as the "quality on a scale of 1 to 10" of a module or a programmer's recollection several weeks later of the time expended on a project. But the disadvantages of subjective measurements are myriad. First, there is the problem of non-replication. Subjective measurements are, by definition, based on individual ideas about what the metric should be. In all likelihood, this meaning will differ with different observers. Furthermore, with a subjective measurement, the method of assigning a value can change as an observer changes over time: that is, given the same situation, an observer may assign the metric different values today and one year from now. Obviously, it is then difficult to compare subjective measurements gathered in different studies. It can also be more costly to compute some subjective measurements, especially those that are based on the observations of several people and involve discussions among them.

Objective, or algorithmic, measurements avoid many of these problems; that is,

> *An objective, or algorithmic, measurement is one that can be computed precisely according to an algorithm. Its value does not change due to changes in time, place, or observer.*

In theory, there should be no question of the replicability of an objective measurement. An algorithm should not change over time or among several observers. Any observer at any time should assign the same value to the same metric. Thus, software metrics that can be measured objectively should be comparable among several studies that allow the combination of data for research and analysis purposes. Furthermore, the algorithms for measurement may be included in software analyzers that compute objective metrics so that little human time is needed to obtain these values.

However, we would be dishonest if we led the reader to believe that metrics that can be measured objectively are a panacea. There are a few problems inherent in their use. First, in establishing computational algorithms, it can be very tedious to include all cases. For example, there is a software metric called the *operand*. (It will be defined and described in Sections 2.2 and 2.3.) Intuitively an operand is anything that is "operated on" in a computer program, such as variables, constants, and labels. But, what about user-defined types in languages that allow them? Every possibility like this has to be considered or the algorithm derived will be incomplete.

A related problem in creating algorithms for determining software metrics is the difference of opinion among researchers concerning how to define a metric. This situation will become apparent in Section 2.2 where we present the various competing algorithms for computing the most classical software metric, lines of code. We attempt in this book to present consensus definitions or to create them when none presently exists. Thus, although we will present alternative algorithms for a metric in several sections of this book, we will usually identify our own choice and justify why we think it is superior to the others. In spite of this effort, realistically we conclude that this problem of competing algorithms based on different definitions will remain unsolved for at least the foreseeable future.

Perhaps the most serious problem facing the researcher who desires metrics that can be measured objectively is the fact that there are some abstract concepts for which there are no attractive algorithms that capture them. For example, the concept of software complexity (discussed in the previous section) has often defied agreement among researchers. We all know that some software is more complex than others. This knowledge is generally based on a combination of impressions left by such factors as size, control structure, algorithms used, and data structure. It is possible to construct an algorithm to measure these components, but there is the question as to what validity it has.

Faced with the task of constructing an objective algorithm to measure an abstract concept such as software "quality," one could measure the quality based on such items as the number of errors uncovered in testing, defects discovered per thousand lines of code, or time between the last two software failures. It is also possible to create functional combinations of these items as well. Certainly, it can be argued that to count the number of errors discovered in testing is objective. But does that number bear any relation to the abstract concept of quality? Despite the difficulty in defining and applying metrics, there is no shortage of complexity metrics.[13] However, many of those proposed are very difficult to compute, or have very little supporting evidence on their utility. We have identified several "popular" metrics for discussion in this book, which are described in detail in Chapter 2.

1.3.3 Process and Product Metrics

Measurements of software characteristics can be useful throughout the software life cycle. Software metrics are often classified as either *process* metrics or *product* metrics, and are applied to either the development process or the software product developed. Specifically,

---

Process metrics quantify attributes of the development process and of the development environment.

Process metrics include resource metrics, such as the experience of programmers, and the cost of development and maintenance. Examples of metrics for the levels of personnel experience are the number of years that a team has been using a programming language, the number of years that a programmer has been with the organization, the number of years that a programmer has been associated

---

13. Dr. Bill Curtis, a researcher at Microelectronics and Computer Technology Corporation (MCC) in Austin, Texas, said at a colloquium given at Purdue University that there were probably more complexity metrics than computer scientists, since many were responsible for defining several of them.

with a programming team, and the number of years of experience constructing similar software. Other factors related to development include such items as development techniques (the use of top-down or bottom-up development techniques, structured programming, and other software engineering techniques), programming aids (the use of design languages and systems, editors, interactive systems, and version control systems), supervisory techniques (such as the type of team organization and number of communication paths), and resources (human, computer, time schedule, and so on). In many cases, the value of a metric could be either 0 or 1, representing the absence or presence of a particular technique or process. A numeric value can also be used to represent the degree of usage.

On the other hand,

> *Product metrics are measures of the software product.*

Note that they may reveal nothing about how the software has evolved into its current state. Product metrics include the size of the product (such as the number of lines of code or some count of tokens in the program), the logic structure complexity (such as flow of control, depth of nesting, or recursion), the data structure complexity (such as the number of variables used), the function (such as type of software: business, scientific, systems, and so on), and combinations of these.

It may be difficult to classify certain metrics as either process- or product-related. For example, the number of defects discovered during formal testing depends both on the product (the number of code segments that are erroneous), and on the process used in the testing phase (the extensiveness of testing). In general, it is possible for a product metric to be influenced by the process used, and vice versa. A metric should be classified according to the factor that is believed to provide the major influence. (More details on these types of metrics are given in Chapter 2.)

1.3.4 Models of the Software Development Process

In this book we will present several models of the software development process. Just as a municipal electric company constructs a mathematical model to explain (and ultimately predict) energy usage, we could create mathematical models that deal with the software development process. Inputs to the electric company model may include temperature, humidity, day of the year, day of the week, time of day, geographical location, and many more. Factors potentially included in software development models are process and product metrics described earlier.

A model for the software development process (or a part of it) may be represented by the general form

$$y = f(x_1, x_2, \cdots, x_n) \tag{1.9}$$

The *dependent* variable y is normally a process metric of interest, such as the total effort, development cost, or quality in terms of the number of post-release defects. It is a function of the *independent* variables $x_1, x_2, \cdots, x_n$, which can be either product- or process-related. When considering the parameters to be included in a software development model, the model developer must decide how to formulate the specific model. There are two basic choices: *theoretical* or *data-driven* models. Theoretical models are based on hypothesized relationships among factors. These are developed independent of any data. For example, if we believe that the effort involved in software development increases quadratically with the size of the product, our theoretical model will likely contain a relationship of the form

$$effort = \cdots size^2 \cdots$$

in addition to any other theoretical relationships that we include.

Data-driven models are generally the result of statistical analyses with little concern about sensibility or intuition for the formulas developed. Thus, if a statistical analysis of our data yields a model in which

$$effort = \cdots size^{.483} \cdots$$

then the statistically-based model builder might use this model without questioning what the .483 really means.

Probably the most sensible alternative to these two extremes is a model derived via a combination process: that is, our intuition determines the basic shape of the model (very much like the theoretical model building process) as much as possible with constants (e.g., coefficients and multipliers) provided via data analysis. Thus, we might constrain the statistical process to yield a model with effort as a function of size squared, but with a coefficient derived statistically. For example,

$$effort = \cdots 1.5 \times size^2 \cdots$$

Many of the models discussed in Chapters 4 through 7 are of this combined type. We are interested in models that are simple, express an intuitive relationship, and fit the data well.

1.3.5 Meta-metrics

Just as a *meta-language* is used to describe a language, a *meta-metric* is a measure of a software metric. We have already indicated that a useful metric should be measured objectively and algorithmically. The following are some meta-metrics that can be used to evaluate a proposed metric. Unfortunately, some of the meta-metrics can only be evaluated subjectively.

Simplicity — Does the metric lead to a simple result that is easily interpreted? A single, intuitive value—like the number of reported errors as a software quality metric—is simple. However, another metric that provides several numbers or values—like logarithms of other metrics—which are not as easily interpreted is not simple.

Validity — Does the metric measure what it purports to measure? It is easy to see that the lines of code count is a valid measure for program size. But a measure for program comprehension may actually be the score on some multiple-choice test, whose value is, at best, indirectly related to comprehension.

Robustness — Is the metric sensitive to the artificial manipulation of some factors that do not affect the performance of the software? For example, the value of a metric should not be drastically changed by the rearrangement of code, which does not affect the execution of the program.

Prescriptiveness — Can the metric be used to guide the management of software development or maintenance? For example, in order to guide the development process, it is better if the value of the metric can be assessed *during* the development process, rather than only at the end. In this case, the manager may know when a problem occurs, and may take proper corrective action before it is too late.

Analyzability — Can the value of the metric be analyzed using standard statistical tools? For example, the common metric "lines of code" is easily analyzable, while the *binary* metric "use/nonuse of structured programming techniques" is not.

We are interested in metrics that are simple, valid, robust, useful for development, and that can be analyzed properly. The metrics discussed in Chapter 2 are selected on such a basis.

1.4 Empirical Validation of Development Models

The construction of a model, regardless of how difficult it may seem, is really the easy part. Then the process of developing convincing evidence that the model works must begin. It is far too easy to create an attractive, intuitive model without providing data that shows that the model actually does explain the software phenomenon of interest. Attempts to validate programming models have involved collecting data via software analyzers, report forms, and interviews. Statistics have been employed to show relationships among metrics and to try to produce functions of those relationships for explanatory and predictive purposes.

1.4.1 Data Collection

First, data must be collected. There are many techniques for gathering data to use with a software model:

Software analyzers — These can be run automatically as programs are submitted to a compiler. As a side benefit of such analyzers, information can be gathered dynamically (during the course of software development) to help monitor the programming process, and to provide progressively better estimates. Software analyzers are by nature algorithmic and objective.

Report forms (logs) — These are information-gathering forms to be completed by analysts and programmers at various milestones. A report form might have entries like date, time, activity, and number of hours involved. In a more modern situation, this information could be gathered "online" by entering this information into a file via a standard text editor.

Interviews — Report forms suffer because people frequently forget to fill in the information in a timely fashion or because they misunderstand what information is being requested. To avoid this problem, it is possible to conduct interviews with analysts and programmers at regular intervals or at the completion of certain milestones. In an interview, a member of the research staff collects the same information that would have been put on the report form. But, this technique makes it possible to make sure that programmers understand precisely what information is being requested and to ensure that they are following development requirements as asked of them. From the scientist's standpoint, this means that the data collected is more likely to be valid and comparable. From the analyst's and programmer's standpoint, this alleviates any confusion that can be associated with trying to provide data to researchers. There are other benefits of the interview — including the gathering of anecdotal information that may lead to new metrics based on the observations of the experimenters, analysts, and programmers. Also, from a management standpoint, rather than being a time-consuming annoyance, the interview process has the benefit of being a good way to monitor the development process of an ongoing project. However, it should be apparent that conducting such interviews is costly (in terms of experimenter time) and, if not conducted skillfully, can slow down the development process.[14]

---

14. For a description of an interview procedure that yielded substantially better data than the researcher had been able to obtain via logs or other processes, see [WANG84].

The danger of the interview procedure interfering with the software development procedure leads us to consider a significant problem in the use of software metrics. Simply put, is it possible to observe, measure, and quantify any activity without altering it somewhat in the process? Scientists in virtually every discipline have been troubled by this phenomenon. Consider the opinion surveyor who knocks on someone's door and inquires "You're not going to vote for Senator Wilson, that old crook, are you?" There is every likelihood that some responses will be affected by the way that question was phrased. In studies of organizations, this is known as the "Hawthorne effect" — named after the Western Electric plant in Hawthorne, New Jersey, where experimentation in the 1920s first revealed this phenomenon. (For example, see the discussion in [SCHE70].)[15]

Thus, when collecting data, we must distinguish between *obtrusive* and *non-obtrusive* measures. Obtrusive measures require the involvement of the subjects (i.e., through logs and interviews or by submitting programs or plans to analyzers). Obviously, there is a wide range of "obtrusion" possible, from a lot to almost none at all. Furthermore, it is certainly not the case that, because a measure is obtrusive, it will affect the data collected. For example, requiring a programmer to submit a program to a special analyzer that computes software metrics does involve the programmer, but probably does not appreciably affect the person's software development procedure. Obtrusive measures may potentially alter the very process they are being used to quantify, but in many instances they may be the best way of getting usable data.

At the other the extreme of the continuum are non-obtrusive measures: observations of the program development process that are transparent to the subject. For example, consider the recording of programming time and programmer communication time via observations through a one-way mirror. Even in this case, experimental integrity requires that programmers must know what is happening: that is, they must be made aware of what data is being collected and by what means (although the precise use of it may be concealed until the end of the study or collection process to avoid biasing the results). Another example is to infer programming times according to the frequency of job submissions and the interval between submissions, which can be logged automatically by the operating system. Certainly non-obtrusive measures avoid the bias issue, but many are hard to collect and contain more imprecise information than a similar obtrusive measure.

---

15. In the best known of the Hawthorne studies, employees who assembled telephone equipment were removed from the assembly line and brought into a special room that simulated the assembly line. In this room, illumination was better than in the typical work environment. Not surprisingly, productivity levels were also better there. But, when these same employees returned to the assembly line, their productivity levels continued to be high. The experimenters explained this in terms of the feeling of self-esteem created in the subjects who had been selected to participate in this experiment. Thus, it became apparent that the experiment itself had become a major factor in productivity, making it difficult to interpret the "true" meaning of increased productivity.

In software metrics research, another problem is the difficulty in obtaining replicated data. The time-honored method in experimentation has several subjects (or groups of subjects) perform the same task and averages their performance to avoid the biasing effects of a single outstanding or below-average individual. But, in industry, most projects are done by one individual or one team — not several. If researchers collect a set of industrial data, this can lead to problems in analysis. From an experimental standpoint, what can be missing is a control on the type of and differences among the tasks involved. Due to cost consequences, replication is probably not possible in many organizations. (How many times does one company assign three programming teams to work from the same software specifications simultaneously?) However, for researchers, something close to replication may be possible if they can compare data from similar software development processes gathered from several organizations; but they still must be careful about organizational differences that could bias the results.

It should be apparent from this discussion that there are two distinct possibilities available to scientists interested in examining the software development process: experimentation and data gathering during real program construction. In true experimentation, the scientist can set up any situation desired within reason. But, true experiments are seldom possible outside of the artificial university or research organization environment. In data gathering, we are usually limited to non-replicated and non-obtrusive (even after the fact) data collection. But, this may be the best that industry can offer in many situations.

There is a desperate need for researchers to have available to them a large database reporting the salient features of both software and the software development process in industry today. One major effort concerning data collection is currently being fostered by the Rome Air Development Center (RADC) under the STARS program. The lack of accurate data about software system parameters is perhaps the single largest impediment to software metrics research. Information on such factors as effort, productivity, and error rates is almost always considered proprietary by the developing companies and, therefore, is usually not published. Yet the validation of metrics and models is impossible without accurate data about these and other parameters.

We need to develop a national database (or databases) of software project parameters so that researchers can access this information for their studies. These databases should contain project data that span the spectrum of software systems from various representative software groups. At a minimum, the database should include the following project types: military command and control systems, real time systems, operating and utility systems, commercial systems, and scientific applications.

Critical to the successful use of such databases is a common set of definitions and measures. Today, when software groups report on software product measures, they use different definitions of the basic parameters. Even as simple a measure as lines of code is defined differently by each group. For example, some groups include comment lines in this measure, while others do not. The number of variations in the line count can be extremely large.[16] Similar discrepancies exist in the definitions of such common measures as productivity, development effort, error rates, development schedule, and life-cycle phases. It is absolutely essential that common definitions be established so that reported data is interpreted correctly.

The establishment of a national database of software parameters, based on universally accepted definitions of these parameters, is a necessary precursor to the validation of and the search for improved metrics and models. The commonality of definitions will also make possible the development of universal, transportable metric evaluation tools.

1.4.2 The Statistical Interpretation of Data

After data is gathered, the researcher must draw out of that information as many potential relationships as possible. A primary activity when analyzing data is to try to find relationships between and among metrics. Thus, we may discover that size of the software (measured in lines of code) and programming time (measured in hours) are related because as one increases, so does the other. These types of relationships are generally explored via *correlation*, a traditional technique that can be used to suggest generally linear relationships.[17] There are also tests for the *significance* of any presumed relationship.[18]

The scientist usually employs *regression* techniques[19] to demonstrate explanatory and predictive relationships. Regression, an outgrowth of correlation, produces linear and non-linear functional forms via a variety of techniques under the control of the experimenter. The data can be examined as a potential instance of virtually any functional form.

There are roughly two types of studies that can be conducted: *exploratory* and *confirmatory* studies. In exploratory studies, the data gathered is generally quite voluminous so that the experimenter can observe whatever occurs in hopes of including the best parameters in a model. In confirmatory studies, the experimenter conducts an experiment usually with all but one factor controlled in an attempt to confirm a relationship suggested by previous exploratory studies. Thus, we may find that, over several exploratory experiments, team size seems to affect the productivity of each team member. We may then set up a confirmatory experiment with several teams constructing the same software (i.e., controlling the task). By using teams of various sizes (as prescribed by the researchers), we attempt to confirm the relationship observed in exploratory studies. The details on frequently used empirical designs and statistical techniques are given in Chapter 3.

---

16. This point will be discussed in more detail in Section 2.2.1.

17. For more about correlation, see Section 3.4.4.

18. We take a "significant" look at this concept in Section 3.4.3.

19. These are covered in Section 3.4.4.

1.5 The Limitations of Metrics and Models

This book concerns the use of software metrics, their actual measurement, and models of the programming process. Our intention is that this book will promote research concerning the creation of and evaluation of software metrics and models. We also hope that many managers, analysts, and programmers will begin to use software metrics and models in their work. Some concerns that we have as we write this book involve possible misuses of the ideas presented herein, including attempts to use software models developed in one environment in a different one and the use of software metrics as personnel evaluation tools.

First, it should be clear that data analyses can only be useful if one is comparing "apples with apples": thus, scientists and managers must be careful not to combine data containing software metrics with different definitions. In comparing two different sets of data with items called "lines of code," one must be careful that the items are really measuring the same thing. In Section 2.2, it will become obvious that there are many definitions of lines of code. If one set of lines of code excludes comments and declarations while the other includes them, it will be difficult to draw conclusions from the combined data set without introducing serious biases. For this reason, researchers must be careful when analyzing data from different organizations or data gathered under different rules at the same organization.

Second, most software development models that we will present require *calibration*, that is, determining coefficients and constants from historical data gathered in a specific environment. Most software models cannot be transported directly from one environment to another without re-calibrating. The price paid for violating this standard is erroneous or misleading predictions.

Third, the results of software models can support, but not replace, the decision-making process of experienced managers. We consider the models and metrics discussed in this book as valuable tools for decision makers, but the tools cannot ever replace managers since, in general, metrics normally address only a small part of the development process or the product. Furthermore, even when reasonably validated, metrics focus on only a small number of the variables involved and, by their nature, produce measures of average system characteristics. Because of the extreme variations in human performance, such average measures may give a distorted picture when applied to a particular system. Similarly, some metrics and models that produce good results in one environment may produce poor results in a substantially different environment. In particular, managers should be free to disregard implications from software models if they believe the current project to be so "different" in some way that the model is giving an erroneous reading. Their experience and intuition should be their guide. However, model and metric information (when it coincides with intuition) can help to provide greater precision for estimates and decisions.

Finally, a serious concern for all those working in the software metrics research area: software metrics and models are intended to be used for managing products, not for evaluating the performance of technical staff. However, if these metrics and models are successful, management may want to use productivity measures both as a way to predict costs and as a way to assess the relative performance of each programmer. But, programmers will quickly catch on to this use and will begin to maximize and minimize whatever factors are being used; for example, they may produce unnecessary lines of code to increase the lines-of-code/month rate. This will lead to a decaying performance of models for predictive and explanatory purposes, because in effect the metrics and models will be chasing a moving target. We suggest that the measurement process will achieve better cooperation from programmers if metrics and models are not used for programmer comparison, assessment, or evaluation, and are confined instead to prediction and control of the software development process.

In addition to possible misuses of metrics, there are also some limitations that should be addressed. Of paramount importance is the problem that many predictive models rely on estimates of certain variables, which are often not known exactly. For example, most resource models use program size as an input parameter. Yet our ability to estimate size early in the development process is very poor. Unfortunately, the model prediction can be no more accurate than the size prediction.

Another limitation on the use of metrics is the difficulty and cost of computing these metrics. The cost of gathering metrics may outweigh their potential benefits. The most useful metrics are those that can be gathered automatically and with little extra effort by programmers. Software tools for several languages are now available that can compute size, control structure, and other complexity metrics for computer programs.[20] Some installations automatically compute such metrics on all code produced, so that appropriate action may be taken when these metrics exceed certain prescribed thresholds.

As a final limitation, we want to make it clear that predictive models concerning software development should be treated as probabilistic models. The inputs into these models are themselves subject to considerable variability, and some factors must inevitably be omitted from the model.

1.6 Organization of This Book

In the following chapters, we present the current state of software metrics and models. We begin in Chapter 2 by describing most of the important metrics that have been proposed and are now being used. In Chapter 3, we discuss the process of analyzing the relationships among metrics that lead to models.

---

20. Several tools were discussed at the SCORE '82 conference. See Proceedings of *Performance Evaluation Review* (11, 2 and 3), ACM SIGMETRICS, 1982.

Chapter 4 describes small experiments that have led to some simple effort models and that have explored the effects of various programming techniques. This leads to a discussion of several larger models of programming productivity in Chapter 5. Programming team, large-scale effort models are presented in Chapter 6. Chapter 7 is an assessment of where we are in explaining and controlling the defects (i.e., bugs) in software. Finally, Chapter 8 contains our assessment of what needs to be done with the cooperation of both researchers and practitioners in order to get us to the point where software metrics and models are useful tools for prediction and control purposes.

Exercises

1. List the factors that significantly affect software development costs and software quality. Which factor do you feel is the most critical? Justify your answer.

2. What are the activities involved in software maintenance? Which activity has the highest potential to be eliminated by modern programming practices?

3. What are the essential phases of the software life cycle? What is the percentage of cost for each phase? Which phase has the highest potential to be reduced by modern programming practices?

4. If w_{ij} is the weight of the ith level and jth primitive, rewrite Equation (1.3). Is a two-weight scheme better than the one-weight scheme? Justify your answer.

5. What are the laws of software evolution dynamics? Which law is the most essential for metrics research? Justify your answer.

6. Distinguish between process and product metrics, and give an example of each. Define a metric that could be classified as either a product metric or a process metric.

7. What is a software analyzer? Which metrics (process, product, or both) can it produce?

8. What is a meta-metric? Give an example.

9. Why do we need large amounts of metric data for model development?

10. What are the potential problems of using metrics for evaluating personnel performance?

2 Software Metrics

When you can measure what you are speaking about, and express it in numbers, you know something about it; but when you cannot measure it, when you cannot express it in numbers, your knowledge is of a meager and unsatisfactory kind.

(Lord Kelvin, *Popular Lectures and Addresses*, 1889 [COOK82])

2.1 Introduction

There are many features one can measure about computer software: the size in lines of code, the cost of development in dollars, the time for development in workdays, the size of memory required in bytes, and even the number of customer complaints received after delivery. Yet different observers of the same software product may obtain different measurements, even when the same property is measured.

Consider *lines of code* as an example. For a particular program, one observer may count the total number of lines in the listing, including comments and blank lines. Another observer, realizing that comments and blank lines do not affect the performance of the program, may ignore these lines in the count. Yet another observer, knowing that some lines in the program are copied directly from another product, may choose not to count them or at least to adjust that part of the count by some factor that takes into account that copying code involves almost no time or effort. Thus, a precise definition of the *lines of code* measure is needed so that different observers will obtain identical results from the same program.

Only under such conditions can we confidently compare the results of empirical studies conducted at different places or times. The first sections of this chapter discuss the metrics that are related to a program's size, data structure, and logic structure. There are several proposed in each category; even experts cannot agree on which ones are the most important [ZOLN81]. Over the years, a few simple metrics have gradually emerged to become the most popular among researchers. As we have discussed in Section 1.3.3, these are referred to as *product metrics* since they can be derived by an automatic tool that analyzes the software itself. The tool is often a computer program that accepts the program as input and provides counts of various metrics as output.

There are other measurements of a software product that depend mostly on the development environment. These are called *process metrics* as discussed in Section 1.3.3, since they are related to the development process and require no observation of the program itself. An example is measuring the amount of time taken by a programmer to design, code, and test a program. This measurement depends on (among many other things) the difficulty of the assignment, the ability of the programmer, the type of methodology used, and the availability of the computer during the development process. If the same program were developed by another programmer under different circumstances, it would be rare for the amount of time taken to be identical to that of the first programmer. This is not to say that such a measurement is not meaningful simply because it may not be exactly reproducible. In fact, development time is one of the most interesting and useful software metrics. It is informative to know how long it took a programmer to produce a particular module or program. If two programmers develop the same product independently, the average of their time measures may be even more meaningful than either measure considered alone. Furthermore, an average of more than two programmers gives us even more confidence that the mean time is representative for the typical programmer, except when there is a great variance among the times (see Section 3.4.2).

For an average time to be useful and for any set of times to be comparable, we want to be able to compare "apples with apples": the time measure should represent the same sorts of activities by each programmer. Thus, it is important to know what is included in the measure, such as the time spent actually coding the program, as well as what is excluded, such as the time spent on personal telephone calls while working on the program. One attraction of controlled experiments (discussed later in Section 3.3) is the ability to collect exactly those time intervals that we want or to tell programmers exactly what activities to include or exclude from their time logs.

Another benefit of a precise definition of a metric is the capability it gives us to compare different programs. For example, after the time metric is precisely defined, a time measure for one program may be compared to that for another to determine which program takes longer to develop. Of course, it is even better to compare a set of time measures for one program with a set of times for another to determine which program takes longer to develop by a "typical" programmer.

The following sections of this chapter survey some product and process metrics that have been proposed which possess the qualities described in Section 1.3.5. Space limitations prevent us from being completely exhaustive in our software metric survey that follows. The absence of a metric should not be interpreted as a negative evaluation of its quality. However, emphasis is given to those metrics that are employed most often and that have been found to be the most useful by software researchers.

2.2 Size Metrics

Some programs are written in Pascal, some in COBOL, others in FORTRAN, and still others in assembly language. Some programs are for batch processing, and some allow interactive input and output. Some are written using the latest software engineering techniques, while others are developed without adequate planning. Some programs are well-documented with carefully crafted internal comments; other programs are written in a "quick-and-dirty" fashion with no comments at all. But, there is one characteristic that all programs share — they all have *size*.

The size of a computer program used to be easily determined by the number of punched cards it took to contain the program. This metric (which was almost a weight measure for people who had to carry their programs to and from the computing center) is roughly equivalent to the *lines of code* metric that survives to this day. There are many possibilities for representing the size (or magnitude) of a program — including the amount of memory required to contain the compiled version of it. However, in the remainder of this section, we concentrate on the principal size measures that have been found the most useful in characterizing software — such as lines of code, number of tokens, number of functions, and some other measures based on these basic ones.

The size of a program is an important measure for primarily these reasons:

- It is easy to compute after the program is completed.

- It is the most important factor for many models of software development.

- Productivity is normally based on a size measure.

The program listings generated by most compilers or assemblers have a serial number printed for each line of the program. This feature is included to provide a quick way of finding individual program lines in case there are errors in the program. For example, in Figure 2.1 are lines 358—414 of a Pascal program from a Computer Science class at Purdue University. If there had been a syntax error in the READLN statement in function GETEMPLOYEE, then the compiler would have generated an error message referring to line 382.

```
358  (*    EMPLOYEE INPUT AND OUTPUT ROUTINES    *)
359  FUNCTION GETEMPLOYEE : EMPLOYEEPTR;
360  (************************************************************)
361  (*                                                        *)
362  (* THIS FUNCTION READS AN EMPLOYEE RECORD FROM THE EMPLOYEE *)
363  (* FILE, AND RETURNS A POINTER TO IT.  NO ERROR CHECKING IS *)
364  (* DONE WITHIN SETEMPLOYEE. THE FIELDS ARE THOSE DEFINED IN *)
365  (* THE ASSIGNMENT ...                                     *)
366  (*                                                        *)
367  (************************************************************)
```

```
368   VAR
369      I : INTEGER;
370      PERSON : EMPLOYEEPTR;
371   BEGIN
372      NEW(PERSON);   WITH PERSON^ DO   BEGIN
373         READ(DATA,ID);
374         FOR I := 1 TO 10 DO
375            READ(DATA,LAST[I]);
376         FOR I := 1 TO 10 DO
377            READ(DATA,FIRST[I]);
378         READ(DATA,DEPT);
379         JOB := BLANKWORD;
380         READ(DATA,JOB[1]);
381         READ(DATA,JOB[2]);
382         READLN(DATA,SALARY);
383      END;                  (* WITH *)
384
385      GETEMPLOYEE := PERSON;
386   END;                  (* FUNCTION *)
387
388
389   PROCEDURE READED;        (* READ IN DATABASE INTO ED *)
390
391   BEGIN
392      NEMPL := 0;
393      WHILE NOT EOF(DATA) DO   BEGIN
394
395         NEMPL := NEMPL + 1;
396         EPTR := GETEMPLOYEE;
397         ED[NEMPL] := EPTR^;
398         INDEX[BI,NEMPL].TAG := EPTR^.ID;
399         INDEX[BI,NEMPL].IND := NEMPL;
400         INDEX[LN,NEMPL].TAG := CONVERTI(EPTR^.LAST);
401         INDEX[LN,NEMPL].IND := NEMPL;
402         INDEX[PN,NEMPL].TAG := CONVERTI(EPTR^.FIRST);
403         INDEX[PN,NEMPL].IND := NEMPL;
404         INDEX[DP,NEMPL].TAG := EPTR^.DEPT;
405         INDEX[DP,NEMPL].IND := NEMPL;
406         INDEX[JB,NEMPL].TAG := CONVERTI(EPTR^.JOB);
407         INDEX[JB,NEMPL].IND := NEMPL;
408         INDEX[SL,NEMPL].TAG := EPTR^.SALARY;
409         INDEX[SL,NEMPL].IND := NEMPL;
410      END;
411
```

```
412   ° SORT(LN);        SORT(DP);                (* MAKE SURE THEY'RE SORTED *)
413     SORT(FN);        SORT(JB);       SORT(SL);
414   END;
```

Figure 2.1   Lines 358-414 of a Pascal database program.

An added advantage of such line numbers is that, after a program is compiled, a programmer immediately knows the total number of lines in the program. Since everyone agrees that, to a large extent, the amount of effort necessary to construct a program depends upon the number of lines that are written, this size measure naturally becomes a dominating factor in effort-related studies.

However, the line of code measure may not be satisfactory for modern programming languages since some lines (or groups of lines) in a program are more difficult to produce than other lines in the same program. (For example, in Figure 2.1, line 395 is easier to construct than line 402.) Such concern about consistency leads to two opposite approaches:

(1)   Refine the size measure by counting the basic tokens on all lines and ignoring the lines themselves. (For example, line 395 contains the six tokens NEMPL, :=, NEMPL, +, 1, and ;.)

(2)   Generalize the measure by grouping lines that support well-defined functions. (For example, lines 373−382 read in just one employee record from the employee file.)

The following subsections discuss the line of code, count of tokens, and count of functions measures. All of these have been used for cost estimation, comparison of products, and productivity studies.

2.2.1 Lines of Code

As we mentioned earlier, the most familiar software measure is the count of the lines of code. It is represented by the symbol S_s, whose unit is LOC. For large programs, it is appropriate to measure the size in thousands of lines of code (KLOC), which is represented by S. Although this may seem to be a simple metric that can be counted algorithmically, there is no general agreement about what constitutes a line of code. For example, in the FORTRAN program shown in Figure 2.2, if S_s is simply a count of the number of lines, then Figure 2.2 contains 16 LOC. But most researchers agree that the line of code measure should not include comments or blank lines since these are really internal documentation and their presence or absence does not affect the functions of the program. More importantly, comments and blank lines are not as difficult to construct as program lines (in much the same way that making a "Wet Paint" sign is not as difficult as painting the bench to which the sign refers). The inclusion of comments and blank lines in the count may encourage programmers to introduce artificially many such lines in project development in order to create the illusion of high productivity, which is normally measured in LOC/PM (lines-of-code/person-month). When comments and blank lines are ignored, the program in Figure 2.2 contains 14 lines.[1] Furthermore, if the main interest is the size of the program that supports a certain function, it may be reasonable to include only executable statements from the S_s count. The only executable statements in Figure 2.2 are in lines 5−15 leading to an S_s count of 11. Do you agree that Figure 2.1 has 57 lines, 42 lines excluding comments and blanks, and 37 executable statements? Thus, the differences in the counts for Figure 2.2 are 16 to 14 to 11, while the differences for Figure 2.1 are 57 to 42 to 37. One can easily see the potential for major discrepancies for large programs with many comments or programs written in languages that allow (or even require) a large number of descriptive but non-executable statements.[2]

Furthermore, the advantages of programming languages that permit free-format coding create yet another problem. These languages often allow compounding with two or more statements on one line (e.g., line 372 in Figure 2.1), or a single statement to be extended over two or more lines (e.g., line 374 and 375 in Figure 2.1). In Figure 2.3 (containing a part of a program in a Pascal-like language), we may argue that there are alternatively three lines of code (denoted by the three semicolons), five lines (by simply counting every line), or even six (counting every line plus two "lines" on line 1). A solution to this inconsistency is a standard definition for lines of code. Unless otherwise noted, the S_s (in LOC) or S (in KLOC) in this book is defined as follows:

> *A line of code is any line of program text that is not a comment or blank line, regardless of the number of statements or fragments of statements on the line. This specifically includes all lines containing program headers, declarations, and executable and non-executable statements.*

This is the predominant definition for lines of code used today by researchers. By this definition, Figure 2.1 has 42 lines of code, Figure 2.2 has 14, and Figure 2.3 has 5.

---

1. We are not advocating program construction without comments. Comments and blank lines are a valuable aid for most programmers during program development, as well as for later maintenance and modification of a program. (See Section 4.5.1.) They are usually encouraged by management. We are only reporting that they are generally not included in the S_s count.

2. The ENVIRONMENT and DATA divisions in COBOL are examples of declarative statements that constitute a major proportion of code.

```
Line                                                          Level
  1       SUBROUTINE SORT (X,N)
  2       INTEGER X(100),N,I,J,SAVE,IM1
  3     C THIS ROUTINE SORTS ARRAY X INTO ASCENDING
  4     C ORDER.
  5       IF(N.LT.2) GO TO 200                                  1
  6          DO 210 I=2,N                                        2
  7             IM1=I-1                                          3
  8             DO 220 J=1,IM1                                   3
  9                IF(X(I).GE.X(J)) GO TO 220                    4
 10                   SAVE=X(I)                                  5
 11                   X(I)=X(J)                                  5
 12                   X(J)=SAVE                                  5
 13    220            CONTINUE                                  3
 14    210         CONTINUE                                     2
 15    200      RETURN                                          1
 16          END
```

Figure 2.2 A FORTRAN subroutine that sorts an array into ascending order.

```
Line
  1    X := 0;   Y := A^2+LOG(B)+C;
  2    IF X<Y
  3       THEN
  4          R := X/Y
  5    FI;
```

Figure 2.3 A program segment with an unknown number of lines of code.

2.2.2 Token Count

In Section 2.2.1, we discussed a major problem with the S_s measure: it is not consistent because some lines are more difficult to code than others. One solution to this problem is to give more weight to lines that have more "stuff" in them. For example, we suggest that line 402 in Figure 2.1 contains more "stuff" than line 395. Line 402 has a two-dimensional array, pointers, qualified names in data records, and a function call, while line 395 only increments a single variable.

A natural weighting scheme to handle this problem is to use the number of "tokens," which are basic syntactic units distinguishable by a compiler. Such a scheme was used by Halstead in his family of metrics commonly called *Software Science* [HALS77]. A computer program is considered in Software Science to be a collection of tokens that can be classified as either *operators* or *operands*.[3] All Software Science measures are functions of the counts of these tokens. The basic metrics are defined as:

$$\eta_1 = \text{number of unique operators} \tag{2.1}$$

$$\eta_2 = \text{number of unique operands} \tag{2.2}$$

$$N_1 = \text{total occurrences of operators} \tag{2.3}$$

$$N_2 = \text{total occurrences of operands} \tag{2.4}$$

Generally, any symbol or keyword in a program that specifies an action is considered an operator, while a symbol used to represent data is considered an operand. Most punctuation marks are also categorized as operators. Variables, constants, and even labels are operands. Operators consist of arithmetic symbols (such as +, −, and /), command names (such as WHILE, FOR, and READ), special symbols (such as :=, braces, and parentheses), and even function names (such as EOF in line 393 of Figure 2.1).

The size of a program in terms of the total number of tokens used is

$$N = N_1 + N_2 \tag{2.5}$$

Figure 2.4 shows a sample operator and operand analysis of the program in Figure 2.2. Just as there are variations in counting lines of code, there are variations in classifying operators and operands. The original rules established by Halstead excluded the counting of declaration statements (such as line 2 in Figure 2.2) and input/output statements (such as lines 373 or 375 in Figure 2.1). Statement labels were not counted as operands, but rather were considered a part of direct transfers (for example, lines such as GOTO 200 and GOTO 220 were considered two unique operators).

Currently, researchers lean toward counting the tokens in declaration and I/O statements, and most count statement labels as operands wherever they appear (in which case GOTO 200 and GOTO 220 contain two occurrences of the one operator GOTO and one occurrence each of the two operands 200 and 220). This technique has been employed to produce the counts in Figure 2.4. However, there is currently no general agreement among researchers on what is the most "meaningful" way to classify and count these tokens [SHEN83]. The classification is usually determined at the convenience of the programmer who is building the counting tool.

---

3. This is based on the fact that all programs can be reduced into a sequence of machine language instructions, each of which contains an operator and a number of operand addresses.

Operators	Occurrences	Operands	Occurrences
SUBROUTINE	1	SORT	1
0	10	X	8
,	8	N	4
INTEGER	1	100	1
IF	2	I	6
.LT.	1	J	5
GO TO	2	SAVE	3
DO	2	IM1	3
=	6	2	2
−	1	200	2
.GE.	1	210	2
CONTINUE	2	1	2
RETURN	1	220	3
end-of-line	13		
$\eta_1 = 14$	$N_1 = 51$	$\eta_2 = 13$	$N_2 = 42$

Figure 2.4   A token analysis of subroutine SORT.

The rules used are also language-dependent. Furthermore, ambiguities in the counting of unique operators and operands occur frequently. For example, the "−" in Pascal can denote either a unary operator (negation) or a binary operator (subtraction). If both uses occur in a program, do we have two unique operators or two instances of one operator? Figure 2.5. gives a complete set of counting rules for the Pascal language as implemented in the software analyzer distributed by the Purdue University Software Metrics Research Group.

```
(*********************************************************************)
(*                                                                 *)
(*                                                                 *)
(*                  Pascal Counting Strategy                       *)
(*                  _____ _____ _____                       *)
(*                                                                 *)
(*  1.  All of the program including statement parts, program      *)
(*      heading, and declaration parts should be considered.  The  *)
(*      only statements ignored should be comments.                *)
(*                                                                 *)
(*  2.  Variables, constants (including the standard constants      *)
(*      FALSE, TRUE and MAXINT), user-defined types, literals, file *)
(*      names, and the reserved word NIL are counted as operands.   *)
(*      All operands are counted as if they were global in scope.   *)
(*      In other words,local variables with the same name in        *)
(*      different procedures are counted as multiple occurrences of  *)
(*      the same operand.                                           *)
```

```
(*                                                                      *)
(*   3.  The following entities are always counted as single            *)
(*       operators ( * is not differentiated between set and            *)
(*       arithmetic use):                                               *)
(*                                                                      *)
(*       *         /         DIV       MOD       <         <=       ;   *)
(*       <>        >=        >         :=        ^         ,        ..   *)
(*       NOT       AND       OR        IN        PACKED    TO    DOWNTO  *)
(*       INTEGER   REAL      TEXT      CHAR      LABEL     PROGRAM FUNCTION *)
(*       EXTERN    FORWARD   PROCEDURE                                  *)
(*                                                                      *)
(*       CDC Pascal release 3 unique operators:                         *)
(*                                                                      *)
(*       FORTRAN   SEGTEXT   SEGMENTED  ALFA  DYNAMIC  OTHERWISE         *)
(*       RUN                                                            *)
(*                                                                      *)
(*   4.  The following multiple entities are counted as single          *)
(*       operators.                                                     *)
(*                                                                      *)
(*          BEGIN END    CASE END       WHILE DO      REPEAT UNTIL      *)
(*          IF THEN      IF THEN ELSE   FOR DO        WITH DO           *)
(*          SET OF       FILE OF        RECORD END    ARRAY OF          *)
(*                                                                      *)
(*   5.  The following entities or pairs of entities are counted as     *)
(*       single operators subject to the accompanying conditions:       *)
(*                                                                      *)
(*          VAR     is counted as an operator in parameter lists and    *)
(*                  is not counted as a section label.                  *)
(*                                                                      *)
(*          =       is counted as either a relational operator in       *)
(*                  expressions or a definition operator in             *)
(*                  non-executable sections of the program.             *)
(*                                                                      *)
(*          +       is counted as either a unary + or binary +          *)
(*                  depending on its function.  The binary + is not      *)
(*                  differentiated between artihmetic and set usage.    *)
(*                                                                      *)
(*          -       is counted as either a unary - or binary -          *)
(*                  depending on its function.  The binary - is not      *)
(*                  differentiated between arithmetic and set usage.    *)
(*                                                                      *)
(*          .       is counted as either a record component selector    *)
(*                  symbol or a program terminator depending on its     *)
(*                  function.                                           *)
```

```
(*                                                                    *)
(*         :          is a definition operator in the VAR section and *)
(*                    parameter lists.  It is a separation operator   *)
(*                    following CASE or GOTO labels.                  *)
(*                                                                    *)
(*         ( )        is counted as either an argument list  operator or *)
(*                    expression operator depending on the function.  *)
(*                                                                    *)
(*         [ ]        is counted as either a subscript operator or set *)
(*                    operator depending on the function.             *)
(*                                                                    *)
(*   6.  Procedure and function calls are counted as operators.  The  *)
(*       subprogram name following FUNCTION or PROCEDURE is not       *)
(*       counted, though it actually is the operand for the FUNCTION  *)
(*       or PROCEDURE operator.                                       *)
(*                                                                    *)
(*   7.  GOTO statements (i.e., GOTO and an accompanying label) are   *)
(*       counted as the operator GOTO and the operand "label".        *)
(*                                                                    *)
(*   8.  Declarations of labels are not enumerated - all tokens after *)
(*       the LABEL operator through the next semicolon (inclusive)    *)
(*       are ignored.                                                 *)
(*                                                                    *)
(*   9.  The following are syntactic devices and are not counted:     *)
(*                                                                    *)
(*          CONST   TYPE    VAR (for variable sections)               *)
(*                                                                    *)
(* 10.  The following are rules pertaining to Pascal 6000 release 3:  *)
(*                                                                    *)
(*          VALUE is a syntactic device and is not counted.          *)
(*          commas, () and = in VALUE sections are counted as in the  *)
(*             TYPE section.                                          *)
(*          OF in VALUE sections is a syntactic device and is not     *)
(*             counted.  OTHERWISE is counted as another CASE label.  *)
(*                                                                    *)
(* 11.  McCabe's v(g) metric is counted as follows:                  *)
(*                                                                    *)
(*        increment on keywords :                                     *)
(*                                                                    *)
(*        WHILE   FOR   REPEAT     IF        OTHERWISE                 *)
(*        AND     OR    PROCEDURE  FUNCTION  PROGRAM                   *)
(*                                                                    *)
(*        AND and OR include loops/branches controlled by             *)
(*        Boolean variables.  Conditionals couldn't be counted        *)
```

```
(*       directly as Boolean functions and variables would not be   *)
(*       counted correctly.                                         *)
(*                                                                  *)
(*       also count CASE labels by:                                 *)
(*                                                                  *)
(*       incrementing on:                                           *)
(*                                                                  *)
(*               colons in the executable part of the program but   *)
(*                   outside a WRITE(LN) parameter list.            *)
(*                                                                  *)
(*               commas in a CASE label list (on scanning a colon,  *)
(*                   add the number of commas since the last        *)
(*                   semicolon).                                     *)
(*                                                                  *)
(*       decrementing on:                                           *)
(*                                                                  *)
(*               LABEL keyword.                                     *)
(*               commas in a LABEL statement.                       *)
(*                                                                  *)
(*       The decrement is necessary to remove the GOTO labels, if   *)
(*       any.                                                       *)
(*                                                                  *)
(*   12.  VARS is computed by subtracting the number of numeric     *)
(*       constants and character strings in the program from the eta2 *)
(*       count.                                                     *)
(*                                                                  *)
(********************************************************************)
```

Figure 2.5 Pascal counting rules.

In Figure 2.4 note that $N_1 = 51$ and $N_2 = 42$ and the size called "length" by Halstead is $N = N_1 + N_2 = 93$. The Software Science metric N may be converted to an estimate of S_s via the relationship $S_s = N/c$, where the constant c is language-dependent. For FORTRAN, it is thought to be about 7. Notice that $93/7 \approx 13$, which is close to the actual S_s (14) in Figure 2.2.

Software Science defines additional metrics using these basic terms. The first is *vocabulary*, which is defined as

$$\eta = \eta_1 + \eta_2 \tag{2.6}$$

The term vocabulary accentuates the fact that, if you have a programming vocabulary consisting of only these η operators and operands, you could successfully construct this program; or more precisely that, from a programmer's large vocabulary of operators and operands, these η have been chosen as the set to be used in writing this program.

This leads to another measure for the size of a program, called the *volume:*

$$V = N \times \log_2\eta \qquad\qquad (2.7)$$

The unit of measurement of volume is the *bit,* the common unit for measuring the actual size of a program in a computer if a uniform binary encoding for the vocabulary is used. For the subroutine in Figure 2.2 (analyzed in Figure 2.4), $N = 93$ and $\eta = 27$. If a binary number scheme is used to represent each of the 27 items in the vocabulary, it would take 5 bits per item, since a 4-bit scheme leads to 16 unique codes (which is not enough), and a 5-bit scheme leads to 32 unique codes (which is more than sufficient). Each of the 93 tokens used in the program could be represented in order by a 5-bit code, leading to a string of $5 \times 93 = 465$ bits that would allow us to store the entire program in memory. Notice that this size analysis is based on storing not a compiled version of the subroutine, but a binary translation of the original FORTRAN program. We could then say that this program occupies 465 bits of storage in its encoded form. However, also notice that a 5-bit scheme allows for 32 tokens instead of just 27 tokens, so instead of using the integer 5, Equation (2.7) for volume uses the non-integer $\log_2\eta = 4.75$ to arrive at a slightly smaller volume of 442.

A study of over one thousand commercial assembly language and PL/S modules found that S_s, N, and V were linearly related, and appeared equally valid as relative measures of program size [CHRI81]: that is, S_s seems to be measuring the same program characteristic as N which in turn seems to be measuring about the same program characteristic as V). The size metrics N and V are "robust": even a significant variation of the rules in the classification of operators and operands has virtually no effect on the resulting size [ELSH78].

2.2.3 Function Count

Many researchers have found units larger than the line of code (LOC) useful measures for characterizing the size of programs, especially for large programming products. Some have tried to use the *module* as a unit — usually defined as a segment of code that is independently compilable (for example, see [BASI79]). For large programs, it may be easier to predict the number of modules than the number of lines of code. However, unless there are strict guidelines about the way a program is divided into modules, this metric may give us little information. For example, if modules are required to be nearly x lines long, then a prediction of m modules will lead immediately to a projected size of $m \times x$ lines of code. Many managers suggest that modules should be approximately 100 LOC long. If under such circumstances, a programmer reports that a program will require 120 modules, then a good size estimate is 12,000 LOC.

However, most of us divide a program into modules based upon other considerations — such as a module should be the subprogram for one algorithm (such as input the data, find the maximum value in the table, insert a new item in the inventory), or consist of all operations on one data structure (such as all push, pop, and read operations for a stack, or all make, check, and cancel reservation operations for an airline flight). With this way of constructing modules, there is little chance that all modules will be nearly the same size. This phenomenon has been observed in a study of a large number of commercial products, where the sizes of modules ranged from less than 10 to nearly 10,000 lines of code [SMIT80].

A *function* in a program is defined as a collection of executable statements that performs a certain task, together with declarations of the formal parameters and local variables manipulated by those statements. A function is an abstraction of *part* of the tasks that the program is to perform. This idea is based on the observation that a programmer may think in terms of building a program from functions, rather than from statements or even modules. For example, if you show Figure 2.2 to an experienced programmer and ask what it does, the experienced programmer might report that this is an "interchange sort." Thus, to an experienced programmer, this subroutine does not contain several lines of code, but a single function. In fact, most modules can be divided into one or more functions by an experienced programmer. In psychology, the term for this way of thinking is "chunking" [COUL83].

A module consists of one or more functions. A function may compute a single arithmetic value. It may also change the values of data structures or files. The count of the functions in a program may not be easy to obtain unless the programmer has constructed each as a separate module. Furthermore, different programmers may not use the same logic to break a program into the same functions. For example, a less-experienced programmer might consider that Figure 2.2 consists of several functions, one of which is a swap function in lines 10−12.

The number of lines of code for any function will usually not be very large. One reason for this observation may be the limit on the human mental capacity: a programmer cannot manipulate information efficiently when the amount is much greater than that limit [WOOD81b]. For example, constructing a program that symbolically solves the Rubik's cube may seem overwhelming, but constructing a subprogram (either a module or function) that rotates one edge is mentally manageable. If we put several such mentally manageable functions together, ultimately we will have a Rubik's cube solution program.

Some authors advocate that module sizes be limited to 50−200 LOC, arguing that such sizes increase understandability and minimize errors [BAKE72, BELL74]. The overhead involved, both mental and syntactic, discourages the definition of functions that are too small. It is probably easier to put together three 40-line functions to make a program, than to put together twelve 10-line functions or 120 one-line functions. Thus, the variation of size in LOC for functions may not be as great as that for modules. Indirect support is found in a study of student projects, which shows that programmers use a similar number of functions to solve a given problem, but use a different number of modules [BASI79].

2.2.4 Equivalent Size Measures

It is important to realize that programmers do not always develop *new* software. In fact, a good deal of programming work involves modifying existing code. This is done in order to produce a product that is new in the sense that it does things that the previous software did not, but not totally new in the sense that it involves software borrowed from a previous version or from a similar program. For example, suppose that you had been given the task of constructing the program represented by the excerpt in Figure 2.1. If you had already constructed a GETEMPLOYEE function, or knew where you could find one from some other program, you might decide to include it to avoid writing the code in lines 359−386.

Such activity is greatly discouraged in school situations, where it may be called cheating in some cases. But, in business programming positions, such initiative is likely to be rewarded; how many times have we been told not to "reinvent the wheel"? Currently in industry about 50−95% of what programmers do is modifying existing programs. In these cases, they add new code while reusing old code. It has been reported that, at IBM's Santa Teresa Laboratory, 77% of all program code is written in order to add new features to existing products [PAUL83].

However, code reuse creates problems when using many of the software models we present later. In general, these models make no distinction between what portion of software is new and what portion is being reused. Figure 2.1 is from a 537-line Pascal program. If we want to use one of the effort models in Chapter 5 to predict the effort necessary to construct this program, do we use 537 lines as the size parameter? This will probably lead to an incorrect result if 125 lines (including function GETEMPLOYEE) were lifted from another program. So, should we use 537 or 412 (412 = 537−125) or some number in between? Next, we attempt to provide some approaches to answer that question.

It should be clear from our discussion that, for many programs, size has two components: S_n for newly written code and S_u for code adapted from existing software (or reused code). The components of size may be expressed in any of the previously discussed metrics (line of code, token count, or function count). In any case we are interested in an equivalent size measure S_e, which is a function of S_n and S_u. This means that the effort required to develop the software with S_n and S_u (new and reused code) is "equivalent" to the effort of developing a product with S_e "from scratch" (all new code and no reused code). In the example based on Figure 2.1 discussed earlier, $S_n = 412$ and $S_u = 125$. S_e should probably not be greater than the simple sum of S_n and S_u. However, there is a possible undesirable situation in which it actually costs more to put together several existing program segments than it would to construct equivalent software from scratch.

Notice that in the definition of S_u, we called it "code adapted from existing software." This introduces a more subtle point: often when we use existing software, it is necessary to adapt it to fit the rest of the program. For example, suppose that function GETEMPLOYEE in Figure 2.1 must be changed to accommodate a new situation in which employee names will be entered as first name followed by last name. This would require alterations to lines 375 and 377, but the function could still be easily used. Sometimes it is even necessary to write some new code or to delete some that is not needed. This makes it more difficult to compute S_n and S_u. But, at least in theory it should still be possible to delineate the new code from the reused code. The reused code could include revised code. So, if lines 375 and 377 needed revision, we would still report that $S_n = 412$ and $S_u = 125$.

A function is proposed by Boehm for his COCOMO effort estimation models [BOEH81; see also Chapters 5 and 6 of this book]. This function is

$$S_e = S_n + \frac{a}{100} S_u \tag{2.8}$$

where the adjustment factor a is determined by the percentage of modification required of the design (DM), of the code (CM), and of the effort necessary for the integration of the modified code (IM). Boehm proposes another formula to determine the adjustment factor:

$$a = 0.4(DM) + 0.3(CM) + 0.3(IM) \tag{2.9}$$

Note that the maximum value of a is 100, which corresponds to the case in which it is equally difficult to adapt used code as to rewrite it completely. This approach requires the subjective determination of the factor IM, in addition to the uncertain assumption that we have the information before and after modification to obtain CM and DM.[4] Thus, we have no record of its successful application except in the original COCOMO studies [BOEH81].

A similar formula that was proposed by Bailey and Basili [BAIL81] is

$$S_e = S_n + kS_u \tag{2.10}$$

A value of $k = 0.2$ for all programs was found to be reasonable for the projects studied in [BAIL81].

However, a fixed value for k is probably not realistic and should be considered only a first-order approximation. Let us consider two extremes: First, we include a well-defined mathematical function into a software product, the only effort required is to make sure that the correct calling sequence is used. This is

---

4. The data published in Table 29-1 of [BOEH81] shows that (ADJ KDSI) = AAF × (TOT KDSI), or $S_e = a(S_n + S_u)$. This is apparently an approximate relationship derived from the application of Equation (2.8) to individual modules.

seemingly independent of the size of the code for the mathematical function. Thus, $k = 0.2$ may be too large in this case. Second, an included program may need to be enhanced. This process may involve a uniform distribution of changes throughout the body of the program and may require a thorough understanding of the entire reused program. This could lead to an adjustment factor close to 1.0.

Thebaut [THEB83] agrees that new and reused code should contribute to equivalent size differentially, but he makes a different assumption — that the contribution of adapted code is nonlinear. He proposes

$$S_e = S_n + S_u^{\,k} \tag{2.11}$$

where k is a positive constant *no greater than* 1. Using some databases for which S_n and S_u were available, Thebaut found by using regression analysis that $k \approx 6/7$. For values of S_u up to about 98,000

$$S_u^{6/7} > 0.2 S_u$$

Table 2.1   A Comparison of the Equivalent Size Formulas

S_n	S_u	Equation (2.8) $S_e = S_n + \left(\dfrac{0.004 S_u}{100}\right) S_u$	Equation (2.10) $S_e = S_n + 0.2 S_u$	Equation (2.11) $S_e = S_n + S_u^{.857}$
5000	0	5000	5000	5000
4750	250	4753	4800	4864
4500	500	4510	4600	4706
3750	1250	3813	4000	4201
2500	2500	2750	3000	3317
0	5000	1000	1000	1479

It is interesting to observe the effects of all three models on the equivalent size count if we keep the sum $S_n + S_u$ constant, but change the proportion of new code to used code. Table 2.1 shows a comparison of the three models represented by Equations (2.8), (2.10), and (2.11) for three different situations involving 5000 LOC. For Equation (2.8), we assume that the percentage of modification is linearly related to the amount of $S_u (a = 0.004 S_u)$.[5] For Equation (2.10), we use $k = 0.2$, as suggested by [BAIL81]. For Equation (2.11), we choose $k = 0.857$ (that is 6/7) since this worked best in [THEB83]. All three formulas show a decreasing S_e as S_n decreases. The nonlinear feature of Equation (2.11) can be observed by considering the first three rows of the table.

---

5. Since we have no presumed values for *DM*, *CM*, and *IM*, $a = 0.004 S_u$ is chosen to make Equation (2.8) identical to Equation (2.10) when $S_n = 0$.

Note that a decrease of 250 LOC in S_n from row 1 to row 2 and from row 2 to row 3 leads to an exact 200 LOC decrease in S_e in Equation (2.10) in both instances. However, for Equation (2.8) with the hypothetical a, the first 250 LOC decrease in S_n leads to a 247-line S_e decrease, and the next 250 LOC decrease leads to a 243-line S_e decrease. The corresponding values for Equation (2.11) are 136 and 158. These different characteristics should be considered carefully before a model is selected.

There is no consensus about how to compute equivalent size. Intuitively, formulas such as these seem very appropriate. In the rest of this book, we will indicate the method used in studies where such an equivalent size measure is employed.

2.3 Data Structure Metrics

Essentially, the reason for software, programming, and most of the other activities discussed in this book are to *process data*. Some data is input to a system, program, or module; some data may be used only internally; and some data is the output from a system, program, or module. A few examples of input, internal, and output data appear in Figure 2.6.

Program	Data Input	Internal Data	Data Output

Payroll	Name
	Social Security No.
	Pay Rate
	Number of
	  hours worked
		Withholding rates
		Overtime factors
		Insurance premium
		  rates
			Gross pay
			Withholding
			Net pay
			Pay ledgers

Spreadsheet	Item names
	Item amounts
	Relationships among
	  items
		Cell computations
		Subtotals
			Spreadsheet of
			  items and totals

Software Planner	Program size No. of programmers on team	Model parameters Constants Coefficients	Est. project effort Est. project duration

Figure 2.6 Some examples of input, internal, and output data.

Thus, an important set of metrics are those that capture the amount of data input to, processed in, and output from software. For example, assume that a problem can be solved in two ways, resulting in programs A and B. A has 25 input parameters, 35 internal data items, and 10 output parameters. B has 5 input parameters, 12 internal data items, and 4 output parameters. We can assume that A is probably more complicated, took more time to program, and has a greater probability of errors than B.[6]

A count of the amount of data input to, processed in, and output from software is called a *data structure metric*. This section presents several data structure metrics. Some concentrate on variables (and even constants) within each module and ignore the input/output dependencies. Others concern themselves primarily with the input/output situation. As stated in Section 2.2, there is no general agreement on how the line of code measure (the classical and best-known software metric) is to be counted. Thus, it is not surprising that there are various methods for measuring data structures as well. In the following subsections, we will discuss the metrics proposed to measure the amount of data, the usage of data within modules, and the degree to which data is shared among modules.

2.3.1 The Amount of Data

Most compilers and assemblers have an option to generate a cross-reference list, indicating the line where a certain variable is declared and the line or lines where it is referenced. Such a list is useful in debugging and maintenance, and can help determine the amount of data in the program. For example, a simple Pascal program appears in Figure 2.7. It inputs work hours and pay rates, and computes gross pay, taxes, and net pay. The Pascal compiler produces a cross-reference listing for this program, which appears in Figure 2.8.

One method for determining the amount of data is to count the number of entries in the cross-reference list. Be careful to exclude from the count those variables that are defined but never used. The definitions of these variables may be made for future reference, but they do not affect the operational characteristics of the program or, more importantly, the difficulty of development, and should not be counted. Such a count of variables will be referred to as *VARS*. Thus, for the program **payday** appearing in Figure 2.7, *VARS* = 7. For the sample program **SORT** in Figure 2.2, *VARS* = 6 (from a cross-reference listing that identified X, N, I, J, SAVE, and IM1 as the variables in the program). The count of variables *VARS* depends on the following definition:

> *A variable is a string of alphanumeric characters that is defined by a programmer and that is used to represent some value during either compilation or execution.*

---

6. You may find two programs somewhere that defy this generalization, but you probably would have to look a long time.

```
1    program payday (input,output);
2    type check = record
3            gross : real;
4            tax : real;
5            net : real
6         end;
7    var pay: check;
8        hours, rate: real;
9    begin
10      while not eof (input) do begin
11         readln (hours, rate);
12         pay.gross := hours * rate;
13         pay.tax := 0.25 * pay.gross;
14         pay.net := pay.gross - pay.tax;
15         writeln (pay.gross, pay.tax, pay.net)
16      end
17   end.
```

Figure 2.7   A simple Pascal payroll program.

check	2	7			
gross	3	12	13	14	15
hours	8	11	12		
net	5	14	15		
pay	7	12	13	13	14
	14	14	15	15	15
rate	8	11	12		
tax	4	13	14	15	

Figure 2.8   A cross reference of program payday.

Although a simple way to obtain *VARS* is from a cross-reference list, it can also be generated using a software analyzer that counts the individual tokens, as described in Section 2.2.2.

While it may sound simple to determine the value of *VARS* — certainly, counting the number of variables in a program seems straightforward — there are some items in the cross-reference listing of the program in Figure 2.7 that we deleted. These items are listed in Figure 2.9. The items eof, input, and output are related to I/O. The cross-referencing software called the name of the program payday a variable. However, because none of these are variables in the sense of variables that we create to produce a program, we deleted them from Figure 2.8. But it should be clear that this "algorithmic" metric *VARS* is, in fact, a little subjective. In determining this metric, as with all other software metrics including lines of code, we attempt to establish guidelines that eliminate as much subjectivity as possible. But, the reader is well advised to realize that total objectivity is impossible.

```
eof      10
input     1   10
output    1
payday    1
```

Figure 2.9   Some items not counted as *VARS*.

Among all the variable names in line 13 of Figure 2.7 is the constant 0.25. This program assumes that all pay will be taxed at a 25% rate. Also, in line 4 of Figure 2.2, the constant 2 is used to avoid sorting arrays with less than two elements, and the label 200 is used to provide an exit from the program if the array is too small to sort. None of these constants — 0.25, 2, or 200 — are counted as *VARS*, and yet they play special purposes in the programs. Furthermore, mathematical constants such as π and ϵ are important for programs involving trigonometric or logarithmic applications. Even array references with an explicit index, such as A[11], may indicate some special meaning for that particular location.[7]

Halstead [HALS77] introduced a metric that he referred to as η_2 (Equation (2.2)) to be a count of the operands in a program — including all variables, constants, and labels.[8] Thus,

$\eta_2 = VARS$ + unique constants + labels.

The sample SORT program in Figure 2.2, which is analyzed in Figure 2.4, has 6 variables (X, N, I, J, SAVE, IM1), 3 constants (1, 2, 100), and 4 labels (SORT, 200, 210, 220), so that $\eta_2 = 13$. The name of the subroutine SORT is treated as a label since it is the label that will be used by any other program or subprogram that wants to access SORT. The program payday in Figure 2.7 has 7 variables (check, gross, hours, net, pay, rate, tax), 1 constant 0.25, and 1 label (payday) which is the name of the program. Thus, its η_2 is 9.

---

7. For example, if the A-array has ten *bona fide* values, then A[11] may be the location to store the range of values to be used by a plotting routine.

8. We, like many researchers, have chosen to include labels as operands, although the original work by Halstead incorporated labels with their related direct transfers. For example, in Halstead's work, GOTO 200 is counted as an distinct operator from another operator GOTO 220. The labels 200 and 220 are not considered separate tokens, just as the GO in GOTO is not.

Note that η_2 is the count of the number of *unique* operands. Thus, this metric fails to capture an important feature of the "amount of data" — namely the total operand usage. For example, given the nine operands in Figure 2.7, it is possible to construct the program shown or to construct a much larger and more complicated program.[9] In order to measure the quantity of usage of the operands, Halstead further defined the metric *total occurrences of operands*, and named it N_2. Figure 2.10 repeats Figure 2.7 and encloses each operand occurrence in brackets.

```
1    program [payday] (input,output);
2    type [check] = record
3            [gross]: real;
4            [tax]: real;
5            [net]: real
6        end;
7    var [pay]: [check];
8        [hours], [rate]: real;
9    begin
10     while not eof (input) do begin
11         readln ([hours], [rate]);
12         [pay].[gross] := [hours] * [rate];
13         [pay].[tax] := [0.25] * [pay].[gross];
14         [pay].[net] := [pay].[gross] - [pay].[tax];
15         writeln ([pay].[gross], [pay].[tax], [pay].[net])
16     end
17   end.
```

Figure 2.10   Program `payday` with operands in brackets.

The program `payday` uses the 9 operands 32 times: some are used several times (like `pay`) and some are used sparingly (`payday` is used only once). Thus, $N_2 = 32$ for this program. (As an exercise, perform a similar analysis to determine that $N_2 = 42$ for the SORT program in Figure 2.2.)

The metrics *VARS*, η_2, and N_2 are the most popular data structure measures. They seem to be robust: slight variations in algorithm computation schemes for computing them do not seem to affect inordinately other measures based upon them. For example, counting labels as part of the operators as Halstead has suggested will yield the same count for *VARS*, 10 for η_2, and 35 for N_2 in Figure 2.2. The following subsections discuss more exotic data structure metrics.

---

9. We will, of course, have to be careful not to introduce new operands in the latter case.

2.3.2 The Usage of Data within a Module

In Figure 2.11 the program bubble inputs two related integer arrays (a and b) of the same size up to 100 elements each. It uses a bubble sort on the a-array, interchanges the b-array values to keep them with the accompanying a-array values, and outputs the results. Prior to Figure 2.11, all of our examples have illustrated small, single-module programs or subroutines. Figure 2.11 contains a main program in lines 15−38 and a subprogram procedure swap in lines 7−13. We can compute several metrics on the main program and the subprogram. For example, $VARS = 7$ for the main program and $VARS = 3$ for procedure swap. We can now characterize the main program and subprogram.

Several other metrics (including all those in Section 2.3.1 and this section) may be computed for individual modules. In order to characterize the intra-module data usage, we may use the metrics *live variables* and *variable spans*, which are described below.

Live Variables While constructing program bubble, the programmer created a variable last. Analyze Figure 2.11 carefully to see that all array elements beyond the "last" one are ordered. While the program is running, if size = 25 and last = 14, then all items a[15]−a[25] and b[15]−b[25] are in order even though the first 14 elements of each array are not yet ordered. (If you didn't know it already, this is the way that a bubble sort works.) A beginning value for last is established in line 20, decremented in line 24, and used in the logical expression in line 26.

There are only three statements in this program in which last appears, excluding the declaration in line 3. Does this mean that we do not need to be concerned with last while constructing the statements other than 20, 24, and 26? Certainly not. Between statements 20 and 26, it is important to keep in mind what last is doing. For example, statements 21−22 are used to set up a potentially never-ending loop. However, even though these statements never mention last, the programmer realized that each time an a-value "bubbles down" to its appropriate position, last will be decremented by one. Eventually on some cycle through the a-values none will be swapped and the loop begin-ning in statement 22 will be exited. As we will show later, last has a lifespan that begins at statement 20 and extends through statement 26.

Thus, a programmer must constantly be aware of the status of a number of data items during the programming process. A reasonable hypothesis is the more data items that a programmer must keep track of when constructing a statement, the more difficult it is to construct. Thus, our interest lies in the size of the set of those data items called *live variables* (LV) for each statement in the program.

As suggested earlier, the set of live variables for a particular statement is not limited to the number of variables referenced in that statement. For exam-ple, the statement being considered may be just one of several that set up the parameters for a complex procedure. The programmer must be aware of the

```
1    program bubble (input,output);
2    type intarray = array [1..100] of integer;
3    var i, j, last, size: integer;
4        continue: boolean;
5        a, b: intarray;
6
7        procedure swap (var x: intarray; k:integer);
8        var  t: integer;
9        begin
10         t := x[k];
11         x[k] := x[k+1];
12         x[k+1] := t
13       end;
14
15   begin
16      read (size);
17      for j := 1 to size do begin
18          read (a[j],b[j])
19      end;
20      last := size;
21      continue := true;
22      while continue do begin
23         continue := false;
24         last := last -1;
25         i := 1;
26         while i <= last do begin
27            if a[i] > a[i+1] then begin
28               continue := true;
29               swap (a,i);
30               swap (b,i)
31            end;
32            i := i+1
33         end
34      end;
35      for j := 1 to size do begin
36         writeln (a[j],b[j])
37      end
38   end.
```

Figure 2.11   A Pascal bubble sort program.

entire list of parameters to know that they are being set up in an orderly fashion, so that no variables needed later are disturbed by any statement in the group. Therefore, there are several possible definitions of a live variable [DUNS79]:

(1) A variable is *live* from the beginning of a procedure to the end of the procedure.

(2) A variable is *live* at a particular statement only if it is referenced a certain number of statements before or after that statement.

(3) A variable is *live* from its first to its last references within a procedure.

The first definition, while computationally simple, does not correspond to the idea of the live variable. According to this definition, both the variable last with a 7-statement lifespan (lines 20−26) and the variable size with a 20-statement lifespan (lines 16−35) can be considered alive throughout the procedure. The second definition might work, but there is no agreement on what a "certain number of statements" should be and no successful use has been reported.

The third definition meets the spirit of the live variable idea and is easy to compute algorithmically. In fact, a computer program (a software analyzer) can produce live variable counts for all statements in a program or procedure. Table 2.2 gives an example of counting the sample program in Figure 2.2 using the third definition.

Table 2.2   Live Variables for the Program in Figure 2.2

Line	Live Variables	Count
5	N	1
6	N,I	2
7	I,IM1	2
8	I,IM1,J	3
9	I,J,X	3
10	I,J,X,SAVE	4
11	I,J,X,SAVE	4
12	J,X,SAVE	3
13		0
14		0
15		0

It is thus possible to define the *average* number of live variables ($\overline{LV}$), which is the sum of the count of live variables divided by the count of executable statements in a procedure. This is a complexity measure for data usage in a procedure or program. The average live variables for the program in Figure 2.2 is 22/11 = 2. The live variables in the program in Figure 2.11 appear in Table 2.3. The average live variables for this program is $\overline{LV} = 110/28 = 3.9$. (As an exercise, compute the live variables and average live variables for the programs shown in Figures 2.1 and 2.7.)

Table 2.3   Live Variables for the Program in Figure 2.11

Line	Live Variables	Count
9		0
10	t,x,k	3
11	t,x,k	3
12	t,x,k	3
13		0
15		0
16	size	1
17	size,j	2
18	size,j,a,b	4
19	size,j,a,b	4
20	size,j,a,b,last	5
21	size,j,a,b,last,continue	6
22	size,j,a,b,last,continue	6
23	size,j,a,b,last,continue	6
24	size,j,a,b,last,continue,i	6
25	size,j,a,b,last,continue,i	7
26	size,j,a,b,continue,i	7
27	size,j,a,b,continue,i	6
28	size,j,a,b,i	6
29	size,j,a,b,i	5
30	size,j,a,b,i	5
31	size,j,a,b, i	5
32	size,j.a,b, i	5
33	size,j,a,b	4
34	size,j,a,b	4
35	size,j,a,b	4
36	,j,a,b	3
37		0

As shown, live variables depend on the order of statements in the source program, rather than the dynamic execution-time order in which they are encountered. A metric based on run-time order would be more precisely related to the life of the variable, but would be much more difficult to define algorithmically (especially in a non-structured programming language).

Variable Spans   Two variables can be alive for the same number of statements, but their use in a program can be markedly different. For example, Figure 2.12 lists all of the statements in a Pascal program that refer to the variables a and b. Both variables are alive for the same 40 statements (21−60), but a is referred to three times while b is mentioned only once. A metric that captures some of the essence of how often a variable is used in a program is called the *span* (*SP*). This metric is the number of statements between two successive references to the same variable [ELSH76]. The span is related to the third definition of live variables. For a program that references a variable in n statements, there are $n-1$ spans for that variable. Thus, in Figure 2.12, **a** has 4 spans and **b** has only 2. Intuitively this tells us that **a** is being used more than **b**.

```
      ...
21    read (a,b);
      ...
32    x := a;
      ...
45    y := a-b;
      ...
53    z := a;
      ...
60    writeln (a,b)
      ...
```

Figure 2.12   Statements in a Pascal program referring to variables **a** and **b**.

Furthermore, the size of a span indicates the number of statements that pass between successive uses of a variable. A large span can require the programmer to remember during the construction process a variable that was last used far back in the program. In Figure 2.12, **a** has 4 spans of 10, 12, 7, and 6 statements, while **b** has 2 spans of 23 and 14 statements. It is simple to extend this metric to "average span size," in which case **a** has an average span size of 8.75 and **b** has an average span size of 18.5. (As an exercise, show that the number of spans at a particular statement is also the number of live variables at that point.)

Making Program-wide Metrics from Intra-module Metrics   Each of the metrics discussed in this section is intended to be used within a module, as indicated. But it is possible to extend each one into an inter-module metric. For example, if we want to characterize the average number of live variables for a program of m modules, we can use this equation

$$\overline{LV}_{\text{program}} = \frac{\sum\limits_{i=1}^{m} \overline{LV}_i}{m}$$

where $\overline{LV}_i$ is the average live variable metric computed from the ith module.

Furthermore, the average span size $(\overline{SP})$ for a program of n spans could be computed by using the equation

$$\overline{SP}_{\text{program}} = \frac{\sum\limits_{i=1}^{n} SP_i}{n}$$

2.3.3 The Sharing of Data among Modules

As noted earlier, each of the metrics discussed in the last subsection is intended to be used within a module. But a program normally contains several modules. Often it is desirable and useful to know how data is shared among the modules.

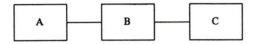

Figure 2.13   Three modules from an imaginary program.

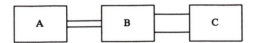

Figure 2.14   "Pipes" of data shared among the modules.

For example, Figure 2.13 shows a schematic of a program consisting of the three subprograms A, B, and C. If we include information that represents the amount of data "passed" among the subprograms, we could envision pipes between the subprograms. The diameter of each pipe could represent the quantity, or volume, of data sent from one subprogram to be used in the other. Figure 2.14 shows the same three subprograms with pipes representing data shared between A and B and between B and C. Note that the A−B shared data is implicitly less than the B−C shared data. Figure 2.15 shows a pictorial representation of the data shared between the main program of bubble and procedure swap both from Figure 2.11. In bubble, the main program invokes the procedure swap in order to get it to swap the ith and $(i+1)^{st}$ members of the a-vector and the b-vector.

In this section, we will introduce metrics that can be used for measuring this concept of sharing of data between modules. Keep in mind that the "bigger the pipe" is between any two modules, the more complex is their relationship. In theory, every module in a program is related to every other module. If this

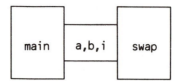

Figure 2.15   The data shared in program **bubble**.

were not true, the modules would not have been put into the same program. But, in practice, some modules may share no data directly with another, as shown by modules A and C in Figure 2.14. The data structure employed in A should have little effect on module C, while the data structure employed in B is obviously important to C since they have such a large pipe between them.

The relationship between subroutine SORT in Figure 2.2 and any program that invokes it is simple since only two variables are passed between them. One of the variables (N) is not changed. However, a module with a long list of parameters of different types, and some "global" data structure which is shared with several modules should be more difficult to construct or comprehend.

In the following discussion, assume that a *global variable* is one that is available to any and all modules in a program. Most programming languages allow the declaration of variables that can be accessed anywhere in the program. Contrast a global variable with a *local variable*, which is declared in a specific module, and whose name is unknown outside that module. A local variable is available to another module only when specifically mentioned in a parameter list passed to that module (in a procedural language), or when referred to in a module completely contained in the one where the local variable is declared (in a block-structured language). Global variables are not so limited, and are known and usable everywhere in the program.

In a study concerning program development strategy, Basili and Turner employed approximately 20 different metrics [BASI75]. Two of the metrics measured the sharing of data as global variables among modules. A *segment-global usage pair* (P, R) is an instance of a segment or module P using global variable R. The value of variable R is either set or read by module P. The count of the number of such pairs among all modules and global variables represents the complexity of the way that the data is shared. In a programming language that allows the definition of individual scopes for global variables, a module can access a global variable, but it can make neither set nor read operations. Thus, the metric can be normalized by dividing the count of potential pairs into the actual count. This metric is called the *relative percentage usage pairs*. The usage pair metric can be further refined to represent the binding of data between two modules. A binding is represented by a triple (P, R, Q), which infers that global variable R is set by module P and read by module Q.

Note that the triple (P, R, Q) requires the existence of pairs (P, R) and (Q, R). The count of the number of such triples for a program is a metric for the sharing of data among modules. It can also be normalized by dividing the count of potential triples into the actual count.

The complexity of data sharing can also be viewed at the module level. Suppose we extend the definition of the data binding triple so that the variable R could be either a global variable or a parameter.[10] Henry and Kafura [HENR81] define the *fan-in* of the module Q to be the number of unique modules P in the program so that at least one of the following conditions holds:

(1) There exists a variable R so that the triple (P, R, Q) is a valid data binding triple.

(2) There exist a module T and variables R, S so that the triples (P, R, T) and (T, S, Q) are valid data binding triples.

The fan-in for a module is the number of modules that pass data to the module either directly or indirectly. Similarly, we can define the *fan-out* for a module as the number of modules to which data is passed either directly or indirectly. A family of *information flow metrics* are proposed in [HENR81] for a module in a programming product as follows:

$$fan-in \times fan-out$$

$$(fan\text{-}in \times fan\text{-}out)^2$$

$$S_s \times (fan\text{-}in \times fan\text{-}out)^2 \tag{2.13}$$

where S_s is the size of the module in LOC.

2.4 Logic Structure Metrics

The logic structure of a program allows it to perform different operations dependent upon different input data or intermediate calculations. For example, Figure 2.7 shows a little program to calculate pay, assuming that there is no overtime pay due. However, in the program of Figure 2.16, employees who work more than 40 hours will receive "time and a half" for all overtime hours. All employees with 40 hours or less are paid at their standard rate. This differential processing is accomplished by the well-known and time-honored IF statement in line 12. Depending upon the hours input, it is now possible for statement 13 or

---

10. An empirical study on the alternative use of global variables and formal parameters was conducted by Lohse and Zweben [LOHS84]. However, there were no conclusive results concerning program modifiability.

15 to be executed while the other one is skipped. Thus, there is no single path through this program any more. There are now two.

```
Line                                                                    Level
  1   program bigpay (input,output);
  2   type check = record
  3           gross: real;
  4           tax: real;
  5           net: real
  6         end;
  7   var pay: check;
  8       hours, rate: real;
  9   begin
 10       while not eof (input) do begin                                  1
 11         readln (hours, rate);                                         2
 12         if hours <= 40 then                                           2
 13             pay.gross := hours * rate                                 3
 14         else                                                          3
 15             pay.gross := (40 * rate) + 1.5 * (hours-40) * rate;       3
 16         pay.tax := 0.25 * pay.gross;                                  2
 17         pay.net := pay.gross - pay.tax;                               2
 18         writeln (pay.gross, pay.tax, pay.net)                         2
 19       end
 20   end.
```

Figure 2.16   A Pascal payroll program that pays overtime.

In addition to the computer's power to store and access large amounts of data, it has the ability to test data and to take action dependent upon the outcome of the test. The orderly tests and associated action form the basis of all computer programs, and are called *algorithms*. (In fact, the claim *Algorithms + Data Structures = Programs* is implicitly made through the use of this phrase as the title for a classical textbook on programming [WIRT76].) The structure of an algorithm is often represented by a directed graph called the *flowchart* or *flowgraph*. It is conventional to highlight the points in a flowchart at which a test is performed and from which there are two or more possible branches. The actions taken in a branch after a test are often grouped together. Figures 2.17 and 2.18 are flowcharts for the programs in Figures 2.2 and 2.7 respectively. The part of the algorithm dealing with the tests made and branches after tests is called the *logic structure* of the program.

In a study in which experts rated complexity metrics, eight of nine product metrics considered important were related to measures of a program's logic

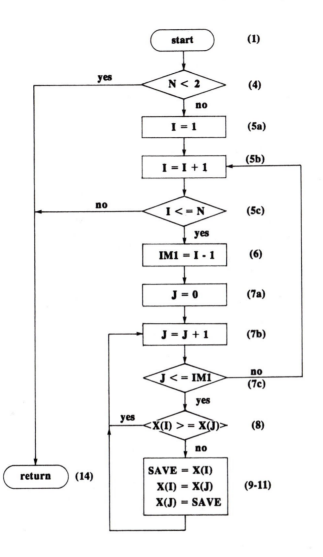

Figure 2.17   The control-flow graph for the program in Figure 2.2.

structure [ZOLN81]. (The ninth important metric was related to data.) As with the metrics for data, there is no agreement on which logic metric is the most important. Even for metrics with the same name and intention, different researchers have used different counting schemes. The following subsections introduce the most popular counting methods for several representative metrics for the logic structure of programs.

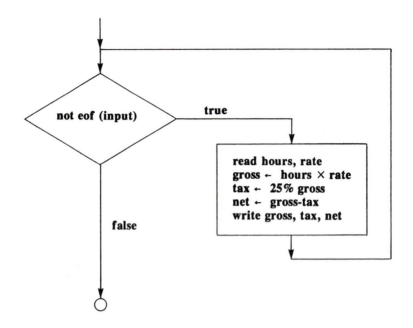

Figure 2.18   The control-flow graph for the program in Figure 2.7.

2.4.1 Decision Count

The flow of control in a computer program normally proceeds sequentially. It is interrupted in three possible situations:

A forward branch — This follows a conditional test that leads to a choice between at least two possible actions. An example is shown in Figure 2.19.

A backward branch — Used to create loops, this may be unconditional (see example in Figure 2.20), or may follow a conditional test that allows either another iteration or the termination of the loop (see example in Figure 2.21).

A horizontal branch — Typically a transfer of control to a procedure or subroutine, this situation is not normally considered an interruption, since the procedure is supposed to return control to the statement following the branch when it terminates.

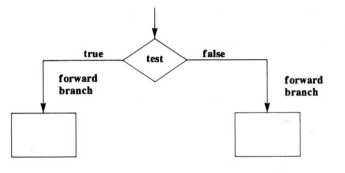

Figure 2.19   A conditional test that leads to a choice.

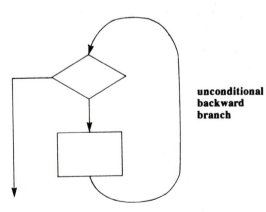

Figure 2.20   An unconditional backward branch used to create loops.

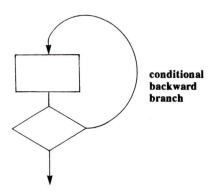

Figure 2.21   A backward branch following a conditional test.

Figures 2.17 and 2.18 contain examples of the first and second flow interruptions. In Figure 2.17, note the forward transfers in boxes labelled 4, 5c, 7c, and 8, and the backward transfers in boxes labelled 7c, 8, and 9−11. Note that **DO** statements in FORTRAN are actually abbreviations of three substatements (as shown by the breakdown into 5a, 5b, and 5c, and 7a, 7b, and 7c. In Figure 2.18, note the two forward transfers and the single backward transfer.

A simple control structure metric called *decision count* (*DE*), for a program is the count of **IF, DO, WHILE, CASE** and other conditional and loop controlstatements. Thus, in Figure 2.2, $DE = 4$, and, in Figure 2.7, $DE = 1$. A program with a larger *DE* (as in Figure 2.2) is believed to be generally more complex than another program with a smaller *DE* (as in Figure 2.7).

Many programming languages allow the use of compound conditions in **IF** and other conditional and loop-control statements. For example, let c_1 and c_2 be two conditions and let s be a statement (or group of statements). The statement

IF c_1 **AND** c_2 **THEN** s

is equivalent to either

IF c_1 **THEN IF** c_2 **THEN** s

or

IF c_2 **THEN IF** c_1 **THEN** s

The flowchart representation in Figure 2.22(*a*) shows the single decision point if the compound condition is treated like a simple condition. In Figure 2.22(*b*), the breakdown of the compound predicate leads to two decisions. However, in Figure 2.22(*c*), it does not matter whether the compound conditions are connected by the logical operators AND or OR. Although the flowchart differs in obvious ways, the OR connection also leads to two decisions.

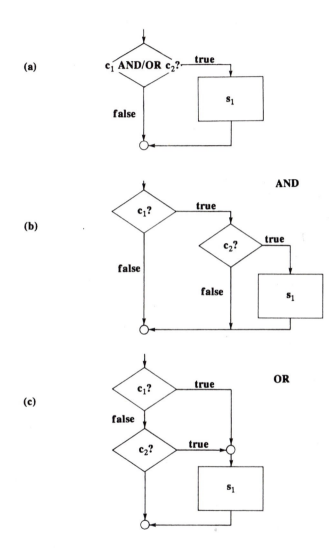

Figure 2.22   The flowchart representation of a compound conditional.

Thus, it is reasonable to count an IF statement with two simple conditions as contributing two to the count of decisions. These simple conditions called *predicates* should be counted as *DE* in a program, instead of the number of occurrences of the keyword (in most languages the keyword IF) for conditional statements. Similarly, a CASE statement is considered to be an IF statement with multiple predicates. If a tool to count some basic software metrics is available, it can easily be extended to include the count of decisions (*DE*) [SHEN85].

A more sophisticated and better known metric based on the number of decisions seems to be the *cyclomatic complexity number* (*v(G)*) proposed by McCabe [MCCA76]. This metric was originally designed to measure the number of "linearly independent" paths through a program, which in turn is believed to relate to the testability and maintainability of the program. Since a program with a backward branch potentially has an infinite number of paths, a measure that is a count of the number of some distinct "basic" paths, rather than all possible paths, is probably more meaningful.

The cyclomatic complexity is defined in a manner similar to that of the *cyclomatic number* in a directed graph such as a flowgraph (see, for example, [WILS72]):

$$v(G) = e - n + p \tag{2.14}$$

where e is the number of edges, n is the number of nodes, and p is the number of connected components in the flowgraph.[11] The cyclomatic complexity differs from the standard cyclomatic number in that it has a branch from the exit node to the entry node in a flowgraph before computing the measure. Therefore, for a flowchart with e edges and n nodes,

$$v(G) = e - n + 2 \tag{2.15}$$

For example, in the flowgraph given in Figure 2.23, if the rectangles are statements and diamond boxes are decision points in a program, this figure displays a flowgraph with thirteen nodes and sixteen edges. Therefore,

$$v(G) = 16 - 13 + 2 = 5$$

Note that the node count includes both rectangles and diamonds.

A good way of conceptualizing the cyclomatic complexity number is to imagine that it represents the number of edges that must be removed in order to reduce the flowgraph (while ignoring directions on its edges) to its "skeleton" — that is, one without "circuits" or loops. A simple flowgraph such as Figure 2.24(a), which represents a linear sequence of code, has $v(G) = 1$. Therefore, a linear set of nodes, like those in Figure 2.24(a), can be reduced to a single node (cf. Figure 2.24(b)) without changing the cyclomatic number. Also, programs with the same number of conditions and branches, and whose flowgraphs are "homeomorphic", have the same cyclomatic number. While the two flowgraphs in Figure 2.25(*a*) and (*b*) represent markedly different programs with differing numbers of nodes and edges, both have the same $v(G) = 4$. Note that for a given program module (single connected component), the cyclomatic

---

11. An "edge" in a flowgraph is a line connecting blocks of code that indicates flow of control. The blocks of code are considered "nodes". A procedure is considered a "connected component".

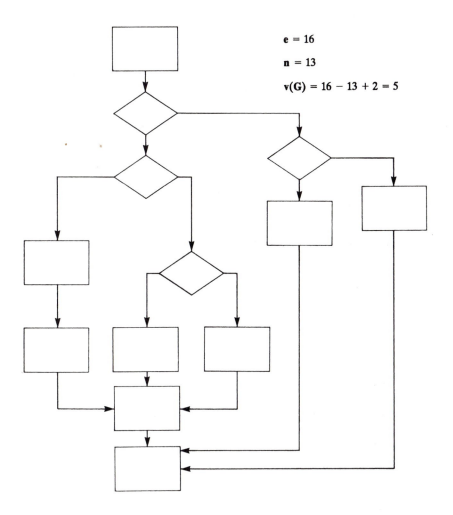

$e = 16$

$n = 13$

$v(G) = 16 - 13 + 2 = 5$

Figure 2.23   A flowgraph with thirteen nodes and sixteen edges.

complexity differs from the cyclomatic number of the flowgraph by 1, and the complexity of the simplest flow graph is 1. McCabe believed that $v(G) = 10$ is a reasonable, but not magical upper limit for proper testing.

Constructing a software tool that generates the flowgraph for analysis is complicated. However, since the cyclomatic complexity depends only on the total number of edges and nodes in the graph, and not on how they are connected, the mechanical generation of $v(G)$ can be simplified greatly. In fact, it is not even necessary to construct the graph if we remember some key points. First, a node in a flowgraph normally has only one edge leading out, unless it is

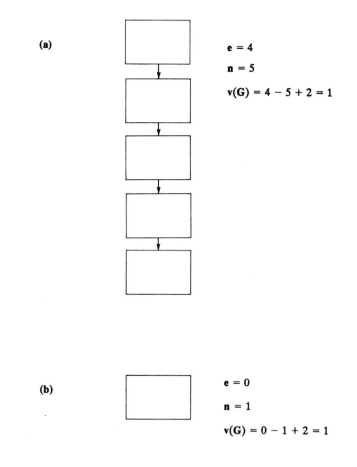

(a)

$e = 4$

$n = 5$

$v(G) = 4 - 5 + 2 = 1$

(b)

$e = 0$

$n = 1$

$v(G) = 0 - 1 + 2 = 1$

Figure 2.24   A simple flowgraph of a linear sequence of code.

the terminal node in the graph, or unless it is a conditional or loop control statement. A node that contains a direct transfer (i.e., GOTO statement) has only one edge leading out. Refer back to Figure 2.24 which had no conditionals and for which $e = n - 1$. (The -1 results from the fact that the terminal node has no edge leading out). It is obvious that this relationship between e and n will hold, regardless of the number of nodes, as long as there are no conditionals or loops. Since each conditional has two edges emanating from it, the conditional statements in a program increase e by 1 for each conditional. For example, if γ is the number of predicates,

$$e = n - 1 + \gamma \tag{2.16}$$

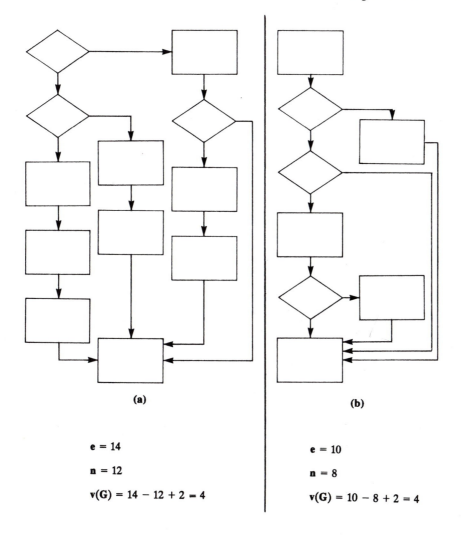

(a)

(b)

e = 14

n = 12

v(G) = 14 − 12 + 2 = 4

e = 10

n = 8

v(G) = 10 − 8 + 2 = 4

Figure 2.25   Two flowgraphs with differing numbers of nodes and edges that both have the same $v(G)$.

or stated equivalently

$$e - n \ = \ \gamma - 1 \tag{2.17}$$

Therefore, by adding 2 to both sides, we get

$$v(G) \ = \ e - n + 2 \ = \ \gamma + 1 \tag{2.18}$$

What have we done? We have taken a fairly complex, graphical metric $v(G)$ and reduced it to a simple computational algorithm. Furthermore, from our earlier discussion of predicates, it should be clear that γ and DE are the same thing. Thus, a computationally tractable formula for $v(G)$ is

$$v(G) = DE + 1 \tag{2.19}$$

This can be easily provided by a simple software analyzer. The counting rules for $v(G)$ or DE for Pascal is shown in Figure 2.5. For example, consider the sample program in Figure 2.17. It clearly has $e = 15$ and $n = 12$, leading to $v(G) = 5$. But, it also has 4 predicates represented by the 4 diamond boxes, so $\gamma = DE = 4$, also leading to $v(G) = 5$.

A program with a certain number of modules has a flowgraph with the same number of connected components. For example, consider the modules in Figure 2.26. Program 1 has e_1 edges and n_1 nodes. From one of those nodes, program 2 is invoked with its e_2 edges and n_2 nodes. Recall that

$$v(G_1) = e_1 - n_1 + 2 \tag{2.20}$$

and

$$v(G_2) = e_2 - n_2 + 2 \tag{2.21}$$

Figure 2.26 shows that invoking program 2 adds both a "call" and a "return" edge. Thus, for the whole program, the cyclomatic complexity becomes

$$v(G) = (e_1 + e_2 + 2) - (n_1 + n_2) + 2$$
$$v(G) = (e_1 - n_1 + 2) + (e_2 - n_2 + 2)$$
$$v(G) = v(G_1) + v(G_2) \tag{2.22}$$

Therefore, the cyclomatic complexity for a multi-module program is simply the sum of the $v(G)$'s for the individual modules. For example, for a program with m modules,

$$v(G_{\text{program}}) = \sum_{i=1}^{m} v(G_i) = \sum_{i=1}^{m} e_i - \sum_{i=1}^{m} n_i + 2m \tag{2.23}$$

where $v(G_i)$ is the cyclomatic complexity of the ith module. Since $v(G_i) = DE_i + 1$,

$$v(G_{\text{program}}) = \sum_{i=1}^{m} DE_i + m. \tag{2.24}$$

2.4.2 Minimum Number of Paths and Reachability Metrics

Schneidewind and Hoffmann [SCHN79] defined metrics for the *minimum number of paths* in a program and the *reachability* of any node. In order to determine N_p, the minimum number of paths, one approach is to describe each path — a unique sequence of arcs from the start node to the terminal node. This path analysis also leads to the determination of reachability R, the number of unique ways of reaching each node.

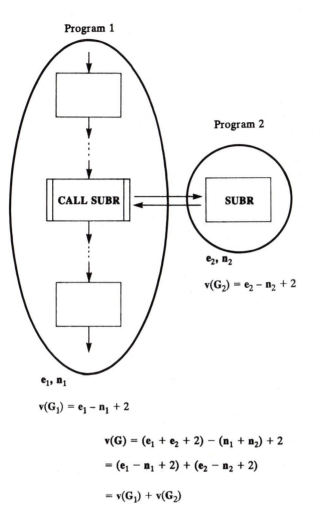

$$v(G_2) = e_2 - n_2 + 2$$

$$v(G_1) = e_1 - n_1 + 2$$

$$v(G) = (e_1 + e_2 + 2) - (n_1 + n_2) + 2$$

$$= (e_1 - n_1 + 2) + (e_2 - n_2 + 2)$$

$$= v(G_1) + v(G_2)$$

Figure 2.26 Program 1 calls Program 2 (subroutine **SUBR**).

Obviously, the number of paths could be large, or even infinite, when loops exist. The determination of N_p excludes paths with backward loops traversed more than once. For example, in Figure 2.17, there are 5 unique paths (i.e., $N_p = 5$):

1,4,14
1,4,5a,5b,5c,14
1,4,5a,5b,5c,6,7a,7b,7c,5b,5c,14
1,4,5a,5b,5c,6,7a,7b,7c,8,7b,7c,5b,5c,14
1,4,5a,5b,5c,6,7a,7b,7c,8,9−11,7b,7c,5b,5c,14

However, this technique may be awkward to use on large programs. Shooman proposes a method to estimate N_p based on algebraic considerations (see Chapter 4 of [SHOO83]). The reachability R of each node in Figure 2.17 can be determined from the information in Table 2.4. For example, Table 2.4 shows that there are 4 unique paths to node 5b, but only one unique path to node 5a. The average reachability ($\bar{R}$) is computed from the total number of paths divided by the number of nodes:

$$\bar{R} = \frac{26}{12}$$

Table 2.4   The Reachability (R) of each Node in Figure 2.17

node	R	paths
1	1	(1)
4	1	(1,4)
5a	1	(1,4,5a)
5b	4	(1,4,5a,5b) (1,4,5a,5b,5c,6,7a,7b,7c,5b) (1,4,5a,5b,5c,6,7a,7b,7c,8,7b,7c,5b) (1,4,5a,5b,5c,6,7a,7b,7c,8,9-11,7b,7c,5b)
5c	4	(1,4,5a,5b,5c) (1,4,5a,5b,5c,6,7a,7b,7c,5b,5c) (1,4,5a,5b,5c,6,7a,7b,7c,8,7b,7c,5b,5c) (1,4,5a,5b,5c,6,7a,7b,7c,8,9-11,7b,7c,5b,5c)
6	1	(1,4,5a,5b,5c,6)
7a	1	(1,4,5a,5b,5c,6,7a)
7b	3	(1,4,5a,5b,5c,6,7a,7b) (1,4,5a,5b,5c,6,7a,7b,7c,8,7b) (1,4,5a,5b,5c,6,7a,7b,7c,8,9-11,7b)
7c	3	(1,4,5a,5b,5c,6,7a,7b,7c) (1,4,5a,5b,5c,6,7a,7b,7c,8,7b,7c) (1,4,5a,5b,5c,6,7a,7b,7c,8,9-11,7b,7c)
8	1	(1,4,5a,5b,5c,6,7a,7b,7c,8)
9-11	1	(1,4,5a,5b,5c,6,7a,7b,7c,8,9-11)
14	5	(1,4,14) (1,4,5a,5b,5c,14) (1,4,5a,5b,5c,6,7a,7b,7c,5b,5c,14) (1,4,5a,5b,5c,6,7a,7b,7c,8,7b,7c,5b,5c,14) (1,4,5a,5b,5c,6,7a,7b,7c,8,9-11,7b,7c,5b,5c,14)

26/12=2.2 average reachability $\bar{R}$

It is just coincidental in Figure 2.17 that N_p and $v(G)$ are both 5. But Figure 2.27 shows a program flowchart similar to one in the Schneidewind and Hoffman paper. In this figure, $v(G) = 4$ (note the 3 decision boxes), but there are 6 unique paths (i.e., $N_p=6$):

1,2,4,10
1,2,3,2,4,10
1,2,4,5,6,7,9,10
1,2,4,5,6,8,9,10
1,2,3,2,4,5,6,7,9,10
1,2,3,2,4,5,6,8,9,10

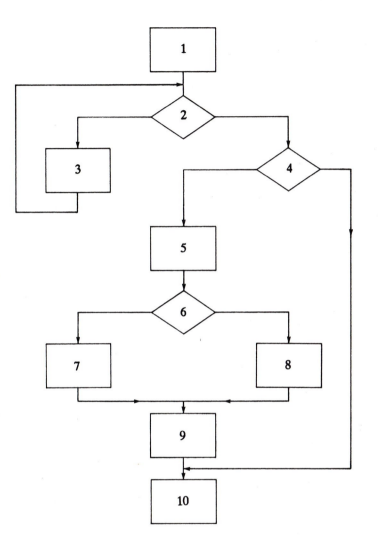

Figure 2.27   A program flowchart adapted from Schneidewind and Hoffmann [SCHN79].

Since every decision leads to at least one extra path, it is always true that $N_p \geq v(G)$. The reachability of each node in Figure 2.27 can be determined from the information in Table 2.5.

In an attempt to validate the usefulness of N_p and $\bar{R}$, Schneidewind and Hoffman gathered data on 64 errors found during debugging and testing of actual software products. They found high correlations between N_p and $\bar{R}$ and some complexity measures (see Section 3.4.4). For example, the correlation

Table 2.5   The Reachability (R) of each Node in Figure 2.27

node	R	paths
1	1	(1)
2	2	(1,2) (1,2,3,2)
3	1	(1,2,3)
4	2	(1,2,4) (1,2,3,2,4)
5	2	(1,2,4,5) (1,2,3,2,4,5)
6	2	(1,2,4,5,6) (1,2,3,2,4,5,6)
7	2	(1,2,4,5,6,7) (1,2,3,2,4,5,6,7)
8	2	(1,2,4,5,6,8) (1,2,3,2,4,5,6,8)
9	4	(1,2,4,5,6,7,9) (1,2,4,5,6,8,9) (1,2,3,2,4,5,6,7,9) (1,2,3,2,4,5,6,8,9)
10	6	(1,2,4,10) (1,2,3,2,4,10) (1,2,4,5,6,7,9,10) (1,2,4,5,6,8,9,10) (1,2,3,2,4,5,6,7,9,10) (1,2,3,2,4,5,6,8,9,10)
24/10=2.4 average reachability $\bar{R}$		

coefficients were 0.76 (number of errors found and N_p), 0.77 (number of errors found and $\bar{R}$), 0.90 (time to find errors and N_p), and 0.90 (time to find errors and $\bar{R}$).

2.4.3   Nesting levels

Consider line 5 of the Pascal program segment in Figure 2.28. Can you quickly decide what must be true to reach line 5? The answer is given later, but it should be obvious that nesting is a useful programming method. Nesting allows the programmer to avoid excessive compound conditionals in any one IF or WHILE statement by taking advantage of conditions in effect due to previous IF or WHILE statements. Thus, the IF statement in line 4 ensures that decrementing will not lead to a negative x[i] and from the WHILE statement in line 3, it is possible to assume that x[i] is larger than x[i+1] before decrementing. But, moderation in all things is a virtue: excessive nesting can lead to circumstances in which it is difficult for programmers to comprehend what must be true for a particular statement to be reached [DUNS79]. In Figure 2.28, x[i] (for only i values of 1 through n−1) must be positive, larger than x[i+1], and at least as large as the decrement value in order to reach line 5.

```
Line                                              Level
1    for i := 1 to n-1 do begin                    1
2        if x[i] > 0 then begin                     2
3            while x[i] > x[i+1] do begin           3
4                if x[i] >= decr then begin         4
5                    x[i] := x[i] - decr            5
6                end
7            end
8        end
9    end;
```

Figure 2.28   A Pascal program segment with extensive nesting.

Thus, another important complexity metric is the *depth of nesting* [ZOLN81]. For example, a simple statement in the sequential part of a program, such as line 5 in Figure 2.2, may be executed only once. A similar statement, such as line 9, is executed in the order of n^2 ($O(n^2)$) times (n is the size of the array and is stored in variable N) since it is part of an inner loop. The higher the depth or *nesting level*, the more difficult it is to assess the entrance conditions for a certain statement. Such difficulty leads to the definition of the metric *average nesting level* $(\overline{NL})$ [DUNS80]. In order to compute this metric, every executable statement in a program must be assigned a nesting level. A simple recursive procedure for doing this is described as follows:

(1) The first executable statement is assigned nesting level 1.

(2) If statement a is at level l and statement b simply follows sequentially the execution of statement a, then the nesting level of statement b is l also.

(3) If statement a is at level l and statement b is in the range of a loop or a conditional transfer governed by statement a, then the nesting level of statement b is $l+1$.

In Figure 2.2 all executable statements have been assigned a nesting level via this procedure. In order to determine the average nesting level $(\overline{NL})$, add all statement nesting levels and divide the sum by the number of statements. For this program with 11 executable statements, the sum is 34 and the average nesting level is 3.1. Similarly, the $\overline{NL}$ for Figure 2.16 is 2.2 and the $\overline{NL}$ for Figure 2.28 is 3.0.

2.4.4 Transfer Usage

In a classic letter denouncing the use of the GOTO statement, Dijkstra suggested that a wise programmer should strive to narrow the conceptual gap between the static program and the dynamic process that it represents [DIJK68]. This means that a program is easier to understand if successive statements in the program text also correspond to successive actions in time. The use of direct transfers (or GOTO statements) disrupts such correspondence. Thus, Dijkstra claimed that he "...had been familiar with the observation that the quality of programmers is a decreasing function of the density of GOTO statements in the programs they produce." If Dijkstra is right, a simple count of direct transfers will serve as a useful metric. However, such a measure is not meaningful in certain popular languages such as FORTRAN, where the GOTO statement is essential even in writing structured programs. (Note that this is not applicable to FORTRAN 77 which is a structured language.) In such a case, the count of GOTO statements is not as useful as the measure of its uncontrolled use.

```
1           IF (X.GT.Y) GOTO 200
2               Z=X
3               GOTO 300
4    200        Z=Y
5                .
6                .
7                .
8               GOTO 200
9    300 CONTINUE
```

Figure 2.29   GOTOs in FORTRAN.

For example, in Figure 2.29, there are three distinct GOTO statements. The ones in lines 1 and 3 are used with the IF statement to produce the effect of an IF–THEN–ELSE (and thus are being used in a structured manner). However, the GOTO statement at line 8 simply transfers control backwards in the program in an unstructured manner.

In this spirit, a metric for the uncontrolled use of GOTO statements is the measure *knots* proposed by Woodward, Hennell, and Hedley [WOOD79]. They observed that, during program development or debugging, a FORTRAN programmer often laid out the listing and proceeded to draw lines with arrows on the margin indicating the flow (or the interruption thereof) of control. Figure 2.30 reproduces the sample program in Figure 2.2 and shows the possible flow lines. In this case, there is no knot as the two GOTO statements do not cross each other. In addition to forward transfers, backward arrows are drawn at the end of each loop. Suppose for some reason we modify the program by

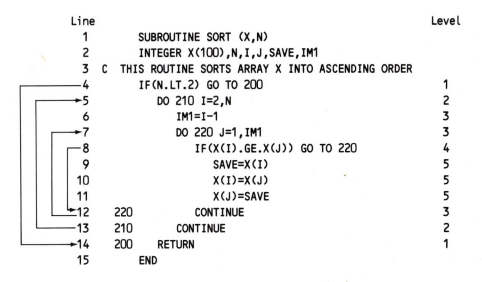

```
Line                                                      Level
  1        SUBROUTINE SORT (X,N)
  2        INTEGER X(100),N,I,J,SAVE,IM1
  3    C  THIS ROUTINE SORTS ARRAY X INTO ASCENDING ORDER
  4        IF(N.LT.2) GO TO 200                             1
  5          DO 210 I=2,N                                   2
  6            IM1=I-1                                       3
  7            DO 220 J=1,IM1                               3
  8              IF(X(I).GE.X(J)) GO TO 220                 4
  9                SAVE=X(I)                                5
 10                X(I)=X(J)                                5
 11                X(J)=SAVE                                5
 12    220      CONTINUE                                    3
 13    210    CONTINUE                                      2
 14    200  RETURN                                          1
 15        END
```

Figure 2.30 A FORTRAN subroutine that sorts an array into ascending order.

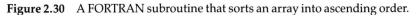

```
Line                                                      Level
  1        SUBROUTINE SORT (X,N)
  2        INTEGER X(100),N,I,J,SAVE,IM1
  3    C THIS ROUTINE SORTS ARRAY X INTO ASCENDING ORDER
  4        IF(N.LT.2) GO TO 200                             1
  5          DO 210 I=2,N                                   2
  6            IM1=I-1                                       3
  7            DO 220 J=1,IM1                               3
  8              IF(X(I).LT.X(J)) GO TO 230                 4
  9                GO TO 220
 10    230        SAVE=X(I)                                5
 11                X(I)=X(J)                                5
 12                X(J)=SAVE                                5
 13    220      CONTINUE                                    3
 14    210    CONTINUE                                      2
 15    200  RETURN                                          1
 16        END
```

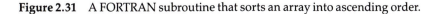

Figure 2.31 A FORTRAN subroutine that sorts an array into ascending order.

reversing the direction of the test in line 8 and add a GOTO statement, as shown in Figure 2.31. This is an awkward way to sort correctly, but it shows that this is a case in which there is one knot. To define the knots metric, assume that the lines in a program are numbered sequentially. Let an ordered pair of integers (a,b) indicate that there is a direct transfer from line a to line b. Given two pairs (a,b) and (c,d), there is a knot if one of the following two cases is true:

(1) $\min(a,b) < \min(c,d) < \max(a,b)$ and $\max(c,d) > \max(a,b)$

(2) $\min(a,b) < \max(c,d) < \max(a,b)$ and $\min(c,d) < \min(a,b)$

The ordered pairs for the program in Figure 2.31 are (4,15), (8,10), and (9,13). The pair (4,15) does not form a knot with any other pair; (8,10) and (9,13) satisfy Case (1). This example shows that an inappropriate use of the conditional statement may increase the structural complexity, which is reflected by the knot count.

For languages that allow multiple statements on one line, we must reformat the source listing so that all direct transfers are on individual lines before applying this definition to obtain the number of knots. In certain situations, we can rearrange some statements in a program in a way that will not change the function of the program, but will change the knot count [WOOD79]. For these equivalent programs, the ones with the lower knot count are believed to be better designed.

2.5 Composite Metrics

Imagine how difficult it would be to try to assess a human being with just one measure. Candidates for such a measure might be height, weight, or level of intelligence. But, it is obvious that not one of those metrics gives a complete picture of a person. (Surely you would not like to be evaluated by means of only your weight!) When describing people, we recognize that it takes several measures even to attempt to give a meaningful description.

It is just as naive to think that a single metric will ever be adequate to represent the complexity of software. Since the previously discussed metrics are designed to measure different features of computer programs, a straightforward approach is to consider a *vector* of such metrics. For example, we could use a pair of numbers (a,b) so that a and b are metrics. A partial ordering can then be formed: program P_1 with metric (a_1,b_1) is more complex than program P_2 with metric (a_2,b_2), if $a_1 \geq a_2$ and $b_1 \geq b_2$ (as long as one of the pairs is ">" rather than just "$\geq$"). Using this technique, we can order the programs in

Table 2.6 from the least to the most complex, if a is the size metric S_s and b is the logic structure metric $v(G)$.

Table 2.6   Ordering Software Complexity with a Vector of Metrics

Complexity	S_s	$v(G)$
Least	300	7
.	320	9
.	320	11
.	350	11
.	400	15
.	500	16
Most	500	22

Myers made such an attempt by considering cyclomatic complexity [MYER77]. He recognized the potential inconsistency between the count of IF statements and the count of predicates. He proposed that a more reasonable metric for logic structure is the pair (*CYC-mid, CYC-max*) where

CYC-min =   count of all conditionals and loops and including CASE statements

CYC-mid =   CYC-min + number equal to 2 less than the number of selections in a CASE statement.

CYC-max =   CYC-mid + each logical operator (AND or OR) in a conditional statement. (*CYC-max* is equivalent to our definition of $v(G)$ given in Equation (2.18).)

Another attempt has been made by Hansen [HANS78]; in which the pair is (*CYC-min, operation count*). This idea is supported by the work of Baker and Zweben who proposed a composite metric of Software Science E (discussed in the next section) and McCabe's $v(G)$ [BAKE80]. Oviedo proposed a composite program complexity metric C based on control flow complexity CF (the cardinality of a set based on the control flow graph), and a data flow complexity DF based on the count of variable definitions and references in each block [OVIE80]. In it simplest form

$$C = \alpha CF + \beta DF \tag{2.25}$$

for some weights α and β.

However, the compositing of metrics by simply including them in a vector may only increase the confusion since the relationship between programs not covered by the partial ordering is not defined. In our example, it is not clear which of the two programs is more complex if $a_1 > a_2$ but $b_1 < b_2$. For example, where in Table 2.6 would you put a program with $S_S = 375$ and $v(G) = 10$? The possibility of confusion also increases when more metrics are included in the vector. Think of the possibilities if the implied vector in Table 2.6 is extended to include η_2 and $\overline{NL}$. As a result, such compositing has not been of much interest to many researchers.

2.6 Software Science Composite Metrics

In Sections 2.2 and 2.3, we introduced several metrics that are part of a collection known as *Software Science*, created by the late Prof. M. H. Halstead at Purdue University in the 1970s. In particular, we discussed his η_1, η_2, N_1, N_2, and V. All except the V metric are basic token counts that, other than minor variations in their definitions, are noncontroversial. In this section, we will discuss the definitions of several more Software Science metrics that are based on Halstead's model of the programming process. All of them are functions of the four basic metrics η_1, η_2, N_1, and N_2. The model envisioned by Halstead was very simple: a program of N_1 operators and N_2 operands is constructed by selecting from among η_1 unique operators and η_2 unique operands. This idea is illustrated in Figure 2.32. From this model, Halstead derived presumed answers to several interesting questions related to programming, such as the level of implementation of a program, the implementation effort, and the level of the programming language used.

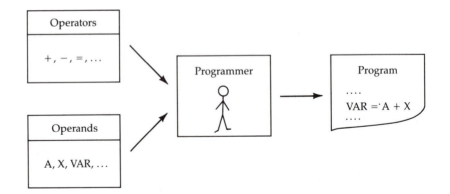

Figure 2.32 A model of the programming process.

However, many of the "composite metrics" we will discuss are those that have been met with some controversy and opposition from some researchers concerning their theoretical basis and empirical support. In general, these metrics have been used only sparingly by practitioners. They are described here for the purpose of completeness and to show the richness of the theory proposed by Halstead. We will conclude this section with a discussion of what we contend to be the *real* contributions of Halstead's work. In our opinion the value goes far beyond the handful of metrics that he proposed.

2.6.1 The Estimated Program Length

As discussed in Section 2.2.2, one measure of the size of a program is the total number of tokens — referred to in Software Science as the *length N*, which is the sum of the total operator and operand usage ($N = N_1 + N_2$). The first hypothesis of Software Science is that the length of a well-structured program is a function only of the number of unique operators and operands. This function, called the *length equation*, is denoted by $\hat{N}$ and is defined by

$$\hat{N} = \eta_1 \times \log_2\eta_1 + \eta_2 \times \log_2\eta_2 \qquad (2.26)$$

For example, the sorting program in Figure 2.2 has 14 unique operators and 13 unique operands, as shown in Figure 2.4. Suppose that these numbers are known before the completion of the program, possibly by using a program design language and knowing the programming language chosen.[12] It is then possible to estimate the length $\hat{N}$ of the program in number of tokens using Equation (2.26):

$$\hat{N} = 14 \times \log_2 14 + 13 \times \log_2 13$$
$$= 14 \times 3.81 + 13 \times 3.70$$
$$= 53.34 + 48.11$$
$$= 101.45$$

Thus, even before constructing the sorting program, Equation (2.26) predicts that there will be about 101 tokens (operators and operands) used in the completed program, which is within 10% of the program's actual length N of 93 tokens (Figure 2.4).

There are several major flaws in the derivation of the formula in Chapter 2 of [HALS77], which we include as Equation (2.26). These flaws are discussed in [SHEN83]. Several researchers have attempted to provide a better theoretical justification for this equation [for example, see SHOO83]. While these theoretical formulations are not entirely convincing, Equation (2.26) may still be empirically justified in the sense that, while it may not be a precise equality for a specific program, it may be considered valid statistically over a large collection of many programs. Indeed there have been several empirical studies that do support the relationship [SHEN83]. Therefore the length equation can be viewed as

---

12. The early estimation of these important factors is discussed in Section 4.3.8.

a relationship that explains "typical" performance, while almost certainly failing to achieve precision in specific instances. It is also known that certain poor programming practices, referred to as *impurities* in programs in [HALS77], can make the length equation a poor predictor of N.

2.6.2 The Program Volume

The model envisioned by Halstead also provides another interpretation of the measure *volume* given earlier as a size metric (Equation (2.7)). Halstead suggested that

$$V = N \times \log_2 \eta \tag{2.27}$$

may also be interpreted as the number of *mental comparisons* needed to write a program of length N. This interpretation assumes that, during programming, the human mind follows a "binary search" process to select the next token from the vocabulary of size η. In our sorting program example shown in Figure 2.2, notice that $\eta = 14 + 13 = 27$ and $N = 93$, so that

$$V = 93 \times \log_2 27$$

$$= 93 \times 4.75$$

$$= 442$$

Thus, Software Science theory suggests that 442 mental comparisons must be made in order to write our sorting program: we must select the 93 tokens each time from a field of 27 possibilities using a binary search technique. Some programmers may feel that they do not program in this way and that programming is a good deal more sophisticated than just determining the next token to use from an available set. For this reason, some researchers found the interpretation of V in this manner to be questionable (for example, see [COUL83]).

2.6.3 Potential Volume and Difficulty

An algorithm may be implemented by many different but equivalent programs. Among these programs, the one that has minimal size is said to have the *potential volume* V^*. Halstead argued that the minimal implementation of any algorithm was through a reference to a procedure that had been previously written. The implementation of this algorithm would then require nothing more than invoking the procedure and supplying the operands for its input and output parameters. Halstead showed that the potential volume of an algorithm implemented as a procedure call could be expressed as

$$V^* = (2 + \eta_2^*)\log_2(2 + \eta_2^*) \tag{2.28}$$

The first term in the parentheses, 2, represents the two unique operators for the procedure call — the procedure name and a grouping symbol that separates the procedure name from its parameters.[13] The second term, $\eta_2{}^*$, represents the number of "conceptually unique" input and output parameters. For the sorting program example in Figure 2.2, the parameters are

X — the array holding the integers to be sorted

N — the size of the array to be sorted

We set $\eta_2^* = 3$ since X is used both as input and output. Thus the potential volume V^* of the sorting program is

$$V^* = 5\log_2 5 = 11.6$$

While $\eta_2{}^*$ can probably be determined for small application programs, it is much more difficult to compute for large complicated programs, such as a compiler or an operating system. In these cases, it is difficult to identify precisely the conceptually unique operands.

In Software Science, any program with volume V is considered to be implemented at the *program level L*, defined by

$$L = V^*/V \tag{2.29}$$

The value of L for a program is a maximum of 1, with $L = 1$ representing a program written at the highest possible level (i.e., with minimum size). Thus, our sorting program may be said to be implemented at level

$$L = \frac{11.6}{442} = 0.026.$$

Halstead called the inverse of the program level the *difficulty D*:

$$D = 1/L \tag{2.30}$$

As the volume V of an implementation of a program increases, the program level L decreases and the difficulty D increases. Thus, programming practices such as the redundant usage of operands, or the failure to use high-level control constructs will tend to increase the volume metric as well as the difficulty metric. For our sorting program,

$$D = 1/.026 = 38.5.$$

The program level L of a particular implementation of an algorithm depends upon the ratio of the potential volume V^* and the actual volume V, as shown in Equation (2.29). But, as we have already discussed, the potential

---

13. Halstead intended that procedures could be invoked as follows
      procedure name, parameter, ..., parameter
in which case the two unique operator argument makes sense. This is somewhat confusing since the syntax of most programming languages leads to procedure invocation as follows
      procedure name (parameter, ..., parameter)
that seems to require three unique operators. This is a syntactic quirk, since two unique operators really are sufficient.

volume metric is usually very hard to determine, so Halstead offered an alternate formula that *estimates* the program level

$$\hat{L} = \frac{1}{\hat{D}} = \frac{2}{\eta_1} \times \frac{\eta_2}{N_2} \tag{2.31}$$

An intuitive argument for this formula is that programming difficulty increases if additional operators are introduced (i.e., if $\eta_1/2$ increases) and if an operand is used repetitively (i.e., if N_2/η_2 increases). Every parameter in Equation (2.31) may be obtained by counting the operators and operands in a finished computer program. The potential volume V^* may then be deduced using Equation (2.32) with L equal to $\hat{L}$. For our sorting program, $\eta_1 = 14$, $\eta_2 = 13$, and $N_2 = 42$, so that

$$\hat{L} = \frac{2}{14} \times \frac{13}{42} = 0.044$$

which is not very close to the 0.026 level we determined earlier using the count of conceptually unique operands. From this result and Equation (2.29) we can suggest that

$$\hat{V}^* = V \times \hat{L} = 442 \times .044 = 19.4 \tag{2.32}$$

The discrepancy between V^* and $\hat{V}^*$ for this simple example does not inspire confidence in the application of this portion of Software Science theory to larger more complicated programs.

2.6.4 Effort and Time

Halstead hypothesized that the effort required to implement a computer program increases as the size of the program increases. It also takes more effort to implement a program at a lower level (higher difficulty) than another equivalent program at a higher level (lower difficulty). Thus, the *effort E* in Software Science is defined as

$$E = V/\hat{L} = \hat{D} \times V = \frac{\eta_1 N_2 N \log_2 \eta}{2\eta_2} \tag{2.33}$$

The unit of measurement of E is *elementary mental discriminations*. For our sorting program

$$E = 442 \,/\, 0.044 = 10045$$

Therefore, 10,045 elementary mental discriminations are required to construct our program.

A major claim for Software Science is its ability to relate its basic metrics to actual implementation time. A psychologist, John Stroud, suggested that the human mind is capable of making a limited number of elementary discriminations per second [STRO67]. Stroud claimed that this number β (called the

Stroud number by Halstead) ranges between 5 and 20. Since effort E uses "elementary mental discriminations" as its unit of measure, the programming time T of a program in seconds is simply

$$T = E/\beta \qquad\qquad (2.34)$$

β is normally set to 18 since this seemed to give the best results in Halstead's earliest experiments, which compared the predicted times with observed programming times, including the time for design, coding, and testing. Halstead claimed that this formula can be used to estimate programming time when a problem is solved by one proficient, concentrating programmer writing a single-module program [HALS77]. Thus, to complete our sorting program example

$$T = 10045 / 18 = 558 \text{ seconds} \approx 10 \text{ minutes}$$

This is probably a reasonable time to produce the program, which is very simple.

At first, a formula for estimating time seems a valuable tool. However, we should note that Stroud's work and the Stroud number are *not* favored by psychologists and many software engineers today, because of the lack of empirical evidence and the poor analogy between the domain of Stroud's work and that of programming. A more thorough discussion of the use of psychological results in Software Science may be found in [COUL83].

2.6.5 Language Level

There are now literally hundreds of programming languages. In some organizations, several languages may be used on a regular basis for software development. For example, in some large companies, software is being developed using FORTRAN, Pascal, COBOL, and assembly language. There are proponents of each major language (including those of newcomers Ada, C, and Prolog — as well as the late-blooming APL) that argue that their favorite language is the best to use. These arguments suggest the need for a metric that expresses the power of a language. Halstead hypothesized that, if the programming language is kept fixed, as V^* increases, L decreases in such a way that the product $L \times V^*$ remains constant. Thus, this product, which he called the *language level* λ, can be used to characterize a programming language:

$$\lambda = L \times V^* = L^2 V \qquad\qquad (2.35)$$

When Halstead analyzed a number of programs written in different languages using Equation (2.31) for L, average language level metrics were determined to be 1.53 for PL/1, 1.21 for Algol, 1.14 for FORTRAN, and 0.88 for CDC assembly language [HALS77]. These average λ's follow the intuitive rankings of most programmers' for these languages, but they all have large variances. Figure 2.33 shows the ± 1 standard deviation range for each language based on data from several programs, which demonstrates the tremendous overlap among the so-called "constants." Such fluctuations in a hypothesized fixed value are not entirely unexpected since the language level metric depends on the language itself, the nature of the problem being programmed, and on proficiency and style of the programmer. Nevertheless, studies by other researchers [CHRI81, CONT82] have failed to confirm that λ is statistically constant for any language. Instead, these studies show that λ is a decreasing function of program size.

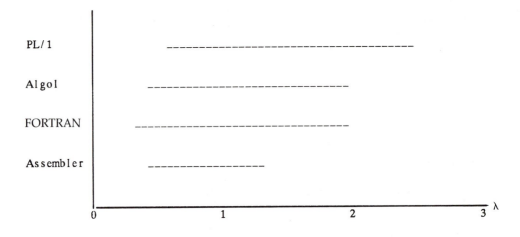

Figure 2.33   Overlapping λ values (+ 1 and − 1 standard deviation ranges).

Equation (2.35), if valid, can be useful in selecting a programming language for an application area. Arithmetic manipulations of Equations (2.28), (2.33), and (2.35) yield

$$E = \frac{V^{*3}}{\lambda^2} \tag{2.36}$$

Thus, for a given problem with fixed V^*, the programming effort E is inversely related to the square of the language level λ. This relationship may help the manager to decide, based on the availability, reliability, and efficiency of various compilers, the appropriate language for the given problem.

For our sorting program,

$$\lambda = .044^2 \times 442 = .86$$

which suggests that the program was written in something slightly below the CDC assembly language level listed earlier.

2.6.6 The Real Contributions of Software Science

A sound theory not only should have an intuitive set of definitions, but also should provide a useful set of hypotheses, which may be derived and validated from the basic model. Although some of the derivations in Software Science are tenuous as discussed in [SHEN83], many interesting aspects of programming are covered. They include the size of a program as a function of the basic metrics, an estimator of the program level (and difficulty), the time to construct a program by a concentrating programmer, and a method to evaluate programming languages. In fact, Software Science is the most comprehensive theory yet attempted of the software development process.

However, the true contribution of Software Science may be best seen from an historical perspective. Halstead's work was very nearly the first software metrics work done in this country. Furthermore, it received more publicity than any other metrics work in the mid-1970s. Many researchers embraced Software Science and promoted it with a missionary-like zeal. However, others disliked its theoretical underpinnings (or the lack thereof, as some of them would say) and argued that Software Science was not a useful body of metrics. However, even as the controversy continued, it made many observers aware of the *need* for metrics and their potential uses. Some researchers proposed and developed metrics for such characteristics as complexity, size, and effort, having been inspired (or shocked!) by Halstead's metrics.

As we write this book in the mid 1980s, we must conclude that many of Halstead's most controversial measures (such as, λ, V^*, and E) have not been shown to have good *construct validity:* they probably do not measure exactly what Halstead hoped they would. However, some of the basic Software Science metrics — especially η_1 and η_2 — have been shown to be strongly correlated to program size and error rates. Researchers are therefore continuing to find these metrics useful as a basis for size and effort models. Thus, Halstead's work served to stimulate a great deal of interest in software metrics, as well as to contribute some basic metrics that survive to this day.

2.7 Effort and Cost Metrics

If you go to a carnival, you are almost certain to see a weight guesser in action. This performer offers for 50 cents to guess a person's weight within 3 pounds or, failing that, to present that person with an expensive stuffed animal. In this timeless bit of Americana, there are two critical quantities involved. One is the performer's *estimate* of the weight, as surely determined by highly some theoretical process, and the other is the *actual* weight, as measured by the performer's accurate scale. The object of the performance is to produce an estimate as close as possible to the actual weight.

We would like to think that the world of software management is as far removed as possible from the carnival world. But a similar process goes on when we try to produce accurate estimates of such factors as effort, cost, and defects. Certainly the costs of such estimates are far more than 50 cents, and the losses due to bad estimates are far more than a stuffed animal.

In this book, we discuss models and methods for producing estimates (see Section 2.6 and Chapters 4—7). In this section and the next, we concentrate on how to obtain actual effort, cost, and defect figures. Such quantities are necessary to determine whether an estimator is really working. Furthermore, even in the absence of estimators, these quantities are needed for effective management of software development.

The effort required to construct a program can be measured in many units. They range from Halstead's elementary mental discriminations, to the actual time in minutes for a programmer to do the job, to the common measure of work in person-months. Also, even though effort (usually measured in time) is important, in a true sense the most important effort metric really is the *cost*. You would certainly be willing to pay 3 programmers $100 per day to produce a payroll system in one 5-day week with the total effort equalling 15 programmer-days, and the total cost equalling $1500 rather than 1 programmer $500 per day to produce the same payroll system in the same 5-day week, with the total effort equalling 5 programmer-days, and the total cost equalling $2,500. At the end of this section, we will return to the consideration of the relationship between effort and cost.

The fact that acceptable effort and cost figures are important to management cannot be stressed strongly enough. Even if no attempt is being made to estimate or predict these quantities, the knowledge of effort and cost are vital to management in such areas as profitability, feasibility of projects, and productivity of programmers. The manager who does not know how much effort and cost have been expended on past projects of various sizes and functions cannot even make a reasonable intuitive estimate on upcoming projects. This same manager could not possibly use most of the effort models described in this book, since many require a knowledge of historical results from within the organization.

The precision of a measure is generally determined by the type of application intended. For example, the micron and the light-year are both measures of distance. The first is used to measure the distance between molecules in crystals, whereas the second is used to measure the distance between stars in the universe. Similarly, effort and cost measurements differ in degree of precision dependent upon their intended usage. Thus, small projects may be measured in days or hours, while large projects may be measure in programmer-months or programmer-years. The units and method of measurement of effort are often divided into two categories: the micro-level of measurement for effort expended by individual programmers on small projects, and the macro-level of measurement for effort expended by teams of programmers on large projects.

2.7.1 Micro-levels of Effort and Cost

Micro-level projects are defined as small projects usually completed by a single programmer in a few days or weeks. Programming teams are not involved, and these projects do not require several months' effort. The most appropriate effort metrics are units of time in minutes, hours, or at most days. Since only one individual is involved, the time is directly convertible to the normal effort measure, the person-hour. Note that such projects are uncommon in industry, but are quite common in small organizations and in experiments that investigate various questions concerning software development.

As discussed in Chapter 1, the development process is often divided into three phases: design, coding, and testing. For micro-level projects, the time spent on individual phases can be measured using an ordinary clock or, in some cases, a stopwatch. The time may be recorded by the programmer or by an independent observer. In any case, records should be made *during* the development process, rather than later to avoid the introduction of errors. Such errors may be due to faulty recollection, or intentional bias toward the time the process *should* have taken. For example, Figure 2.34 shows a form used to record time during an experiment conducted at Purdue University [WOOD79].

The times for coding and testing phases can be substantiated with computer logs if a terminal is used during software development. *Traps* built into the system allow a copy of the source code to be saved (with a time stamp) each time the program is submitted for compilation or execution. These traps have been found to be useful in detecting irregularities in effort data collected via logs.

Since the total time in micro-level projects is often just a few hours, interruptions such as phone calls or coffee breaks may have a biasing effect on the data. Thus, in single-programmer experiments, the only time to be recorded is the time directly related to the software development. This requires programmers (or their observers) to ignore time blocks spent on other activities. Another approach (typically used in the experimental context) is to eliminate interruptions and to strive for a high degree of concentration by keeping subjects in rooms with terminals that are reserved for a block of time. Leaving the room while the experiment is in progress is strongly discouraged.

Thus, a substantive issue in the determination of effort and cost at the micro-level is whether to include or exclude so-called overhead costs.[14] In experiments, we usually do not include any overhead so that the results will reflect actual design, coding, and programming times to be contrasted with models thereof. However, when measuring actual effort in a small organization, it may be decided to include overhead — since this will be a more acceptable measure of the actual cost of producing software. It is important for managers and researchers to decide what amount of overhead to include and to attempt to collect effort data in a manner congruent with such decisions.

---

14. These are costs associated with management, secretarial support, computing facilities, and the physical plant.

NAME   DATE

PROBLEM   SOC. SEC: NUMBER

START TIME: _____

END READING TIME: _____

END DESIGN TIME: _____

END CODING TIME: _____

FIRST CLEAN COMPILATION TIME: _____

FINISH TIME: _____

KEY PUNCH TIMES:

Start: _____   _____   _____

End: _____   _____   _____

Start: _____   _____   _____

End: _____   _____   _____

Start: _____   _____   _____

End: _____   _____   _____

Figure 2.34   A sample form used to collect data in [WOOD79].

Another problem in the measurement of effort is the overhead concerning understanding the task and the proficiency of programmers. For example, suppose a group of programmers is to construct a program that sorts an array of integers using the "quick sort" algorithm (for example, see [KNUT73]). It may take a programmer less than one hour to code and test the program if that person is familiar with the algorithm. On the other hand, it may take another programmer several hours just to read a reference text in order to understand how the algorithm works. If the programming language selected does not support recursion, it may even be impossible for someone who has never tried to simulate recursion using arrays as stacks. Thus, for the effort metric to be meaningful for micro-level projects, we may need to exclude some amount of effort related to understanding the problem for someone who is not at a minimal plateau, or to exclude certain types of programming effort for a programmer unfamiliar with a language or with standard programming techniques. Otherwise, the time recorded will include an element related to the education of programmers, which may seriously confound empirical results that were not designed to include the education element.

While uncommon, there are actual effort metrics other than time. For example, a metric that measures the number of runs submitted during development could be treated as an effort metric. But, since it may be unclear how to relate such a metric to time and cost, and since it is usually just as easy to collect time, time is typically the effort metric of choice. (There is a problem with the metric for the number of runs submitted during development: some programmers submit a lot of runs while expending only a little effort between each one; others agonize for hours over program changes before submitting the next run. Thus, it is unlikely that any simple function can be found that relates the number of runs submitted during development to effort.)

The micro-level effort measurements are useful for controlled experiments. The results from these experiments can be used to gain a better understanding of the isolated factors being tested. However, the controlled condition may be different from a real world situation. Thus, results may not be replicable when some of the factors are not controlled exactly. (Problems with the validity of experiments will be discussed in Section 3.3.)

2.7.2 Macro-levels of Effort and Cost

Macro-level projects are defined as large projects usually completed by a team of at least two programmers in weeks, months, or years. The most appropriate effort metrics are person-months or person-years. When person-months or person-years are used to measure effort in macro-level projects, they refer to the resources expended by professionals in the design, coding, and testing of the software product, including direct management and documentation activities. In industry, this information can be collected directly during the software development process, or can be recovered from the accounting records after the project is completed. Since each organization establishes its rules according to its own needs, consistency between organizations is uncommon. The ever-intensifying software crisis may have also forced certain changes in the accounting rules within an organization, making effort data inconsistent over the years: for example, programmers may have recorded overtime hours in the past, but now are directed to exclude them. Thus, we must be cautious when comparing programming effort for projects developed at different organizations or at different times within the same organization.

Macro-level effort differs from micro-level effort in another aspect. An analogy may be found in the world of sports — specifically track: the times needed for a runner to cover a fixed distance differ significantly between the 100-meter dash and the 26-mile marathon. Someone who could run each 100 meters of a marathon in 10.2 seconds would be considered superhuman. Similarly, one cannot expect the intensity in programming during a small controlled experiment to persist over the months required to complete a team project.

Furthermore, there is again the issue of overhead. But in this situation, the problem is even more serious. Even if the programmers work just as hard in a team situation, there are necessary interruptions over a period of time. Times for coffee breaks, lunches, meetings with supervisors, meetings with other programmers, informal discussions with other programmers, sick days, vacations, and personal business are normally charged to the project. One manager observed that "Typically only 4 to 5 hours of an 8-hour day are applied to the project ..." [PUTN78]. Furthermore, all overhead related to understanding specifications, techniques, and programming language features, as well as unit testing, are generally included. Thus, results on programming productivity in small controlled experiments can seldom be applied to large team projects.

Just as logs can be used to collect effort measurements in micro-level projects, we can use logs, forms, and even on-line data collection facilities in a similar manner for macro-level projects. Analysts and programmers can be required to complete forms detailing the effort expended at the end of, for example, each work session, each day, or each milestone. Such a technique has been used in research-related software development at the NASA Goddard Space Flight Center [BASI83]. During a university research project, Wang used a milestone interview technique for collecting effort and other software metrics that could be adapted to the macro-level setting [WANG84]. A word of caution: the manager and researcher must take care that the amount of overhead involved in the data collection activity does not become substantial, or this will both distort the data collected and discourage programmers.

It is important to realize that, in the macro-level setting of the "real world," there are some even more subtle barriers to gathering valid effort data. If effort is recorded in any fashion that allows the programmer to "decide" how much time was spent, then under- and overestimates are possible. A programmer may underestimate actual effort to make management believe the programmer is very efficient. A programmer may overestimate actual effort to make management believe the programmer is overworked. Such biased figures may even be unconsciously furnished by conscientious programmers.

Furthermore, there is a problem if the effort-gathering mechanism is both a project- and employee-management tool: The manager wants precise data on the project, but this data may make the programmer look bad and may sway the programmer to over- or underestimate for precisely the reasons just mentioned. We suggest that employee evaluation be separated from the project management process as much as possible — encouraging employees to give as accurate effort estimates as possible.

And what about overtime? In some organizations, programmers freely record such time as it is expended and "charge" it to a project. At the other extreme are organizations in which no overtime is ever worked, and if it is, it is not charged to the project. Should this be recorded for management purposes? Should it be included in the effort and cost reported (or charged) for a project? The answers to these questions entirely depend on the situation.

Finally, we focus upon the conversion of effort to cost. The macro-level effort estimate can be converted into a dollar cost usually by computing an average salary per unit time of the technical staff involved, and multiplying this average salary by the estimated effort required. It is common to use such a *burdened* average salary in carrying out this computation; for example, a burdened salary might include fringe benefits, some types of overhead, or clerical support. The means of computing the burdened average salary will also vary with the organization. A cost model must also consider other direct charges in arriving at a final cost estimate. These charges might include computer time, travel costs, and general and administrative expenses. For example, within a particular organization, programmers may be typically paid $15 per hour. If a project has taken 1000 hours, then ostensibly its cost has been $15,000. But to account for all types of programmer, hardware, and organization overhead, the "burdened" cost of a programmer may be $45 per hour. Then, the actual cost was probably closer to $45,000. The inclusion of many factors that depend primarily on environment easily make the cost as an effort measure not transportable from one organization to another.

2.8 Defects and Reliability

Despite recent advances in programming technology, it is not yet possible for programmers to produce error-free code consistently. As a result, a significant amount of effort is typically allocated to the testing and correcting of commercial software before its delivery. Evidence of increased attention toward removing program defects includes a book [MYER79], a tutorial sponsored by the IEEE Computer Society [MILL81], a conference sponsored by ACM SIGSOFT/SIGPLAN [JOHN83], and numerous papers and reports [for example, see BASI84, HALE84, and SHEN85].

A software product is considered defective when it does not perform according to the user's expectations. Let us begin with a definition:

> A fault *is an error in software that causes the software to produce an incorrect result for valid input.*

Such "incorrect results" can range from wrong (but ostensibly right) output, to obviously invalid output, to a software "crash" (i.e., failure to conclude normally). Software may fail for several distinct input sets because of the same fault. On the other hand, a certain input set may reveal several different faults. While it is difficult to identify and fix all the faults in a program, we will concentrate on the evidence of the presence of faults by counting the number of defects. Another definition states,

> A defect *is the evidence of the existence of a fault.*

The actual number of defects can only be determined dynamically as follows: An error is fixed. If the input sets that caused failures earlier now yield correct results, there was only one defect. If an input set still yields incorrect results, then there were originally at least two defects, or fixing the first defect has created a second defect. It is desirable that the input sets used to test the software be *independent*, in the sense that the failure or success of one test run does not necessarily imply the failure or success of another.

In order to manage the testing and maintenance phases of the software life cycle, it is often desirable to estimate the number of defects in software. Some of the models that are designed to produce such estimates are discussed in Chapter 7. However, this section concerns the actual measurement of defects via some standard techniques that can be applied during software development.

2.8.1 Defect Metrics and the Software Life Cycle

In this section, we will consider the four software life cycle phases (from Section 1.2.1) that are logically similar from the standpoint of introducing, discovering, and fixing defects:

Design Phase — Defects can be caused by poor understanding of (maybe resulting from unclear) requirements or specifications. This can lead to incorrect design that will lead later to incorrect code. Defects can be fixed in this phase by recognizing that the design does not satisfy the specifications.

Coding Phase — Defects can be caused by either poor understanding of the design, or poor choices of data structures or algorithms, or by errors in logic or syntax. Defects are fixed generally by changing the code, or occasionally by changing the design to match the code in place (the "what you really want is what I have written" fix).

Testing Phase — Defects may not be caught unless either appropriate test data is used or some method like formal code verification is employed.[15] Defects may also be caused by corrections of other defects.[16] Defects are fixed in this phase generally by code changes.

Maintenance Phase — When the software is actually used, every run really constitutes new "test" cases. Defects are fixed in a manner similar to the testing phase, with the exception that there is a reluctance to change code as long as the software is reliable, in which case documentation may be changed instead. Inadequate performance of software in this phase may be due to many reasons other than incorrect code, including poor documentation, or even poor understanding of the software or documentation by the user.

Since it is frequently easier to change the documentation than to change code, it is not uncommon for software vendors to remove program defects by changing documentation. Since there is no easy way to determine which documentation changes are due to genuine documentation errors, the study of program defects will have to concentrate on errors that lead to design and code changes.

There are three typical metrics for assessing the defects in software:

The metric *number of changes required in the design* — Beginning with the Design phase, this metric results from faulty understanding of specifications. We exclude design changes due to dynamic specification changes — the moving target that all programmers complain that they have trouble trying to hit. Design changes can occur anywhere in the life cycle from the Design phase on, whenever a defect is discovered. The method of computing the "number of design changes" is subject to a count based on the analyst's assessment of the number of "separate" items changed.

The metric *number of errors* — When defects are discovered from the coding phase on and especially during the testing phase, they can be counted. After a program reaches the point where it is written, any errors uncovered via hand-checking, walk-throughs, or testing can be counted in this metric. In many settings, there are formal error reports filed whenever errors are found, and a count of different error reports can be used as a defect metric. The definition we gave earlier of a defect and the way to determine when multiple defects are present can be used to compute this metric.

---

15. See the article on Program Verification in *Encyclopedia of Computer Science and Engineering,* 2nd edition, Van Nostrand Reinhold (1983).

16. A recent study at Purdue University showed that 1 out of 5 defects was caused by earlier fixes [YU85].

The metric *number of program changes* — This algorithmic defect metric is based upon the fact that defects are usually fixed by means of program code changes. In the same way we score a target shooter by observing holes in the target, we can observe program code changes to determine where defects must have been present. This metric depends on our ability to exclude any program changes related to changed specifications and to include only those involved in fixing an errant program.

One "program change" is concerned with a contiguous set of statements that represent a single abstract action [DUNS80]. According to this concept, each of the following text changes to a program represent one program change:

- One or more changes to a single statement.

- One or more statements inserted between existing statements.

- A change to a single statement followed by the insertion of new statements.

The third instance represents a situation in which an existing statement is insufficient and must be altered and supplemented by additional statements to implement the abstract action intended. The insertion and deletion of debugging statements, comments, and blank lines are not counted as program changes, since they do not directly relate to program defects. Even simple deletions of statements are not counted since they are normally countered by insertions elsewhere. A defect report may lead to more than one program change. Thus, the complexity or even seriousness of a defect may be reflected by the number of program changes it takes to correct the defect. We should recognize, however, that both the insertion of one statement and the insertion of a 500-statement procedure are counted as one change in the algorithm presented earlier.

An example of counting program changes appears in Figures 2.35 and 2.36. Figure 2.35 is a payroll program that has (intentionally) been constructed with several defects. Notice that after the changes are made that lead to Figure 2.36, we have the same program as appears in Figure 2.16. There are 3 program changes because of the "one or more changes to a single statement" in line 7 (that is, adding the operator not), the "one or more statements inserted between existing statements" in lines 2.5−2.7, and the "change to a single statement followed by insertion of new statements" in lines 14 and 14.5. No change is counted for the deletion of line 10. It is often difficult to obtain the number of program changes as defined in [DUNS80] when we work with historical data. But many commercial software producers maintain a list of software modules changed for each valid defect report. Thus, a program change is counted when a module is modified in response to a defect report.

It is reasonable that larger software will have more errors and, thus, more program changes. The raw count of number of errors or program changes is not very meaningful for discerning whether software has a lot of defects or just a few. Our 17-line program in Figure 2.35 required 3 program changes. This is

```
Line
1    program bigpay (input,output);
2    type check = record
3         end;
4    var pay: check;
5        hours, rate: real;
6    begin
7        while eof (input) do begin
8            readln (hours, rate);
9            if hours <= 40 then
10               pay.gross := 40 * rate
11               pay.gross := hours * rate
12           else
13               pay.gross := (40 * rate) + 1.5 * (hours-40) * rate;
14           pay.tax := pay.gross - pay.net;
15           writeln (pay.gross, pay.tax, pay.net)
16       end
17   end.
```

Figure 2.35   A defective Pascal payroll program that pays overtime.

poor performance. But, 3 program changes for a 17,000-line program would be considered astonishingly good! In order to compare the defects in software meaningfully, it is customary to normalize the raw count of defects or program changes — usually by the size of the software. Thus, the most common metric for defect comparison purposes is

defect density $=$ number of defects$/S$

where S is the program size in thousands of lines of code. However, the defect density seems to vary as a function of program size. In Chapter 7, we will show that this measure is actually inappropriate in many situations.

There are other characteristics of defects than just the number of or even the density (normalized number) of them. For example, in a payroll program, an error that caused one employee's paycheck to be erroneous by 20 cents would be considered much less "severe" than one that led to half the paychecks being $0.00. Even more severe would be a defect that caused the software to crash, producing no paychecks at all. Therefore, it is possible to think in terms of the "severity" of defects. If a severity number or index is desired, this metric can be obtained by running the software with a set of test cases. The percentage of runs judged as failures can be used as a severity metric — assuming that some attempt has been made to produce independent test cases. Thus, in this payroll program, if there are 1000 employees in the organization, the 20-cent

```
Line
1     program bigpay (input,output);
2     type check = record
2.5         gross: real;                                    line inserted
2.6         tax: real;                                      line inserted
2.7         net: real                                       line inserted
3         end;
4     var pay: check;
5         hours, rate: real;
6     begin
7       while not eof (input) do begin                      line altered
8         readln (hours, rate);
9         if hours <= 40 then
11          pay.gross := hours * rate                       previous line deleted
12        else
13          pay.gross := (40 * rate) + 1.5 * (hours-40) * rate;
14        pay.tax := 0.25 * pay.gross;                      line altered
14.5      pay.net := pay.gross - pay.tax;                   line inserted
15        writeln (pay.gross, pay.tax, pay.net)
16      end
17    end.
```

Figure 2.36   The corrected Pascal payroll program that pays overtime.

error in one paycheck would represent a severity of 0.1%, the zero paychecks a severity of 50%, and the crash 100%.

The metric *number of changed lines of code* — This metric is another way to account for the differing severity of defects. In this metric, a 500-statement change is counted as 500 times more severe than a single-statement change. This metric is simply the "weighted sum" of the metric of program changes.

Still another concern with defects is the difficulty of fixing them. This issue is usually independent of their severity. Thus, a very serious error such as the crash in the payroll example may require only a single statement change and a few minutes to repair. On the other hand, less severe defects such as the 20-cent error may require hours of analysis to determine the particular set of circumstances that cause them. Thus, defects may be characterized by either the time required to repair them or the estimated time for defects not yet repaired. Furthermore, this time can be made comparable for various programs by normalizing by the number of thousands of lines of code or even the number of defects.

2.8.2   Discovering and Correcting Defects

In this section, we concentrate on the points in the software life cycle where defects occur (i.e., when the error enters) and where they are discovered (i.e., when they first can be identified). Defects can enter as early as in one of the design phases caused by misunderstanding the specifications and, whenever they enter, they may not be discovered until the maintenance phase. We also discuss the costs of defects in this section.

As discussed in Chapter 1, modern development methodologies call for regular reviews and inspections (or "walk-throughs") during the design and coding phases. These can be conducted both formally and informally. A group of reviewers, including the principle designer or programmer, gathers together to discuss and evaluate the progress of software development. The reviewers are expected to study the current form of the software (design or code) ahead of time and to prepare comments on its completeness, accuracy, and quality. During the review, the analysts and programmers present an overview of the design and any code already generated. They then "walk" the reviewers through the structure in detail so that the concerns of the reviewers are either explained away or identified as action items. The number of recorded action items can be considered as the number of defects in the design or code. All three metrics discussed earlier — number of design changes, number of defects found, and number of program changes — can be used.

Toward the end of the coding phase, a programmer is also expected to test separate modules using appropriate data according to the modules' input/output specifications. This activity is sometimes called the *unit test* since the modules are tested individually for correctness. The number of defects found and number of program changes can be recorded as the code is changed in order for the module to work properly.

The number of defects discovered during the design and coding phases is represented by d_0. Be careful: in addition to the inherent quality of the design, d_0 depends upon several other factors — the quality of specifications, the frequency of reviews, and the thoroughness of the reviewers. Many changes may also be the normal consequence of the evolutionary nature of the design process. If the programmer attempts to construct a complete program during the design and coding phases with the intention that it should run correctly without effort, then d_0 may be an accurate measure for the quality of coding. If the programmer prefers to let the code evolve into the final state through successive testing and changes, d_0 may not be meaningful. Since it is difficult to record consistently and algorithmically the reasons for changes that are made, defect measures during the design and coding phases have not been thoroughly investigated.

During the testing phase, most commercial software products are tested before release by groups independent of the original programming teams. During this phase, the number of defects found and number of program changes can be especially useful. The testing group for a product assembles a large number of test cases based on the product specifications. When the product is a revised version of a previously existing product, many test cases assembled for the earlier version may be reused. Defects found during the formal testing phase are normally sent back to the designers and programmers to be fixed.

The number of defects discovered during the testing phase is represented by d_1. In order to make sure that all defect reports are handled promptly, on-line reporting mechanisms are often used by both the development and testing teams. For example, a particular software firm has a tool that, when an apparent error occurs, allows the tester to enter into the system the nature of the problem, the on-line location of the test case causing the problem, and the perceived "severity" of the problem. (A problem is considered extremely severe if the system crashes as a result, making further testing impossible.) The defect reports are scanned regularly by a member of the development team. Depending upon the nature, severity, and area of the problem, current defect reports are placed in a priority queue to be serviced by available programmers. A defect report may be "resolved" by changing code, or documentation, or by identifying the defect to be a duplicate of some previously reported problem. The defect may also be categorized as "invalid" if the programmer cannot reproduce the problem with the same test case, or if the defect is due to the erroneous application of the test case. The originating tester is notified automatically when a defect report is resolved.

The existence of a defect-reporting mechanism provides an objective measure for the metric d_1. However, the total number may not be appropriate unless we remove the reports that are invalid or that duplicate earlier reports. Even so, the possibility of partial orderings among test cases may still cause problems.[17]

As discussed in Chapter 1, the maintenance phase of a product's life cycle begins at the point of the product's external release. Changes can still be made during this phase: to correct errors, to add features, or to improve performance characteristics. All three metrics — number of design changes, number of defects found, and number of program changes can be determined from the count of error reports made by customers or the count of program changes made as the result of error reports. Generally, a relatively large number of defects is discovered by customers shortly after release. When a certain threshold of usage is reached, fewer and fewer errors are discovered over time, dropping to zero when the next version of the product is released. The number of defect reports over time for three versions of a popular commercial compiler is shown in Figure 2.37.

The number of defects discovered after release and during the maintenance phase is represented by d_2. Since most errors are removed before the

---

17. Assume that test cases A and B are ordered if failure of A implies failure of B. An example is the input format of a constant; an error in the input procedure leads to failures of all test cases using that constant.

RANGE OF X AXIS: 0 6.25
RANGE OF Y AXIS: 0 8.75

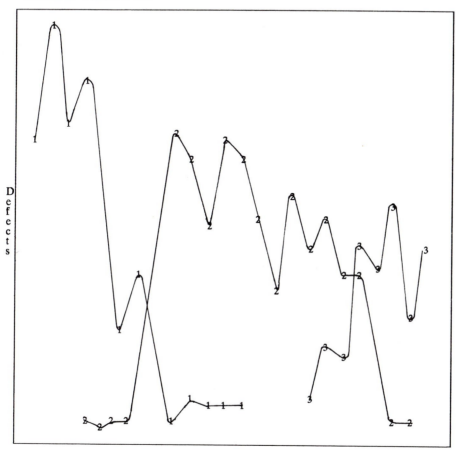

JUNE 81 to MAY 83

Figure 2.37 Defects reported for three versions of a commercial compiler.

maintenance phase, we do not expect to find many defects or to observe many program changes for a module in the maintenance phase. In a recent study of IBM products, most modules were defect-free, and those that did have defects after release typically had only one or two [SHEN85] (see Section 7.2.5). Thus, a measure representing the module's *probability* of having one or more defects,

$$P[d_2 > 0]$$

was more meaningful in that analysis.

In the remainder of this book, we will use the following designations for numbers of defects found in the various software development phases:

d_0 = defects found in the Design and Coding phases

d_1 = defects found in the Testing phase

d_2 = defects found in the Maintenance phase

$d_{tot} = d_0 + d_1 + d_2$ = total defects

2.8.3   Software Reliability

Since software is an essential component of many systems, such as space shuttles, heart monitors, and nuclear reactors, the reliable operation of such systems critically depends on the reliable operation of their software components. The theoretical basis for methods of estimating the reliability of hardware systems is well-developed (for example, see [BARL75]). A hardware component may fail due to a design error, poor fabrication quality, momentary overload, deterioration, or a combination of these factors. An example is a flaw in a mask used to produce a VLSI chip, which caused the spacing between two separate diffused regions to be placed closer than designed. The circuit functioned normally until a random voltage surge one day caused it to fail. The failure in the circuit led to the failure of the whole system. The random nature of system failures enables the estimation of system reliability using probability theory.

The application of hardware reliability theories to software is often viewed skeptically (for example, see [ZELK78]). A *program* will always produce the same answer for the same input, as long as the hardware does not fail. There is no physical deterioration, and the fabrication, or duplication, of code is a trivial process. Software failure is normally due to the presentation of an input that finally "reveals" a defect present from the beginning. Therefore, there is no random malfunction in software, other than defects revealed by random inputs.

Figure 2.38(a) shows the history of defect detection for a certain software system. Each defect is represented by a dot on the line of defect history. If we assume that the detection of software defects is a stochastic process, the distribution of the time interval between defect recordings may be represented by the function $F(\tau)$ for $\tau \geq 0$. This function is interpreted to be the probability that a defect is detected by time τ, as shown in Figure 2.38(b). The *reliability*, $R(\tau)$, of the software is the probability that there is no failure during the time interval of length τ.

$$R(\tau) = 1 - F(\tau) \tag{2.37}$$

This definition assumes that the software being studied is in use continuously during the time interval. For many applications, it may be more appropriate to use the number of *runs* instead of the real time, since no defects can be detected

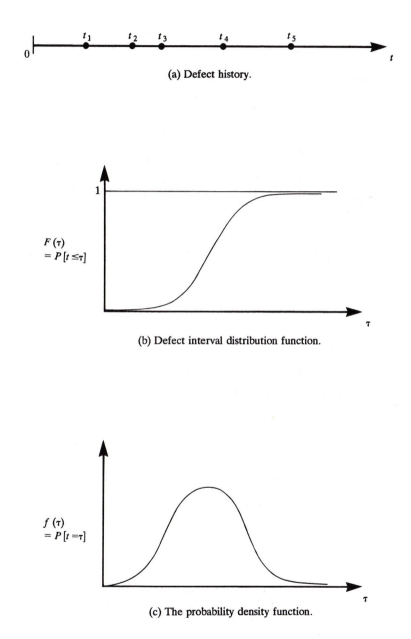

(a) Defect history.

(b) Defect interval distribution function.

(c) The probability density function.

Figure 2.38   The distribution of defects.

unless the program is being run. In this case, the reliability is the probability that there is no failure over n runs:

$$R(n) = 1 - \frac{d_n}{n} \tag{2.38}$$

where d_n is the number of defects detected over the n runs.

If $f(\tau)$ is the probability density function

$$f(\tau) = \frac{dF(\tau)}{d\tau}$$

then $f(\tau)d\tau$ is the probability that the software fails during the semi-open interval $(\tau, \tau + d\tau]$. Such a probability density function is shown in Figure 2.38(c). The *hazard rate*, $h(\tau)$, is defined as the probability that the software fails during the interval $(\tau, \tau + d\tau]$, given that it has not failed before τ:

$$h(\tau) = \frac{f(\tau)}{1 - F(\tau)} \tag{2.39}$$

The right-hand side of Equation (2.39) is actually the derivative of $\ln(1 - F(\tau))$:

$$h(\tau) = -\frac{d}{d\tau}\ln(1 - F(\tau)) = -\frac{d}{d\tau}\ln R(\tau) \tag{2.40}$$

As a result,

$$\ln R(\tau) = -\int_0^\tau h(x)dx \tag{2.41}$$

Therefore, we have another way to represent the reliability $R(\tau)$:

$$R(\tau) = e^{-\int_0^\tau h(x)dx} \tag{2.42}$$

Another measure of interest is the *mean time to failure* (MTTF), which is defined as

$$\text{MTTF} = \frac{1}{n}\sum_{i=1}^{n} t_i \tag{2.43}$$

where t_i is the time interval between the $(i-1)^{th}$ and i^{th} failures. As n approaches infinity, this mean value converges to the expected value of the random variable (for example, see the discussion on the law of large numbers in [FELL68]):

$$\text{MTTF} = \int_0^\infty \tau dF(\tau) = \int_0^\infty \tau f(\tau)d\tau \tag{2.44}$$

It is possible to compute MTTF from $R(\tau)$ by substituting $F(\tau) = 1 - R(\tau)$ into Equation (2.44) and integrating "by parts." Therefore,

$$\text{MTTF} = \int_0^\infty \tau d(1 - R(\tau)) \tag{2.45}$$

$$= -\int_0^\infty \tau dR(\tau)$$

$$= -\tau R(\tau)\big|_0^\infty + \int_0^\infty R(\tau)d\tau$$
$$= \int_0^\infty R(\tau)d\tau$$

The reliability of a software component can be represented by $R(\tau)$ or MTTF. Both can be derived if we know the distribution of the time interval between defect recordings $F(\tau)$ by using Equations (2.37) and (2.45). They can also be derived if the hazard rate calculated by Equation (2.39) is known, by using Equations (2.42) and then (2.45). Therefore, in addition to the count of defects, it is important to record the times of their detection so that a reliability measure may be computed.

2.8.4 The Cost of Repairing Defects

Software engineers have long stressed that a defect found early in the software life cycle can be repaired at much less expense than later in the life cycle. For example, if a design review uncovers that a proposed algorithm will not handle certain classes of input, it will be far less costly to repair this than if the algorithm is coded and the error discovered during the testing or maintenance phases. As we mentioned in Section 1.3.2, errors introduced during design but discovered during maintenance may cost 100 times more than if discovered and repaired during design [BOEH81].

Still another concern is how to apportion the time available during program development among the design, coding, and testing phases in order to ensure that the fewest defects possible survive to the maintenance phase. A common approach is to lengthen the testing phase since it is generally cheaper by an order of magnitude to correct a defect than if the same defect is discovered before the software is delivered to a customer.[18] As a result, the effort expended in testing a product is typically comparable to that expended in its initial development (for example, see [BROO75]). There have also been attempts to strengthen the testing phase by allocating test resources more intelligently. Thus, it is important to have a consistent method to measure defects so that different testing strategies can be evaluated.

A *static defect measure* — whether it is the number of defect reports or the number of program changes — inherently depends on the completeness of the test cases. A low count of defects may be the result of good design and coding, of bad testing, or a combination of both. It is therefore probably inappropriate to use such measures to evaluate the quality of different products. Since the test cases for a given product may exercise certain modules in the product more than others, even the evaluation of the quality of modules within a product using a defect measure is questionable. The problem can be more complicated

---

18. Experience at IBM's Santa Teresa Laboratory shows that the ratio of the cost of a defect found during the design and coding phases, the testing phase, and by the customer is approximately 1:20:80 [REMU80].

since the correction of a defect may inadvertently introduce other defects into the software [YU85]. Thus, the total number of defects as defined in this section is not a precise and accurate measure.

When a software product is adequately and uniformly tested,[19] a *dynamic defect measure*, which incorporates the time of defect detection, *may* be used to evaluate the reliability of the software product. Its accuracy depends on both the accuracy of defect counts and the accuracy of the recording of times when those defects are detected. The measures of reliability will be meaningful only if the intervals between failures are independent of each other.

Nevertheless, a concerted effort must be made within an organization to measure defects (via number of errors, density of errors, number of program changes, or some other metric) in an algorithmic manner. As we have pointed out, it is also critical that test cases be as independent and exhaustive as possible. Such procedures are necessary if a defect metric is to be helpful in determining the quality of software or in determining the effect of changes in the software development process.

2.9 Design Metrics

As the study of other metrics in this chapter indicates, program complexity increases with size: large programs are more difficult to understand and write, they contain more errors, and they are more difficult to debug. To reduce this complexity, software designers have increasingly turned to program modularization and structured design methodologies. Among the many claimed advantages of program modularization are the following:[20]

Comprehensibility — Both the programmer and the user can more easily understand the overall program logic.

Manageability — Managers can more readily assign personnel to modules and responsibility is more localized.

Efficiency — Implementation effort should be reduced.

Error reduction — Testing modules independently should be easier.

Reduced maintenance — Identification of the modules should be easier since different functions are performed by different modules.

It can also be argued that there are some disadvantages to modularization. For example, as the number of modules grows, the need for proper interfacing

---

19. These assumptions will be discussed in more detail in Section 7.3.

20. There will be another discussion of modularity later in Section 4.3.3.

among the modules and for coordination among people assigned to code the modules may increase both the effort to write a program and the time needed to debug a program due to potentially more interface errors. Many structured design methodologies have been proposed that, while allowing for modularization, attempt to minimize intermodule complexity. One consideration in these methodologies is the criteria by which modules are chosen. As discussed in Section 2.2.3, some authors advocate that module sizes be limited to 50−200 lines of code in order to increase understandability and minimize errors. Others advocate functional modules that, regardless of size, perform one specific function. Still others advocate that modules be limited according to some complexity metric value — such as modules whose cyclomatic complexities do not exceed 10 (see Section 2.4.1). Another important consideration is the structure imposed on the modules. Turner [TURN80] advocates the use of hierarchical tree-structured designs. In such a design, a module at a given level can only be called by a single module at the next higher level. Sharing data among modules at the same level or with more than one module at a higher level is not allowed. However, such tree-structured designs are not suited to all types of programs. In particular, it may be difficult to design system programs and real-time control programs using simple tree structures since some modules need to be accessed repeatedly by modules from several different levels.

In any case, the solution to a given problem can be designed in many different ways, even assuming that all designs are structured. Some of these designs may lead to more interface errors that show up primarily during systems integration. Some may be easier to understand, and some may lead to more efficient implementation and lower cost. Given two or more designs for a given problem specification, we can ask, "Which design is of better *overall* quality?" To answer this question, we must first define "overall design quality", then identify specific metrics that correlate with design quality, and finally establish that a valid relationship exists between these design metrics and observed quality.

Several different metrics have been proposed for comparing designs. Some of these are generalizations of internal product metrics that have been widely used. For example, one study has shown how the operators and operands of Software Science can be redefined in terms of the elements of a graphical representation of a design [SZUL81]. Hall and Preiser [HALL84] suggest a generalization of McCabe's cyclomatic complexity applied to a hierarchically structured node representation of a design. Here, we shall assume that design quality is measured by the number of modifications made to a system after the individual modules have been coded, unit tested, and delivered for system integration.[21]

Troy and Zweben have studied the correlations (see Section 3.4.4) between a number of primitive metrics and design quality, as measured by the number of modifications [TROY81]. In this study, a large product was divided into modules using several different designs. In all, some 73 designs for the entire

---

21. There is a discussion of program changes in Section 2.8.

product or for subsystems were studied. Each module was coded, unit-tested, and delivered for system integration. Any changes made in a module after delivery were recorded. Each design implementation was also accompanied by a structure chart. A structure chart of a design implementation is simply a graphic representation of the modules in the design and of their interconnections. (Further details about structure charts are contained in [YOUR79].) A segment of a typical structure chart appeared in [TROY81] and is presented in Figure 2.39. Twenty-one primitive metrics were defined for such structure charts.

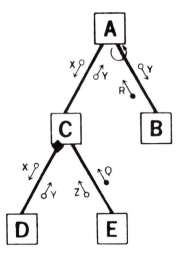

Figure 2.39   An example of a Structure Chart Segment.

Structured design methodology suggests that the quality of a design is related to five design principles. These principles may be objectively measured by one or more of the primitive metrics studied. The principles and example metrics are:

Coupling − Coupling is measured by the number of interconnections among modules. For example, coupling increases as the number of calls between modules increases, or as the amount of shared data increases. The hypothesis is that designs with high coupling will contain more errors. Primitive metrics related to the number of interconnections per box (or node) of the structured chart can be used to quantify coupling.

Cohesion − Cohesion is a measure of the relationships of the elements within a module. In a cohesive design, related functions are located in a single module. The hypothesis is that designs with low module cohesion will contain more errors. Primitive metrics related to the sharing of data among modules (Section 2.3.3) can be used to quantify cohesion. Lower cohesion is evidenced by higher number of fan-in's, for example.

Complexity — A design should be as simple as possible. Design complexity grows as the number of control constructs grows, and as the size in number of modules grows. The hypothesis is that designs with high complexity will contain more errors. Primitive metrics related to the number of boxes in the structure chart and the depth of the chart can be used to quantify complexity. Higher complexity is evidenced by a large number of such boxes, for example.

Modularity — The degree of modularization affects the quality of a design. Over-modularization is as undesirable as undermodularization. The hypothesis is that low modularity indicates more errors. Some of the primitive metrics used to quantify complexity can also be used to quantify modularity, but in an opposite way: a very low number of boxes may indicate undermodularization, for example.

Size — A design that exhibits large modules or a large depth of the structure chart is considered undesirable. The hypothesis is that large programs will contain more errors than small programs. Some of the primitive metrics used to quantify complexity can also be used to quantify size.

The major conclusion of the Troy and Zweben study was that the coupling metrics yielded the best correlations with error counts, while the complexity metrics were next in importance. The correlation coefficient for coupling metrics and errors was 0.73. Although this is a significant result, the value also indicates that there are other variables that affect software quality (see Section 3.4.4). Since coupling is essentially a measure of the data and control interconnections among modules, this result implies that the quality of software design can be improved by minimizing the number of these interconnections. Some specific suggestions for using coupling metrics to improve designs are given in [BEAN84].

2.10 Summary and Conclusions

Sections 2.2 through 2.6 discuss metrics that are product-related. All of them can be derived from analyzing the software itself using an automatic tool. The most common metric is one that is related to program size — S_s (LOC), S (KLOC), or N (number of tokens). Comments and blank lines are usually not included. These metrics can be evaluated easily and objectively, except when parts of the program are adapted or copied from existing programs. There is no consensus on how adapted code should be counted. However, it is important to denote how much of the code is newly developed, how much is copied with-out change, and how much is modified — as well as the extent of modifications.

If a tool that works like the lexical phase of a compiler is available, then it is easy to make more detailed measurements. Metrics such as η_1, η_2, N_1, N_2, *VARS*, and *DE* can be evaluated in one pass. Again, the counts may be mis-leading if parts of the code are adapted. The Software Science composite met-rics discussed in Section 2.6 can be easily computed from the four basic metrics.

Sections 2.7 and 2.8 discussed the metrics that are process-related. The effort related to the development and testing phases should be recorded carefully and at the module level if possible. The number of code changes are frequently counted as the number of program defects. Recording the actual times of defect detection is also useful. Systematic collection of these and other useful metrics is a necessary prerequisite if the software development process is ever to achieve the status of an engineering discipline.

Exercises

1. A proposal is made to count the size of Pascal programs by the number of semicolons, except those occurring within literal strings. Discuss the strengths and weaknesses of this size measure when compared with the lines of code count (S_s).

2. Consider the FORTRAN subroutine: is it always a module, as defined in Section 2.2.3? A function?

3. Many programming languages support a feature to include previously writ-ten code at compilation time, like a macro. Software metrics could be derived either *before* or *after* macro expansion. Discuss the advantages and disadvantages of each approach.

4. Count *VARS*, η_2, $\overline{LV}$, $\overline{SP}$, *DE*, $v(G)$, and $\overline{NL}$ for the programs in Figures 2.1, 2.2, 2.3, 2.7, 2.11, 2.16, 2.28, and 2.31.

5. Show that the value of *SP* at a particular statement is also the value of *LV* at that point.

6. According to the Pascal counting rules given in Figure 2.5, each label within the CASE statement will increase the count of $v(G)$ by one. Draw the control graph for a CASE statement, and see if the counting rule is con-sistent with the definition of $v(G)$. If it is not, modify the counting rule to make it consistent with the definition of $v(G)$.

7. How do you count *DE* or $v(G)$ for APL programs, where most decisions are not explicitly stated? For example, do you consider array operations to be one or more loop statements and increase the count accordingly?

8. Many researchers have found that almost all software complexity metrics are highly correlated with the program size. Is it reasonable, then, to ignore all metrics except the size metric in measurements and models? Justify your answer.

9. Is it always possible to transform a FORTRAN program so that there is no "knot" in it? Justify your answer by either giving a set of steps to transform a program with knots, or giving a sample program that cannot be transformed.

10. Discuss the advantages and disadvantages of using the total CPU time as an effort measure.

11. What are the differences between micro- and macro-level effort measures? List those activities that are included in the macro-level effort metric, but not in the micro-level metric.

12. The nature of hardware defects is quite different from that of software defects. Discuss the differences.

13. The definitions of defects all assume that the software specifications are correct. Which of the definitions will become less meaningful if the specifications are incorrect? Modify these definitions if possible.

14. Is it possible to detect defects before the end of the coding phase? How can these defects be objectively measured?

15. Is it reasonable to define "thresholds" for software modules? For example, is a module acceptable if its $v(G) \leq 10$, or $\eta_2 \leq 25$? Justify your answer.

16. For the control flowgraph G on page 112

    (a) find $v(G)$.

    (b) find and list the minimum number of paths N_p.

    (c) compute the reachability metric for each node and average reachability $\bar{R}$.

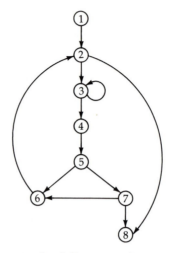

17. Compute the knot count in the following subroutine:

```
        IF (CN.NE.0) GOTO 10
        IF (CN.LT.CT) GOTO 5
        IE = 1
        GOTO 25
5       IE = 0
        GOTO 25
10      IF (CN.LT.TR) GOTO 20
        IE = 1
        GOTO 25
20      IE = 0
25      IF (IE.NE.1) GOTO 40
            ...
            ...
            ...
40      RETURN
        END
```

Measurement and Analysis 3

There are three kind of lies: lies, damned lies, and statistics.
    Attributed to Isaac D'Israeli, 19th century, by Darrell Huff,
    How to Lie with Statistics.

3.1 Introduction

The term *structured programming* has been used extensively by computer professionals since Dijkstra introduced it in 1972 [DIJK72]. However, the lack of a precise definition has allowed people to use it as they wished. Structured programs are considered to be more readable, easier to maintain and modify by someone other than the original programmer, and more likely to be correct (for example, see the entry for Structured Programming in *Encyclopedia of Computer Science and Engineering*, Second Edition [A. Ralston and E. D. Reily, eds.], Van Nostrand Reinhold, 1983.) Structured programming appears to be the panacea for the current software crisis. A quick check in the Purdue University library showed that the term appeared in the titles of at least 40 recently published textbooks. However, for a given computer program, it is not always possible to determine if structured programming techniques have been applied during its creation. Questions such as those about the effect of structured coding on productivity; the percentage cost reduction; the degree that the program is made easier to read, maintain, and modify; and the amount of error reduction (if any) have never been adequately answered (see discussions in Sections 4.5.3 and 5.5).

The variability of the human element in software development is probably the principal cause of the lack of quantification in the claims associated with structured programming and other related issues. For example, it is conceivable that for a given problem, a particular programmer who has not been exposed to structured programming techniques may solve it much faster and with fewer errors than another particular programmer who has. Even the same programmer may perform quite differently on different occasions due to such factors as health, motivation, or familiarity with the problem. In order to avoid drawing conclusions of any kind based on small and possibly biased samples, it is important to study substantial amounts of data using statistical methods to try to answer questions related to the programming process. This chapter discusses two major sources of data: historical records and controlled experiments.

Statistical methods that are applicable to such data are presented. We also give the criteria that we consider useful in the evaluation of models of the software development process.

3.2 Historical Records

The usefulness of software metrics in the management of software development not only should be justified theoretically, but also should be supported by empirical results. The results from controlled experiments, which will be discussed later, are usually limited by economic constraints to small projects by individual programmers, and are usually performed only in universities. Such results are useful in providing insights to certain parameters of the programming process, but are not normally generalizable to team programming and large projects, which are common in industry. Thus, it is frequently necessary to use historical data from industry to confirm the existence of relationships suggested by theoretical analysis and controlled experiments. In this way important trends remain observable in industrial data even after many uncontrolled factors are introduced.

3.2.1 The Difficulty of Gathering Data

In our research, we are interested in the values of all metrics defined in Chapter 2. If records on project data are kept by a commercial concern, they most likely include only gross information, such as the size (in lines of code), the structure (in number of modules), the effort (in person-months charged by project personnel), and the number of defects discovered by customers. Unless project managers are still available, it is often difficult to determine the meaning of some historical data. For example, we may not know whether comments were included in the original count of lines of code. Questions about the percentage of previously existing code used in software development and the difficulty of integrating it with new code may never be answered. A round number (such as 15,000 lines) indicates that the size may just be an estimate, instead of the actual count.

The values of certain product metrics may be accurately determined if the software source code is still available. We can apply an automatic counting tool to the source to collect the various measures. There are now several tools available to count Halstead's Software Science metrics, McCabe's $v(G)$ or DE, and lines of code (for example, see [SHEN80], [CONT82], [PAUL83], or [BASI83]). However, most useful software undergoes changes over time (for example, see the conclusion of [COME81]). The changes may be minor, such as code patches made in response to defect reports. However, these changes may also be major, including the addition or deletion of entire modules.[1] Significant errors can be introduced if the source code available for analysis now is not the same version for which development data and defect counts were collected.

As good management practice, managers must keep accurate and timely records of the development process, just as any manager keeps track of a project. A weekly report should be filled out by individual programmers, indicating the times spent on each module in the system. These times should be partitioned into at least the design, coding, and testing phases. The time for other work related to the project, such as documentation or meetings, should also be recorded. Although daily reporting may be more desirable, this probably adds too much overhead and could affect morale. It is also important for the project manager to prepare a weekly report, summarizing the times charged to the project by various personnel. This provides a reasonable check on the validity of programmers' records to prevent systematic errors. Such a system was used in a recent study in which the projects with more reliable data produced results closer to the researchers' expectations [BASI83a].

A researcher should have accurate and efficient tools available to collect data on various product metrics. Most organizations do not mind if large amounts of text processing and counting can be scheduled during the slack times of the computer system. Special care should be taken to ensure that the product counted is exactly the version associated with the effort and defect data given. Such confusion may be reduced if there is a long-term arrangement with project management so that product metric data are collected at the time when modules are integrated into the system. In any case, the researcher should take an active role during data collection to ensure the data collected are the data desired.

3.2.2 Data Transportability

Collecting consistent data for projects at commercial installations is difficult. A recent attempt at a major research organization employing several hundred programmers turned up exactly one data point — a project consisting of newly created code, complete with size and effort information within acceptable accuracy.[2] Statistical analysis really requires more than one data point! Thus, researchers frequently must combine project information from several environments for studies concerning software development. One of the major studies

---

1. A major problem encountered in a recent study of IBM products was to identify the particular version of a product with which a defect report was associated. The problem was complicated by the fact that several versions of the product were in use during the same time period, and some modules in different versions had identical names. The results were published in [SHEN85].

2. Private communication with Linnea Cook, Lawrence Livermore Laboratory, 1982.

by Boehm began with 12 completed projects, which were primarily aerospace applications. That number later expanded to 36, then to 50, then to 56, and finally to 63 (Chapter 29 of [BOEH81]). A wide variety of environments were involved in the expansion process. He noted that "considerable effort" was devoted to ensuring that the data was consistent. Boehm apparently adjusted the data for a number of projects where he suspected the inclusion of comment lines in the size count, the exclusion of design effort and management effort, and "the like".

Managers must keep detailed descriptions of the programming environment where the software is produced. Special items such as the availability of the computer during development, the use of special software tools, and the accounting method used should be noted. Such information may be used by researchers to identify similar projects for analysis.

A researcher should remember the definition of all metrics needed for a study. If a discrepancy is noted between the definition and actual collection mechanism, adjustment should be made as soon as possible. The original data, the adjusted values, and the reason for adjustment should be kept with the data. To maintain credibility of the research and the integrity of the results, no adjustment can be made *after* analysis has begun. If possible, original data from different environments should be segregated and analyzed separately. Since programming procedures and metric definitions may differ among different environments, combining such data should only be used as a last resort.

3.2.3 The Aging of Data

Programming methodologies have undergone significant changes over the years: from machine code to assembly language, to higher-level languages, and to functional programming; from paper tapes to cards, to video display terminals, and to intelligent terminals; from manual manipulation of cards to on-line manipulation of text that use line- or full-screen editors. Underlying these changes is the trend to improve the efficiency of humans who use the machines, rather than improving the efficiency of machines. Although the improvement has never been fully documented, we believe that process metrics such as effort and defects have also been significantly affected over the years. For example, the use of "modern programming practices" (the factor MODP) has been determined to affect programmer productivity by up to 51% in [BOEH81].

It is important that the researcher know the dates of the project data. Only projects developed during the same period of time — thus possibly using the same programming technology — should be combined for analysis. Managers should also note the time period during which a study was made before applying any of its results. For example, it makes no sense to use data from the mid-1970s to estimate the programming productivity today.

3.3 Controlled Experiments

A controlled experiment is ideal for the evaluation of software development and testing models. In such an experiment, a number of subjects are enlisted to perform a task that involves an activity related to the development process. All factors associated with the task are controlled except any factor being investigated in the experiment. The goal of the experiment is to attribute any changes in performance to changes in the factors that have been allowed to vary. It is often desirable either to test subjects before they perform the task in order to ensure that they have similar abilities, or at least to evaluate their relative abilities for comparisons later.

For example, suppose we want to investigate the "learnability" of the programming languages Pascal and FORTRAN. The initial screening called the *pretest*, could be to interview a number of potential subjects who wish to become computer programmers. The objective of this interview will be to select those subjects who have not yet been exposed to any programming language. The task involved called the *treatment*, would be to teach half of the subjects to program in Pascal, and the other half in FORTRAN. The same number of lectures and identical exercises are given during the teaching phase. The final evaluation called the *posttest*, would be to give the subjects a problem to solve and to compare the times taken by the subjects in solving that problem. In our case, a simple problem — such as the sorting of an array of integers — is given to a group of 30 subjects. Half of the group is to write the sorting procedure in Pascal, while the other half is to solve it in FORTRAN. All subjects must use reserved computer terminals to develop their programs, and then they must test them using a common set of test cases. Let us assume that, after everyone has finished testing, we discover that the average time to solve the problem (that is, to code and test the algorithm) for the Pascal subjects is 27 minutes, whereas the average time for the FORTRAN subjects is 35 minutes. We might be tempted to conclude that Pascal is more powerful than FORTRAN. But is this conclusion valid? Section 3.3.1 explores the issues that must be considered before any such conclusion can be drawn.

3.3.1 The Validity of Experiments

The first question we may ask about any empirical result is whether the difference in the treatment is the reason for the difference in the observed results in the groups of subjects. This is referred to as the *internal validity* of the experiment (for example, see [CAMP63]). For the example just given, we have two experimental groups: one group is learning to program in Pascal, and the other is learning to program in FORTRAN. There are a number of factors, called *confounding factors*, that may affect the internal validity of the experiment:

History — During the experiment some specific "external" events occurred that may have affected the measurements. For our experiment, suppose that during the teaching phase an article written by a prominent computer scientist, who claims that FORTRAN will soon be replaced, appears in the campus newspaper. That may have discouraged the subjects in the FORTRAN group from learning the language well because they thought that their efforts were being wasted. Thus, experiments should be planned so that the chance of the subjects being exposed to biasing external events is minimized.

Maturation — During the experiment, some specific "internal" changes occurred that may have affected the subjects. For our experiment, since the subjects are students, they may be taking other courses at the same time. The programming skills of certain subjects may improve faster than others during the experiment because of the courses they take. Thus, experiments should be planned so that the chance of the "aging" process affecting the measurements is minimized.

Testing — Knowing that one is being tested may affect performance. For our experiment, if most subjects have never had the experience of being closely monitored, their performance may be significantly different from normal. In experiments that require subjects to be tested several times, the scores of later tests may also be affected by the earlier ones.

Instrumentation — Changes in the measurement device during the experiment may produce changes in the results. For our experiment, if the number of terminals available for the posttest is limited, it may be necessary to plan several sessions over different time periods and to let each subject sign up for the most convenient time slot. If a hardware problem causing degraded computer response occurs during a session when most subjects are from the FORTRAN group, their performance will be adversely affected. Even if each session is balanced, a temporary shutdown may still affect some subjects more than others, depending on their stages of development: if the language choice encourages one group to spend more time in design than the other, an early downtime would favor the first group who may not yet need the computer when it goes down. Thus, experiments should be planned so that the chance of specific events occurring between measurements and affecting them is minimized.

Selection — The method used to divide subjects into the two groups may have inherent biases. For our experiment, if the subjects' language preference is used in the selection, the Pascal group may contain more students in Computer Science, who are motivated in learning to program. The other group may contain more students from other departments, who do not care which language they learn. The results are then expected to be different; in fact, one group may be able to complete the final test in less time than the other, regardless of the language choice. Thus, it is important to use a random method to divide the subjects into groups whenever it is possible.

Mortality — The rate of loss of subjects from the comparison groups may be different. For our experiment, if two of the subjects from the Pascal group and ten of the subjects from the FORTRAN group fail to complete the program, then the results may be questionable. The difference in the loss may be the result of different abilities of the subjects in the two groups, or the ease of use of the languages, or other factors. Differing mortality rates — such as 13% vs. 67% in the case just examined — may signal that a serious bias has been created in the data from the characteristics of the subjects who remained.

The second question we may ask about any empirical result is whether the observed difference can be expected in other situations when Pascal and FORTRAN are the language choices. In other words, we may ask whether the result will be generalizable. This characteristic is referred to as the *external validity* of the experiment. For our subjects, we know that the average time to solve the sorting problem in Pascal is less than the average time to solve it in FORTRAN. We cannot say that for *all* programmers, since our subjects are just beginning to learn programming. Nor can we say that, for our subjects, the average time to solve any problem in Pascal is less than the average time to solve it in FORTRAN, unless the sorting problem is representative of all programming problems. If we disregard the difference between 27 and 35 minutes, which will be discussed in Section 3.4, our experiment far from enables us to say that Pascal is more powerful than FORTRAN.

To design experiments that are valid both internally and externally is often difficult. This is especially true when concerns about internal validity may jeopardize concerns about external validity, and vice versa. For example, to balance the group selection for our experiment, we choose subjects who are very similar in programming ability — who have no experience, in fact. This uniformity necessarily makes the sample not representative of the population of all programmers, thus making the result not generalizable to all programmers. However, if we use professional programmers and commercial software, external validity will be enhanced, but at the expense of introducing a lot of sources of internal "invalidity." However, designing experiments that are strong in both types of validity must remain the goal of all researchers. The following subsections describe several popular designs and discuss their validity.

3.3.2 Pre-experimental Designs

Before the discussion of any experimental design, let us introduce the notation we will use that we have taken from [CAMP63]. The symbol X will represent the *eXposure* of a group to a certain treatment and the symbol O will represent the *Observation*, or measurement, of the results of the treatment. The progress of the experiment over a group of subjects will be represented by a sequence of X's and O's, interpreted from left to right. The symbol R preceding any X or O indicates the subjects in the group are chosen as a *Random* sample from a certain population. When two or more rows (representing different groups) of X's, O's, and R's are used to describe an experiment, the vertical alignment of the symbols indicates that the activities are simultaneous. Additional notations will be introduced when necessary.

We discuss three forms of *pre-experimental* designs,—*pre-* in the sense that they may be used only to strengthen or weaken intuitions, but have very little scientific value. They may only serve as "pilot" studies for true experimental designs to be conducted later.

The One-Shot Case Study   This particular design may be represented by

$$X \qquad O$$

A single group is exposed to a treatment presumed to cause change, followed by the measurement of the results. For example, suppose we are interested in the "learnability" of Ada. This design calls for a group of subjects to learn Ada, to solve a number of problems using Ada, and to testify that it is great to program in Ada.[3] The implicit comparison is with the subjects' experience in other programming languages and the feeling about what would have happened if another language had been used to solve the same problems. It is almost impossible to quantify the differences since the comparison is made with other events that are casually observed and remembered. Since there is no control on any of the factors that might affect the presumed difference, this case study cannot be used as a benchmark to compare with future studies of the treatment. A possible use of this design is to gain confidence with the treatment; that is, to know for sure that the given problems can be solved in Ada using reasonable effort. Such a pilot study helps the planning of a true experiment later by providing some estimates on its time and expense.

The One-group Pretest-Posttest Design   This design may be represented by

$$O_1 \quad X \quad O_2$$

First, certain characteristics of a single group are measured; then the group is exposed to a treatment; and finally these characteristics are measured again for changes. For example, to investigate Ada, a group of subjects unfamiliar with

---

3. We could also gather data on, for example, the time to write programs, or the "correctness" of those programs. Note, however, that there is no control data with which to compare this.

the language is told to solve a sorting problem using a programming language that they are familiar with, and the individual times are recorded as the first observation. The group is then taught Ada; afterwards, the subjects are told to solve a similar problem in Ada, with the individual times recorded as the second observation.

Almost all of the confounding factors described in Section 3.3.1 are *not* controlled in this design. The history and maturation factors are not controlled since it may take for instance, a week to teach Ada. Many events may have happened between the first and second observations. The testing factor is not controlled since, after the subjects have solved the problem given during pretest, solving another *similar* problem during the posttest ought to take less time, even with a "worse" language. If different observers are employed during pretest and posttest, the instrumentation factor may vary since one observer may exclude the short interruptions during programming from the total time, while another may not. Thus, it is difficult to attribute the difference in performance to the teaching of Ada alone.

So, while the One-group Pretest-Posttest design may provide some insight to planning a real experiment, it is insufficient by itself for controlling most biasing factors.

The Static-group Comparison   This particular design may be represented by

$$X \quad O_1$$
$$O_2$$

A group that has been treated by X is compared with another that has not. The observed difference, if any, is then attributed to the treatment.[4] For example, we would compare the times needed to solve a problem for subjects who have been taught Ada with that of subjects who have not. This design can control the factors of history, maturation, testing, and instrumentation. However, the selection factor may confound the results if the two groups are composed in some nonrandomizing way, such as two classes, two clubs, or two dormitory teams. The group taught Ada may be composed of those motivated to learn programming, while the other group may not. Subjects in the first group may perform better whether Ada is taught or not. It will be important to study the background of all subjects to make sure that they are "comparable." This may not be possible since all subjects in the first group *choose* to be taught Ada, while other subjects do not. Even if the groups have once been "identical," different mortality rates may affect the composition at the posttest time.

---

4. Especially note the absence of the letter R in the experimental design: the two groups are *not* obtained by randomly dividing potential subjects.

The shortcomings of the three pre-experimental designs lead us to the following true experimental designs, which should be used whenever possible.

3.3.3 The Pretest-Posttest Design

This design should be used to evaluate the differences for several treatments X_1, X_2, ..., X_n, whenever possible. It may be represented by

$$
\begin{array}{cccc}
R & O_1 & X_1 & O'_1 \\
R & O_2 & X_2 & O'_2 \\
\cdot & \cdot & \cdot & \cdot \\
\cdot & \cdot & \cdot & \cdot \\
\cdot & \cdot & \cdot & \cdot \\
R & O_n & X_n & O'_n
\end{array}
$$

The subjects are randomly divided into n groups. They are first given a pretest $(O_1, O_2, ..., O_n)$. The groups are then treated by $X_1, X_2, ..., X_n$. They are given the posttest to obtain $O'_1, O'_2, ... , O'_n$. The difference between O_i and O'_i can be compared with that between O_j and O'_j for all i and j. This design can be used to ascertain the effects of just two treatments

$$
\begin{array}{cccc}
R & O_1 & X_1 & O'_1 \\
R & O_2 & X_2 & O'_2
\end{array}
$$

and if X_2 is simply no treatment at all, this becomes

$$
\begin{array}{cccc}
R & O_1 & X_1 & O'_1 \\
R & O_2 & & O'_2
\end{array}
$$

This is called the *Pretest-Posttest Control Group design*, where the second group is the control group. In this case, care must be taken to make sure that the activities of the control group while the first group is receiving X_1 do not add ambiguity to the results. This means that the second group should be kept occupied for the same amount of time and with similar activities as the first group. For example, they may be taught something about programming — but *not* Ada.

Furthermore if $n > 2$, one of the n groups may be considered a control group. Thus, for an experiment on comprehending software, we may use header comments (appearing only at the front of a module), block comments (before each major function in the module), interspersed comments (before every few lines), and no comments at all. In this case, $n = 4$, which could be represented as

$$
\begin{array}{llll}
R & O_1 & X_1 & O'_1 \\
R & O_2 & X_2 & O'_2 \\
R & O_3 & X_3 & O'_3 \\
R & O_4 & X_4 & O'_4
\end{array}
$$

in which case X_4 is no comments (and is a control group.) X_4 could be diagrammed as

$$
\begin{array}{llll}
R & O_1 & X_1 & O'_1 \\
R & O_2 & X_2 & O'_2 \\
R & O_3 & X_3 & O'_3 \\
R & O_4 & & O'_4
\end{array}
$$

Our example described at the beginning of Section 3.3 is a Pretest-Posttest design, provided that the subjects are randomly divided into the two groups

$$
\begin{array}{llll}
R & O_1 & X_1 & O'_1 \\
R & O_2 & X_2 & O'_2
\end{array}
$$

or more specifically

$$
\begin{array}{llll}
R & O_1 & \text{Pascal} & O'_1 \\
R & O_2 & \text{FORTRAN} & O'_2
\end{array}
$$

For this example, the pretest refers to the initial screening of subjects to make sure that none has been exposed to any programming language. This kind of pretest may not provide any quantitative data. Consequently, the differences in the time taken to solve the sorting problem (O'_1 and O'_2) are attributed to the different treatments.

The Pretest-Posttest design controls the factors of history and maturation, since their effects on $O_i - O'_i$ should be the same for all groups. If identical tests are used on the groups at the same time, this design also controls the factors of testing and instrumentation. The factors of selection and experimental mortality are controlled by the random assignment of the subjects to the groups.

The question of external validity is more complicated. For example, in our example, the results on the "learnability" of programming languages may only apply to those subjects who have not been exposed to any language at all. Thus, we are logically unable to generalize to the large population of programmers, for whom the results would be more interesting. Such is the problem plaguing researchers conducting controlled experiments about software and its development. The results cannot usually be generalized directly to experienced programmers.

3.3.4 The Posttest-Only Design

This design is very similar to the Pretest-Posttest design and is used in similar situations, except that a pretest is not feasible and therefore is not used. It may be represented by

$$
\begin{array}{ccc}
R & X_1 & O_1 \\
R & X_2 & O_2 \\
\cdot & \cdot & \cdot \\
\cdot & \cdot & \cdot \\
\cdot & \cdot & \cdot \\
R & X_n & O_n
\end{array}
$$

The subjects are randomly divided into n groups. The groups are treated by X_1, X_2, ... , X_n, and then tested to obtain O_1, O_2, ... , O_n. Just like the Pretest-Posttest design, the Posttest-Only design can be used to ascertain the effects of a single treatment (there is no X_2 when only two groups are involved). Or, any of the X_i's can be a control treatment.

The reasons why a pretest may not be used vary from cost (it is more expensive to do both a pre- and posttest), time (omitting the pretest leaves more time to spend on the treatment and posttest), to bias affects (for example, a pretest using a text editor may so bias the subjects to that editor that their use of another may be strongly affected).

Since the pretest in our Ada example does not provide any quantitative data, our example may also be considered to be the Posttest-Only design. The comments on internal and external validity for the Pretest-Posttest design generally apply also to the Posttest-Only design. When it is feasible to apply a pretest to obtain quantitative data on the subjects' performance before treatment, there exist more sophisticated statistical tools to analyze the results. Some of these tools will be discussed later in Section 3.4.

3.3.5 Counter-Balanced Design

If the number of treatments is large or if the number of subjects is small, it may not be feasible to divide the subjects into groups for either the Pretest-Posttest or the Posttest-Only designs, while maintaining a reasonable number of subjects per group. Experimental control can still be achieved if we let each subject be exposed to all treatments. The "Latin square" arrangement is a typical approach for balancing the effects of extraneous factors. An example with four treatments is shown on the following page:

	t_1	t_2	t_3	t_4
Group A	X_1O	X_2O	X_3O	X_4O
Group B	X_2O	X_4O	X_1O	X_3O
Group C	X_3O	X_1O	X_4O	X_2O
Group D	X_4O	X_3O	X_2O	X_1O

In this design, the subjects are divided into four groups. The four treatments are applied to each group in an order such that, during any one time period, each group is being exposed to a different treatment. The design is further "balanced" in the sense that each treatment precedes each other treatment exactly twice, and follows each other treatment exactly twice.[5] Only posttests are used after each treatment.

Notice that the trade-off here is "number of subjects" for "time:" although fewer subjects are needed in the counter-balanced design, their time involvement can be significantly greater since they must receive each treatment and posttest.

Suppose that we have four individuals and want to investigate the use of mnemonic variables. We can define four levels of mnemonic variable usage. For example, in a payroll program where the pay rate and salary of employees are frequently referenced, the four modes may be illustrated as follows:

	Rate	Salary
Very Mnemonic	RATE	SALARY
Somewhat Mnemonic	RT	SAL
Non-mnemonic	A	I
Anti-mnemonic	SALARY	RATE

Such different levels of mnemonic variables can be created for other types of programs. The hypothesis is that different levels of mnemonicity affect programmers' understanding of programs, which lead to differing performance when making changes to programs. The experiment would be to use four different programs, each written in four versions using the four different levels of mnemonicity. Associated with each program is a quiz on its functions, which can be completed correctly only if a programmer fully understands it. The percentage of correct answers represents the percentage of understanding. The programs and associated quizzes are given to the subjects according to the arrangement shown in the Latin square. At the end of the experiment, we have 16 scores to analyze — 4 for each mnemonicity level. Of course, more scores will be available if we have four groups instead of just four individuals.

The Latin square design controls the history factor since, in any one time period, all treatments are being applied to the experiment groups. The balanced

5. This could be important if exposure to one treatment is likely to bias performance in any way for another treatment.

sequence for each group in theory prevents the repeated testing and maturation from affecting the results. Selection and mortality would not be issues of concern if the subjects are randomly distributed into the groups.

The number of possible Latin squares with n treatments can be very large.[6] As a result, there is no published complete table of Latin squares from which an experimenter might make a random selection. However, it is possible to generate one for any number of treatments using the following method:[7]

(1) Construct a "standard" square where each row is obtained by shifting the elements of the previous row (by one) cyclically. For example, a 6-treatment "standard" square is:

$$
\begin{array}{cccccc}
A & B & C & D & E & F \\
B & C & D & E & F & A \\
C & D & E & F & A & B \\
D & E & F & A & B & C \\
E & F & A & B & C & D \\
F & A & B & C & D & E
\end{array}
$$

Note that each treatment (represented by a capital letter) appears only once in each row and each column.

(2) Construct a new square by selecting the middle column first (where middle $= \dfrac{n+1}{2}$ if n is odd, and middle $= \dfrac{n}{2} + 1$ if n is even).

(3) Continue to add columns to the square in the order middle, middle-1, middle$+1$, middle-2, middle$+2$, and so on, until all columns are in the square.[8]

---

6. For $n = 6$, the number of possible squares is 812,851,200 including those that are not balanced [GILL78].

7. This technique was developed by one of the authors of this book and was then found to be functionally equivalent to a method described in [KEMP52].

8. Let us look at the reason why this technique works. Notice that the standard square is very unbalanced (e.g., B is before C 5 times and C is before B only once [in row 3]). This algorithm reverses the order of the relationships before the middle column, as well as half of the premiddle column and postmiddle column relationships. Thus, it balances the relationships. Notice that in the resultant Latin square B is before C 3 times and C is before B 3 times. These is no unique balanced Latin square; this algorithm produces only one of several. Note that, in the 4 treatment case, it selects columns 3, 2, 4, 1 to produce

$$
\begin{array}{cccc}
3 & 2 & 4 & 1 \\
4 & 3 & 1 & 2 \\
1 & 4 & 2 & 3 \\
2 & 1 & 3 & 4
\end{array}
$$

which differs from the one shown at the beginning of this section.

Note that, from our six-treatment square, middle = 4, which places columns 4, 3, 5, 2, 6, and 1 in the Latin square as shown below:

$$
\begin{array}{cccccc}
D & C & E & B & F & A \\
E & D & F & C & A & B \\
F & E & A & D & B & C \\
A & F & B & E & C & D \\
B & A & C & F & D & E \\
C & B & D & A & E & F
\end{array}
$$

3.4 Statistical Analysis

In Section 3.3, we described an experiment in which a group of subjects had been instructed to solve a problem in Pascal, while another group of subjects had been instructed to solve the same problem in FORTRAN. The average time to solve the problem in Pascal was 27 minutes, and in FORTRAN 35 minutes. We know from experience that whenever human subjects are involved there is a degree of randomness in their behavior: the times taken by the subjects in the Pascal group may range from 12 to 46 minutes, while those for the FORTRAN group may range from 20 to 44 minutes. A set of hypothetical data is given in Table 3.1. The average times for the two groups are expected to be somewhat different. The observed difference may have occurred purely by chance. The important question is whether the probability of such a difference occurring purely by chance is low enough, so that we may have confidence that a "real" difference actually exists. All empirical results should be analyzed to determine if they are "statistically significant."

For example, if we toss a coin 1000 times, in theory we should see 500 heads and 500 tails. But, purely by chance, we may actually see 509 heads and 491 tails. This is not significant in the sense that we should not conclude that a head is more likely than a tail on any future toss. However, if we think the coin is fair and see 400 heads and 600 tails, this *is* significant and is conclusive evidence that the coin is unfair. In the following subsections, we shall describe some basic concepts of statistics to enable a researcher to interpret the empirical results intelligently and to determine the significance of the results.

3.4.1 Types of Measurement Scales

Before we talk about the statistical tools that might be used in analyzing data, it is important to understand the type of data we may have. Statisticians recognize four basic types or scales.

Table 3.1   Programming Times and Analysis for a Sorting Experiment (in minutes)

SUBJECT	PASCAL	FORTRAN
1	12	20
2	13	21
3	14	25
4	19	26
5	21	31
6	25	35
7	27	38
8	27	38
9	28	39
10	30	40
11	32	41
12	34	42
13	36	42
14	42	42
15	46	44
mean	27	35
median	27	38
mode	27	42
s	10.2	8.2
skewness	0.13	-0.58
kurtosis	-1.04	-1.30

The *nominal* scale refers to data that categorizes objects of interest. The only property is equality (and, of course, inequality). For example, the sex of human beings is important information in the analysis of behavior. Numbers may be used for computer analysis of such data, possibly with 0 representing male and 1 representing female. It is reasonable to compare the sex designator of a subject with that of a group to see if the subject is a member of that group, but it is not reasonable to compute the "average" sex of a group of subjects from both sexes. The numbers on the jerseys of football players are also an example of the nominal scale, even though it is conventional to assign low numbers to lighter players (such as quarterbacks and wide receivers) and high numbers to heavier ones (such as linemen). In metrics research, data on whether a particular strategy is used, or whether a module has defects for example, are from nominal scales.

Ordinal scale data can be ordered. This scale has both the properties of equality and rank. For example, the class rank of students, the education level of employees, or the place of finish in races can be given numerical representations, but the average value is not meaningful. Although we can talk about items of the same rank, we cannot say (without additional information) that the difference between the first and second finishers of an auto race is the same as the difference between second and third finishers. There are many factors that can be used to rank data in metrics research. We have talked about the "mnemonic levels" of programs; other items such as levels of programmers' experience, levels of program complexity, or scores on comprehension tests may also be from ordinal scales.

Interval scale data refers to numbers that have meaningful differences, in addition to the properties of equality and rank. Fahrenheit temperatures are from an interval scale because the difference between 70° F and 85° F is the same as the difference between 75° F and 90° F. We can also say that the average temperature of a city is 70° F, but not that it is "twice as hot" as another city whose average temperature is 35° F.

The most desirable scale is the *ratio* scale, for which a broad range of statistical tools can be applied. This scale has all the properties of equality, rank, meaningful differences and meaningful ratios. The absolute temperature (K°) is such an example; for example, 400° K is indeed twice as hot as 200° K, with the difference measurable in several physical characteristics. A key characteristic of ratio scale data is the existence of an *absolute zero*. Most product metrics discussed in Chapter 2 are from ratio scales. Examples are lines of code, number of decisions, and the various token counts and composite metrics based on these basic metrics. The four scales of data and the appropriate operations on them are summarized in Table 3.2.

Table 3.2   Summary of Measurement Scales

SCALE	OPERATIONS*	DESCRIPTION	EXAMPLES
nominal	$=, \neq$	categories	sex, race
ordinal	$<, >$	rankings	rank in class
interval	$+, -$	differences	F°, C°(temp.)
ratio	$\div$	absolute 0	K°(temp.)

*The operations listed are appropriate for all scales

listed beneath it as well.

It is often difficult to determine to which scale a metric belongs. For example, in the recorded defects for software modules, we notice that there are certain modules with no defects, indicating the presence of absolute zero. But is the number of defects really from a ratio scale? The answer to this question depends on whether it is appropriate to consider a module with eight defects "twice as error-prone" as another module with just four. The function of the module with eight defects may be to print different diagnostic messages for a compiler depending on the error code. Each defect may represent a misprint in the stored messages, which is trivial to correct. On the other hand, the function of the module with 4 defects may be syntactic analysis. Four critical constructs of the language may not have been properly implemented, requiring major changes of the design. In this case, it is probably *inappropriate* to consider the eight-defect module more error-prone, or even more so to consider it twice as error-prone. Similarly, the number of defects may not be from an interval scale because the types of defects within a module may be quite different. Their summation is therefore meaningless. Even the ranking of modules according to the number of defects may be questionable; a recent analysis of commercial software shows that most modules of the products from one company have zero defects after release [SHEN85]. For the modules that do, most have only one or two defects. Therefore, there are a large number of modules "tied" in the rankings, making the ordinal scale not very useful.

However, assume that we want to investigate 10 programs written to satisfy the same specifications. If each program is run with the same 100 test cases, then the number of failed test cases could probably allow us to rank the 10 programs by ordinal scale, and could possibly even allow us to consider relative differences or ratios by interval or ratio scales. In conclusion, a researcher must be aware of the scale of the data being analyzed in order to select the appropriate statistical tools.

3.4.2 Measures of Central Tendency and Variability

When we have a set of numbers representing some measurement, the simplest way to describe the set is to find its *central tendency* or *average*. For example, when an anthropologist reports that the average height of a certain Micronesian tribe is five feet, two inches, the report gives us a good idea of the stature of people living on that island. We expect that a large number of people on that island *are* five feet, two inches tall, that many are quite close to that height, and that the number of people taller than the average is about equal to the number of people shorter than the average. This and many other natural phenomena follow what is called a *normal distribution*, a bell-shaped curve showing the number of samples plotted against the range of their values. Figure 3.1 shows such a curve.

There are at least three formal ways to describe the central tendency of a set of numbers. They are the *mean*, *median*, and *mode*. Let the set of numbers be represented by $X = (x_1, x_2, \cdots, x_n)$, where the elements x_i are sorted in ascending order. The *mean*, often represented as μ, is defined as

$$\mu = \frac{\sum_{i=1}^{n} x_i}{n} \tag{3.1}$$

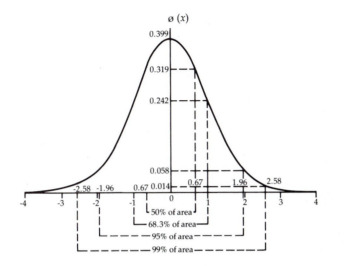

Figure 3.1   A normal distribution curve.

It is also called the *average*. The *median* is defined as $x_{\lceil n/2 \rceil}$. (The "ceiling" function, which is the same as $(n+1/2)$ is used to select the middle subscript when n is an odd number). This definition has the characteristic that half of the samples are lower than the median value, and the other half are higher than the median. The *mode* of a set of numbers is the value where the distribution curve peaks: the mode is the value that occurs most often in a set of data.[9] In a normal distribution, the mean, the median, and the mode have the same value.

Suppose that a sociologist reports that the average annual income for members of that Micronesian tribe is $10,500. This high figure may lead us to conclude that the islanders are rich, possibly because of the recent oil and gas discoveries. However, depending on the socio-economic structure of the tribe, the majority of the people may still be very poor while the family of the tribal chief is exceedingly rich. Such a skewed distribution of wealth may have the form shown in Figure 3.2. Depending on the specific situation, the mean income may be much higher than the median and mode. The distribution curve is a graphical method that gives us a good idea of the wealth of the people living on that island.

Note that we may compute the mean, median, and mode of interval and ratio scale data. However, since differences may not be meaningful for ordinal

---

9. For example, in the set of data (3, 5, 5, 5, 7, 7, 8, 9), the mode is 5 because there are three of them. In the set of hair colors (black, brown, red, black, blonde, black, brown, black), black is the mode.

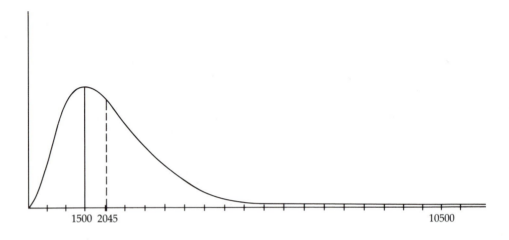

1500 2045   10500

Figure 3.2   A skewed distribution curve.

data, only the median and mode should be used. For nominal data, only the mode can be used. Thus, it makes sense and is more useful to report the median Micronesian income of $2045, or the mode of $1500, rather than the mean.

In addition to the central tendency of data, we may be interested in how data vary relative to the mean value. The measurement of variability includes the *minimum* and *maximum values* (x_1 and x_n for our example) and their difference called the *range* $(x_n - x_1)$. Another popular measure of variability is the *standard deviation* σ, defined as

$$\sigma = \left[\frac{\sum\limits_{i=1}^{n} (x_i - \mu)^2}{n} \right]^{1/2} \tag{3.2}$$

It is the square root of the mean squared difference between data values and the mean value of the data (μ). A large σ indicates that there is a number of data values that are quite different from the mean. For data that follow a normal distribution, we expect 68% of the observations to occur within one standard deviation, and 28% between one and two standard deviations, tapering off as shown in Figure 3.1. A related measure is the *variance*, which is simply the square of the standard deviation:

$$\sigma^2 = \frac{\sum\limits_{i=1}^{n} (x_i - \mu)^2}{n} \tag{3.3}$$

The formulas given for μ and σ are intended for data from the entire population. In practice, most data we encounter are *samples* from populations. It is more appropriate in statistics to compute the *unbiased estimate* of the standard deviation using the formula

$$s = \left[\frac{\sum\limits_{i=1}^{n} (x_i - \mu)^2}{n-1} \right]^{1/2} \tag{3.4}$$

when dealing with data samples. This formula is used by standard software packages such as SPSS [NIE75]. The change of the denominator from n to $n-1$ does not affect the result much when n is large. The unbiased estimation of μ is

$$\bar{x} = \frac{\sum\limits_{i=1}^{n} x_i}{n} \tag{3.5}$$

(i.e., computed exactly like μ).

We can also measure the *skewness* of a distribution using the formula

$$skewness = \frac{\sum\limits_{i=1}^{n} ((x_i - \bar{x})/s)^3}{n} \tag{3.6}$$

The skewness has value zero when the distribution is a completely symmetric curve such as the normal and uniform distributions. A positive value indicates that the data are clustered more to the left of the mean, with most of the extreme values to the right (as in Figure 3.2); a negative value indicates that the data are clustered to the right. Nonzero skewness signals that the mean may not be as useful a measure of central tendency as the median or mode. Another measure called the *kurtosis* indicates the relative flatness of the distribution. It is defined as

$$kurtosis = \frac{\sum\limits_{i=1}^{n} ((x_i - \bar{x})/s)^4}{n} - 3 \tag{3.7}$$

A normal distribution has a kurtosis of zero. A positive value indicates that the distribution is more peaked than the normal distribution; a negative value indicates that it is flatter. However, many statisticians question the validity of using a single number to represent the "peakedness" of any distribution.

Let us return to our earlier example comparing programming in Pascal and programming in FORTRAN. Table 3.1 shows the raw data on the posttest for the two groups and their central tendencies and variability.[10] From the table, we know that the distributions for both groups are somewhat flatter than the

---

10. Note that this is artificial data made up by us and not from a real experiment.

normal distribution (negative kurtosis), with the Pascal group skewed to the left (positive skewness) and the FORTRAN group skewed to the right (negative skewness). Since there are two Pascal programmers with programming times larger than most FORTRAN programmers, it is not immediately obvious whether the different average times (27 minutes vs. 35 minutes) show that the different treatments imply different performance. The following subsection discusses the application of statistical tests that may answer the question of statistical significance.

3.4.3 The Experimental Paradigm

In software metrics research, experiments are often conducted to determine the acceptability of hypotheses that we derive from our intuitive understanding of the programming process. After establishing an hypothesis, which may be a part of a proposed theory, we collect data from historical records or controlled experiments in order to evaluate the hypothesis. The analysis of such empirical data may lead us to retain, revise, or reject the hypothesis and the associated theory. There are a number of statistical tests that we can use to evaluate an hypothesis objectively. The following procedure is often used; the individual steps will be discussed in more detail later:

(1) State the *null hypothesis* (H_0).

(2) Choose an appropriate statistical test for H_0.

(3) Specify a *significance level* (α) as the criterion of rejection.

(4) Compute the statistic and determine its p-value. The null hypothesis H_0 is rejected if and only if the p-value is no larger than α.

The Null Hypothesis   The null hypothesis (H_0) is formulated for the express purpose of being rejected. It is usually an hypothesis of *no difference:* the observed data for two empirical groups are simply random samples from the same population. If it is rejected, we may then accept the alternative hypothesis (H_1), which is actually the hypothesis we are interested in.

In our example, the null hypothesis is that there is no difference between the performances of the Pascal and FORTRAN groups. More specifically, let μ_1 be the mean time to solve the problem in Pascal and μ_2 be that in FORTRAN, then

$$H_0: \ \mu_1 = \mu_2$$

and

$$H_1: \ \mu_1 \neq \mu_2$$

The alternative hypothesis H_1 may also be either $\mu_1 > \mu_2$ or $\mu_1 < \mu_2$, if the theory predicts the Pascal time will be more than the FORTRAN time or vice versa.

The Choice of the Statistical Test   There are often several statistical tests available for a given situation. The first consideration should be the *power* of tests; a powerful test has a large probability of rejecting H_0 when it is false, which is exactly the kind of performance we want. However, the most powerful tests are those that require the most extensive assumptions about the distribution of data. An example is the commonly used t test, which can be used to test the hypothesis for our Pascal and FORTRAN programming times. The test has the following assumptions:

(1) The observations must be independent.[11]

(2) The observations must be drawn from normally distributed populations.

(3) These populations must have nearly the same variance, or standard deviations.

(4) The measurements must be in *at least* an interval scale as described in Section 3.4.1.

These conditions are typical of a family of statistics known as *parametric* tests. The validity of using a parametric statistical test depends upon the validity of the assumptions on the actual data. For our case, we can consider the measurements to be independent since a programmer's time in solving a given problem should not be affected by other programmers' times.[12] It is hard to say that human performance follows the normal distribution, but our study on skewness and kurtosis shows that the data are not far from normal. The standard deviation for the Pascal group is around 10; the standard deviation for the FORTRAN group is around 8. Are they nearly the same? Yes — they certainly have the same order of magnitude. The data in our case *is* at least in an interval scale. Thus, we can defend our use of the t test for this experiment.

A *non-parametric statistical test* requires fewer and weaker assumptions. The observations must still be independent, but there are no conditions on the distribution of data and the variances. Most nonparametric tests can be used on data from an ordinal scale, and some apply also to data from a nominal scale (see Section 3.4.1). Although nonparametric tests can be applied to more situations, we should still try to use parametric tests whenever possible, since the latter take advantage of additional information and can give significant results with fewer data points. Nonparametric statistics require fewer assumptions because they ignore the actual data and use only their ranks. However, parametric statistics, use the actual data. (Refer to [HOLL73] or a similar text book for a comprehensive discussion on the merits of the different tests.)

---

11. In general, using different subjects in experimental groups and forbidding interaction among experimental subjects will ensure independence.

12. Although this may not be true in general, the experiment can be controlled so that no subject is aware of what others are doing.

The Significance Level In any experiment, the data we collect is but a sample from some larger population. There is usually a large set of possible results that could occur when the null hypothesis H_0 is true.[13] However, a result (a set of data) may be so extreme that the probability is very small that it is a member of the set when H_0 is true.[14] For any set of data, we can compute a statistic and determine its p-value. We reject H_0 if the p-value is no larger than a certain value α, which is called the *significance level*. Common values of α for software metrics research are 0.05 and 0.01. If our observed difference between Pascal and FORTRAN programming performance occurs purely by chance with probability less than 0.05, we will conclude that the performances are really different. The α value is the probability that a true null hypothesis will be rejected. For example, $\alpha = 0.05$ indicates that there is a 5% chance that our conclusion may be false. Depending on the circumstances, larger (such as 0.10) or smaller (such as 0.005) levels are sometimes chosen.

Take note of both the classical and the more modern methods of determining the significance of experimental results. In the classical paradigm, an α level is established before any data is collected. This α is based upon subjective criteria on the part of the scientist, as well as on tradition. After conducting the experiment, if the p-value is at least as small as α, the classical experimenters report that their "results are significant and that H_0 can be rejected at the α level." Otherwise, they report that "the results are not significant and H_0 cannot be rejected." But this rigid technique can lead to some ridiculous situations — such as a p-value of 0.011 is not significant if α is 0.01. More modern experimenters report the p-value, offer their own interpretation of its significance while taking into account any predetermined α, and leave the final significance judgment somewhat to the intelligent reader.

Computation of Statistical Tests Many computer systems provide statistical packages that perform a variety of tests. An example is the SPSS system, which contains the t test and the analysis of variance, both of which are parametric tests [NIE75]. The IMSL library [IMSL82] has a large number of parametric and nonparametric tests from which a researcher may choose. It is not our purpose to discuss the available tests in any detail. However, using our example of Pascal and FORTRAN programming, we shall illustrate the use of one parametric test, the t test, and one non-parametric test, the Mann-Whitney U test.

The t test is used when we assume that the conditions for parametric tests are met. Let $\bar{x}_1$ and s_1 be the mean and standard deviation for the Pascal group, and $\bar{x}_2$ and s_2 be those for the FORTRAN group. Compute

---

13. For example, a 509 heads and 491 tails example with a fair coin after 1000 tosses.

14. For example, 400 heads and 600 tails.

$$s^2 = \frac{(n_1-1)s_1^2 + (n_2-1)s_2^2}{n_1 + n_2 - 2} \tag{3.8}$$

and

$$t = \frac{\bar{x}_1 - \bar{x}_2}{\sqrt{s^2/n_1 + s^2/n_2}} \tag{3.9}$$

where n_1 and n_2 are the number of data points in each group. For our case, $n_1 = n_2 = 15$, we have $s^2 = 85.2$ and $t = 2.33$. With this t value, we can refer to a table of critical t values. Such a table is given in Appendix A (Table A.1) and in many statistical books. Each row in Table A.1 corresponds to some "degrees of freedom" — that is, $df = n_1+n_2-2$. Since our H_1 is of the form $\mu_1 \neq \mu_2$, it is considered a "two-tailed" test.[15] The significance level is 0.05 since row 28 has 2.0484 (<2.33) for 0.05, and 2.4671 (>2.33) for 0.02. Therefore, we can conclude that the performance for the two groups are different, with H_0 rejected at the 0.05 level.[16]

If the conditions for the parametric test cannot be met, then the nonparametric Mann-Whitney U test can be used to determine whether the two samples are from identical populations. The U test is a most useful alternative to the parametric t test. To find U, we first rank the 30 programming times as shown in Table 3.3. In case of tied scores, the rank for each tied score is the average of the ranks that the scores would have had if we had more precise measurements to reveal the minute differences. After the ranks are established, compute $U = \min(U_1, U_2)$ where

$$U_1 = n_1 n_2 + \frac{n_1(n_1+1)}{2} - R_1 \tag{3.10}$$

and

$$U_2 = n_1 n_2 + \frac{n_2(n_2+1)}{2} - R_2 \tag{3.11}$$

with $R_i = \sum_{j=1}^{n_i} RANK_i$ for group i. In our case, $R_1 = 183.5$ (Pascal) and $R_2 = 281.5$ (FORTRAN). Consequently, $U_1 = 161.5$ and $U_2 = 63.5$, leading to $U = 63.5$. Table A.2 in Appendix A shows that H_0 can be rejected at the 0.05 level, but not at the 0.02 level. This is the same result obtained by using the t test.[17]

---

15. That is either $\mu_1 > \mu_2$ or $\mu_1 < \mu_2$ would satisfy $\mu_1 \neq \mu_2$.

16. Note that in this case we really did not compute the p-value. We were able to take a statistic $t = 2.33$ directly to a table and determine which α-value is most appropriate. If we had used a statistical package, it would have reported that $t = 2.33$, $df = 28$ leads to a p-value $= .0298$, from which we would show the same conclusion (i.e., $.02 < .0298 \leq .05$).

17. If there are too many tied scores, the Mann-Whitney U test becomes too conservative and fails to reject H_0 when it should. There is a technique to adjust this statistic if several ties are present [SIEG56]. However, with our data in Table 3.3, there are only five sets of tied scores — too few to affect the test appreciably.

Table 3.3   Ranks of Programming Times for the Sorting Experiment

SUBJECT	PASCAL	RANK	FORTRAN	RANK
1	12	1	20	5
2	13	2	21	6.5
3	14	3	25	8.5
4	19	4	26	10
5	21	6.5	31	15
6	25	8.5	35	18
7	27	11.5	38	20.5
8	27	11.5	38	20.5
9	28	13	39	22
10	30	14	40	23
11	32	16	41	24
12	34	17	42	26.5
13	36	19	42	26.5
14	42	26.5	42	26.5
15	46	30	44	29

Suppose the performance of the subjects in the FORTRAN group is that shown in Table 3.4, instead of that in Table 3.1. Even though the mean performance is the same as the FORTRAN group, there is a much wider range of values. The standard deviation is about twice that of the Pascal group, possibly making the use of the t test inappropriate. It is still possible to use the U test, which does not have assumptions on the distribution of data. The computation is shown in Table 3.5. In this case, H_0 cannot be rejected at the 0.20 level. Therefore, we cannot conclude that the times for the two groups are different.

The two sets of programming times by the FORTRAN group show that mean values alone are not sufficient to allow the researcher to conclude whether the Pascal group is different from a FORTRAN group. We need to select an

Table 3.4   Programming Times and Analysis for the Sorting Experiment

SUBJECT	PASCAL	FORTRAN
1	12	3
2	13	5
3	14	7
4	19	12
5	21	19
6	25	28
7	27	28
8	27	40
9	28	41
10	30	47
11	32	48
12	34	49
13	36	60
14	42	62
15	46	71
mean	27	35
median	27	40
mode	27	28
s	10.2	22.1

appropriate statistical test and to analyze all experimental data. Even with a positive test result, the conclusion can only be stated in probabilistic terms.

When we wish to test to see whether more than two samples come from populations with the same mean, we could apply the t test to pairs of samples if

Table 3.5   Ranks of Programming Times and Analysis for the Sorting Experiment

SUBJECT	PASCAL	RANK	FORTRAN	RANK
1	12	4.5	3	1
2	13	6	5	2
3	14	7	7	3
4	19	8.5	12	4.5
5	21	10	19	8.5
6	25	11	28	15
7	27	12.5	28	15
8	27	12.5	40	21
9	28	15	41	22
10	30	17	47	25
11	32	18	48	26
12	34	19	49	27
13	36	20	60	28
14	42	23	62	29
15	46	24	71	30
R_1	208	U_1	137	
R_2	257	U_2	88	
U	88	α	>0.20	

the assumptions are met, and the U test if they are not. However, if the null hypothesis can be stated as

$$H_0: \ \mu_1 = \mu_2 = \ \cdots \ = \mu_k$$

and the alternative as

$$H_1: \ \mu_i \neq \mu_j, \text{ for some } i,j \ \ 1 \leq i < j \leq k$$

a more general "one-way analysis of variance" test can be used. Examples are the F test (parametric), and the Kruskal-Wallis test (nonparametric). Both tests allow a number of samples (including the case of two samples) and are available in most statistical packages. They are frequently used in place of the t and U tests, even for the two-sample case, since researchers can easily be familiar with a limited set of tools that have a broad range of applications. The basic concepts of the analysis of variance will be discussed later.

3.4.4 Relationships among Sets of Measures

A major area of metrics research is the testing of two sets of measures to find out whether they are related in some way. The measures in question normally have properties that are attributable to a common feature. For example, a hospital may keep a large number of records on patients that include their weights and heights. An intuitive hypothesis would be that a tall person is heavier than a short person; in other words, weights and heights are "positively" related. This hypothesis can be tested by collecting all weights of patients as one set of measures, and all heights of patients as the other set. The only requirement is that, for every weight measure, there is a corresponding height measure for the same person. Similarly, if we are interested in knowing whether larger programs use more unique variables, we can analyze a set of programs and obtain the lines of code (S_s) and variable count ($VARS$) for each program. We then have two sets of measures: for each size measure in lines of code, there is a corresponding variable count for the same program.

A strong relationship between two sets of measures may not imply that one is caused by the other. For example, suppose that data from a company reveals that team size (such as the number of programmers on a programming team) is best related to program size (such as the number of lines of code produced). Suppose that this is a positive relationship: larger team sizes correspond to longer program sizes. Can we conclude that the team size is the *cause* of the program size? If we want a small software package, can we simply assign a small team to work on a problem? No! If there *is* a causal relationship here, it probably works the other way: small problems lead to small software that can be written by small teams, while large problems require large programs that in turn require large teams.

When there is no causal relationship between two sets of measures, both may still be caused by a third measure, which may not be available. For example, consider the salaries of programmers in dollars per month, and performance in lines of code per month on a certain project. Both measures are related to programmers' ability, which is difficult to quantify. Although generally increased salary leads to higher performance, increasing the salary of poor programmers will not immediately make their performance better.

The following subsections describe methods to determine whether two sets of measures are related. If so, we are interested in the type and strength of the relationship. Methods to find models that approximate a relationship are also discussed.

Table 3.6   The Metrics η_1, η_2, *VARS*, and *N* for a Sample of 24 Programs [WANG84]

Program	η_1	η_2	*VARS*	*N*
1	127	413	211	12171
2	117	451	204	7086
3	125	588	325	11270
4	81	144	84	3111
5	96	427	234	10825
6	82	118	73	2196
7	141	1020	646	20031
8	115	729	297	13490
9	96	380	236	7548
10	118	440	223	11719
11	139	690	475	12479
12	89	172	96	2564
13	149	666	397	11209
14	98	369	161	4219
15	86	182	133	2890
16	93	308	186	5090
17	89	295	161	6723
18	97	295	195	3790
19	181	756	564	13348
20	121	517	327	6941
21	337	1073	703	29699
22	122	439	255	9066
23	170	761	483	15698
24	269	952	743	27729

Scatter Diagrams   Often the first step taken in the analysis of the relationship between two sets of measures is the *scatter diagram*, which is a two-dimensional graph with a number of points plotted on it. The coordinate for each point is a pair of measures corresponding to an item for which the two measures are taken. The measure used as the abscissa is often called the *independent variable*, whereas the measure used as the ordinate is often termed the *dependent variable*. For example, a study was made in 1983 to determine the relationship between the unique variable count (*VARS*) and total program length (*N*) for a sample set of Pascal programs [WANG84]. Table 3.6 shows the data and Figure 3.3 shows the scatter diagram.[18] The diagram suggests that programs with a

---

18. Additional data on the η_1, η_2 metrics are also given for discussion later.

RANGE OF X AXIS: 73 743
RANGE OF Y AXIS: 2196 29699

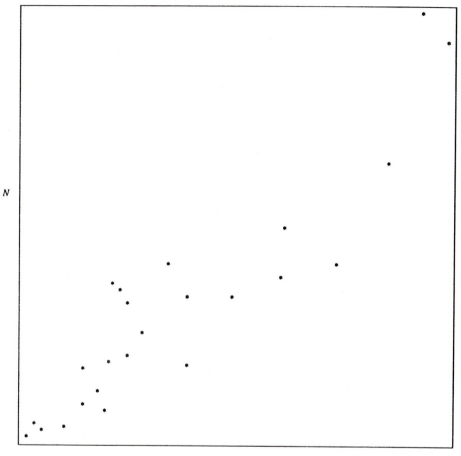

Figure 3.3   *N* versus *VARS*.

higher number of unique variables (larger *VARS*) are generally longer (larger *N*). Furthermore, the relationship appears to be linear; the formula

$$N = a + b \ VARS \tag{3.12}$$

may be a good approximation of the relationship. An examination of the scatter diagram may suggest suitable models for the relationship. The appropriateness of the model or the strength of the relationship can then be analyzed using other quantitative methods.

Correlation   *Correlation* is a colloquial term used to mean many different things. Someone may say, "My past experience correlates well with the job I now have," or "There is a strong correlation between health and happiness". However, in this book when we use the term *correlation*, we mean a statistical relationship between two sets of measures, or metrics, in which interval changes in one measure are accompanied by interval changes (not necessarily the same interval) in the other measure. Correlation may be "positive" in which case changes are in the same direction, or "negative" in which changes are in opposite directions. For example, if a one-year increase in a person's age is typically (unfortunately!) accompanied by a five-pound increase in weight, then these two metrics may be said to be positively correlated. On the other hand, if one hour of testing time is typically associated with three fewer defects in delivered software, then these two metrics are negatively correlated.

Thus, the strength of a relationship between two sets of measures can often be evaluated using the *correlation coefficient*. Depending upon the type of data, there are both parametric and nonparametric correlation procedures. As we discuss later, the parametric procedure depends on the assumption that the relationship is *linear*. The parametric correlation coefficient also depends on the usual parametric assumptions, such as interval scale data, independent data, or nearly equal variances. However, the nonparametric correlation coefficient depends only on the fact that the two sets of data come from ordinal scales.

Parametric Correlation   For data in interval or ratio scales that also meet the other requirements for parametric statistics, the *Pearson product-moment correlation* is often used to assess the strength of the linear relationship between two sets of measures. The symbol for the correlation coefficient is r, whereas the symbol for the corresponding parameter of the population is ρ:

$$\rho = \frac{1}{N} \sum \frac{(x - \mu_x)}{\sigma_x} \frac{(y - \mu_y)}{\sigma_y} \tag{3.13}$$

where the symbol N represents the population size, x and y are the N pairs of related data items, μ_x and μ_y are means of the populations, σ_x and σ_y are standard deviations of the populations; and

$$r = \frac{1}{n-1} \sum \frac{(x - \bar{x})}{s_x} \frac{(y - \bar{y})}{s_y} \tag{3.14}$$

where the symbol n represents the sample size, x and y are the n pairs of related data items, $\bar{x}$ and $\bar{y}$ are means of the samples, and s_x and s_y are standard deviations of the samples. The computations for these terms are defined in Equations (3.1) to (3.5). Thus, ρ represents the correlation between x and y in the entire population while r is the approximation of this correlation as determined from the sample of size n.

RANGE OF X AXIS: 1 20
RANGE OF Y AXIS: 1 20

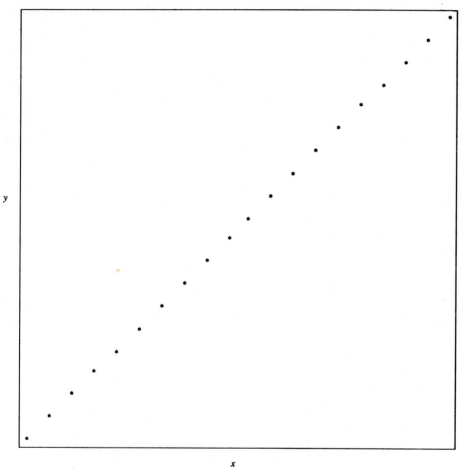

y

x

Figure 3.4   A perfect positive linear relationship.

The formula for r has the characteristic that $r = 1$ when there is a perfect positive linear relationship between two sets of measures as shown in Figure 3.4, and $r = -1$ for the perfect negative relationship shown in Figure 3.5. When there is little or no linear relationship between the measures, r has a value close

RANGE OF X AXIS: 1 20
RANGE OF Y AXIS: 1 20

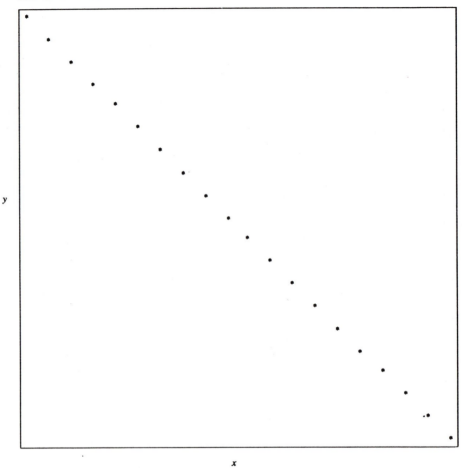

Figure 3.5   A perfect negative linear relationship.

to zero (see Figure 3.6).   The correlation coefficient for the unique variable count (*VARS*) and total program length (*N*) in Table 3.6 is 0.92.

Since the absolute value of a correlation coefficient is always a number between 0 and 1, it is reasonable to ask whether the relationship is "significant": Is a correlation coefficient like 0.92 (or even 0.54) different enough from zero to conclude that the data is really related?   If we stop 100 people on the street and ask them to report their shoe size and last 4 digits of their telephone number,

RANGE OF X AXIS: -20 20
RANGE OF Y AXIS: -20 20

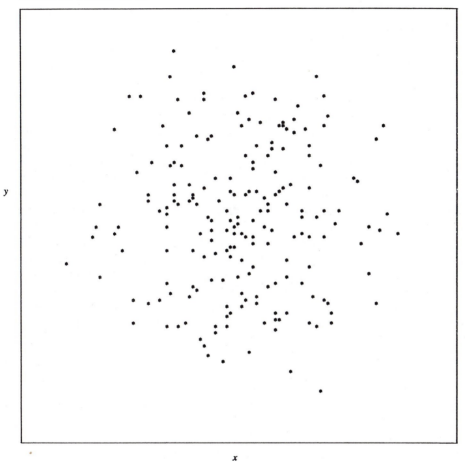

y

x

Figure 3.6   A completely random *x-y* relationship.

we would certainly expect these two measures to be unrelated. If we find that the correlation coefficient between the two is 0.17, this is *not* 0.00. However, as in the coin tossing that we described earlier, slight deviations from a 0.00 correlation coefficient may still occur even when the data truly is unrelated. Thus, a correlation coefficient of 0.17 may (we sincerely hope!) be insignificantly different from zero.

To determine the significance (or the lack thereof) of a correlation coefficient, the null hypothesis is generally that there is no correlation between the two populations:

$$H_0: \rho = 0$$

The alternative is then

$$H_1: \rho \neq 0$$

The probability of obtaining various non-zero values of r when there is no correlation can be computed and compiled into a table of "critical" r values. Such a table is given in Table A.3 of Appendix A . Note that for a desirable α level, the critical r value becomes smaller as the sample size grows. Thus, the more data we gather in an experiment, the more likely we will be to reject the null hypothesis for a given α level if it indeed is not true. If the alternative hypothesis does not indicate a direction,[19] it is called a *two-tailed test* for which the α value is twice that indicated. For the data in Table 3.6, the correlation coefficient 0.92 is larger than the critical value for $n = 20$, $\alpha = 0.01$. Therefore, it is significant at the 0.01 level. Note that *significance* means "significantly different from 0," rather than "significantly close to 1." In Table A.3, if we had 100 pairs of data (rather than just 20), we could reject the null hypothesis at the 0.01 level with a correlation coefficient as small as 0.26.

The formula to compute correlation coefficients may be given in another form to simplify computation: that is, it can be shown that Equation (3.14) is equivalent to

$$r = \frac{n\sum(xy) - (\sum x)(\sum y)}{\sqrt{(n\sum x^2 - (\sum x)^2)(n\sum y^2 - (\sum y)^2)}} \tag{3.15}$$

Instead of computing $(x - \bar{x})/s_x$ and $(y - \bar{y})/s_y$, it is possible to tabulate x, x^2, y, y^2, and xy to find individual sums to use in Equation (3.15) to calculate r.

Note that a low correlation coefficient implies a lack of *linear* relationship, not a lack of relationship. For example, the correlation coefficient for the 10 data points shown in Figure 3.7 is -0.17. It is not statistically significant according to Table A.3. However, for each pair of (x, y),

$$y = 1 + \sin(x)$$

for $x = 1, 2, \dots 10$.

Non-parametric Correlation   As we have already discussed, there are occasions when it is inappropriate to use the Pearson parametric correlation coefficient. For data in the ordinal scale — when they can be ranked — *Spearman rank correlation* correlation is often used. The symbol for this correlation coefficient is r_S and is defined as follows:

---

19. This is common when dealing with correlation coefficients and is true for our example as well.

$$r_S = 1 - \frac{6}{(n^3 - n)} \sum_{i=1}^{n} d_i^2 \tag{3.16}$$

where the symbol n represents the sample size and d_i represents the *difference in ranks* of the ith pair of data. For example, Table 3.7 shows the computation of the rank correlation using the data in Table 3.6. The sum of d^2 is 219.5. Using Equation (3.16), we have $r_S = 0.90$. It can be shown that r_S ranges from -1 to 1, as does r. A value near either 1 or -1 indicates that there is a strong linear relationship between the ranks of the two measures.

Table 3.7   The Unique Variables *VARS* and the Length *N* for a Sample Group of Programs

Program	VARS	rank	N	rank	d	d^2
1	211	10	12171	17	-7	49
2	204	9	7086	10	-1	1
3	325	16	11270	15	1	1
4	84	2	3111	4	-2	4
5	234	12	10825	13	-1	1
6	73	1	2196	1	0	0
7	646	22	20031	22	0	0
8	297	15	13490	20	-5	25
9	236	13	7548	11	2	4
10	223	11	11719	16	-5	25
11	475	19	12479	18	1	1
12	96	3	2564	2	1	1
13	397	18	11209	14	4	16
14	161	5.5	4219	6	-0.5	0.25
15	133	4	2890	3	1	1
16	186	7	5090	7	0	0
17	161	5.5	6723	8	-2.5	6.25
18	195	8	3790	5	3	9
19	564	21	13348	19	2	4
20	327	17	6941	9	8	64
21	703	23	29699	24	-1	1
22	255	14	9066	12	2	4
23	483	20	15698	21	-1	1
24	743	24	27729	23	1	1
						219.5

It is also possible to test whether the relationship r_S is significant. The probability of obtaining various nonzero values of r_S when there is no correlation can be computed and compiled into a table of critical r_S values. Such a table is given in Appendix A (Table A.4). Using an approach similar to that for the table of critical r values described earlier, the data in Table 3.7 is found to be significant at the 0.01 level.

Figure 3.8 shows a relationship $y = x^3$, for $x = 1, 2,..., 20$. Since it is not linear, the Pearson correlation $r = 0.92 < 1$. However, the related data points

RANGE OF X AXIS: 1 10
RANGE OF Y AXIS: 4.10757253e 1.98935825

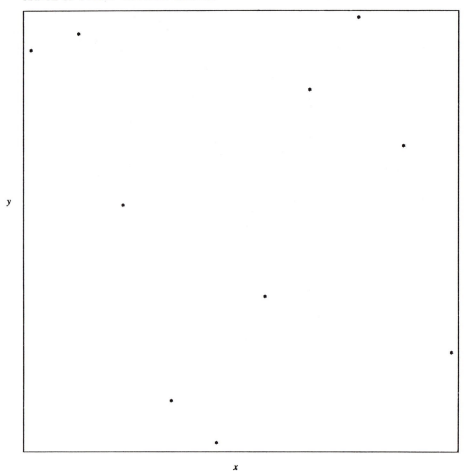

Figure 3.7 $y = 1 + \sin(x)$.

rank perfectly, so that $r_S = 1$. It may be useful, even for data in the interval scale, to compute both the Pearson and Spearman correlations to identify the model that best represents the relationship between two sets of measures.

Coefficient of Determination   The measure r^2 is called the *coefficient of determination*. This may be interpreted as the percentage of variance in one measure accounted for by the other. Since $0 \leq |r| \leq 1$, it must also be the case that

$0 \le r^2 \le 1$. For example, for our $r = 0.92$, $r^2 = 0.85$. Thus, we can say that *VARS* accounts for approximately 85% of the variance of N, and vice versa. This implies that knowing one of these two metrics gives us a good deal of information about the other, which is not surprising since the correlation coefficient is so high. Furthermore, it also implies that 15% of the variance in each is not accounted for by the other. (This will be covered later when we discuss Analysis of Variance in this section.)

Linear and Multilinear Regression   When there is a linear relationship between two sets of numbers, it is often desirable to express the relationship in an analytic form: let y be the dependent variable, and let x be the independent variable. We are looking for coefficients b_0, b_1 such that

$$\hat{y} = b_0 + b_1 x \tag{3.17}$$

is a reasonable approximation to y. The coefficient b_0 is called the *y-intercept*, and the coefficient b_1 is called the *slope*. A frequently used method to determine b_0 and b_1 is the method of least squares: b_0 and b_1 are chosen so that the sum of the squared errors $(\sum_{i=1}^{n}(y_i - \hat{y}_i)^2)$ is minimized. It can be shown that these coefficients can be determined by the following formulas:

$$b_1 = \frac{\sum(x_i - \bar{x})(y_i - \bar{y})}{\sum(x_i - \bar{x})^2} \tag{3.18}$$

$$b_0 = \bar{y} - b_1\bar{x} \tag{3.19}$$

These yield unbiased coefficients (i.e., they do not systematically over- or underestimate). A straight line approximation obtained by least squares is usually called the *regression line*.

For the data given in Table 3.6 and plotted in Figure 3.3, $\hat{N} = -56 + 34VARS$. The regression line is shown in Figure 3.9. It is always possible to find the regression line even for data that is not really linearly related. For example, the regression line for $y = x^3$ is $\hat{y} = -1894 + 390x$, for $x = 1, 2, ..., 20$, which is shown as a solid line in Figure 3.10.

The *aptness*, or appropriateness, of a linear regression model can be evaluated by inspecting the scatter diagram of *residuals*, which are simply the difference between the actual and predicted values $(y - \hat{y})$. For example, the residuals for the data of an N versus *VARS* model is shown in Figure 3.11. The linear model is considered apt since the residuals, which are errors for individual estimates, appear to be distributed with the same variability over the range of *VARS*. Figure 3.12 shows the trend for the residuals for a *curvilinear* relationship, $y = x^3$. Note the systematic change in the distribution of the residuals. Thus, the linear regression model does not appear to be an appropriate one in this case (which should not be surprising).

RANGE OF X AXIS: 1 20
RANGE OF Y AXIS: 1 8000

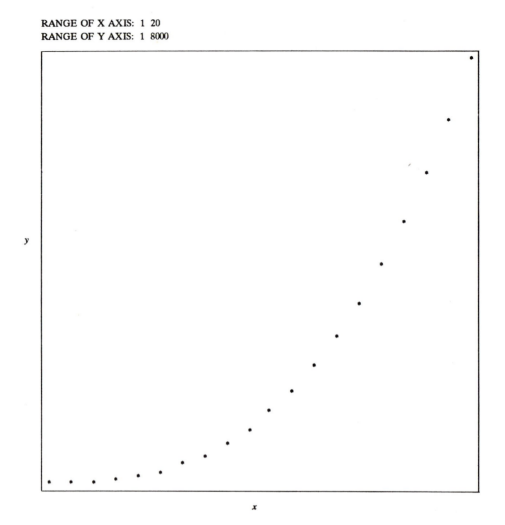

y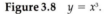

x

Figure 3.8 $y = x^3$.

It is sometimes desirable to "force" the regression line through the origin by requiring that $b_0 = 0$. For example, the relationship between a person's height and weight should be such that a person with zero height has zero weight. A program with zero lines of code should also have zero defects. A program with no variables should have zero or near-zero length. The dashed line in figure 3.10 shows such a straight line fit to the function $y = x^3$, $x = 1, 2, ..., 20$.

RANGE OF X AXIS: 0 743
RANGE OF Y AXIS: -56 29699

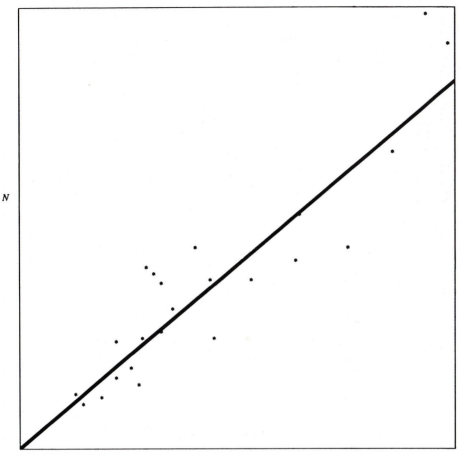

Figure 3.9   *N* versus *VARS*.

It can be represented as $\hat{y} = 252x$. The sum of the squared errors is larger than the case when $\hat{y} = -1894 + 390x$ (36,303,696 versus 18,801,288).

Many statistical packages support regression with more than one variable, called *multivariate* or even *multilinear regression:*

$$\hat{y} = b_0 + b_1x_1 + \cdots + b_nx_n \tag{3.20}$$

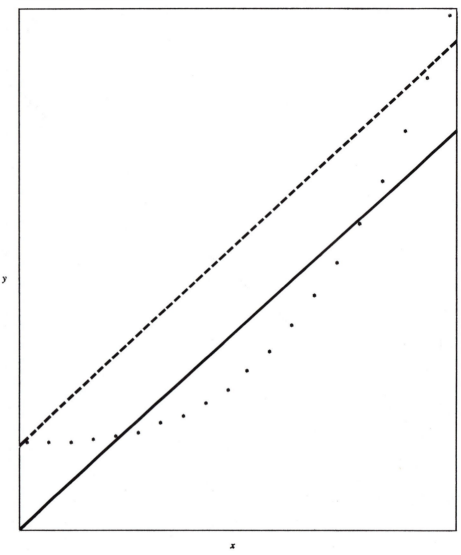

RANGE OF X AXIS: 0 20
RANGE OF Y AXIS: -1894 8000

Figure 3.10 $y = x^3$.

For a set of independent variables x_1, x_2, $\cdots$ x_n, such a program finds a set of coefficients b_0, b_1, $\cdots$ b_n so that $\sum(y_i - \hat{y}_i)^2$ is minimized. Normally, the more variables used, the smaller the squared errors that are expected. Note that

RANGE OF X AXIS: 73 743
RANGE OF Y AXIS: -5789.4634 5831.1986

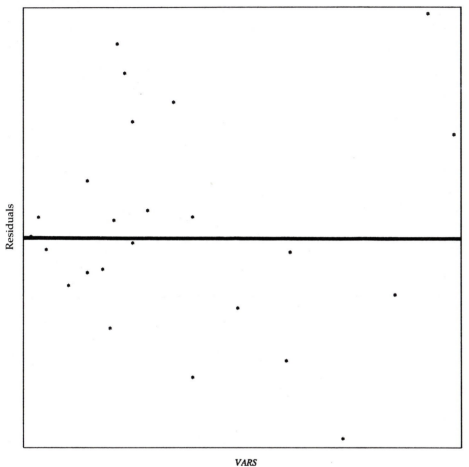

VARS

Figure 3.11   Residuals for N versus *VARS*.

in multilinear regression, the coefficients obtained for highly correlated independent variables *do not* suggest the relative importance of the variables in predicting the dependent variable.

Using the metrics η_1, η_2, and *VARS* in Table 3.6 as independent variables,

RANGE OF X AXIS: 1 20
RANGE OF Y AXIS: -1069.2 2086.2

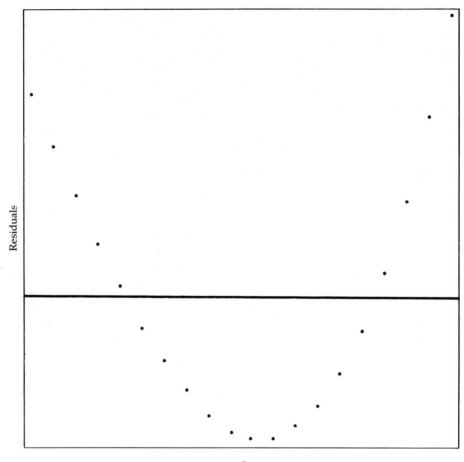

Figure 3.12   Residuals for $y = x^3$.

multi-linear regression yields

$$\hat{N} = -4468 + 59\eta_1 + 16\eta_2 - 3\ VARS$$

The introduction of η_1 and η_2 in the formula produces a better approximation for N than using $VARS$ alone, in terms of a higher coefficient of determination ($r^2 = 0.93$ versus 0.85), and lower sum of squared errors (94,732,693 versus 200,689,465).   The three "independent" variables are actually *not* independent from each other, with $r_{\eta_1, \eta_2} = 0.82$, $r_{\eta_1, VARS} = 0.86$, and $r_{\eta_2, VARS} = 0.96$.

Therefore the regression formula should *not* be interpreted to show that η_1 has more influence on $\hat{N}$ than η_2 or *VARS*, or that *VARS* has *negative* influence on $\hat{N}$.

Analysis of Variance   *Analysis of Variance* (ANOVA) is a technique for showing the amount of variance in a dependent variable "explained" by independent variables. For example, suppose we have a dependent variable y and a set of independent variables $x_1, x_2, ..., x_n$. As we discussed earlier in this section, we can determine the relationship between each of the independent variables x_i and y to obtain some idea about how each is related to the dependent variable. However, this type of analysis may not give a clear picture of what really affects y. In particular, ANOVA allows us to see how combinations of independent variables affect the dependent variable.

For example, suppose we collect data on programming time (the dependent variable y), the size of each program, the number of team members, the average years experience of each team member, and the number of code walk-throughs during development (the independent variables x_1 to x_4). This data for 25 projects appears in Table 3.8(a). This data was input to a standard Analysis of

Table 3.8(a)   Data for 25 Imaginary Projects

Time	Size	Members	Experience	Walk-throughs
120	1000	8	5	3
240	5000	4	6	5
1280	40000	73	3	6
2400	100000	34	4	0
40	300	2	1	10
160	2500	6	3	24
960	15000	2	7	12
1920	50000	47	8	8
80	3000	19	8	7
960	25000	4	6	8
5760	500000	70	7	5
120	1200	3	5	7
1920	80000	57	4	48
1360	35000	230	2	3
480	7000	54	3	6
960	17000	23	5	28
1920	58000	50	6	6
2400	65000	34	1	7
1120	3100	68	2	39
2560	74000	34	3	5
3840	120000	57	5	6
1640	7500	33	4	2
120	2000	4	6	7
960	8100	6	8	8
2090	90000	57	7	3

Table 3.8(b)   Analysis of Variance of Data for 25 Imaginary Projects

Correlation with Time
(Main Effects)

Independent Variable	Correlation Coefficient	Coefficient of Determination
(1) Size	.8750	.7656
(2) Members	.3352	.1123
(3) Experience	.0890	.0079
(4) Walk-throughs	-.1128	.0127

Correlation with Time
(Interactions)

Independent Variable(s)	Correlation Coefficient	Coefficient of Determination
(1)	.8750	.7656
(1) (2)	.8854	.7839
(1) (2) (3)	.8860	.7850
(1) (2) (3) (4)	.8862	.7854

Variance package and reveals the following in Table 3.8(*b*):[20]

(1)   There is a significant correlation (0.8750) between the size of each program and the total programming time. Remembering the coefficient of determination (discussed earlier in this section), the size of each program explains approximately 76.56% (which is 0.8750^2) of the variance in total programming time.

(2)   There is a smaller correlation (0.3352) between the number of team members who worked on each program and the total programming time. Thus, number of team members explains only about 11.23% of the variance in total programming time.

(3)   There is a small nonsignificant correlation (0.0890) between the average years experience of each team member who worked on each program and the total programming time. Thus, average years experience explains less than 1% of the variance in total programming time.

(4)   There is a small nonsignificant negative correlation (-0.1128) between the number of code walk-throughs during development and the total

---

20. This is not real data, just some we have concocted for this example.

programming time. Thus, number of code walk-throughs explains about 1% of the variance in total programming time. Furthermore, the negative correlation suggests that, as the number of code walk-throughs went up, the total programming time went down (which is what any software engineer would hope would happen).

Thus, we learn from these so-called "main effects" that the size of the program is the most important parameter related to programming time.[21] But, in addition to what we learn from these four results, the ANOVA also tells us that knowing the size of the program and the number of people on the programming team allows us to account for 78.39% of the variance (only up a little from the 76.56% accounted for by program size alone). In fact, the ANOVA reveals that knowing all four of the independent variables (program size, team size, average experience, and number of code walk-throughs) increases the variance accounted for in programming time only to 78.54%. We can easily conclude from this analysis that the other 3 independent variables simply do not tell us much more about programming time than we can learn from program size.

Thus, ANOVA is used in experimentation to determine the "significant" simple relationships among variables, as well as any more complex relationships if they exist.

Nonlinear Regression   Earlier in this section, we showed a situation in which a relationship between two metrics was *nonlinear*. In that example, there was a relationship of the form $y = x^3$. However, as we saw earlier, it is often possible to approximate a linear relationship even with nonlinear data. This suggests that analyzing a scatter diagram is the best way to begin looking at the relationship between two metrics. If the scatter appears approximately linear, then correlation, regression, or ANOVA will probably be appropriate. On the other hand, if the scatter appears nonlinear, then nonlinear regression may be the answer. Analyzing a scatter diagram of the residuals may confirm the initial observations.

Again, there are many statistical packages with a nonlinear regression tool to be used to establish a nonlinear relationship between two sets of measures. Their use is about as easy as linear regression or ANOVA. In some cases, the tool may include automatically several powers of an independent variable (like x, x^2, x^3, etc.), several standard functions (like e^x, log x, etc.), and even some combinations of multiple independent variables (like $x_1 \times x_2$). With some other nonlinear regression tools, it is necessary for the user to specify which of these various manipulations of the independent variables to try.

As in the case of linear regression, the result of nonlinear regression is a regression equation in terms of some manipulations of the independent variables. For example, suppose we have data on a dependent variable y and 4

---

21. Remember that this is just artificial data to show how ANOVA works.

independent variables x_1, x_2, x_3, x_4, and we have examined some scatter diagrams that suggest that nonlinear regression is appropriate. Nonlinear regression may yield the following equation as the best approximation:

$$y = b_0 x_1 + b_1 e^{b_2 x_4} + b_3 x_2 x_3$$

It is then the responsibility of the researcher to determine why such a non-linear relation is sensible.

Factor Analysis   If we employ correlation or regression to examine the relationship between several independent variables and a dependent variable, we usually find that some of the independent variables are strongly related to each other. For example, earlier in this section, we found that program size and programming team size were strongly correlated (and we explained why this makes sense from a management standpoint).[22] Furthermore, we found that, after we knew the program size, very little additional information was provided by knowing the team size. Often it is tempting for researchers (or managers) to think that if they gather hundreds of metrics and combine the results in some way, they must be able to produce a more accurate model than if we just have a few parameters.

However, often this is not the case. In our hypothetical example in the discussion of ANOVA, a model composed of four factors really was not any better than one including only the program size. Some metrics are often strongly related to each other but not to some other metrics. For example, let us suppose that data has been gathered about the programming process at a particular company in which we have information on a dependent variable (such as, programming time) and some ten independent variables, which for this example we will call simply x_1, x_2, ..., x_{10}. We may decide to perform regression analysis, which may produce a regression equation involving all ten independent variables. However, further analysis could reveal that a regression equation with just 4 of those variables might do just as well. The economic implications should be obvious: if we have a software development model with 4 parameters (rather than 10), it will probably be cheaper and easier to use this in actual practice.

To determine which variables are really needed, we can turn to a statistical technique known as *factor analysis.* Once again, many statistical packages include factor analysis as a tool. In this case, we provide the dependent variable and all 10 independent variables; the factor analysis tool classifies the independent variables for us into as many equivalence classes (or factors) as are warranted. The factors are such that, within each class, the variables are strongly interrelated, while among factors they are relatively independent.

As a practical consideration, any variables included in the same factor will have high correlation coefficients with each other (like program size and team

---

22. Remember that this data was fabricated for this example.

size in our earlier example). Variables in different factors will have very low correlation coefficients (e.g., program size and average experience of team members).

Let us assume in this example that factor analysis reveals the following 4 factors:

$$(<x_1, x_5, x_7, x_8>, <x_2, x_9>, <x_3, x_6, x_{10}>, <x_4>)$$

The variables x_1, x_5, x_7, and x_8 are related to each other (like program size, number of variables, number of modules, and Software Science N). However, each is fairly independent of x_2 and x_9, which are related. What we learn from factor analysis in this case is that a model for y composed of one variable from each factor (such as, x_5, x_2, x_6, and x_4) will account for nearly as much variance in y as a model composed of all ten independent variables.

Data Transformations When two sets of measures are linearly related, the regression methods described earlier may be used to find the approximate relationship; that is, one in which the sum of squared errors is minimized. When the relationship is not linear, the more complicated nonlinear regression packages may be applied. However, there exist several relationships that are *intrinsically* linear: even though they are *not* linear, linear regression can be used to obtain the appropriate coefficients. This means that there exist simple transformations that enable the researcher to employ linear regression to get the coefficients. Several examples are the following.

Example 1. $\hat{y} = b_0 x^{b_1}$ ⠀⠀⠀⠀⠀⠀⠀⠀⠀⠀⠀⠀⠀⠀⠀⠀⠀⠀⠀⠀⠀⠀(3.21)

This power equation can be linearized by taking the natural logarithm of both sides to yield

$$\ln \hat{y} = \ln b_0 + b_1 \ln x$$

If we now set

$$Y = \ln \hat{y}, \; B = \ln b_0, \; X = \ln x$$

we obtain the linear form

$$Y = B + b_1 X \qquad\qquad\qquad\qquad (3.22)$$

If we apply linear regression to the form in Equation (3.22) to obtain the best fit constants B^*, b_1^* we can then return to the power form in Equation (3.21) by taking inverse logarithms. This yields

$$b_0 = e^{B^*}, \; b_1 = b_1^*$$

Example 2. $\hat{y} = b_0 b_1^x$ ⠀⠀⠀⠀⠀⠀⠀⠀⠀⠀⠀⠀⠀⠀⠀⠀⠀⠀⠀⠀⠀⠀(3.23)

Transforming this equation by taking natural logarithms leads to

$$\ln \hat{y} = \ln b_0 + x \ln b_1$$

On setting

$$Y = \ln y, \ B_0 = \ln b_0, \ B_1 = \ln b_1$$

we obtain the apparently linear equation

$$Y = B_0 + B_1 x \tag{3.24}$$

Least squares regression applied to Equation (3.24) yields the best fit constants B_0^*, B_1^*. The use of inverse logarithms then allows us to return to the non-linear form in Equation (3.23) via

$$b_0 = e^{B_0^*}, \ b_1 = e^{B_1^*}$$

Other useful transformations include relationships like $\hat{y} = b_0 + b_1/x$ and $\hat{y} = \dfrac{1}{b_0 + b_1 x}$. The reciprocal function can be applied to either the independent or the dependent variable.

Another reason for performing data transformations is to reduce some variance in the data: a logarithmic transformation has a smoothing and condensing effect on a set of data. Often, it may even yield a linear relationship where one does not exist with the raw data. Sometimes, transforming one of the variables, while leaving the others alone, may be just what is needed to obtain statistical significance.

For example, suppose we have some interval scale data that has one or two bad *outliers*, which are points that are many standard deviations away from the mean of the data distribution. A transformation like a logarithmic one, or even taking the square root, on that data will have the effect of making the outliers less so.

However, there are some serious problems when researchers resort to this technique in data analysis. Suppose that we are able to show that the logarithm of x is correlated with the square root of y. What does this really mean about the relationship between x and y? Perhaps nothing. If a model shows that the logarithm of programming team size explains 85% of the variance in the square root of programming time, what have we learned that a manager can use? We don't assign members to programming teams by considering the logarithm of team size, nor does the square root of time mean very much to us.

Note that nonparametric statistics are really a form of data transformation — transforming each measure into its own rank. This process smooths, eliminates bad outliers, and may allow a linear statistic to show significance where it would not with the raw data itself. Thus, a researcher should be aware of the fact that if a nonparametric statistic suggests a significant relationship while its equivalent parametric statistic does not, this may be a sign of a nonlinear relationship.

The Chi-square (χ^2) Test   Often, software metrics research may yield data that one can only say comes from a nominal scale. Examples of nominal scale data are the presence or absence of defects in software modules, the use or non-use of structured programming techniques in software development, or the use of one of the languages Ada, Pascal, C, or COBOL for implementation. It is still possible to perform some statistical tests even for such nominal data — the best-known (and probably most useful) of which is the *chi-square (χ^2) test* [SIEG56].

The χ^2 assumes only that data can be classified into two or more categories and that the number of data items that "should" fall into these categories can be determined. For example, in its simplest form, the χ^2 can be used to see if data meets null hypothesis expectations.

Suppose that, for years in our company, we have found that 30% of all modules contain at least one defect prior to the formal testing phase. We have recently introduced a new software development procedure intended to reduce the number of defects during design and coding. In order to investigate whether the new procedure is having its desired effect, we gather data for the last 85 modules produced in our company and find that only 12 of them had defects that showed up in formal testing. Since 12 is only 14% of 85, we are tempted to say that the procedure is working. But, we can test this using the χ^2 in a way that will allow us to assign a significance level.

Table 3.9   Hypothetical Data (1) to Illustrate the x^2 Test

Modules with defects	Modules without defects
$E_1 = 25.5$	$E_2 = 59.5$
$O_1 = 12$	$O_2 = 73$

Hypothetical data is shown in Table 3.9. The null hypothesis in this instance is

H_0:   30% of modules have defects.

We hope to reject this in favor of the alternate hypothesis

H_1:   the number of modules with defects is a percentage different from 30%.

Actually, we will only consider the new procedure a success if the percentage is less than 30%. However, for ease in statistical analysis, let us use H_1 as shown. In Table 3.9, E_i refers to the expected numbers for each category. Thus, E_1 (which is 30% of 85) is the number of modules we expect to have defects under the null hypothesis (and if the new procedure is having no effect).

Similarly, E_2 (70% of 85) is the number of defect-free modules under H_0. O_1 is the number of defect-laden modules we actually observe in our data and O_2 is the count of defect-free observed modules.

In order to compute the χ^2 statistic, we only need to do the following:

$$\chi^2 = \sum_{i=1}^{n} \frac{(O_i - E_i)^2}{E_i} \qquad (3.25)$$

$$df = n - 1 \qquad (3.26)$$

For our example, we have

$$\chi^2 = \frac{(12-25.5)^2}{25.5} + \frac{(73-59.5)^2}{59.5} = 182.25/25.5 + 182.25/59.5 = 10.2$$

$$df = 1$$

In order to determine whether our χ^2 value of 10.2 is significant or not, we look in Table A.5 of Appendix A at the line for 1 degree of freedom and find that 10.2 is larger even than 7.879. Thus, we may reject the null hypothesis at an α level of 0.005, and conclude that our new software development procedure has had an effect (in fact, the type of effect we wanted) on defects. However, had our data been as shown in Table 3.10, this would lead us to a totally different conclusion:

$$\chi^2 = \frac{(22-25.5)^2}{25.5} + \frac{(63-59.5)^2}{59.5} = 12.25/25.5 + 12.25/59.5 = .69$$

$$df = 1$$

Table 3.10   Hypothetical Data (2) to Illustrate the x^2 Test

Modules with defects	Modules without defects
$E_1 = 25.5$	$E_2 = 59.5$
$O_1 = 22$	$O_2 = 63$

This value of χ^2 (with one degree of freedom) is not significant; the best α level we can assign is 0.75. Thus, we may not reject the null hypothesis and, in this case, we conclude that our new software development procedure has had no appreciable effect on defects.

The χ^2 procedure may be used in more complicated instances, as well. For example, suppose that in a particular environment we have found that programmers rate their team leaders as Excellent, Good, Fair, and Poor at the following percentages: 45%, 25%, 15%, and 15%. A new team leader training program has been used over the past year, and now we ask our 175 programmers to rate their team leaders. Our fabricated data is shown in Table 3.11. We can compute

$$\chi^2 = \frac{(96-78.75)^2}{78.75} + \frac{(52-43.75)^2}{43.75} + \frac{(2-26.25)^2}{26.25} + \frac{(25-26.25)^2}{26.25}$$

$$= 3.78 + 1.56 + 22.40 + 0.06$$

$$= 27.80$$

$$df = 3$$

Table 3.11   Hypothetical Data (3) to Illustrate the x^2 Test

Excellent	Good	Fair	Poor
$E_1 = 78.75$	$E_2 = 43.75$	$E_3 = 26.25$	$E_4 = 26.25$
$O_1 = 96$	$O_2 = 52$	$O_3 = 2$	$O_4 = 25$

This value of χ^2 (with 3 degrees of freedom) is significant at the 0.005 level. Thus, we may reject the null hypothesis, and conclude that our new team leader training procedure has had an effect on programmer ratings of their team leaders.

From a practical standpoint, note that more leaders are now rated as both "excellent" and "good" than the old percentages (our null hypothesis) suggest. Almost none are rated as "fair." However, take special note of the "poor" category: There are almost as many "poor" ratings as under the old (before-training) system — indicating that our new training may be making good or marginal leaders better, but is probably not doing anything for poor ones.

Thus, we have seen how the χ^2 procedure can be used to analyze data when it is possible only to categorize the data, as when a nominal scale is all we can justify.

3.5 Model Evaluation Criteria

As we discussed in Section 1.3.4, the general form of a model is

$$y = f(x_1, x_2, \cdots, x_n). \tag{3.27}$$

In software metrics research, the dependent variable y is normally a process metric[23] of interest, such as programming effort, development duration, or defect probability. The independent variables x_1, x_2, ... x_n are product or process metrics that can be objectively (and usually algorithmically) determined. Note that the creation of such a model, using theoretical or empirical methods or their combinations, is only a first step. It is necessary to try to confirm that the model explains or predicts actual metric values for data collected through controlled experiments or from historical data. The model *should* work well for the data used to develop it. The ideal model should also be applicable without much modification for all data collected during different times and from different environments.

Since a critical problem faced by all software project managers is that of accurate effort and cost estimation, models of programming effort have been of particular interest in recent years. As a result, a large number of effort and cost models have been proposed (for example, see [MOHA81], Section 29.7 of [BOEH81], or [BOEH84]). Unfortunately, for a single project or for a set of similar projects these models generally yield substantially different estimates of cost or effort; while we expect some differences due to the imprecise nature of most models of physical processes, the differences are too great to inspire much confidence in their general usefulness.[24]

We know that it is impossible for any model to consider all possible factors that might affect the cost or effort to develop a software product, and that it is difficult to obtain precise measures of the factors that are considered. Thus, an estimate of cost or effort is expected to differ somewhat from what actually happens. A model can be evaluated using historical data, which is actually a set of *accidental* data, rather than a *random* sample of software projects. Therefore, data is collected from whatever sources happen to be available until the sample reaches some designated size, or the time allotted for data collection expires, or there are no additional sources. Even though the statistical analyses and tests described in Section 3.4 are often used on the data, the assumption of having a *random* sample is generally not met. This is one of the principal reasons that a model that seems to be appropriate for one set of historical data may not be appropriate at all for another set. In this section, we discuss objective ways to evaluate the performance of models so that the difference between actual and predicted values can be quantified. The criteria discussed in the following subsections may be independent of each other; for example, a model that performs well according to one criterion may perform poorly according to another. It is still the researcher's responsibility to decide which model is best by weighing the objective scores *subjectively* when they do not provide consistent results.

---

23. Refer to Section 1.3.3 for a discussion of product and process metrics.

24. In chapter 6, there is a discussion of a study done by Mohanty [MOHA81] in which he compared 13 cost models and their cost estimates of a hypothetical software system. The estimates ranged from a low of $362,500 to a high of $2,766,667 — nearly an order of magnitude difference.

As an example to illustrate the different criteria for the evaluation of models, we shall use some project data collected by the Software Engineering Laboratory, Department of Computer Science, University of Maryland [BAIL81]. The data is described in more detail in Section 3.6, and the actual values are given in Table B.3 of Appendix B. The equivalent sizes of the projects when there are both new and reused code are obtained by using Equation (2.10), which is reproduced here with $k = 0.2$ and $S_u = S_{\text{tot}} - S_n$:

$$S_e = S_n + 0.2S_u \tag{3.28}$$

Using this data, we have developed several regression models for estimating the effort E (i.e., computing an $\hat{E}$) as a function of equivalent project size S, given in thousands of lines of code or project duration T in months. These models are not necessarily good models (i.e., they probably are not the best we could have found); they are only sample models to illustrate the points in this section. The regression models are the following:

(1) Linear function of program size

$$\hat{E} = 5.03 + 1.67\ S$$

(2) Linear function of program development duration

$$\hat{E} = -4.12 + 6.77\ T$$

(3) Linear function of size and duration

$$\hat{E} = -2.59 + 1.48\ S + 2.62\ T$$

(4) Power function of size

$$\hat{E} = 2.09\ S^{.95}$$

The scatter diagrams for the four models are shown in Figures 3.13 through 3.16. It appears that the linear model of size (model 1) performs better than the linear model of development duration (model 2) for this set of data. However, the performances of models 1, 3, and 4, appear very similar. Therefore, objective measures are needed to decide if one model performs differently from another, and how to decide which is the best. There are many such objective criteria that have been used to compare the performance of different models (for example, see [THEB84]). All of them have limitations and strengths. The following have been found to be the most useful in software metrics studies. Since the effort model is chosen as the example, we denote the actual effort expended on a software project by E and the effort predicted by a model by $\hat{E}$. This same technique is also used on other measures of interest as well.

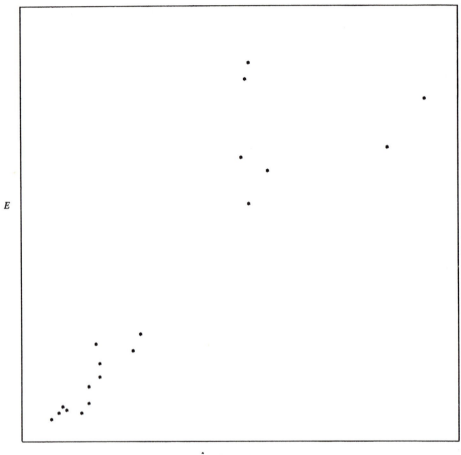

$$\hat{E} = 5.03 + 1.67\,S$$

Figure 3.13 E versus $\hat{E} = 5.03 + 1.67\,S$.

3.5.1 The Coefficient of Multiple Determination (R^2)

The *coefficient of multiple determination* (R^2) is among the most popular measures used to indicate the extent to which E and $\hat{E}$ are *linearly* related. R^2 is defined for n pairs of E and $\hat{E}$ values as

RANGE OF X AXIS: 0 160
RANGE OF Y AXIS: 0 160

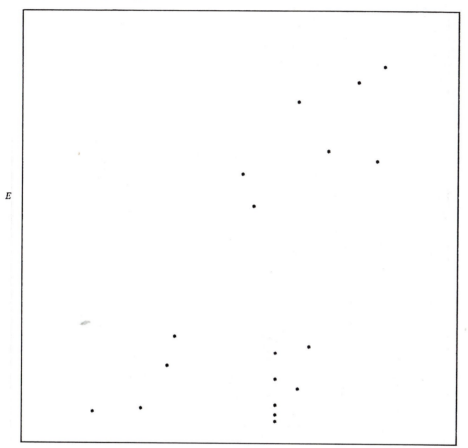

$$\hat{E} = -4.12 + 6.77\,T$$

Figure 3.14 E versus $\hat{E} = -4.12 + 6.77\,T$.

$$R^2 = 1 - \frac{\displaystyle\sum_{i=1}^{n}(E_i - \hat{E}_i)^2}{\displaystyle\sum_{i=1}^{n}(E_i - \bar{E})^2} \tag{3.29}$$

It can be shown that R^2 is the same as r^2 (which is discussed in Section 3.4.4) when only one independent variable is involved. When $\hat{E}$ is obtained through

RANGE OF X AXIS: 0 160
RANGE OF Y AXIS: 0 160

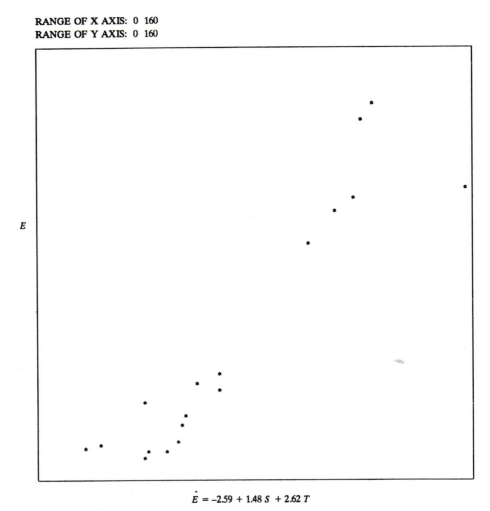

$$\hat{E} = -2.59 + 1.48\,S + 2.62\,T$$

Figure 3.15 E versus $\hat{E} = -2.59 + 1.48\,S + 2.62\,T$.

multilinear regression, R^2 is frequently used to denote the percentage of variance accounted for by the independent variables used in the regression analysis. A high value of R^2 suggests either that a large percentage of variance is accounted for, or that the inclusion of additional independent variables in the model is not likely to improve the model much. The value of R^2 does not reflect how closely E and $\hat{E}$ correspond to one another in an absolute sense.

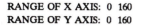

RANGE OF X AXIS: 0 160
RANGE OF Y AXIS: 0 160

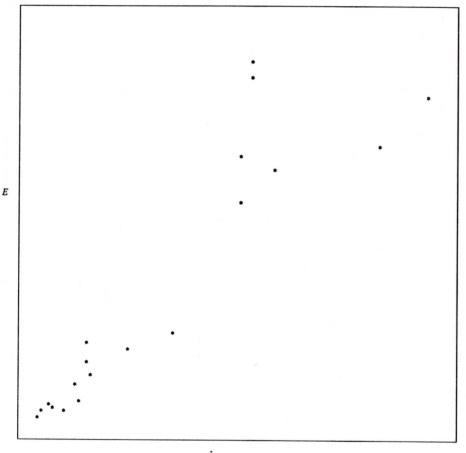

$$\hat{E} = 2.09\ S^{.95}$$

Figure 3.16 E versus $\hat{E} = 2.09\ S^{.95}$.

The R^2 values for models 1, 2, 3, and 4 are 0.82, 0.35, 0.86, and 0.82, respectively. Models 1, 3, and 4 perform better than model 2 as suggested by the scatter diagrams. Model 3 shows that the inclusion of both S and T provides a slight improvement in R^2 over model 1, which is expected.

3.5.2 The Relative Error (*RE*) and the Mean Relative Error ($\overline{RE}$)

To see how the actual values of E and $\hat{E}$ relate to each other, we define the relative error by

$$RE = \frac{E - \hat{E}}{E} \qquad (3.30)$$

If $\hat{E} > E$, then *RE* is negative; if $\hat{E} < E$, then *RE* is positive. When $RE > 0$, it must be between 0 and 1; when $RE < 0$, it is essentially unbounded in magnitude. We can also define the mean relative error of a set of n projects by the formula

$$\overline{RE} = \frac{1}{n} \sum_{i=1}^{n} RE_i. \qquad (3.31)$$

If a model is a good representation of effort expenditure, it will lead to small values of *RE* and generally to a small $\overline{RE}$. However, since it is possible that large positive *RE*'s can be balanced by large negative *RE*'s, a small $\overline{RE}$ may not imply that a model is a good one. Hence, this measure may not be useful in practice.

The $\overline{RE}$ values for models 1, 2, 3, and 4 are -0.24, -1.37, -0.22, and -0.05, respectively. In this instance, all four models overestimate E on the average.[25] Model 4 appears to produce the least amount of overestimate (as shown by the smallest $\overline{RE}$).

3.5.3 The Magnitude and Mean Magnitude of Relative Error (*MRE* and $\overline{MRE}$)

In view of the problem with *RE* and $\overline{RE}$ discussed earlier we define the magnitude of the relative error as

$$MRE = |RE| = \left| \frac{E - \hat{E}}{E} \right| \qquad (3.32)$$

Thus, the smaller the value of *MRE*, the better the prediction. Even more important, positive and negative relative errors do not balance each other, so that the larger the value of *MRE*, the worse the prediction. For a set of n projects, we can compute the mean magnitude of the relative error by

$$\overline{MRE} = \frac{1}{n} \sum_{i=1}^{n} MRE_i \qquad (3.33)$$

If $\overline{MRE}$ is small, then the model produces on average a good set of predictions. However, even when $\overline{MRE}$ is small, there may be one or more predictions that can be very bad. We consider $\overline{MRE} \leq 0.25$ as acceptable for effort prediction models.

---

25. It could just as easily have been that any one or more could have underestimated.

The $\overline{MRE}$ values for models 1, 2, 3, and 4 are 0.37, 2.03, 0.68, and 0.27, respectively. All models (except model 4) are far from being acceptable under this criterion.

3.5.4 Prediction at Level l (PRED(l))

Let k be the number of projects in a set of n projects whose $MRE \leq l$. Then we define a measure as

$$PRED(l) = \frac{k}{n} \tag{3.34}$$

For example, if $PRED(0.25) = 0.83$, then 83% of the predicted values fall within 25% of their actual values. We have concluded that an acceptable criterion for an effort prediction model is $PRED(0.25) \geq 0.75$. This measure would also permit some extremely poor predicted values. In particular, there is no limit on the MRE of the other estimates that exceed 25% of the actual values.

The $PRED(0.25)$ values for models 1, 2, 3, and 4 are 0.37, 0.05, 0.32, and 0.63, respectively. Since there are 19 data points, the numbers of estimates that are within 25% of actual values are 7, 1, 6, and 12 for the models. Figure 3.17 shows the performance of the four models for l level ranging from 0 to 1.0. Generally, if the curve for a model lies on top of that for another, this model is considered better than the other in terms of this criterion.[26] It is clear from the figure that model 4 performs better than the other models at all l levels. At $l = 0.5$, 90% of the estimates from model 4 are within 50% of the actual values. The corresponding percentages for models 1, 2, and 3 are 79%, 42%, and 63%. It is also interesting to note that the curves for models 1 and 3 cross at $l = 0.25$. Such "irregularities" would be expected for small data sets (like this one) when the exclusion or inclusion of a few projects in terms of MRE has a large impact on the value of $PRED(l)$.

3.5.5 The Mean Squared Error ($\overline{SE}$) and the Relative Root Mean Squared Error ($\overline{RMS}$)

Given a set of n projects, we define the *mean squared error* ($\overline{SE}$) as

$$\overline{SE} = \frac{1}{n} \sum_{i=1}^{n} (E_i - \hat{E}_i)^2 \tag{3.35}$$

This error is meaningful for regression models only. It represents the mean value of the error minimized by the regression model. From $\overline{SE}$, we can

---

26. This makes sense if we consider that curves that are more "concave-down" (i.e., that rise sharply) and stay close to the $PRED(l)$ axis represent models with which there is a large percentage of projects that meet the criterion of $MRE \leq l$ for each l. If curve a is on top of curve b, then it demonstrates this type of behavior and is intuitively better than curve b.

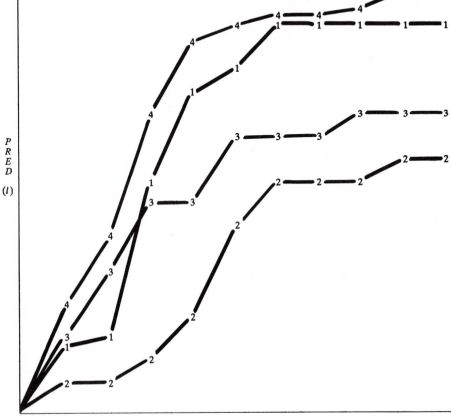

Figure 3.17   *PRED (l)* Curves.

compute the *root mean square error (RMS)*

$$RMS = (\overline{SE})^{\frac{1}{2}} = \sqrt{\frac{1}{n} \sum_{i=1}^{n} (E_i - \hat{E}_i)^2} \tag{3.36}$$

and the *relative* root mean square error $(\overline{RMS})$ defined by

$$\overline{RMS} = \frac{RMS}{\frac{1}{n} \sum_{i=1}^{n} E_i} \qquad\qquad (3.37)$$

The RMS for models 1, 2, 3, and 4 are 21, 40, 18.5, and 21, respectively, while the $\overline{RMS}$ values are 0.40, 0.75, 0.35, and 0.40. Model 3 has the least such error possibly because it uses two independent variables, compared to only one for the others. We consider $\overline{RMS} \leq 0.25$ as acceptable performance for a model.

3.5.6 A Comparison of the Criteria

The performance of the four models as measured by the five criteria described is shown in Table 3.12. Notice that model 3 is best for R^2 and $\overline{RMS}$, but model 4 is best for $\overline{RE}$, $\overline{MRE}$, and $PRED(0.25)$. It is unfortunate that these criteria — namely R^2, $\overline{RE}$, $\overline{MRE}$, $PRED(l)$ and $\overline{RMS}$ — are often not in agreement for a set of models and projects in the sense that we cannot say which model is best without making a subjective judgment on the relative importance of the evaluation criteria. In this case, we may wish to pick model 4, since it involves only one independent variable and makes predictions that have smaller average errors. There are also more predictions that fall within 25% of the actual values.

Table 3.12   A Comparison of Measures of Goodness

	Model 1	Model 2	Model 3	Model 4
R^2	.82	.35	.86*	.82
$\overline{RE}$	-.24	-1.37	-.22	-.05*
$\overline{MRE}$	.37	2.03	.68	.27*
$PRED(.25)$	.37	.05	.32	.63*
RMS	21.05	39.79	18.7*	20.89
$\overline{RMS}$	0.40	0.56	0.35*	0.39

* Best under this criterion.

Table 3.13   A Comparison of Measures of Goodness

Data Set	No. Projects	$\overline{MRE}$	PRED (.25)	$\overline{RMS}$
1	23	.16	.78	.34*
2	28	.19	.75	.51*
3	15	.16	.80	.30*
4	19	.11	1.00	.13
5	17	.14	1.00	.20
6	33	.27*	.64*	.46*
7	40	.24	.73*	.95*
8	12	.28*	.83	.12

* Measure is "not acceptable."

A model that works well for one data set may not work well for others. For example, one model that we have tested led to the measures shown in Table 3.13. From these projects, it appears that the $\overline{RMS}$ measure is more conservative than the $\overline{MRE}$ measure, although for set 8 this is not so. Moreover, the more heterogeneous the projects in a data set, the worse the $\overline{RMS}$ measure is likely to be. This conclusion is based on the fact that the $\overline{RMS}$ measure is acceptable only on sets 4, 5, and 8. We have additional information that they are the only homogeneous sets in the table. However, there appears to be closer agreement between $\overline{MRE}$ and $PRED(0.25)$. Indeed if we term the simultaneous satisfaction of the two measures

$$\overline{MRE} \leq .25 \quad \text{and} \quad PRED(.25) \geq .75 \qquad (3.38)$$

as constituting acceptable performance, then the model performance is acceptable on Sets 1−5 but not acceptable on Sets 6−8. On the whole, however, the $\overline{MRE}$ and $PRED(l)$ measures appear to suggest overall acceptable performance of the model, while the $\overline{RMS}$ measure leaves the performance in some doubt. In the analysis of models later in this book, some common criteria for evaluation is needed. Since there is no generally accepted standard, we have chosen the criteria defined by Equation (3.38) and will try to apply these to all models whenever it is possible to do so.

3.6 Data Collection Used in this Book

The authors of this book are part of the Software Metrics Research Group, Department of Computer Science, Purdue University, West Lafayette, Indiana. This group has collected and maintains what we call the Software Metrics Data Collection (SMDC) [YU84]. The collection includes data describing commercial software developed at several industrial environments and controlled experiments conducted mostly at Purdue University. Since there are several sources involved, it is difficult to have a uniform definition for each software metric in the SMDC. The following subsections describe the information normally available for the projects included in the collection.

3.6.1 Size in Lines of Code (S_s or S)

We have collected size information in lines of code (S_s) for small projects, and in thousands of lines of code (S) for large projects. As has been discussed in Section 2.2, this count includes lines of executable statements and declarative statements, but excludes comments and blank lines. For many large projects, some code is new and some code is reused. Information about the percentage of new and reused code is also kept when it is available from the source.

3.6.2 Effort in Person-hours or Person-months (E)

We have collected effort information in person-hours for small projects. For large-scale projects, effort is measured in person-months, where a person-month is defined to be 160 person-hours (40 hours/week $\times$ 4 weeks). Reported effort refers to development effort — the effort required to design, code, unit test, and system test. Ideally, we would like effort to be measured in a controlled environment, so that programmers work only on the assigned software without distractions. It is also preferable to have an objective and algorithmic method to record effort. We are also interested in the effort between certain milestones when it is possible to collect them. For small programs, these milestones occur after the end of the specification, design, coding, and testing phases. For large projects, the milestones should be the completion of the specification, design, coding, unit testing, integration testing, publication, and performance evaluation phases.

3.6.3 Development Duration (T)

Duration T is defined as the elapsed time in hours or months during which development effort proceeds without interruption. For a one-person project, this is the same as the effort. For projects completed by two or more programmers, the effort is always greater than or equal to the duration.

3.6.4 Token Counts

Many complexity measures can be derived from the count of tokens (as defined in [HALS77] and in Chapter 2). When it is possible to apply an automatic code analyzer to the source code, we have collected the unique operators (η_1), unique operands (η_2), total operators (N_1), total operands (N_2), unique variables (*VARS*), decisions (*DE*) and the cyclomatic complexity ($v(G)$). Since software may be written in different languages and, therefore, analyzed by different counting tools, there may be minor variations in the counting rules. The large amount of data in our data collection probably makes the inconsistencies inconsequential. Also, token counts are not available for all data from some of our commercial sources.

3.6.5 Defect Counts

As discussed in Section 2.8, a software defect is difficult to define and measure. The defect data collected in our SMDC may have different meanings for different environments. Whenever possible, the defect count is the number of software changes made in response to errors found during formal testing or after releasing the product to customers.

3.6.6 Description of Several Collections of Commercial Data

Some chapters in this book discuss various models of the software development process and of productivity. The data in our SMDC is often used to investigate and compare the performance of different models. The most frequently referenced data are the six sets of commercial projects for which the size, development effort, and development duration are recorded consistently within each set. The encoding used to identify the six sets of data and the number of projects included in each is given in Table B.1 of Appendix B. Sets A and B, as well as the major part of Set D, were acquired from recently published material. Set C was obtained directly from a large software-producing company. Set E is based on data gathered during an industry-wide project survey conducted by a private consulting firm. Set F was obtained from an internal report of a special study on resource estimation models prepared by the U.S. Army. Publication references to each data set appear in the individual discussions that follow.

Set A This data comes directly from Boehm's well-known book *Software Engineering Economics* [BOEH81], and represents what is perhaps the most detailed collection of project development statistics for a large number of commercially developed products that is generally available. Boehm has avoided giving information that might suggest the identity of individual products, development groups, or companies. He has also adjusted certain measures for selected projects in the attempt to obtain "a consistent set of well-defined measures" for the products included in the set. In this data set, size S is defined as source lines of code in thousands excluding comments.

Set B The data for Set B was obtained from a paper written by Belady and Lehman, "The Characteristics of Large Systems" [BELA79]. Gross statistics for 37 programs are given and are described simply as "statistics for programs developed by a large software house." Of the 37 programs, only 33 include measures of program size, development effort, and development duration. The information regarding these 33 programs is given in Table B.2. Precise definitions of these measures were not given in the paper.

Set C The third set consists of data for 40 program products and has been obtained from a large software-producing company that wishes to remain anonymous. The programs include information retrieval systems, special-purpose operating systems, device support packages, and language products. Of the 6.1 million source instructions represented by the 40 products, approximately 70% are written in assembly language; the remainder are written in a higher-order language. All of the products were developed between 1977 and 1982. An equivalent size measure is used that incorporates measures of new and reused delivered source instructions. Source instructions include all executable or declarative statements, but exclude comments. The actual data contained in Set C cannot be published due to its proprietary nature. The original set C contained 41 projects. One of the projects in this set has an average productivity in KLOC/PM at least one order of magnitude greater than that of the other projects. It is considered an "outlier" and is eliminated from most analyses.

Set D This data comes from the Software Engineering Laboratory, Department of Computer Sciences, University of Maryland,[27] and corresponds to 19 products developed at the NASA Goddard Space Flight Center since 1976. A subset of the data has been used in a previous study at the University of Maryland and has been published in [BAIL81].[28] Most of the programs in this set are ground support routines for various spacecraft projects. The primary language used is FORTRAN with some assembly language programs. Projects are supervised by NASA personnel, but involve the use of some programmers supplied by outside contractors. The size metric here includes comment lines,[29] as well as an adjustment for reused code. The data used in this study is included in Table B.3.

---

27. Data was supplied by V. R. Basili and J. W. Bailey.

28. Much of the descriptive material appearing here has been taken from this source.

29. Bailey indicates that comments typically comprise 30−50% of the total lines of source code for a product in this set [BAIL82].

Set E   This set of data is based on the results of the *Yourdon 78—80 Project Survey* conducted by Tom DeMarco.[30] Companies with a new software project in an early stage of development were invited to provide detailed information on the progress of their efforts on a monthly basis. DeMarco provided forms for this purpose, which specified the information sought and the assumptions to be used. Besides the monthly progress reports, initial and final project questionnaires and a follow-up report were requested. Although 19 projects were available to us, one was eliminated because it was terminated prior to completion, and another was eliminated for being an outlier on productivity, similar to the case eliminated from Set C. The great majority of products represented by this set are associated with business applications and were written in COBOL. The 17 products are known to have been developed in different environments. While it is generally a questionable practice to compare development statistics accumulated separately, the problem has been minimized in the case of the *Yourdon Survey* by DeMarco's establishing a common set of measurement definitions and data reporting forms. The size metric here includes comment lines. These products are characterized by very high productivity rates, which imply that significant amounts of reused code were incorporated. However, explicit information about the amount of reused code was not given. The projects from this data set are given in Table B.4.

Set F   This set of data was gathered from a report issued by the Department of the Army in 1982, "USACSC Evaluation of the Software Lifecycle Management Model (SLIM)" [WING82]. The projects in the set appear to be entirely of a "business application" type and all were written in COBOL. Of the 15 projects, 11 are classified as "historical systems," while the other 4 are classified as systems under development. The size metric here excludes comment lines. There is no information on the breakdown between new and reused code for the 11 historical systems. The data used in this study is shown in Table B.5.

3.7 Summary and Conclusions

We have attempted to discuss the essential aspects of conducting empirical studies related to software. Not all studies with data can be called empirical studies; only carefully controlled studies may provide truly useful results. Of all controlled experiments, the "Posttest-Only" design (Section 3.3.4) is probably the most popular, but there are other designs that have been, and may be, used productively for software research.

---

30. Yourdon, Inc. is a private consulting firm.

Depending on the metrics studied, either "parametric" or "nonparametric" statistical analysis may be used. Since it is very expensive to conduct a well-controlled experiment, it is essential to formulate the hypothesis to be tested beforehand in order to obtain meaningful results (Section 3.4.3). Many computing facilities provide adequate tools for statistical analysis. The most popular are SPSS (for parametric analysis) and IMSL (for parametric and non-parametric analyses). Some of the basic tools were discussed in Sections 3.4.3 and 3.4.4. Read the documentation carefully before applying any of the tools provided. We have tried to emphasize the assumptions that must be met before applying each statistical test. The analyses presented later in this book use tools that are part of the SMDC system at Purdue University [YU84].

The model evaluation criteria discussed in Section 3.5 are those that we consider the most appropriate for metric studies. The threshold values for acceptance may, of course, be set differently for different applications.

Exercises

1. Concerns about internal validity often jeopardize the concern about external validity. For each of the six confounding factors, give an example to show how its control might lead to problems with external validity, and vice versa.

2. What are the advantages of the Pretest-Posttest design over the Posttest-Only design?

3. Construct a counter-balanced design with five treatments.

4. Design an experiment to test if comments can help programmers debug. Which design do you wish to employ? Why? What are the treatments in this experiment?

5. For Table 3.1, take the scores from the first 10 Pascal subjects and the last 10 FORTRAN subjects, and perform the t and U tests.

6. Compute r and r_s for the first 20 η_2 and VARS pairs of Table 3.6. Test if they are significantly different from zero.

7. Is it always true that $r_s > r$? Prove it or give a counter-example.

8. Compute the regression constants b_0 and b_1 for the first 20 data points of Table 3.6 using VARS as the independent variable and N as the dependent variable.

9. The following is the summary of the mortality of a certain experiment:

outcome	male	female
stay	40	30
drop	30	25

    Apply the χ^2 test to see if sex has any effect on the mortality. Hint: To compute the E_is, note that of the 125 people there are 70 males (56%) and 55 females (44%). Assume those percentages should hold in all "stay" and "drop" cells.

10. Discuss "meta-criteria" that can be used to evaluate the criteria given in Section 3.5.

11. Regression models minimize the squared error $(SE = \sum(Y_i - \hat{Y}_i)^2)$. Suppose we wish to minimize the squared relative error, defined as

    $$\sum(1 - \frac{\hat{Y}_i}{Y_i})^2$$

    Derive the formula for computing the coefficients of the model (assuming that $\hat{Y}_i = b_0 + b_1 x_i$).

    (This is a hard problem requiring some skills not taught in this book.)

12. Using the data from Table B.3 (with size adjustment), derive the first two regression models discussed in Section 3.5 (which are shown immediately after Equation (3.28)).

13. For the regression models in Exercise 12, compute the measures R^2, $\overline{RE}$, $\overline{MRE}$, $PRED(0.25)$, and $\overline{RMS}$.

Small Scale Experiments, Micro-models of Effort, and Programming Techniques

4

He who is faithful in a very little thing is faithful also in much; and he who is unrighteous in a very little thing is unrighteous also in much.

Jesus Christ, *Luke 16:10, New American Standard Bible,* The Lockman Foundation, La Habra, CA (1960).

4.1 Introduction

Programming is a complex endeavor affected by many factors, such as the problem, the hardware, the language, the algorithm used, the time allotted, the tools available, and the programmer's ability. Programming would certainly be easier if there were a complete axiom system and theorems that could help answer any questions about procedure changes or management decisions. Unfortunately, such knowledge about the programming process does not yet — this is a hopeful "yet" — exist.

We have two alternatives. First, we could declare that the programming process is uncontrollable and nonunderstandable and that our intuition is all we can use in dealing with it. Or second, we could try to understand what goes on in carefully crafted situations to gain some insight into the software development process in general. Fortunately, researchers have decided to follow the second alternative.

In order to understand software and the software development process better, some software researchers have conducted experiments. Ideally, these experiments should be made under "real-world" conditions, so that "real-world" models can be developed. But, this is difficult and expensive. Such experiments would require hundreds of professional programmers organized into several programming teams with each team constructing real-world software to the same set of specifications. This would cost thousands of dollars and could delay ongoing work by months. Therefore, researchers have turned to small-scale experiments, usually using specifications that lead to small programs and university student programmers as a viable alternative.

> *A small-scale experiment is one involving a few subjects, usually working alone on a relatively simple task, that can be completed in a matter of a few hours or less.*

In such experiments, it is (at least in theory) possible to control all factors except the one being investigated. For example, if we want to study how the use of modularity affects the debugging process, we can construct programs that are identical in terms of what they do and their bugs, but differ only in the types of modularity used. Furthermore, subjects can also be isolated, and their times and other interesting metrics precisely measured. From such small experiments come *micro-models*.

> *A micro-model is a relationship among factors generally supported by small-scale experiments.*

These micro-models are formulas or statements that postulate the effect of some independent variable, such as modularity usage, on a dependent variable, such as debugging time. Many micro-models have resulted from small-scale experiments developed to establish a relationship between effort and simple product metrics. In this chapter, *effort* will refer to effort in either program construction, program comprehension, or program modification depending upon the context.

However, the small-scale experiment and micro-model process has its limitations. Inherently, such experiments (and the models resulting therefrom) may suffer from lack of *external validity* (see Section 3.3.1). Typically, in small-scale experiments, programmers work as individuals, rather than as members of programming teams. Resource limitations often restrict the tasks attempted to mostly small ones that can be finished in less than one hour. None of the resultant models can be assumed to be good approximations of commercial-environment projects, where teams of programmers frequently spend months or years together in designing, coding, and testing.

There is yet another problem. Many researchers have conducted experiments on programming by attempting to keep all but one or two of the potentially related factors fixed. However, the variability of the results still could not be attributed conclusively to the factors that were allowed to vary in the experiments. The failure of these experiments to establish cause-and-effect relationships implies that programming is actually more complex than anyone has imagined.

Nevertheless, in this chapter, we will report on the results of small-scale experiments. We consider them a valuable basis for software metrics research. Unless we learn as much as we can about the factors that are involved in programming through small experiments (described via simple models), we cannot convince anyone that more complicated models with interacting factors can be trusted in real-world situations.

The models that apply to commercial-environment projects involving teams of programmers are called *macro-models*.

> *A macro-model is a relationship among factors generally supported by large-scale experiments.*

Success in the development of micro-models *may not* lead to success in macro-models. However, failure in the development of micro-models can be detrimental to our confidence in macro-models.

It is, of course, possible that some imaginative individual could create a valid macro-model based purely upon intuition. But, we believe that a surer way to create good macro-models is to begin with sound small-scale experiments and micro-models.

In this chapter, the assumptions of each empirical study are stated, the major results presented, and the implications and potential for future work suggested. In our opinion, more careful and thorough studies of micro-models are clearly warranted. Finally, we conclude the chapter with a section on small-scale experiments related to *programming techniques*.

> *A programming technique is an activity exhibited by a programmer over which the programmer has some choice as to the degree to which the activity will be used.*

Examples of programming techniques are the use of comments, mnemonic terms, and flowcharts. Each can be used in practice and in experiments in various ways (including not at all). In most cases, the micro-models related to these experiments are strikingly simple — that the use of a technique such as commenting aids in the software development process, while the nonuse or misuse does not.

4.2   Small-scale Experiments

Our discussion of small-scale experiments will proceed as follows: we will discuss the types of activities generally involved in such experiments — software construction, comprehension, and maintenance. In each section, we will talk about the typical experiments and the usual metrics collected, such as time, or number of errors. For all three areas of experimentation it is typical that experiments conducted are of the posttest-only variety. (Review this type in Sections 3.3.3 and 3.3.4). Some are occasionally counter-balanced designs (see Section 3.3.5).

4.2.1   The Construction Process

Programmers are not interchangeable, as any software development manager will attest. The performance of different programmers varies a great deal. In his book on software productivity, Mills asserts that the differential of 10 to 1 in productivity is "undisputed" among professional programmers [MILL83]. Another study on small, one-person programming jobs shows that the differential can be as large as 26 to 1 [SACK68]. A common measure of productivity is lines of code per person-month (LOC/PM). The use of this measure implies a model of effort for program construction is simply a linear function of program size in lines of code. The model assumes that it takes more effort to produce larger programs and that this first-order approximation for the relationship is a reasonable one.

We have already discussed the difficulty in counting lines of code for programs in Chapter 2. Even if they can be counted consistently, there are many situations where the construction effort might actually be *inversely* related to the size of a program. An example is the implementation of a procedure that operates in real-time, such as the scheduler of an operating system. A certain programmer might use a straightforward implementation and produce a lot of lines in a short period of time, suggesting high programming productivity. Another programmer might spend more time in programming in order to create a design that does the work more efficiently with fewer lines of code and that makes his or her company more competitive in the market place. It is evident that the second programmer is more productive, although the productivity in LOC/PM will be less than that of the first.

One possible reason that the lines of code metric is not an appropriate measure for productivity in the scheduler example is that the *complexity* of the implementation is not taken into account. The implementation with the smaller size might have many conditional statements and loops, whereas the implementation with the larger size might be mostly sequential code. Therefore, researcher have been interested in finding metrics and their combinations that more closely model the construction effort, rather than just measure size. In Section 4.3, we discuss studies that attempt to formulate models based on product metrics for construction effort.

In the discussion of these micro-models, it will be apparent that they are not the result of controlled experiments. They come from studies more like the pre-experimental designs discussed in Section 3.3.2. In these studies, all of the analyses were done "after the fact": the metrics were obtained through the analysis of the finished programs, for which effort information had been recorded. The goal of these studies was to identify the metrics or their combinations that are important factors in influencing effort.

Although the complexity of software that affects construction effort is an interesting concept, current complexity metrics fail to correlate significantly better with actual effort than size-related metrics. This is not surprising since the most popular complexity metrics such as Halstead's E (and the related $\hat{T}$) and McCabe's $v(G)$ (and the related DE) are all related to the size metric.

None of the micro-models to be presented meets our expectations (e.g., $PRED(0.25) \geq 0.75$). We do not know whether there exist more appropriate metrics that can produce better results; the large errors are quite typical of experiments when human subjects are involved. However, since the study of metrics is still in its infancy, it is too early to conclude that there will never be a metric better than some measure of size for construction-effort prediction.

One should really take the view of an optimist: although none of the current metrics account for all the variability of effort data, the chances of finding another metric that will account for more of the variability are still reasonable. Even if size is the primary measure that is related to effort, metrics that are related to size *and* can be obtained *early* in the development process are still valuable in a predictive sense.

Experiments that explore software construction generally involve subjects writing programs or parts of programs. Typically, the ability of size or complexity metrics to explain the software construction process is determined by how well these metrics relate to programming time, the quality of the resulting software, or the number of bugs present in the software.

4.2.2 The Maintenance and Comprehension Processes

Software maintenance is a major effort among professional programmers.

> *Software maintenance refers to any activity that involves changing software. It can be for the purpose of error correction (usually called* debugging*) or to change or to add capabilities to the software (usually called* modification *or* enhancement*).*

Thus, maintenance involves considerably more than just error correction; the implementation of design changes or enhancements is often considered part of the maintenance activity. As a result, the financial resources required for maintenance have been estimated to be at least as much as that of software development [SHOO83], or even three times as much [CURT79a] .

The probability of program changes after initial development is also almost certain for small programs originally designed for private use [COME81]: a program that does something useful *will* be used by others. As the program increases in popularity, the pressure for changes to make it more useful will also increase. Even if it remains in private use, the time will come for it to be moved to a new machine. Thus, all programs should be written with the expectation that they will be changed later. They should be judiciously modularized, well-commented, and written in proper style so that the effort required to understand them later in order to make changes is significantly less than that of starting over.

In Sections 4.3 and 4.4, there are discussions of studies that attempt to evaluate the effectiveness of certain programming techniques, including modularization techniques and the use of comments and mnemonic variable names. In many cases, the dependent variable of interest is related to comprehension — such as whether or not some technique or procedure makes a program more understandable. It is almost certain that programs that are the most comprehensible will also be the ones easiest to modify.

Experiments that investigate software comprehension generally involve subjects reading programs or parts of programs. Typically, the ability of size or complexity metrics to explain the software comprehension process is determined by how well these metrics relate to scores from multiple-choice, fill-in-the-blank, and open-ended tests.

The modification of a program is a complex process: we need (1) to understand the functions of the existing program, (2) to understand the specifications of the desired change, and (3) to implement the change correctly. Note that implicitly we must comprehend what a program does before we can modify that program.

In most scientific pursuits, if part of a complex problem does not yet have a satisfactory solution, then it is not attractive to try to obtain a satisfactory solution to the whole problem. However, this may not be a serious obstacle for the comprehension and subsequent modification of computer programs, since the three parts of the modification process may be interrelated. For example, a thorough understanding of the existing program (high comprehension effort) may make the implementation much easier (low implementation effort). Similarly, a superficial understanding of the program (low comprehension effort) may make the implementation very difficult, sometimes requiring re-reading of the original program (high implementation effort). Thus, it is not unreasonable to study the whole problem, with the hope that complementary effects can be masked. The effort required to make modifications is the effort of interest to all.

Experiments that explore software maintenance generally involve subjects modifying programs or parts of programs. Typically, the ability of size or complexity metrics to explain the software maintenance process is determined by how well these metrics relate to either the time needed to modify software according to some new specifications, or the correctness of the modifications.

4.3 Micro-models of Effort

Included in this section are descriptions of several studies of the effort involved in the programming process. Models, experiments, and results are presented for a wide range of studies.

4.3.1 Halstead's Time Estimator Study

The first known experiments regarding construction effort models were those conducted by Halstead. We have discussed the equations to compute the effort E and the related time T of Software Science in Chapter 2. As discussed in Section 2.6.4, the combination of Equations (2.33) and (2.34) shows that the time in seconds to produce a program ($\hat{T}$) can be expressed as

$$\hat{T} = \frac{\eta_1 N_2 N \log_2 \eta}{2 \eta_2 \beta} \tag{4.1}$$

where the variables η_1, η_2, η, N_2, N, and β are defined in Chapter 2. Even though the equation only gives the duration of development, it is directly related to actual effort since it is the duration that the task would take when only one programmer is involved. This model for programming effort, which is Halstead's time estimator model, must be subjected to experimental verification before it can be considered useful.

Experiment 1 This experiment involved a single subject, a graduate student doing his Ph.D. thesis research under the direction of Halstead. He and Halstead selected 12 algorithms published in the *Communications of the ACM* in the early 1960s. Each algorithm (all were stated in ALGOL) was

Table 4.1   Prediction of T (actual time) using Halstead's Model ($\hat{T}$)

CACM Number	First		Second		Third	
	T	$\hat{T}$	T	$\hat{T}$	T	$\hat{T}$
(14)	33	13	15	16	25	29
(16)	135	123	77	102	44	53
(17)	33	22	10	6	11	10
(19)	7	3	10	9	9	5
(20)	12	9	14	7	6	5
(21)	43	51	30	47	39	63
(23)	21	17	13	5	13	3
(24)	16	22	8	7	6	6
(25)	62	101	45	74	20	42
(29)	25	5	35	9	16	17
(31)	20	17	11	15	7	8
(33)	4	1	3	1	3	1
Sum	411	384	271	298	199	242
$\overline{RE}$		.21		.10		-.01
$\overline{MRE}$		.41		.43		.37
PRED (.25)		.33		.25		.58
Correlation		.92		.92		.94
Rank Corr.		.82		.79		.85

implemented in three languages: PL/1, FORTRAN, and APL. The order of the implementation for each algorithm was determined by a random process in order to minimize learning effects. The arrangement was similar to the counter-balanced design with respect to the three languages, which was described in Section 3.3.5. The time recorded for each implementation of an algorithm included the times for coding and "desk checking," while the subject maintained "a high degree of mental concentration." The entire project lasted five months. The results were published as Table 8.2 in [HALS77], which is excerpted in Table 4.1, with several evaluation criteria added. Each of the "First," "Second," and "Third" columns provides the actual implementation time (T) in the chosen language, and the estimated time ($\hat{T}$) using Equation (4.1). One third of the implementations for each column is in one of the three languages.

The proximity of the sums of T and $\hat{T}$, and the high correlations in the three implementations support the validity of the $\hat{T}$ model given in Equation (4.1). Correlation coefficients of about 0.92 mean that $\hat{T}$ accounted for about 85% of the variance of T. Even though the $\overline{MRE}$ and $PRED(0.25)$ measures are not very impressive,[1] the results of this experiment are still interesting, considering the assumptions under which the theoretical model Equation (4.1) was derived.

It is reasonable to ask, however, whether the model performs significantly better than a simple model based only on the size metric. Halstead addressed this issue by comparing the lines of code count in the original ALGOL representation of the algorithm with the *average* T and $\hat{T}$ for the three implementations for that algorithm. He found that the correlation coefficient between T and $\hat{T}$ was higher than that between T and the ALGOL lines of code count. We do not consider such comparisons meaningful since the hypothesized relationship is between the construction effort and the actual implementation, not a *representation* of the implementation in a different language. The result may be further confounded by the difficulties in counting ALGOL lines. Instead, we think that the use of another size measure — the token count length N — is more appropriate. It is also possible since the value of N is readily available in Table 8.1 of [HALS77]. The results are shown in Table 4.2, with $\overline{RE}$, $\overline{MRE}$, and $PRED(0.25)$ computed using $\hat{T}_N$, the estimated values obtained from linear regression. By comparing the performance of the $\hat{T}$ model in Table 4.1 and the performance of the $\hat{T}_N$ model in Table 4.2, we *cannot* assert that there is much difference. The phenomenon is probably the result of the fact that T, $\hat{T}$, and N are highly correlated with each other. Nevertheless the $\hat{T}$ model should be preferred since it produces equally satisfactory results without using regression.[2]

The empirical setting can be criticized on several grounds. The results might have been confounded by history or maturation, since the experiment lasted five months. Some of the algorithms studied were quite small; the

---

1. Each $\overline{MRE}$ is greater than 0.25 and each $PRED(0.25)$ is less than 0.75 — the acceptability criteria established in Section 3.5.

2. The same formula, Equation (4.1), was used for the $\hat{T}$ model in all cases without change, whereas three different regression formulas were used for the $\hat{T}_N$ model:

First: $\hat{T}_N = -7.4 + .25N$

Second: $\hat{T}_N = -2.1 + .15N$

Third: $\hat{T}_N = 1.3 + .096N$

Table 4.2   Prediction of T (actual time) using a Linear Model ($\hat{T}_N$)

CACM Number	First			Second			Third		
	T	N	$\hat{T}_N$	T	N	$\hat{T}_N$	T	N	$\hat{T}_N$
(14)	33	115	21	15	103	14	25	138	15
(16)	135	526	123	77	505	74	44	450	44
(17)	33	159	32	10	154	21	11	151	16
(19)	7	44	3	10	63	7	9	51	6
(20)	12	97	17	14	80	10	6	84	9
(21)	43	203	43	30	256	37	39	262	26
(23)	21	100	17	13	82	10	13	86	10
(24)	16	163	33	8	158	22	6	143	15
(25)	62	342	77	45	260	37	20	284	29
(29)	25	139	27	35	153	21	16	129	14
(31)	20	107	19	11	122	16	7	111	12
(33)	4	24	-1	3	18	1	3	22	3
$\overline{RE}$	.07			-.11			-.20		
$\overline{MRE}$	.36			.48			.44		
PRED (.25)	.58			.42			.25		
Correlation	.97			.93			.86		
Rank Corr.	.88			.61			.73		

smallest had just a single ALGOL statement. This, and the fact that most algorithms published in the *Communications of the ACM* are well-polished, further limits the external validity of the experiment. However, the most serious problem is that only *one* subject was involved. Unless the subject was really a "typical" person, the results may not be applicable in general. The fact that this subject had a vested interest in the success of the experiment (that is, the completion of his own Ph.D. thesis) could be a biasing factor in the results. Nevertheless, deficiencies such as these are not unusual in exploratory studies when there are severe resource constraints. This suggests that we should remain skeptical of single experiment results until they are confirmed in independent experiments conducted by independent investigators.

Experiment 2   In an attempt to confirm the results reported previously, another graduate student under Halstead's supervision was enlisted for this experiment. As in Experiment 1, he and Halstead selected 11 algorithms from two textbooks using some subjective criteria. The subject then implemented them at the rate of one a day. All implementations were done in FORTRAN and were objectively tested. The times recorded were for reading specifications, design, coding, and testing until each program passed an acceptance test. Time to key in the source code was not included. The results are reported in Tables 8.4 and 8.5 of [HALS77], and are reprinted in a somewhat-revised form in Table 4.3. We have again used the linear regression model for the two size metrics to obtain the values for $\overline{RE}$, $\overline{MRE}$, and $PRED(0.25)$. The result that there is not much difference between the $\hat{T}$ model and the two regression models based on size seems to be confirmed by this study.

The empirical setting is subject to the same criticisms that we stated for Experiment 1. The projects are also very small. However, the most serious problem is still the use of a single subject. We do have more confidence, though, since the two experiments produce generally consistent results.

Summary   Halstead's work was instrumental in making metric studies an issue with computer scientists. Although the model of the programming process he proposed has limited empirical support, his work suggested that it was possible to apply a rigorous scientific approach to the programming process, which for years had been considered an art. We cannot say that the $\hat{T}$ model is much better than a linear model based on program size, but it did give reasonable results without depending on regression-derived constants. Independent validation using more data from more programmers and under more controlled conditions is needed to find the range of application for the model.

4.3.2 Woodfield's Time Estimator Study

The interest in metrics research remained strong at Purdue University after Halstead's death in January 1979. Several pilot studies were conducted that indicated that further experimentation with the $\hat{T}$ model might be fruitful. The goal was to find a setting where the selection of both the subjects and the problems to be solved were under the control of someone other than the researcher, in order to see if the model could explain software development time in a situation free from any potential experimenter bias.

Table 4.3   Prediction of T (actual time) using Size or Halstead's Model ($\hat{T}$)

Program Number	T (mins.)	S_t (LOC)	N	$\hat{T}$ (mins.)
1	5	7	53	5
2	5	8	50	5
3	21	11	73	2
4	30	15	131	7
5	16	18	113	16
6	19	18	110	15
7	24	18	128	23
8	39	32	244	44
9	92	36	428	82
10	43	38	228	49
11	91	59	483	129
Sum	385	260	2041	377
$\overline{RE}$		-.15	-.09	.12
$\overline{MRE}$		.35	.22	.25
PRED (.25)		.18	.64	.73
Correlation		.89	.98	.93
Rank Corr.		.85	.94	.82

The ACM Programming Team   An opportunity to collect a substantial amount of data appeared during the summer of 1979, while the student chapter of the Association for Computing Machinery at Purdue University was selecting and training its team to participate in the Fourth Annual ACM National Scholastic Programming Contest. A number of practice sessions were conducted at that time to select the participants, who later finished second in the national contest [*Communications of the ACM* (23, 4), April 1980, pp.259−260]. All of the participants were students experienced in FORTRAN programming. They were given problems selected from diverse areas, and worked in an isolated environment that permitted a high degree of concentration. These built-in controls appeared to fit the conditions of the $\hat{T}$ model. An observer from the Software Metrics Research Group recorded the programming times in a consistent manner using the form shown in Figure 2.34. Time measurement began when a programmer started working on a problem and ended when the program ran successfully with official test data. All metrics for the programs were determined using an automatic code analyzer, and part of the raw data was published in [WOOD81b]. A set of 33 programs was collected in the summer, and another set of 30 programs was collected about 5 months later. The properties of the 2 sets are presented in Table 4.4.

Table 4.4   Properties of two sets of Woodfield's Data

	Set 1	Set 2
No. programs	33	30
No. problems	10	12
No. modules	143	77
Range of T	0.9–4.83 hours	0.33–2.97 hours
Range of S_s	57–265 LOC	18–196 LOC

Time Estimators for Multi-module Programs   The analyzer in use during the experiment provided counts for the size metrics S_s (in LOC) and N, the logic structure metric $v(G)$, and all of the Software Science metrics at both the module level and the program level. Let us review the steps. As discussed in Chapter 2, the metrics η_1, η_2, N_1, and N_2 were defined originally at the module level. Other composite metrics such as E and $\hat{T}$ were naturally also defined at the module level. For a multi-module program, there are actually two ways to compute $\hat{T}$. A straightforward way is to compute the $\hat{T}$ for the individual modules, and then use the sum of all modules to get $\hat{T}_P$, the *physical-module model* (or the $\hat{T}_P$ model):

$$\hat{T}_P = \sum_{i=1}^{m} \hat{T}_i \qquad (4.2)$$

where $\hat{T}_i$ is the estimated time for the ith module, $1 \leq i \leq m$.

Another technique that appears equally reasonable is to ignore the module boundaries in the counting process and to assume that variables with the same name represent the same physical concept in the program, even though they may occur in different modules. This technique is referred to as the *integrated model* (or the $\hat{T}_I$ model). In addition to the two models based on Equation (4.1), we also evaluated linear-regression models using size or a control structure metric. They are referred to as the $\hat{T}_{S_s}$, $\hat{T}_N$, and $\hat{T}_{v(G)}$ *models*. Tables 4.5 and 4.6 show the results for the two sets of data.

Table 4.5   Prediction of T (actual time) using Various Models for Set 1

Criterion	$\hat{T}_{S_s}$	$\hat{T}_N$	$\hat{T}_{v(G)}$	$\hat{T}_P$	$\hat{T}_I$
$\overline{RE}$	-.12	-.10	-.16	-.06	-1.60
$\overline{MRE}$	.30	.28	.34	.29	1.62
PRED (.25)	.61	.55	.49	.61	.12
Correlation	.71	.73	.51	.58	.71
Rank Corr.	.55	.65	.39	.80	.59

Summary   The results in the tables show that the $\hat{T}_I$ model consistently overestimates the actual values by a large amount (about 150%). A possible explanation comes from looking carefully at Equation (4.1). If we assume that $\eta_1 \approx \eta_2$, and N_2 increases in proportion to N, then $\hat{T}$ increases faster than $O(N^2)$. In this case, considering a program with several small modules as a single large module may artificially increase the resulting estimate.

On the other hand, notice that the $\hat{T}_P$ model has a $\overline{MRE}$ of only 0.29 in Table 4.5 (although it has a much worse $\overline{MRE}$ of 0.90 in Table 4.6). Since the $\hat{T}_P$ model appears more reasonable than the $\hat{T}_I$ model for both sets of data, it supports the proposition that the $\hat{T}$ model applies better to single-module programs developed by a single, competent programmer working in an environment that permits a high degree of concentration. This observation also forms the basis for the logical-module model, which will be discussed in Section 4.3.3.

Even though we cannot say that the $\hat{T}$ model performs better than other models based on size or control structure metrics, the fact that it performs

Table 4.6   Prediction of T (actual time) using Various Models for Set 2

Criterion	$\hat{T}_{S_t}$	$\hat{T}_N$	$\hat{T}_{v(G)}$	$\hat{T}_P$	$\hat{T}_I$
$\overline{RE}$	-.18	-.17	-.19	-.45	-1.42
$\overline{MRE}$	.37	.36	.39	.90	1.55
$PRED$ (.25)	.53	.47	.47	.30	.20
Correlation	.80	.79	.78	.54	.70
Rank Corr.	.86	.65	.81	.89	.90

comparably without using regression has kept researchers interested. Of course, it would be interesting if we could show that the same results hold for industrial software.

4.3.3 Modularity

Most programming languages provide facilities for breaking up a complex program into several modules. The purpose of modularization is to break a complex task into smaller and simpler subtasks. A program consisting of modules of properly designed scope is believed to be simpler to design, code, and test. This has been found to be an effective way of organizing a large computer program. Generally, what is included in each module is a segment of code that deals with one function (e.g., to invert a matrix) or one collection of data (e.g., a large airline reservation table). Most programming methodologies deal with the issue of modularity.

> *Modularity is the programming technique of constructing software as several discrete parts.*

The process of modularizing allows the original programmers to segment the process so that each module deals only with some mentally manageable subset of the problem that the entire program is to solve. Furthermore, when a program is modularized, it may be easier to modify since it may not be necessary to understand the entire program just to change some small part of it.

There is general agreement that modularization is useful for constructing and comprehending software. However, it is possible that overmodularization may actually be detrimental: A 1000-statement program divided into four 250-statement routines may be easier to understand. But, if it is divided into 250 4-statement routines (if this ridiculous extreme were possible), then comprehension would probably be detrimentally affected.

A Small Modularity Experiment   The issues of usefulness of modularity and the potential problem with overmodularity are supported by a small experiment we conducted at Purdue University [DUNS85]. We produced three versions of a FORTRAN program (each about 100 statements long) that inserted, deleted, and searched a list of stolen credit card numbers. Three versions of the program were prepared:

- *Unmodularized* — the entire program was written as one routine.

- *Partially modularized* — the program was broken up into a "moderate" number of subroutines (4).

- *Supermodularized* — the program was broken up into more than twice the number of subroutines (9) as the partially modularized version. An attempt was made to make this "super" decomposition as natural (albeit overdone) as possible.

Twenty-six upper-level undergraduate computer science students were assigned randomly as subjects to each of the three treatments. Table 4.7 shows that the median score for a comprehension test for the partially modularized version (31.5) was 65% better than the medians (both were 19) for the unmodularized and supermodularized versions. Statistical analysis revealed that this result was significant at the 0.10 level.

Table 4.7   Effect of modularization on Comprehension

Degree of Modularization	Median Scores
Unmodularized	19
Partially-modularized	31.5
Super-modularized	19

Woodfield's Modularity Experiment   A much larger experiment was conducted by Woodfield, Dunsmore, and Shen that focused on the effects of modularization techniques and the use of comments [WOOD81a]. (The comment results will be discussed in Section 4.4.1.)

The subjects in this experiment were 48 graduate and senior undergraduate students who were all experienced in FORTRAN programming. Only one program was used in the experiment. It was an implementation of a model of program decomposition into physical models based on the histogram of certain metrics. It could be classified as a non-numerical application. To our knowledge, none of the subjects was previously exposed to anything similar to this program. The results may be relevant to the behavior of experienced FORTRAN programmers when confronted with a totally unfamiliar program.

The program was implemented using four different modularization approaches. They were

Monolithic — This was a program of 111 FORTRAN statements that had neither functions nor subroutines. This type of modularization (or the lack of it) was not recommended by any modern programming methodology. The effort involved in comprehension was expected to be high.

Functional Modularization — This version had 8 "physical" modules (i.e., main program, functions, and subroutines) for a total of 139 statements. This type of modularization was recommended by Yourdon and Constantine [YOUR79]. Every distinct function of the program was implemented as a physical module, which communicated with other parts of the program through input/output parameters. The effort involved in comprehension was expected to be low.

Super Modularization — This version had 18 physical modules, none of which had more than 15 statements. The division of the program was still based on the cohesiveness of program statements. However, the larger number of modules required more statements for linkage protocols, which increased the final program size to 192 statements total. This example was designed to illustrate the negative effects of the overzealous use of modules. The additional effort required to understand the relationship between these many small modules was expected to make the total comprehension effort very high.

Abstract Data Type — This version had 8 physical modules for a total of 170 statements. Even though the number of modules was the same as that of the version using functional modularization, they were different in the sense that if several functions shared a global data type, they were placed in the same physical module. It was coincidental that the number of modules was also 8. The distinct functions in a physical module were defined using ENTRY statements. It was interesting to investigate whether this modularization technique had low comprehension effort similar to that of functional modularization.

Another factor manipulated in this experiment was the use of comment statements. There were a total of eight versions: four different modularization approaches, each with or without comments. The experiment was of the posttest-only different treatment design:

$$R \quad X_1 \quad O_1$$
$$R \quad X_2 \quad O_2$$
$$\cdot \quad \cdot \quad \cdot$$
$$\cdot \quad \cdot \quad \cdot$$
$$\cdot \quad \cdot \quad \cdot$$
$$R \quad X_8 \quad O_8$$

The subjects were randomly divided into eight groups of six. The groups were exposed to the eight different versions of the same program as described. In addition, each subject was given a test booklet containing twenty questions on the program that were to be answered sequentially. (The test was identical for all subjects). Fifteen minutes were allotted for instructions, and one hour was allotted for the examination of the programs in order to answer the test questions.

Table 4.8   Average Test Scores in Woodfield's Comprehension Study

Modularization	S_s	No Comments μ	No Comments σ	Comments μ	Comments σ	All μ	All σ
Monolithic	111	46.83	17.03	53.50	8.64	50.17	13.34
Functional	139	38.00	16.48	56.67	15.98	47.33	18.29
Super	192	35.67	16.18	53.83	20.08	44.75	19.81
Abstract Data	170	50.83	17.29	77.33	11.22	64.08	19.61
All		42.83	16.86	60.33	17.00		

Table 4.8 shows the average scores and the standard deviations for the different groups. The group that scored the highest was the one that received the abstract data type version. Analysis of variance (see Section 3.4.4) indicates that the modularity factor was significant at the 0.05 level ($p = 0.022$). There was no significant difference among the monolithic, functional, or

supermodularization versions. However, the abstract data type version is significantly better than the next best monolithic version ($p = 0.056$).

As in many empirical studies, the major weakness of this experiment is the external validity. Even if the subjects are typical, drawing conclusions from a single program (and related versions) is seldom very convincing. Furthermore, there is also some doubt whether results such as these based on relatively small programs apply equally well to large industrial programs. Nevertheless the strong statistical results should encourage the repetition of experiments using different programs.

The results reported in Tables 4.7 and 4.8 suggest that breaking a program up into several functional parts is more useful than constructing a program as a single routine. Furthermore, the results also suggest that modularity, although generally a beneficial process, can be detrimental if overdone.

Logical Modules   The *logical module model* was developed using the first set of 33 programs collected and described in Section 4.3.2. Figures 4.1 through 4.3 show the actual programming times plotted against estimated times using linear models of S_s, $v(G)$, and $\hat{T}_P$, respectively. The $\hat{T}_P$ model is interesting since it performed well in terms of $\overline{RE}$, $\overline{MRE}$, $PRED(0.25)$, and rank correlation in Table 4.5. It has potential for wide application since it did not need a regression-derived constant. The linear model of $\hat{T}_I$, however, is not of interest since it performed poorly in Table 4.5 and Table 4.6, which was obtained later. A close examination of Figure 4.3 shows that there are at least two outliers, which correspond to programs whose estimated times using the physical module model are much larger than the corresponding actual programming times. Examination of these programs reveals that in each program whose $\hat{T}_P$ is an outlier, there is at least one unusually large and complex module or subroutine. As discussed in Section 4.3.2, the value of Halstead's E metric and the corresponding $\hat{T}$ metric increases faster than the square of the program size ($O\ (N^2)$). A model that considers a large module as a collection of small ones has the potential of making the estimates closer to the actual values.

These observations lead to the following hypothesis: There is a limit on the mental capacity of human beings to manipulate information. A person cannot manipulate information efficiently when its amount is much greater than that limit. When we apply this hypothesis to programming, the hypothesis suggests that a programmer normally breaks a complex program into several smaller modules for efficient implementation. These smaller modules could be physical modules clearly defined by the syntax of the programming language. However, a large physical module may actually contain several *logical* modules, each of which has size close to the optimal value. The logical modules are grouped together to form a physical module for various reasons. One possible reason is that they all manipulate some complex data structure, as suggested by the experiment described in the last section. Even so, the programmer actually treats

RANGE OF X AXIS: 0 5
RANGE OF Y AXIS: 0 5

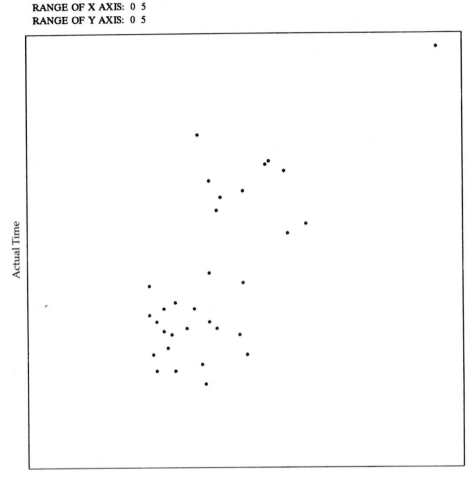

Estimated Time by S_s

Figure 4.1   Actual time versus estimates by S_s.

them mentally as individual modules during implementation. If the programmer does not treat all physical modules as monolithic units, then a time estimate based on $\hat{T}$ for the physical module may be higher than is warranted.

The second hypothesis needed for the logical module model is that a module's complexity must exceed the *optimal* value by some significant amount before a programmer will logically or physically partition it into two or more pieces. This is based on the observation that programmers often resist

RANGE OF X AXIS: 0 5
RANGE OF Y AXIS: 0 5

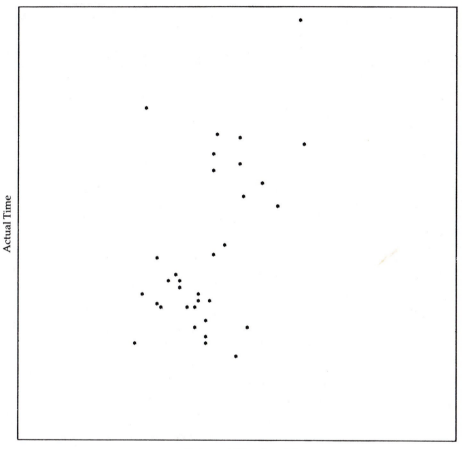

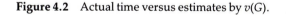

Estimated Time by $v(G)$

Figure 4.2   Actual time versus estimates by $v(G)$.

segmenting a program because of the potential overhead involved, unless its complexity is beyond some *maximum* limit. After this limit is reached, the gains from segmentation exceed the costs, and there is little extra overhead to prevent the programmer from dividing a program to make each piece close to the optimal complexity.

RANGE OF X AXIS: 0 10
RANGE OF Y AXIS: 0 10

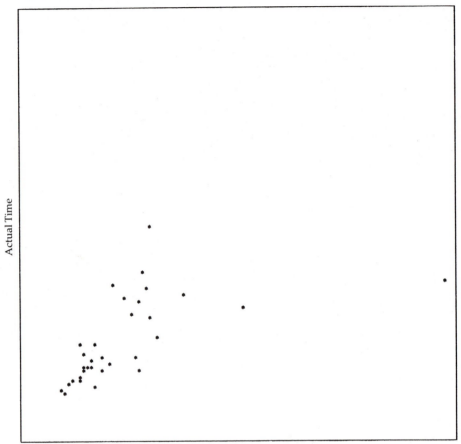

Figure 4.3   Actual time versus estimates by $\hat{T}_p$.

The logical module model can be tested using the following procedure:

(1) Compute $\hat{T}_{P_i}$ for each physical module i, $1 \le i \le m$, where m is the total number of physical modules.

(2) If a module i is considered to contain m_i logical modules using some criteria, compute $\hat{T}_j$ for each logical module j, $1 \le j \le m_i$.

(3) For each physical module i, set

$$\hat{T}_{L_i} = \begin{cases} \hat{T}_{P_i} & \text{if one logical module} \\ \sum_{j=1}^{m_i} \hat{T}_j & \text{if } m_i \text{ logical modules} \end{cases}$$

(4) The estimated time according to the logical module model is

$$\hat{T}_L = \sum_{i=1}^{m} \hat{T}_{L_i}$$

This procedure shows that the estimated time according to the logical module model is the sum of the estimated times for the individual logical modules of the program using Halstead's $\hat{T}$ model. The criteria that Woodfield, Dunsmore, and Shen used to determine if a physical module contained more than one logical module were based on the size in LOC of the physical module and the estimated time $\hat{T}$ for that physical model. A module with size larger than 70 LOC or $\hat{T}$ larger than 2 hours was considered to contain at least two logical modules. Since it is not easy to determine the boundaries of logical modules in a physical module mechanically, an approximation method was used. A physical module i was considered to contain m_i logical modules of *equal* size in LOC, where m_i was the smallest integer so that $\hat{T}_j \le 1$ hour, $1 \le j \le m_i$. The maximum size was chosen based on the suggested maximum module size, 50 LOC, based on [BAKE72]. Woodfield, Dunsmore, and Shen used 70 LOC since it was a number of lines beyond the suggested limit, according to the second hypothesis for logical modules. Independent analysis showed that modules of between 50 and 70 LOC had $\hat{T}$ value around 2 hours. The optimal module size was suggested to be 30 LOC [WEIN70], and modules with 30 LOC had $\hat{T}$ value around 1 hour. While those figures appeared reasonable, a detailed analysis showed that the results were not sensitive to the variations of the chosen limits, which were given as round numbers.

Figure 4.4 shows the result of applying the logical module model to the data used for its development. All of the outliers in Figure 4.3 have been adjusted in the right direction. The numerical analysis is given in Table 4.9, with all the columns (except that of $\hat{T}_l$) in Table 4.5 repeated for comparison. The same model was also applied to the Set 2 data described in Section 4.3.2. The analysis in Table 4.10 appears to confirm that, without any adjustment of constants used, the model performs well on data not used for its development. The linear models based on S_s, N, and $v(G)$ had constants different from those used on the Set 1 data.

RANGE OF X AXIS: 0 5
RANGE OF Y AXIS: 0 5

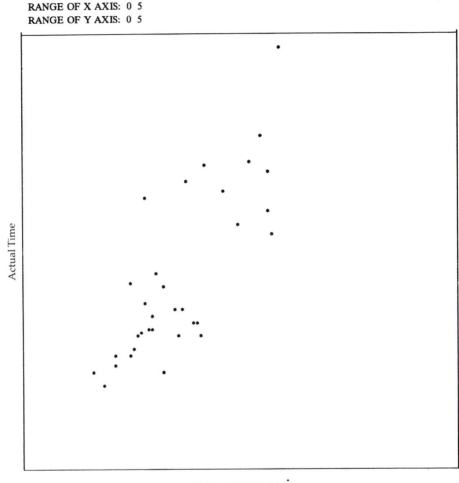

Estimated Time by $\hat{T}_L$

Figure 4.4   Actual time versus estimates by $\hat{T}_L$.

4.3.4 Basili's Program Construction Model

The Software Engineering Laboratory is a joint venture between the University of Maryland, NASA Goddard Space Flight Center, and the Computer Sciences Corporation. The Laboratory collects data from commercial programs that deal with many aspects of the software development process [BASI77]. As the study of metrics has become more popular, it is natural for researchers associated with

Table 4.9   Prediction of T (actual time) using Various Models for Set 1

Criterion	$\hat{T}_{S_r}$	$\hat{T}_N$	$\hat{T}_{v(G)}$	$\hat{T}_P$	$\hat{T}_L$
$\overline{RE}$	-.12	-.10	-.16	-.06	.11
$\overline{MRE}$	.30	.28	.34	.29	.21
$PRED\,(.25)$	.61	.55	.49	.61	.61
Correlation	.71	.73	.51	.58	.79
Rank Corr.	.55	.65	.39	.80	.76

Table 4.10   Prediction of T (actual time) using Various Models for Set 2

Criterion	$\hat{T}_{S_r}$	$\hat{T}_N$	$\hat{T}_{v(G)}$	$\hat{T}_P$	$\hat{T}_L$
$\overline{RE}$	-.18	-.17	-.19	-.45	.23
$\overline{MRE}$	.37	.36	.39	.90	.32
$PRED\,(.25)$	.53	.47	.47	.30	.40
Correlation	.80	.79	.78	.54	.89
Rank Corr.	.86	.65	.81	.89	.92

the laboratory to use the collected data to examine the claims of proposed met-rics. Some preliminary results were published in [BASI81], more comprehensive results were published in [BASI83], and those related to construction effort are summarized in this section.

The Data Collection   The programs analyzed in [BASI83] are the newly devel-oped modules of ground support software for satellites. The parent systems consist of 51,000 − 112,000 lines of FORTRAN code (including comments) in 200 − 600 modules. They were produced by 8 − 23 programmers, who spent

6,900 — 22,300 programmer-hours on their development. Although the raw data on the 731 newly developed modules have not been published, these descriptions suggest that they are generally larger than the typical size of the programs used in the study by Woodfield, Dunsmore, and Shen. The most valuable feature of this data is that all of the modules were developed by professional programmers working in an industrial environment. Software metrics were derived from the source code of these modules using a software tool called SAP [DECK82].

Instead of having independent observers record time as in the study by Woodfield, Dunsmore, and Shen, each programmer was asked to complete a Component Status Report (CSR) every week. The report records effort spent on each module, partitioned into such phases as design, code, test, documentation, meetings, and so on. Since errors and oversights by individuals are normally expected, project managers were also asked to complete a Resource Summary Form (RSF) every week from accounting records. This report records all time charged to the project for the various personnel, but does not break the effort down to the module level. The existence of the two reports enables the selection of projects whose effort records are more accurate than others. One selection criterion used in [BASI83] is defined as

$$V_m = \frac{\text{number of CSRs by programmer}}{\text{number of weeks programmer on RSFs}} \tag{4.3}$$

If a programmer conscientiously submitted each weekly Component Status Report, the number of CSRs submitted by the programmer should equal the number of weeks that the programmer appeared on the Resource Summary Forms. Thus a higher V_m indicates higher reporting frequency, which could lead to more accurate effort records.

Table 4.11 Rank Correlation of T (actual time) with Various Models for Basili's Study

V_m (#modules)	$\hat{T}_{S_t}$	$\hat{T}_N$	$\hat{T}_{v(G)}$	$\hat{T}$
All(731)	.46	.43	.46	.45
80%(398)	.42	.42	.46	.42
90%(215)	.44	.46	.48	.47

The Analysis The relationship between the total development effort with a variety of metrics are reported in Table VI of [BASI83], which is excerpted in Table 4.11. Only the Spearman rank correlations are given, all of which are significant at the 0.001 level. But the correlations are generally lower than those reported in the Halstead and Woodfield studies. Thus, this data suggests that time estimators based on any of the standard size and complexity estimators, while statistically significant, were not terribly accurate. The unavailability of raw data prevents the applications of other criteria, such as the $\overline{RE}$, $\overline{MRE}$, and $PRED(0.25)$. It is also impossible to tell whether the conversion from $\hat{E}$ (the effort estimate) to $\hat{T}$ in Software Science without using a regression constant will lead to reasonable values.

4.3.5 Gordon's Comprehension Study

The importance of writing programs using good style has been demonstrated by the popularity of an interesting book, *The Elements of Programming Style*, by Kernighan and Plauger [KERN74; KERN78]. Using published program segments, all of which had previously appeared in programming textbooks, the authors showed that even experienced programmers could produce examples of bad style. For each example given, the authors discussed the shortcomings of the implementation and then rewrote it in a better way. The revised example was presumed to be in better style and more readable. Examples in this book, as well as those in other articles and texts that have contrasting examples of style, provide a unique collection of data that can be used to develop objective measurements of style. If we accept the authors' subjective opinions on style as prevalent opinions, then any objective measure that produces different results for the two versions of the same example in a consistent fashion will be quite useful. The measure can then be used in the evaluation of readability for existing software, in the evaluation of programmers' ability to produce software in good style, and in the education of student programmers. Forty-six contrasting examples from six such sources formed the basis of Gordon's study [GORD79]. For example, Case 12 was taken from [KERN74]:

12A:

```
        IF (A(I) .GT. GRVAL) GOTO 30
        GOTO 25
    30 GRVAL = A(I)
        ...
    25
```

12B:

```
        IF (A(I) .GT. GRVAL) GRVAL = A(I)
```

It is obvious that version 12B is equivalent to 12A, and is the preferred version of the segment to set GRVAL to be the greatest value of array A.

According to Gordon, an example must satisfy the following conditions in order to be included in the sample:

(1) Both the poorly written version and the corresponding well-written version perform *very nearly* the same task. Enhancements such as parameter validation or error recovery would fail this condition unless the author specifically stated that the improvement, even including the extra code, still required less total effort to comprehend.

(2) The improvement cited has to be in clarity, rather than an improvement in, for example, execution speed, decreased memory requirement, and increased accuracy.

(3) The improvement cannot be limited to the use of more descriptive variable names or more appropriate printing format for the source code.

Gordon contended that a model for program comprehension could be based on a model for program construction. This concept has been shared by many researchers; micro-model examples come from [HALS77], [CURT79a], [CURT79b], and [WOOD80]. The main reason is that, after a programmer fully understands an algorithm, the additional effort required to express it as a program in a language is relatively small.[3] A clear program, which is a representation of the algorithm, enables a programmer to follow the steps of the algorithm easily.

One way to validate a comprehension model empirically is to ask a group of subjects to study the original versions of the program segments, and another group to study the improved versions. The times that the subjects take to complete a comprehension test, one for each program segment, can be considered indicative of the comprehension effort. Any metric (or combination of metrics) that best models the variation of the comprehension effort may then be identified. If expert judgments on the contrasting versions are correct, we expect to see the effort spent by the subjects on the original versions to be higher than that spent by the subjects on the improved versions.

This procedure could be difficult to conduct. The most difficult part is the preparation of the comprehension tests, where a unique test is needed for each sample segment. There is no easy way to make the tests uniform, in the sense that the times required to finish the tests are directly related to the inherent clarity of the program and are measures in at least the ordinal scale. The apparent insurmountable difficulty of this approach led Gordon to make a simplifying assumption: the expert judgments of the clarity of the examples were correct. The problem was then reduced to finding any metric that consistently ranked the program segments according to the subjective ratings.

---

3. This is probably also true for macro-models, where coding is only a small part of the total life cycle effort.

The metrics studied by Gordon were the composite metrics of Software Science. The metric of particular interest was the effort metric E as given in Equation (4.1), denoted as E_c for comprehension effort:

$$E_c = \frac{\eta_1 N_2 N \log \eta}{2\eta_2} \tag{4.4}$$

In addition to the size in lines of code (S_s), raw data for η_1, η_2, N_1, and N_2 were published. Table 4.12 shows the performance of the basic and composite metrics in terms of the number of correctly classified pairs of examples (out of 46).[4] Gordon was convinced that a model for comprehension effort should be based on a model for construction effort and that Halstead's E was a reasonable model for construction. He compared the performance of E_c with the size measures S_s and V, and another composite metric D, which was believed to relate to the difficulty of a program. Table 4.12 shows that E_c indeed classified more examples correctly than these other three metrics. However, a more thorough analysis shows that the metrics N_1 and N exhibit similar performance in terms of the number of examples classified correctly.

4.3.6 Curtis' Debugging Study

Curtis, Sheppard, and Milliman designed an experiment in which the task involved was to locate a bug planted in a computer program [CURT79b]. Subjects were given the listing of a program, input files, desired output, and erroneous output produced after the insertion of the bug. The time that it took for a subject to find the bug was measured to the nearest minute, and this served as the dependent variable. The effort to modify the program in order to remove the bug was not considered. The independent variables were lines of code (S_s), McCabe's cyclomatic complexity ($v(G)$), and Halstead's effort measure (E).

The subjects in this experiment were 54 professional programmers: 30 were civilian industrial employees and 24 were military employees. The participants averaged 6.6 years of programming experience in FORTRAN. Three different programs were developed, each with three different versions of control flow, and were presented to the subjects in three different lengths varying from 25 to 225 lines of code. One of three different types of bugs was inserted in each program, for a total of 81 different treatments. Table 4.13 shows graphically these 81 different programs used in the experiment. Each of the first 27 subjects worked with three of the programs, exhausting the 81 situations. The second 27 subjects replicated the conditions exactly, except that the order of presentation of the tasks was different in each case.

Table 4.14 shows the correlation coefficients relating the time to locate the bug and the complexity metrics. The complexity metrics were computed in two

---

4. A metric is considered to distinguish the two versions correctly if its value is higher for the original. All metrics considered were able to distinguish Case 12 (our example) correctly.

Table 4.12   Correct Classifications of the Comprehension Effort using Various Metrics

Nature	Metric	Number (/46)
Size	S_s	31
	N	41
	V	37
Vocabulary	η_1	31
	η_2	16
Usage	N_1	40
	N_2	28
Compound	D	31
	E_c	40

Table 4.13   The 81 Programs used in Curtis' Debugging Study

3 ×	3 ×	3 ×	3	= 81
Programs	**Control Flow**	S_s	**Bugs**	
sorting	structured	25 - 75	computational	
accounting	naturally structured	100 - 150	logical	
grading	graph-unstructured	175 - 225	data	

ways: one was computed on the subroutine containing the bug, and the other was computed on the whole program. Since there were only 27 versions, the time to locate the bug was the average of six scores — two complete replications of the times to find three different bugs. A detailed analysis of the correlations between metrics showed that all three were highly correlated with each

Table 4.14   Correlations of Metrics with Time to Find a Bug

Source	Number	E	$v(G)$	S_s
Subroutine	27	.66	.63	.67
Program	27	.75	.65	.52

other at the subroutine level, but the correlation of Halstead's E with either $v(G)$ or S_s was substantially lower than the correlation between $v(G)$ and S_s at the program level. Except for S_s, all correlations were significant at the 0.001 level.

This study suggests that complexity metrics such as E and $v(G)$ are also related to the difficulty programmers experience in locating errors in programs. Such information can be used in providing feedback to programmers and their managers regarding the complexity of developed code, so that adequate resources may be allocated for its maintenance.

4.4   Early Size Estimation

In the discussion of the micro-models of effort in Section 4.3 we notice that the program size (S_s, N) or metrics that are related to size such as $v(G)$ and $\hat{T}$ are important factors in programming effort. It is expected that most of the effort models currently in use rely on an estimate of the project size S_s in lines of code or S in thousands of lines of code as a primary factor. Therefore, accurate size prediction is essential to the effective use of any of these models for effort prediction. Moreover for models that incorporate "diseconomies of scale" in which

$$\hat{E} = a\, S^b, b > 1$$

a given percentage error in the size S will result in an even larger percentage error in the estimated effort. For example, if we use the COCOMO Embedded Mode nominal estimator (to be explained in Chapter 6)

$$\hat{E} = 2.8\, S^{1.2}$$

a 50% error in the size estimate S will result in a 63% error in the effort estimate. Thus, significant errors in the size measure can easily swamp the effect of most other parameters involved in cost estimation.

If cost models based on size as a cost driver are to be useful, it is necessary to be able to predict the size of the final product as early and as accurately as possible. This is, unfortunately, an elusive goal. Historically, managers have relied on expert judgment based on experience and on analogy with projects of similar characteristics to estimate the ultimate size of a project. Unfortunately, expert sizing depends on so many subjective factors that different "experts" can arrive at radically different estimates.

In an unpublished report prepared by Yourdon, Incorporated, several experienced managers were asked to estimate the size of 16 completed software projects given only the complete specifications for each project. The average of the expert predictions is given in Table 4.15. Of course, the $\overline{MRE}$ of 61% is very poor, even when based on the average estimate of several experts, as is the $PRED$ (0.25) = 0.25 measure.

Various authors have suggested some quasi-objective methods for improving size estimation. One of these is the PERT sizing technique [BOEH81]. In its simplest form, the researcher estimates the lowest possible size of the product, a, and the highest possible size, b. Then the expected size $\hat{S}$ is the mean of a and b:

$$\hat{S} = \frac{a + b}{2} \tag{4.5}$$

The standard deviation of $\hat{S}$ is

$$\sigma(\hat{S}) = \frac{b - a}{6} \tag{4.6}$$

This implies that, 68% of the time, the actual size of the project should fall within $\hat{S} \pm \sigma(\hat{S})$.

A more sophisticated form of PERT sizing can be based on component-by-component size estimation. For the ith component, the researcher generates three numbers:

a_i = the smallest possible size

m_i = the most likely size

b_i = the highest possible size

The PERT technique then produces the expected size $\hat{S}_i$ and the standard deviation $\sigma(\hat{S}_i)$ by the equations

$$\hat{S}_i = \frac{a_i + 4m_i + b_i}{6} \tag{4.7}$$

$$\sigma(\hat{S}_i) = \frac{b_i - a_i}{6} \tag{4.8}$$

Table 4.15   Actual (S_s) and predicted ($\hat{S}_s$) Size of 16 Products

Product	S_s	$\hat{S}_s$	RE
1	70,919	34,705	.51
2	128,837	32,100	.75
3	23,015	22,000	.04
4	34,560	9,100	.74
5	23,000	12,000	.48
6	25,000	7,300	.71
7	52,080	28,500	.45
8	7,650	8,000	-.04
9	25,860	30,600	-.17
10	16,300	2,720	.83
11	17,410	15,300	.12
12	33,900	105,300	-2.10
13	57,194	18,500	.68
14	21,020	35,400	-.67
15	8,642	3,650	.58
16	17,480	2,950	.83

$r^2 = .07$

$\overline{MRE} = .61$

$PRED\,(.25) = .25$

Finally the estimated total size and standard deviation are given by

$$\hat{S} = \sum \hat{S}_i \tag{4.9}$$

$$\sigma(\hat{S}) = \sqrt{\sum \sigma(\hat{S}_i)^2} \tag{4.10}$$

We can also expect improved results if the estimates a_i, b_i, m_i for each component represent the averages of several different estimators. This technique, while better than simple expert judgment, is still highly subjective. Moreover, experience indicates that most experts err on the low side: they generally underestimate software size. Table 4.15, for example, shows that the average estimates underestimate actual size on 12 of the 16 projects. The tendency of experts to underestimate the size of a product seems to apply also to estimating cost and project duration. While there are several explanations for this tendency to underestimate (including basic programmer optimism and a desire to please management), an important factor is that estimators often assume that all of the members of the project team have a level of capability equivalent to their own.

This discussion underscores the need for more objectively based sizing techniques. The Software Metrics Research Group at Purdue University is currently investigating several techniques for objective early size estimation. We begin with the observation that a number of simple metrics have been found to be highly correlated with program size ([FEUE79], [CURT79a], [CURT79b], [ALBR83]). These include the number of unique variables and constants such as Halstead's η_2 measure ([HALS77], [SHEN83]), the cyclomatic complexity measure $v(G)$ [MCCA76], the mean variable span $\overline{SP}$ [FEUE79], and function points [ALBR83]. We are particularly interested in a measure based on η_2 since it has been shown to be a dominant factor in size prediction for programs written in PL/S and other high-level languages [SMIT80]. Various studies of vocabulary relationships from Software Science have shown that, for highly structured languages, the count of unique operators η_1 tends to remain fairly constant while the count of unique operands η_2 grows as the size of the program grows.

As defined in Section 2.3.1, another useful metric is $VARS$, which is the unique variable count computed by subtracting the number of constants and character strings in a program from the η_2 count [WANG84]. Obviously, there is a strong relationship between $VARS$ and η_2. The correlation coefficient of the two in any program is normally high. However, Wang used $VARS$ in his research because pilot studies had shown him that it was easier for his subjects to estimate this metric early in program development than to estimate η_2.

Wang also hypothesized a linear relationship between the unique variable count $VARS$ and program size S_S in lines of code. Using pilot study data with subjects and programs similar to the ones he would use in his experiment, he established the relationship

$$S_s = 102 + 5.31 \; VARS \tag{4.11}$$

This suggests that each program had about 100 lines of code as a base, and that this number increased by about 5 lines of code for every variable.

Furthermore, Wang contended that, for strongly typed languages such as Pascal, and for projects developed using a top-down design strategy, the $VARS$ metric should be available very early (before coding commences) in the programming process. Even if the actual value of *VARS* is unavailable, its estimate $\hat{VARS}$ should be accurate late in the design process.

In order to test the hypothesis in Equation (4.11) an experiment was conducted at Purdue University in the summer of 1983. Forty-four upper-level undergraduate and graduate students participated in the study. The subjects were directed to construct two approximately 400-line Pascal programs using a top-down design and data-structure-first development strategy. The experiment took place over an 8-week summer session that allowed a $2-3$ week development time ($25-35$ hours programming time) for each program. A systematic attempt was made to collect counts of the *VARS* metric at various stages of the development process. At the end of design and before the beginning of coding, the subjects were asked to estimate the unique number of variables they would use in the program (such as the *VARS* metric), the size of the program in lines of code, and the amount of effort in hours that they would expend when constructing the program.

The results of this experiment appear in Tables 4.16 and 4.17. Each subject was asked to estimate the final size of the program (this is $\hat{LOC}_{PGMR}$ in Table 4.16); in addition, each provided an estimate of *VARS* from which (using Equation (4.11)) LOC_{VARS} was computed. At the end of each program construction, each size estimator was then compared with the actual size. Table 4.16 shows that the size estimates are a little better (although not significantly so) using Equation (4.11) than the subjects' own subjective estimates for both programs 1 and 2.

Table 4.16 Early Size Estimation

Program	Estimate	$\overline{MRE}$	$PRED(.25)$
1	$\hat{LOC}_{VARS}$	.20	68%
	$\hat{LOC}_{PGMR}$	.23	57%
2	$\hat{LOC}_{VARS}$	.30	61%
	$\hat{LOC}_{PGMR}$	.42	52%

Each subject was also asked to estimate the effort in hours to construct the program (this is $\hat{E}_{PGMR}$ in Table 4.17). Using regression, we were also able to compute an effort estimate $\hat{E}_{VARS}$ based on the number of unique variables (*VARS*). At the end of each program construction, each effort estimator was then compared to the actual effort. Table 4.17 shows that the effort estimates

Table 4.17   Early Effort Estimation

Program	Estimate	$\overline{MRE}$	$PRED(.25)$
1	$\hat{E}_{VARS}$	.24	64%
	$\hat{E}_{PGMR}$	.42	57%
2	$\hat{E}_{VARS}$	.28	52%
	$\hat{E}_{PGMR}$	.86	9%

$\hat{E}_{VARS}$ are significantly better (at the 0.10 level) than the subjects' own subjective estimates $\hat{E}_{PGMR}$ for both programs 1 and 2.

The major conclusion of this experiment was that an accurate estimate of *VARS* does indeed lead to a reasonably accurate estimate of size and effort, based on the hypothesis in Equation (4.11). Whether these results (which were obtained in a university environment using small programs) can be generalized to large, industrially produced software remains to be seen. Nevertheless, these initial results are encouraging.

As already stated, strongly typed languages lend themselves more readily to early data structure estimates. The development of the Ada language with its emphasis on the programming environment and the use of program-design languages encourages the top-down design, data-structure-first technique and, thus, should help to make accurate early estimates of the data structure metric possible.

4.5 Experiments on Programming Techniques

As stated earlier, a programming technique is an activity exhibited by a programmer over which the programmer has some choice as to the degree to which the activity will be used. In this section we will consider a few programming techniques (certainly not an exhaustive list) that we and other researchers have investigated: the use of comments, mnemonic terms, control transfers, flowcharts, and debugging aids. Typically, our micro-models for these techniques are based on a simple hypothesis — that the use of a technique aids in the software development process while the nonuse or misuse does not.

4.5.1 Comments

During the software development process, an ongoing concern is documentation, which can be in various forms including flowcharts, diagrams, and manuals. Programmers generally want to remember design and implementation decisions for their own later perusal or for the benefit of maintenance programmers who may follow them. Most programming languages provide a means of including information from the programmer to help understand what the program does. *Comments* are statements that are interspersed within the program code. These are ignored by the compiler, but remain in place with the code for later reference.

Comments are nonexecutable statements in a program describing the intent of various segments of software code.

These are statements in a program that are not instructions but describe what some instruction statements do.

FORTRAN comment —

```
C    COMPUTE OVER-TIME AS TIME AND A HALF OF ALL THE HOURS OVER 40
C    AND ZERO IF THE EMPLOYEE WORKS 40 HOURS OR LESS
```

COBOL comment —

```
NOTE   COMPUTE OVER-TIME AS TIME AND A HALF OF ALL THE HOURS OVER 40
AND ZERO IF THE EMPLOYEE WORKS 40 HOURS OR LESS.
```

Pascal comment —

```
(*   COMPUTE OVER-TIME AS TIME AND A HALF OF ALL THE HOURS OVER 40
     AND ZERO IF THE EMPLOYEE WORKS 40 HOURS OR LESS              *)
```

Figure 4.5   Comments for FORTRAN, COBOL, and Pascal programs.

Figure 4.5 demonstrates comments prepared for three different programming languages. Misleading comments may be more detrimental than no comments at all (for example, see Chapter 8 of [KERN78]). Consider debugging a program in which the comment reads

```
INCREMENT THE COUNTER BY 1
```

but in which the next statement really adds two to the counter. Furthermore, no compiler checks the program against comments to ensure that the comments really reflect what is going on within. Comments are purely a tool for the programmer.

Purdue Experiment We conducted an experiment on the use of comments in which we explored their use as an aid in modification [DUNS85]. We prepared two versions of a FORTRAN program of 27 executable statements. One version had interspersed comments explaining the code contained in the program. The other had no such comments. Given a day, month, year, and day of the week the program determines the day of the week that date will occur in a future year. The modification task was to alter the program to determine the day of the week for a past year. About 40% of the program statements had to be changed to meet this alteration of the specifications.

Our subjects were 31 students in a graduate Computer Science course. The experiment was administered in a one-hour class period. The subjects were randomly divided into two groups. Each person was given a set of specifications for the program, and either a commented or uncommented version of the program. Subjects were told to make modifications to the version of the program they received. As is shown in Table 4.18, the modifications were apparently made more effectively by those subjects using the commented version. The mean scores for those with comments were on the average 20% better than the scores obtained by subjects whose programs had no comments. This result is significant at the 0.15 level.

Woodfield's Experiment The study by Woodfield, Dunsmore, and Shen first discussed in Section 4.3.3 also considered the use of comments [WOOD81a]. Even though some earlier studies on the prolific use of comments did not produce definite results [WEIS74, SHEP78], we considered it interesting to study the effect of the use of short comments. These comments were judiciously placed at the beginning of each function (called logical module) and briefly described the function. They served to define the boundaries of logical modules in the monolithic and abstract data-type versions. All of the variable names were transformed into meaningless combinations of alphanumeric characters and all indentations were removed. Thus, style factors that dealt with the use of mnemonic variables and proper indentation were masked.

Table 4.18   Mean Modification Scores for Subjects Working on Two FORTRAN Programs

	Mean Modification Scores
Comments	52.0
No comments	42.7

Table 4.8 shows that the groups that had commented programs scored consistently higher than those that had uncommented versions, which is expected (60.33 versus 42.83, significant at the 0.001 level).

4.5.2   Mnemonic Terms

Most programmers are taught to name variables things that make sense. Thus, we may use the term **HOURS** to refer to the number of hours worked by an employee. This is usually an easier name to remember than **X** or **J12R4**. Names used in programming are generally chosen to be mnemonic.

Mnemonic names are words that sound and look like what they stand for, such as **SALARY** *as a name for someone's salary.*

Cases of non-mnemonic names usually occur because the purpose of a variable changes drastically during the program construction process. Software engineers contend that the use of mnemonic variables aids in program construction, comprehension, and maintenance.

We conducted three experiments considering the effects of meaningful names [DUNS85]. First, through a pilot study, some lists of data names were compiled. One list, called the *mnemonic list*, consisted of the twenty most-frequently mentioned names for the items; its opposite, called the *nonmnemonic list*, consisted of twenty of the least-frequently mentioned names. The mean length of the data items in both lists was about seven characters, even though some subjects were allowed to use up to twelve characters. Three other lists were compiled consisting of the most mnemonic names of 1−4 characters, 5−8 characters, and 9−12 characters.

In a pair of experiments, subjects were required to answer questions by recalling item names that they had seen earlier. If they did not recall the names unaided, then they were allowed to look them up in a large data dictionary of more than one hundred related names. This procedure simulated a user referring to a data dictionary to find an appropriate item name. Subjects were 52 upper-level undergraduate students from Computer Science and Management. The data recorded were the times required to complete the questions and the number of wrong answers submitted by the subjects. A wrong response drew a penalty of nine seconds. Any responses that took more than nine seconds were adjusted back to nine in order not to penalize a subject for spending a lot of time searching through the item dictionary.

Table 4.19   Analysis of the use of Mnemonic Names and Nonmnemonic Names

	Mnemonic names	Non-mnemonic names
Mean response time	10.6 sec	18.4 sec
Number of wrong responses	7	39

Table 4.20   Analysis of Effect of Name Length

	1-4 characters	5-8 characters	9-12 characters
Mean response time	10.8 sec	10.3 sec	12.1 sec
Number of wrong responses	13	13	19

Table 4.19 shows that in the first experiment recall was clearly better, both in terms of time and errors, for the mnemonic names. Subjects recalled the mnemonic terms in about half the time it took to recall the nonmnemonic terms and made 80% fewer recall errors. This result is significant at the 0.01 level. Table 4.20 shows that, in the second experiment, recall time slightly favored the 5−8 character range. Performance, both time and errors, was obviously worse

with names in the 9—12 character range. These results, however, are not statistically significant.

In a related study, we replicated the experiment concerning the length of mnemonic variable names using strings in the 5—9 character range and the 10—30 character range. This was done because several programming languages allow a virtually unlimited name length. The question was whether longer mnemonic names are better than relatively short mnemonic ones. Subjects were 37 students in a COBOL programming class. In a manner similar to the other mnemonic experiments discussed earlier, subjects were asked to recall item names they had seen earlier. Each was given a data dictionary for study and directed to recall as many of twenty names as possible in a 15-minute interval. Table 4.21 shows that performance was about 20% better for the shorter terms than the longer ones. This result is significant at the 0.05 level.

Table 4.21   Analysis of Length of Names

	5-9 characters	10-30 characters
Mean number recalled correctly	17.0	14.3

Shorter names may not be rich enough to help memory or comprehension. For example, HRS might mean "hours worked" or it could mean "number of horses." Longer names invite excessive creativity that, without guidelines concerning their formation, may lead to names that are hard to remember exactly (and certainly take longer to enter at a keyboard). Thus, HOURS-WORKED might be misremembered as HOURS-WORK, WORK-HOURS, or even EMPLOYEE-HOURS-WORKED, if there is no limit on the number of characters or guidelines on how names are constructed.

4.5.3 Transfer of Control

One of the by-products of the software engineering movement is a programming technique known as *structured programming* (see Section 3.1). The major characteristic of this technique is that it places some strict rules on how control may be transferred within a computer program. Rather than allowing segments of software to bring other segments into execution arbitrarily, structured programming requires that statements be executed sequentially. Non-sequential control flow is done only through carefully constructed IF-THEN-ELSE or WHILE-DO constructs. Figure 4.6 shows the allowable sequence, choice (IF-THEN-ELSE), and repetition (WHILE-DO). The diamond-shaped boxes represent decision points. In the "choice" construct, "if" the decision question is true, "then" the statements on the left are executed, "else" the statements on the right branch are executed. In the "repetition" construct, "while" the decision question is true, the program continues to "do" (i.e., execute) the statements directly below it.

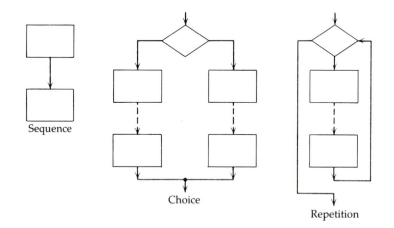

Figure 4.6   Basic program structures in "structured programming."

One aspect of structured programming is its requirement that forward branching be constrained to the strict **IF–THEN–ELSE** process: at any point in a program, if a section of the code is to be skipped, the decision is made by examining the truth or falsehood of a Boolean expression (such as **HOURS ARE GREATER THAN 40**). If the expression is true given the current value of **HOURS**, then a set of predetermined statements (known as the **THEN** clause) are executed — probably those that compute pay with overtime. But, if the expression is false, then another set of statements (the **ELSE** clause) — probably having to do with pay without overtime — are executed. After either case, the program is resumed at some point that is independent of which branch was taken. This means of transfer of control is thus known as *branch-and-join* and is illustrated in Figure 4.7.

```
IF HOURS ARE GREATER THAN 40
  THEN
    SUBTRACT 40 FROM HOURS GIVING OVER_HOURS
    MULTIPLY OVER_HOURS BY 1.5 GIVING OVER_TIME
  ELSE
    MOVE 0 TO OVER_TIME
  END
```

Figure 4.7   An example of a structured **IF–THEN–ELSE** : depending upon the current value of **HOURS** , either the **THEN** or the **ELSE** part will be executed.

However, programmers do not always program like this. Some programming languages allow much more creative (and dangerous) transfers of control. These are called *test-and-branch* situations because, if a Boolean expression is true, the programmer may transfer control to any other point in the program without regard to whether or how it will ever get to the rest of the program.

Table 4.22   Analysis of Certain Program Constructs in Structured and Nonstructured Programs

	Non-Structured Programs	Structured Programs
Percentage of GO TO statements	11.7	2.8
Number of DO-WHILE statements	11	109
Percentage of all IF statements		
with ELSE clauses	17.0	36.4
Average number of statements	853	593

Elshoff [ELSH77] collected 120 programs written by professional programmers before structured programming concepts were taught to them and 34 programs afterwards. Table 4.22 shows some of the data collected. One effect of structured programming is a drastic decrease in the unconditional transfer of control (GOTO) statement that is often used for producing convoluted control structures; their usage drops by 75%. There is also a big increase in the use of the WHILE-DO construct and the ELSE clause. The former is used for establishing structured loops. Finally, the structured programs are more succinct than the nonstructured ones. Of course, these were different programs and cannot be compared directly. But, they were representative of work being done by professional programmers. There is no reason to believe that the structured programs had fewer statements because they were inherently simpler. Instead, the conclusion is that structured programming techniques have led to more succinct programs with less-convoluted control structure.

Furthermore, in an experiment in which 36 professional programmers attempted to understand programs written in both structured and nonstructured FORTRAN [SHEP78], the mean comprehension score for the structured programs, 56%, exceeded that of the nonstructured ones, 42%.

In experiments concerned with only the transfer of control aspect of structured programming [SIME73], eighteen subjects were asked to write programs using two languages. All nine of the subjects who used the structured language solved all five problems assigned to them, and only four of them had any problem with a program not running as originally written. However, only four of the nine subjects using the nonstructured language were able to complete all five assigned problems, and eight of these subjects had problems with program errors. In addition, considering only completed correct solutions, structured programs were written more quickly than nonstructured ones. In the second week, the eighteen subjects used the language they had *not* used the week before. Those who used the structured language during the second week were faster solving the same five problems, while those who used the nonstructured language were slower. Since the first week could be considered as practice for the second week (and people should get better at a task with practice), this latter result really points out the inefficiency of the nonstructured language. Programming is complicated enough without adding layers of complication to those that already exist, so it is not surprising that programmers typically perform better when using structured conditionals.

In later research, Green [GREE77] investigated a syntactical variation of the IF–THEN–ELSE construction (see Figure 4.8) in which the predicate appears more than once. He found that when figuring out the conditions to make a program perform a designated action, mean response times were about six percent shorter with the IF–NOT–END variation, than with the standard IF–THEN–ELSE form.

```
IF HOURS ARE GREATER THAN 40:
      SUBTRACT 40 FROM HOURS GIVING OVER_HOURS
      MULTIPLY OVER_HOURS BY 1.5 GIVING OVER_TIME
NOT HOURS ARE GREATER THAN 40:
      MOVE 0 to OVER_TIME
END HOURS ARE GREATER THAN 40
```

Figure 4.8 The IF–NOT–END version of the IF–THEN–ELSE . Notice that the predicate (HOURS ARE GREATER THAN 40) appears three times.

4.5.4 Flowcharts

One programming technique that enjoyed a good deal of favor in the early days of computing is the *flowchart* (see Figure 4.9). The flowchart is a graphical representation of program structure. It shows how parts of the program are related to other parts, how some parts may be executed conditionally, and how some parts are to be reiterated until some condition is met. A flowchart can be constructed at quite a high level to show only the way that large parts of a program are related to other large parts, or it can be very detailed to reflect nearly a statement-by-statement account of the program.

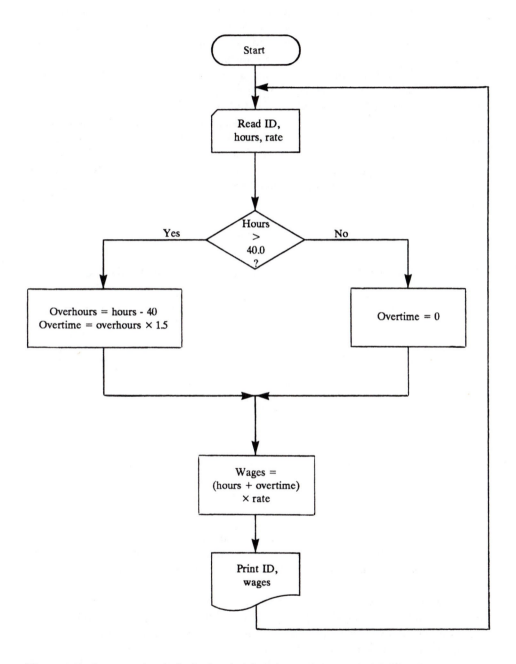

Figure 4.9 An example of a fairly detailed flowchart. The card-shaped object represents input to the program. The diamond is a decision point. Arrows show the way the program executes its various parts. The curly-bottom box indicates output from the program.

Until about 1975, most programmers were taught to construct a flowchart from the program specification and to use it to guide program construction. The benefits they were told were many — making program construction easier via a flowchart, making it easier to understand a program written by someone else (an "alien" program) if that person had provided a flowchart, and making it easier to modify a program that they or someone else had constructed if a flowchart could be referred to before and during modification. However, programmers privately questioned the utility of detailed flowcharts.

In [SHNE77], flowcharting was investigated in a series of experiments involving hundreds of university students and faculty. As Table 4.23 shows, there were no instances to suggest that *detailed* flowcharts are of any value for construction, debugging, comprehension, or modification. The mean scores for subjects doing any of those tasks seemed to be no better or worse with a flowchart than without it.

Table 4.23   The Mean Scores of Programming Activities with and without Flowcharts

		Mean Scores	
Experiment	Activity	Flowchart	No Flowchart
I	Composition	94	95
II	Comprehension	94	93
III	Comprehension and Debugging	39	38
IV	Modification	77	75
V	Comprehension	52	60

Brooke and Duncan [BROO80] noted that the subjects in the Shneiderman experiment were not *required* to use flowcharts and suggested that the results were equivalent because the subjects with the flowcharts simply ignored them. So, Brooke and Duncan replicated the flowchart experiment with the requirement that subjects who received a flowchart received nothing else. They could not cheat and ignore the flowchart in favor of the program. Their results were nearly identical to that in [SHNE77]; the flowcharts led to no improved performance in finding errors by either naive or experienced subjects.

These results occur probably because a detailed flowchart is simply another way of stating what is in the program code itself. This is roughly equivalent to studying a book in English and a translation in French. If one understands the English book, the translation is of very little benefit. However, since the French translation simply repeats what is in the original, it probably is of no help to someone who cannot understand the English version.

Thus, by the mid-1970s computer scientists were no longer teaching the use of flowcharts with the same zeal that they had, and the government and private sector were gradually dropping their insistence on the use of flowcharts. No one has attempted to determine experimentally whether higher-level flowcharts are valuable in planning or understanding a large program or a system of programs, which is generally where and how flowcharts are being used today.

4.5.5 Debugging Aids

Designing and coding software are relatively pleasant tasks. The debugging process is one of the hardest and most unpleasant tasks a programmer faces.[5] Thus, it would be good to be able to provide debugging aids that would help remove some of the drudgery associated with this phase of the programming process.

In a study of the difficulty of finding different types of bugs and the usefulness of several debugging aids by Gould and Drongowski [GOUL74], experienced programmers were asked to find errors in several single-page FORTRAN programs. The programs were seeded with three classes of bugs:

(1) array bugs — in which references are made to members of arrays that cannot exist (an example would be to refer to X(11) when X is an array with only 10 members)

(2) iteration bugs — in which loops are executed an inappropriate number of times (such as going through a set of statements N times when it should really be N-1)

(3) assignment statement bugs — in which variables are given incorrect values (i.e., having the statement X=X+1 if you really mean to add 2)

Subjects were randomly assigned to one of five debugging aid groups:

(1) Control — the subjects were given no debugging aid beyond the program listing

---

5. A popular term used in programming is the word *bug*. This refers to an error in computer software. The origin of the term is debated, but it may have originated with Capt. Grace Murray Hopper, (USN), one of the pioneers of computing. Working on one of the first large scale computers (the MARK II) in the summer of 1945, she found a large moth that had been beaten to death in a relay and that had caused the Mark II to malfunction. Later, when asked why the computer was not running, she announced that she had been removing a *bug*. *Debugging* is a term that has been used by millions of programmers ever since.

(2) Input/Output — in addition to the program, the subjects received a listing of input data and program output

(3) Input/Output+Correct — just the same as (2), the subjects received output that would have resulted if the program had run correctly

(4) Class of Bug — these subjects were given the program listing only and told whether it contained an array, iteration, or assignment statement bug and

(5) Line Number — these subjects were given the program listing only and told in which line the error was

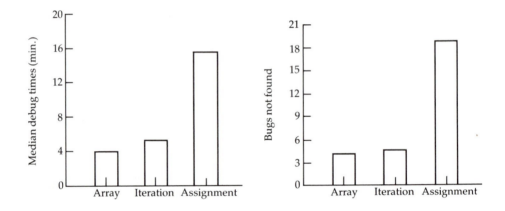

Figure 4.10   Median times to find bugs and numbers of bugs not found.

Figure 4.10 indicates that the most difficult type of error to find was the assignment statement bug. It took about four times as long to find. The number of assignment bugs not found at all was more than four times the number of array or iteration bugs, probably because comments and redundancy do not help much in finding assignment bugs and because the effect of assignment bugs seems to be more localized to a single statement. Finding array bugs can be greatly aided by considering statements where array sizes are declared and iteration bugs frequently make a large segment of code seem suspect.

Figure 4.11 has some striking results. In terms of median debug times, the control group did as well (or better) than three of the treatment groups. Only the Line Number group (which was told in which line the error resided) performed significantly better than the group with only a listing. Thus, this study found no debugging aids superior to pointing out the statement in which the error occurs.

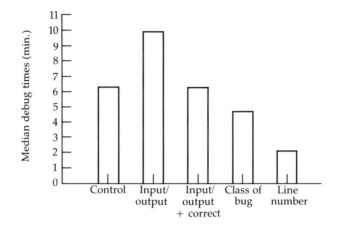

Figure 4.11   Median times for each debugging aid.

The problem is that "pointing out the statement in which the error occurs" is sometimes difficult to do, especially for logic errors. For example, the fact that a program attempts to divide by X, which is zero in line 475, may not be a problem with line 475. Instead, it may reflect a problem with line 452 where X was computed (and given the value zero). Thus, any debugging aids that help programmers isolate such information (such as aids that trace the "execution" of a program by showing the values of items every time they change) might be valuable in the program development process.

4.6 Summary and Conclusions

All the micro-models of effort support the conclusion that program size (S_s (LOC) or N (number of tokens)) is a *major* factor in the effort to construct, comprehend, or debug a program. However, there is no theoretical basis to convert units of size into units of time — different studies propose different regression constants. In any case, none of the metrics of program complexity performs significantly better than a simple model of program size. This is expected since most complexity metrics are highly correlated with size.

The time estimator model proposed by Halstead is unique. Since the E metric of Software Science is related to program size, the performance of Halstead's model is similar to that of size. However, it does not use constants derived by data-fitting, although some adjustment is still required when the range of module sizes is large. One adjustment method that does not require the use of regression-derived constants is the logical module model proposed by Woodfield, Dunsmore, and Shen. The waning interest in micro-level studies leaves this model unconfirmed.

We have discussed several experiments on the use or nonuse of several programming techniques. Generally, the judicial use of such features as comments, mnemonic variable names, flowcharts, or debugging aids are beneficial to the programming process. Although the results are expected and some are not conclusive, it is reassuring to know that some small-scale experiments support our intuition.

Exercises

1. Discuss the importance of small-scale experiments that simulate parts of the large-scale software development process.

2. Design a metric (other than those discussed in the book) to measure the maintainability of a program. Design a small-scale experiment to test the use of this metric.

3. What is the hypothesis of Experiment 1 discussed in Section 4.3.1? Discuss the internal validity and external validity of this experiment.

4. What is the experimental design of the modularity experiment by Woodfield, Dunsmore, and Shen discussed in Section 4.3.3? What are the treatments in this experiment? Discuss the internal validity and external validity of this experiment.

5. What is the relationship between a physical module and a logical module? Describe the relationship precisely using mathematical formulas.

6. Referring to [BASI83], list the criteria used to select data points in the experiment discussed in Section 4.3.4. Which criterion is the most attractive and why?

7. What is the hypothesis of Gordon's experiment discussed in Section 4.3.5? Is there any statistical test discussed in Chapter 3 that can be used to test if the results are significant?

8. What is the experimental design of the experiment by Curtis, Sheppard, and Milliman discussed in Section 4.3.6? What are the treatments in this experiment? Discuss the internal validity and external validity of this experiment.

9. What is the major conclusion of Wang's experiment discussed in Section 4.4? Discuss the internal validity and external validity of this experiment.

10. For all experiments described in Section 4.5, discuss the following:

    (1) The null hypothesis

    (2) The experiment design

    (3) The statistical test

    (4) Data collection and internal validity

    (5) Major results

    (6) External validity

5 Macro-Models of Productivity

The essential features of mass production are (1) manufacture of standardized commodities; (2) long production runs; (3) continuous plant operation; (4) use of specialized production and material handling equipment; (5) plant arrangements minimizing material handling; (6) division of labor to the point where most workers perform short and simplified operation sequences repetitively; and (7) systematic planning, direction and control of manufacture operations.

Encyclopedia Brittanica 14 (1967), 1038.

5.1 Introduction

The features of manufacturing cited are believed to increase productivity, both in terms of the output per time period and the output per worker. Evidence of success was the industrial revolution, which began in the eighteenth century. Further evidence was the application of these ideas on a wide scale in the United States in the beginning of the twentieth century, making this nation a great industrial power in the world. It would be desirable if a *similar* set of features can be applied successfully when software is the commodity manufactured. We say "similar", but not identical, since software is not a commodity that can be standardized. The reproduction of standardized software is basically a magnetic or photographic copying process, which costs very little. Most software production is tailored to a unique and specific need. Since software production is a "labor-intensive" process, it is impossible to keep a long production run or maintain continuous operation. Therefore, our hopes for improved software productivity lie in our ability to provide improved tools for software production, improved development processes, and better planning and control of such processes.

A major goal of the STARS program is productivity improvement. This improvement is necessary both to fill the gap between the supply of and the anticipated demand for computer specialists, and to reduce software development costs, which appear to be growing at an alarming rate. To begin, we need a definition of software productivity. One commonly accepted definition is the following:

234

> *Productivity is the number of lines of source code produced per programmer-month (person-month) of effort.*

As a mathematical equation, this definition becomes

$$\text{productivity} = \frac{\text{size in number of lines of source code generated}}{\text{effort in programmer}-\text{months}} \qquad (5.1)$$

Observed productivity rates vary from 20 to 1500 lines of code per person-month of effort. There are a number of problems with this definition. First, we must define precisely what is included in lines of code (as it was discussed in Section 2.2): Does it include blank lines? Comment lines? Data declaration lines? How do we treat multiple instructions per line? How do we treat programs with significant amounts of reused code? Second, we must define precisely what effort to include in the denominator (as discussed in Section 2.7). Which phases of effort are to be included and which support personnel? Does it include requirements analysis effort? Maintenance effort? Clerical effort? Computer support effort? Or simply the coding effort? It is clear that by varying the definitions of either the numerator or the denominator of Equation (5.1) we can obtain productivity measures for the same product that differ by an order of magnitude or more. Even if we assume that "lines of code" and "effort" can be precisely defined, an even more serious problem arises when we attempt to compare productivity on products written in different languages. The productivity rates for products written in a high-level language are almost always lower than those for products written in assembly language. Indeed both lines of code per unit time and cost per source line appear lower when high-level languages are used. Nevertheless, if we interpret productivity as a measure of work output, then high-level languages do result in greater economic productivity. This paradox is explored more fully in [JONE81]: software development has a fairly high level of fixed costs (e.g., analysis, design, documentation) that is unrelated to coding, and that coding in high-level languages requires fewer lines of code than assembly language coding, as well as less effort in testing. The following example taken from this source illustrates this paradox.

> *Assume two programs are functionally identical, but one is written in assembly language and requires 1000 source lines, while the second is written in PL/1 and requires 250 source lines. (The expansion ratio of 4 to 1 in going from PL/1 to assembly seems to be typical.) Assume that a fully supported person-month costs $5000.*

Table 5.1 lists the typical effort and cost during the life-cycle phases when the program is written in the indicated language. As this example shows, the cost of delivering the product using PL/1 was reduced by 50%, yet productivity measured in lines of source code per person-month dropped by 50% while the cost per source line doubled. This example shows that it is dangerous to use productivity as defined by Equation (5.1) to compare programs written in substantially different languages.

Table 5.1   A Hypothetical Example Concerning Productivity

	Assembler Version		PL/I Version	
Activity	Person-Months	Cost	Person-Months	Cost
Design	1	$5,000	1	$5,000
Coding	5	$25,000	1	$5,000
Testing	2	$10,000	1	$5,000
Documentation	1	$5,000	1	$5,000
Management/Support	1	$5,000	1	$5,000
Total	10	$50,000	5	$25,000
LOC/PM	100		50	
$/LOC	$50		$100	

There have been several attempts to avoid the ambiguity inherent in this definition of productivity. One suggestion is to convert high-level language source lines into an equivalent number of object lines using an appropriate expansion ratio. The observed expansion ratio varies from one language to another. For example the ratio for FORTRAN appears to be about 6.5 to 1, while the ratio for PL/1 is about 4 to 1. Of course, these are average ratios and can vary significantly among programs of different types. Hence this approach too has its limitations.

A second suggestion to avoid the "lines of code" problem is to define the size of a program in terms of the more fundamental metrics — operators and operands. This approach was introduced by Halstead [HALS77] who based his theory of Software Science on these metrics. (Halstead's definitions were described in various sections of Chapter 2.) The productivity would then be measured by the number of tokens produced per person-month. However, we do not have data to show that such productivity is constant (and there is no reason to believe that it should be) when different languages are used to implement a certain software product.

A third suggestion is to abandon lines of code in favor of *function points*, as advocated by Albrecht [ALBR79]. Productivity here is defined in terms of a weighted sum of delivered functional units. Functional units are defined as the number of inputs, the number of outputs, the number of inquiries, and the number of files. Albrecht applied this approach to a set of commercial programs written at IBM's Data Processing Division, and obtained a reasonably smooth fit of his weighted function points to actual costs. However, the programs he studied were all commercial applications, in which the function units are more or less clearly definable and fairly homogeneous. For system programs such as compilers and for other program types, function units are more difficult to define precisely and, in any case, may differ significantly in size and scope. Of course, one could attempt to define function units for different types of programs, but then it becomes more difficult to compare productivity rates across different types of software.

The search for a better definition of productivity continues. In spite of its limitations, it is likely that most organizations will continue to use Equation (5.1) as the preferred measure of productivity for three major reasons: first, it is easily computed; second, it permits easier comparison with historic productivity rate studies which traditionally have used this measure; and third, all alternatives to Equation (5.1) also have problems. As long as appropriate caution is used, productivity rates computed using Equation (5.1) can still yield valuable information about the effects of various software factors on productivity improvements.

5.2 Factors Affecting Productivity

We have already discussed the need for improvements in the definition of programmer's productivity. In spite of its limitations, we adopt the traditional definition of productivity according to Equation (5.1) as

$$L = \frac{S_s}{E} \tag{5.2}$$

where S_s is the number of lines of source code produced and E is the number of person-months of effort charged during development. From this definition, we see that productivity is inversely proportional to effort or cost. We shall focus in this chapter on techniques that increase productivity within the framework of the conventional program development process from analysis and design to systems integration. This approach is evolutionary, as opposed to more revolutionary methods such as automatic program generators, ultra-high-level languages, and reusable program parts that attempt to by-pass the coding process altogether. These promise much greater productivity improvements, if we think of productivity as work accomplished per person per unit time. But, unfortunately these more revolutionary methods are still far from perfected.

The evolutionary school of productivity improvement envisions productivity gains by a factor of 2 to 4 within 10 years by controlling and improving the most significant factors, which are known or believed to affect productivity. The success of this approach is critically dependent upon our ability not only to identify the major factors that affect productivity, but also to produce reasonable measurements of these. In this chapter, we shall attempt to identify and classify some of these factors and their possible effects, and to present various models of productivity as a function of these factors.

There are a large number of factors that appear to affect the software development process and the product produced. The SDC study of 169 projects [NELS66] identified 104 such factors. Without attempting to be all-inclusive we list here some of these factors classified into the four categories: People Factors, Process Factors, Product Factors and Computer Factors.

People Factors — Individual capabilities, years of experience, language experience, experience with similar problems, previous experience with the system being used, the size of the team, organization of the team, experience of the team working together, morale level of individuals, the quality of management.

Process Factors — The programming language, use of a program design or specification language, top down design, HIPO diagrams, use of structured programming, use of chief programmer teams, code walk-throughs, code inspections, milestones, use of a program librarian, testing tools, automatic flowcharters, the development schedule, optimizing compilers, data base system availability, utility tools, multisite development.

Product Factors — Size of the product, size of the data base, real-time requirements, reliability, portability, control structure, data structure, number of modules, module coupling, memory requirements, complexity, the amount of reused code, state of problem definition, the amount of documentation, security restrictions, type of software.

Computer Factors — Response time, turnaround times, hardware under concurrent development, the development machine system volatility, storage constraints, timing constraints.

Undoubtedly, many more factors can be added to this already-lengthy list. In addition to each factor affecting productivity alone, it is also probable that these factors interact in many complex ways to affect productivity. It would be virtually impossible to include all of these factors in a productivity model.

Indeed, one attempt to do so in the SDC study using multi-linear regression led to exceptionally poor results. Some way is needed to reduce the list of factors to those (preferably a small subset) that have a significant and measurable effect on productivity, and to incorporate them into a realistic model. In order to arrive at a set of significant factors, we define some criteria that should be met by a factor for inclusion in the basic set.

Criteria for Factors to Include in a Productivity Model

Measurability and Objectivity — It must be possible somehow to quantify or rate the factor involved. As discussed in Section 1.3.2, the rating level should be more or less independent of the rater: the measure should be algorithmic and objective, yielding reasonably close (if not identical) values for the same software, regardless of time, place, and the rater.

Generality — Is the factor applicable to most software products, or does it arise only in very special products? For example, some models include the number of trips taken or security restrictions as factors. While these factors may affect certain types of military software, they are typically not applicable in most situations. Thus, these factors would not be of value in a general-purpose productivity model.

Significance — A factor should be included only if it can be established that it has a significant effect on productivity in at least one collection of data. Significance can be established by using statistical methods such as regression and tests of significance discussed in Section 3.4. This approach would rule out many factors that have only a minor effect — for example, those that account for only a small percentage of the variance.

Independence — Factors that tend to be highly correlated should be represented by one member of the group. For example, the factors of structured coding, walk-throughs, chief programmer team, and code reading are often used by the same team. Hence, a single factor — such as structured programming — could be used in place of all four. Similar groupings of factors should be possible among all of these the categories. There are factor analysis statistical techniques (see Section 3.4.4) that may be used to determine groups of factors and their best representatives.

5.3 Macro-level Studies on Certain Factors Affecting Productivity

There are few definitive studies of the effects of the factors discussed in Section 5.2 on productivity rates. Some reports have been published that provide at least an indication of the possible magnitude of these effects.

The conclusion from several experiments show that the effect of individual capability on productivity can be very large — as large as 26:1 — on small one-person programming jobs (for example, see [SACK68]). For large team projects, this effect is much less pronounced, although still significant, leading to ratios of perhaps 2:1 to 4:1. The drop off in the variation of productivity rates on large projects is probably due to the need for greater communication among team members and to the averaging effect of differing individual productivity rates.

As shown in various experiments discussed in Chapter 4, even if we attempt to control as many variables as possible, the effect of individual capabilities on various software measures can still be substantial. In the summer of 1983, an experiment was conducted at Purdue University [WANG84] involving 44 students who were asked to write a program to simulate a calculator. The students were mostly graduate Computer Science students of approximately equal experience and training. The program was to be written in Pascal and all subjects had to follow a top-down data-structure-first design strategy (see also Section 4.4). They were asked to complete the program in 2 weeks using prescribed block-work sessions, and to record the time spent on the program carefully. Milestone interviews were held with each student throughout each of 4 development phases, during which intermediate data on various software metrics was collected. The phases included specification, initial design, detailed design, and coding/debugging. The purpose of the experiment was simply to collect data on various software metrics during the development process. The students were assured that there was no connection between performance and grades, and they were not asked to optimize any measure such as effort. In Table 5.2, we give the results on some software metrics collected during the experiment. From this table, we can compute the ratios

$$E_{max}/E_{min} = 3.4$$

$$S_{max}/S_{min} = 2.9$$

$$L_{max}/L_{min} = 4.1$$

Thus, even though an attempt was made to control as many variables as possible — including experience, background, language, motivation, and development strategies — we still find significant differences in productivity and other metrics. It is reasonable to hypothesize that these differences in performance are primarily due to differences in individual capability.

Table 5.2   The Effect of Individual Differences on Software Metrics

Software Metric	min.	max	mean	st. dev.
E (hours)	16	54	27	9
S_s (LOC)	267	784	463	96
L (LOC/hour)	8.2	33.8	18.4	5.4

Harr [HARR69] reported data on some projects produced at Bell Telephone Laboratories. This data is reproduced in Table 5.3. The first two programs that are of control type have a lower productivity rate than the two translator programs. The most distinguishing characteristics of the control programs are in the much larger number of modules and the number of programmers. A possible conclusion is that projects involving large numbers of people or modules will result in lower productivity. A second possible conclusion is that control programs are internally much more complex than translators.

Table 5.3   Harr's Data

Type of Program	No. of Modules	No. of Programmers	Person-Years	Size in Words	Words/PY
Operational/Control	50	83	101	52,000	515
Maintenance/Control	36	60	81	51,000	630
Compiler	13	9	17	38,000	2230
Translator	15	13	11	25,000	2270

Indeed, several studies attempt to determine nominal productivity rates depending on the type of software. Table 5.4 indicates the nominal productivity for software of the indicated type, according to a study at Boeing Computer Services [BLAC77]. These nominal rates are then adjusted up or down depending on a number of other factors. Large products may include components that are of different types so that productivity estimates could involve combinations of some of the rates listed earlier.

Table 5.4   Boeing Productivity Rates

Type of Software	Productivity (LOC/PM)
Mathematical	167
Report/Commericial	125
Logical	83
Signal Proccessing	50
Real Time	25

Some studies show that team experience (the same group of people working together on similar projects) can have a significant impact. One study involved a compiler writing team that was asked to write a translator in a given language for three different computers. The first compiler required 72 person-months of effort, the second compiler took 36 person-months and the third took 14 person-months. If we assume that all three compilers were of roughly the same size and that all other factors were approximately the same, then productivity on the second compiler was twice that of the first compiler, while productivity on the third compiler was about five times that of the first attempt. These productivity improvements are well within the observed bounds of improvements that can be expected, due to experience in writing similar software. In general, experienced programmers seem to be two to four times more productive than less-experienced programmers [BOEH81, THAD84].

Several studies show that interactive computer response times have a significant impact on programmer productivity. One study [THAD84] indicates that it took twice as long to complete a given task at a response time per interaction of 2.0 seconds, compared with a response time of 0.25 seconds. Other studies seem to indicate gains of perhaps 20% in productivity due to rapid response times. Another study suggested that variability of response time is more important than the mean rate [CARB68]. Little performance difference was found when subjects used two systems — one of which was twice as fast as the other, but in which both had constant response rates. However, performance was much worse on a system with the same mean response rate, but with large variability in individual response times. An excellent survey on this issue can be found in [SHNE84].

Hardware constraints — either execution time or storage constraints — can result in reductions in productivity by factors of from 2 to 6, according to studies conducted at Boeing [BLAC77], at General Research Corporation [CARR79], and by Boehm [BOEH81].

The results of these studies are cited to provide a qualitative assessment of the possible effects of various factors on productivity, rather than a precise quantitative assessment. In most cases, the studies were not conducted under controlled conditions and often predominantly reflect the particular environment in which they were done. Any attempt to extrapolate these effects to different environments, and especially the compounding effect of various factors, must be done carefully.

5.4 The Walston-Felix Study of Productivity

Perhaps the first systematic attempt to collect data on software projects under semi-controlled conditions was performed by Walston and Felix at the IBM Federal Systems Division during the early 1970s. An analysis of this data was published in a paper in the *IBM Systems Journal* [WALS77]. Detailed reports from project managers on 60 different projects were collected at various milestones. The collected data included development effort, computer resources, phase completion data, errors, number of modules, degree of use of modern programming practices, pages of documentation, languages used, and so on. The programs were of various types, written in 28 different languages, and ranged in size from 4,000 DSL to 467,000 DSL. (The count DSL (Delivered Source Lines of code) includes comment lines.) Actual productivity ranged from 27 DSL/PM to 1,000 DSL/PM (Delivered Source Lines per Person-Month), with an average productivity of about 300 DSL/PM. Thus, this is an extremely heterogeneous data base.

Among other goals Walston and Felix were interested in producing an effort estimation model based on size alone. The predicted values of effort based on their model showed considerable scatter when compared with the actual effort. In an attempt to explain the scatter in these results, they made a study of the factors other than size. Initially, they identified 68 factors that might account for the variation. A multilinear regression analysis showed that only 29 of these variables were significantly correlated with productivity. Project leaders were then asked to indicate to what extent each of the 29 factors applied to their own project. For each variable, the responses were rated as normal, less than normal, or greater than normal. From these responses, Walston and Felix computed the mean productivity by variable by the indicated rating. Table 5.5 lists each of the 29 variables, the rating scale used, the mean productivity for each rating, and the productivity change.

Table 5.5   Productivity Ranges in the IBM-FSD Data Base

Question or Variable	Response Group Mean Productivity (DSL/PM)			Productivity Change (ΔL)	Productivity Range (L_{high}/L_{low})
	(1)	(2)	(3)	(4)	(5)
1 Customer interface complexity	<Normal 500	Normal 295	>Normal 124	376	4.03*
2 User participation in the definition of requirements	None 491	Some 267	Much 205	286	2.40
3 Customer originated program design changes	Few 297		Many 196	101	2.94*
4 Customer experience with the application area of the project	None 318	Some 340	Much 206	112	2.84*
5 Overall personnel experience and qualifications	Low 132	Average 257	High 410	278	3.11*
6 Percentage of programmers doing development who participated in design of functional specifications	<25% 153	25-50% 242	<50% 391	238	2.56*
7 Previous experience with operational computer	Minimal 146	Average 270	Extensive 312	166	2.14
8 Previous experience with programming languages	Minimal 122	Average 225	Extensive 385	263	3.16*
9 Previous experience with application of similar or greater size and complexity	Minimal 146	Average 221	Extensive 410	264	2.81*
10 Ratio of average staff size to duration (people/month)	<0.5 305	0.5-0.9 310	>0.9 173	132	1.76
11 Hardware under concurrent development	No 297		Yes 177	120	1.68
12 Development computer access, open under special request	0% 226	1-25% 274	>25% 357	131	1.58
13 Development computer access, closed	0-10% 303	11-85% 251	>85% 170	133	1.78

Table 5.5, continued

Question or Variable	Response Group Mean Productivity (DSL/PM)			Productivity Change (ΔL)	Productivity Range (L_{high}/L_{low})
	(1)	(2)	(3)	(4)	(5)
14 Classified security environment for computer and 25% of programs and data	No 289		Yes 156	133	1.85
15 Structured programming	0-33% 169	34-66% –	66% 310	141	1.83
16 Design and code inspections	0-33% 220	34-66% 300	>66% 339	119	1.54
17 Top-down development	0-33% 196	34-66% 237	>66% 321	125	1.64
18 Chief programmer team usage	0-33% 219	34-66% –	>66% 408	189	1.86
19 Overall complexity of code developed	< Average 314		> average 185	129	1.70
20 Complexity of application processing	< Average 349	Average 345	> Average 168	181	2.08
21 Complexity of program flow	< Average 289	Average 299	> Average 209	80	1.43
22 Overall constraints on program design	Minimal 293	Average 286	Severe 166	127	1.77
23 Program design constraints on main storage	Minimal 391	Average 277	Severe 192	198	2.04
24 Program design constraints on timing	Minimal 303	Average 317	Severe 171	132	1.85
25 Code for real-time or interactive operation or executing under severe time constraint	< 10% 279	10-40% 337	> 40% 203	76	1.66
26 Percentage of code for delivery	0-90% 159	91-99% 327	100% 265	106	2.06
27 Code classified as nonmathematical application and I/O formatting programs	0-33% 188	34-66% 311	67-100% 267	79	1.65
28 Number of classes of items in the data base per 1000 lines of code	0-15 334	16-80 243	>80 193	141	1.73
29 Number of pages delivered documentation per 1000 lines of delivered code	0-32 320	33-88 252	>88 195	125	2.56*

In Table 5.5, the productivity change column (ΔL) is obtained by computing the absolute differences of the mean values given in Columns 1 and 3 ($|L_{(1)} - L_{(3)}|$).   It does not give the maximal differences computed from the actual productivity extremes, which is probably a more meaningful quantity. For several attributes, the productivities do not increase or decrease monotonically.   For example with attribute 4, "customer experience with the application area of the project," the average productivities corresponding to the answers "none," "some," and "much" are respectively 318, 340, and 206.   The productivity change as given in Column 4 is $318 - 206 = 112$, while the maximum change of the mean values is actually $340 - 206 = 134$.   While there may in some cases be good reasons to explain the nonmonotone change in productivities, a more likely explanation is that there were too few projects in some response categories to make an average productivity meaningful.

We have also computed in Column 5 the *productivity range* defined by

$$\text{productivity range} = \frac{L_{\text{high}}}{L_{\text{low}}}$$

By examining Column 5, we can quickly see which attributes have the greatest impact on productivity.   The eight attributes having the greatest impact on productivity are identified by stars in Column 5.   Of these eight attributes, three relate to the degree of customer interfacing while four relate to personnel experience and qualifications.   Surprisingly, the number of pages of documentation per 1000 lines of code appears as one of these attributes.   Other researchers omit this attribute entirely as a significant factor.

Some of the attributes that appear to have the smallest potential impact on productivity are "complexity of program flow" (1.43), "design and code inspections" (1.54), "development computer access" (1.58), "top-down development" (1.64), and "hardware under concurrent development" (1.68). While the productivity ranges in Table 5.5 are useful indicators, we must remember that they reflect the projects in this particular environment.   The impact of a particular attribute may be substantially different in another environment.

When we interpret this table, it is important to realize that no attempt was made to factor out the interactions among the attributes or variables.   Many of the variables are strongly related, thus making it difficult to isolate the effect of any one variable.   For example, variables 15 through 18 — "structured programming," "design and code inspections," "top-down development" and "chief programmer team usage" — are highly correlated since managers are likely to insist on the use of all four if they are structured programming devotees.   In any case, it is difficult to know how much of the indicated productivity gain is due to each of the 4 variables or even to all 4 combined.

In an attempt to make the observations from these categories useful to managers for predictive purposes, Walson and Felix first define a productivity index I for each project:

$$I = \sum_{i=1}^{29} W_i X_i \tag{5.3}$$

where W_i is a variable weight defined by

$$W_i = \tfrac{1}{2} \log_{10}(\Delta L_i) \tag{5.4}$$

and X_i is defined as

$$X_i = \begin{cases} 1 \text{ if the variable rating indicates } \textit{increased} \text{ productivity} \\ 0 \text{ if the variable rating indicates } \textit{nominal} \text{ productivity} \\ -1 \text{ if the variable rating indicates } \textit{decreased} \text{ productivity} \end{cases}$$

The weight as defined in Equation (5.4) has two parts. First, the log part provides a "dampened" effect on the productivity range;[1] it is used to adjust the predicted productivity up or down as dictated by X_i. Second, one half of the range is used to adjust the productivity from the "nominal" value, which is in the middle of the range.

The weights W_i range from 0.95 to 1.29. Project managers were asked to rate the productivity variables for their particular project from which an index I was produced for each project. The index I can be negative or positive. $I = 0$ indicates that all of the variables combined had a nominal or average effect on productivity. Next, using linear regression Walston and Felix found the least squares best fit constants in the equation

$$\log L = a + bI \tag{5.5}$$

together with a standard estimate of the error. Thus, Walson and Felix "calibrated" their model for this environment. The actual values found for a and b are not given in the paper but a plot of the results is produced in Figure 5.1.

Equation (5.5) can be used to predict productivity on a new project. First, the manager is asked to rate each of the 29 variables as to expected conditions under which the project was to be developed. This in effect determines X_1, X_2, $\cdots$, X_{29}. Substituting into Equation (5.3) will produce a projected productivity index I^*. Substituting into Equation (5.5) will then produce a predicted productivity rate, together with some confidence intervals that depend on the standard estimate of the error of the least squares fit.

For example, suppose that we find for a new project an index I^*, which

---

1. The term ΔL_i in Equation (5.4) could also be $\dfrac{L_{\mathrm{high}_i}}{L_{\mathrm{low}_i}}$. Walston and Felix did not provide adequate information to show which term was actually used in their analysis.

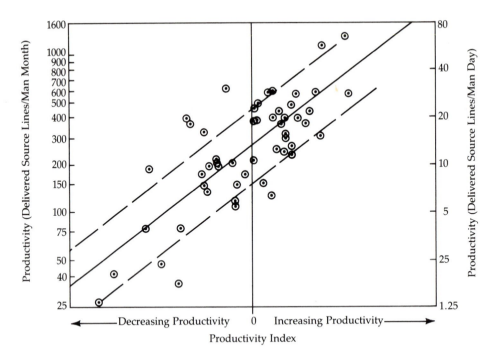

Figure 5.1   Productivity versus productivity index.

when substituted in Equation (5.5) gives

$$L_{\text{expected}} = 200$$

Assuming the standard error of the estimate is   .23 leads to a multiplicative error factor of 1.7, from which we obtain an expected productivity range of

$$115 < L < 340 \text{ DSL/PM}$$

(This is indicated by the dotted lines in Figure 5.1). The project manager can then examine those variables that seemed to have a pronounced effect on productivity to see if they can be improved.

Although Walston and Felix do not provide actual values of the constants in Equation (5.5), the proposed methodology can be applied to a local data base. A major problem with this methodology is that discrete values are assigned to the X_i's. In practice, the influence of any particular variable is likely to vary continuously over a spectrum, rather than take on 3 discrete values. A second problem is the large number of variables involved. Indeed, although Walston and Felix start with a data base of 60 projects, they actually use only 51 in the productivity model described. It would be better to have far more points in order to have confidence in the productivity metrics derived for these 29 variables.

5.5 Structured Programming and Its Effect on Productivity

For some years now, software experts have been exhorting programmers and managers to use a structured approach to software design and programming. This advice is based on the belief that a structured approach reduces errors, increases program clarity, and decreases maintenance effort (see also Section 4.5.3). An interesting question is whether it increases or decreases productivity. On the one hand, we observe that strongly typed languages like Pascal seem to result in more lines of code being written than a language like FORTRAN. This observation may result in an apparent increase in productivity. On the other hand, the structuring process itself usually requires additional effort early, which may lead to a decrease in productivity. There have been few studies that attempt to measure the effect of structured programming objectively. Sime, Green, and Guest [SIME73] did find that novice programmers made fewer errors and completed more programs when using a language with a structured IF-THEN-ELSE, rather than an identical language with only a nonstructured TEST and BRANCH. Green [GREE77] further found that a form of the IF-THEN-ELSE that included redundant predicate information led to superior performance by experienced programmers. In 1980, Brooks analyzed the Walston-Felix data base in an attempt to throw some light on the issue of the effect of structured programming on productivity [BROO81]. He began by observing as we did that, among the 29 productivity variables identified by Walston and Felix, there are four that are directly related to structured programming. Since these four — "structured coding," "top-down development," "chief programmer team usage," and "design and code inspections" — are highly correlated, he decided to use only one of them — "structured coding." Of the 60 projects that Walston and Felix started with, he found only 48 that were appropriate for this study. He classified these 48 by their degree of structuredness as follows:

Unstructured (0%—10% structured) — 17 projects

Partially Structured (11%—89% structured) — 7 projects

Structured (90%—100% structured) — 24 projects

These 48 projects could further be classified by

Size in terms of effort — A project was classified as small if the effort required to produce it was less than 100 person-months; otherwise, it was classified as large.

Complexity of the environment — Environment complexity was measured by the degree of severity of hardware constraints and code complexity.

Programmer experience — Programmers were compared on the basis of years of language experience, previous applications experience, previous experience as a group, and operational machine familiarity.

The object of the study can be stated as follows:

> *With the size of the project held constant, what was the apparent impact of structured coding on productivity at various levels of complexity and/or programmer capability?*

The major conclusions of this study can be summarized as follows:

(1) Within unstructured projects, low productivity is highly correlated with

    a.   Large projects

    b.   High customer interface complexity

    c.   High application complexity

    d.   Timing and storage constraints

    e.   Low personnel experience

    f.   Hardware under concurrent development

(2) Within structured projects, neither complexity nor any of the other constraints seemed to affect productivity with the sole exception of size. This implies that structuring seems to overcome the negative effects of these factors.

(3) Structured programming projects always exhibit a gain in productivity for any classification of projects, but the productivity gain was largest for large projects subject to severe constraints or complexity. For these severely constrained problems, the productivity gain ranged from 200% to 600%. The average productivities by size and degree of structuredness are contained in Table 5.6. The study rules out other possible explanations for the increased productivity observed in structured programs. In particular, neither differences in personnel capability nor code explosion could account for the observed differences.

This study is among the first objective attempts to quantify the potential gains in productivity due to the use of a structured approach to software development. It provides objective evidence that supports the claims of structured programming advocates.

Table 5.6 Productivity Gains due to Structuring

Degree of Structuring	Size	Average Productivity in DSL/MM
Unstructured	Small	293
Structured	Small	405
Unstructured	Large	105
Structured	Large	289

5.6 The ITT Study of Productivity

The International Telephone and Telegraph Corporation has recently formed a group to study software technology within the ITT family. In a recent paper [VOSB84], this group reported on a study designed to identify the factors that most significantly affect productivity. In this report, *productivity* is defined as the number of new or modified statements in a product divided by the number of person-years required during development (LOC/PY). The statement count includes data definitions, declarations, macros, and all executable statements, but excludes comments (unlike the Walston-Felix study).

The researchers studied 44 projects produced within ITT, ranging in size from 5,000 to 500,000 statements. They were written in several different languages and their types included switching systems, tools, defense applications, process control, and operating systems. Data was gathered through questionnaires completed by project managers.

In the first part, the researchers began with a list of some 100 variables that were believed to affect productivity. A *univariate analysis*, which yielded correlations between productivity and each variable considered independently, was used to reduce these 100 variables to 13. (For discussions on related statistical techniques, see Section 3.4.4.) The variables identified as having the greatest impact on productivity were grouped into two categories: *Product-Related Factors*, which are not under project management control, and *Project-Related Factors*, which can to some extent be controlled by management.

These most significant factors are listed in Table 5.7. Each productivity factor was rated on a 2-point or a 3-point scale. Productivity statistics were then determined for all projects falling within a rating scale.

Table 5.7   Most Significant Factors Affecting Productivity in an ITT Study

| | Ratings | | |
Product Related Factors	Low	Medium	High
1. Timing Constraint	0-20%		21-100%
2. Memory Utilization Constraint	0-70%		71-100%
3. CPU Occupancy Limitation	No		Yes
4. Number of Resource Constraints	0-1	2	3
5. Program Complexity	0-40%	41-80%	81-100%
6. Client Participation in Requirements Specification	Low	Medium	High
7. Client Experience with Application	Low	Medium	High
8. Size of Product in Statements	0		
	(Not Supplied)		
Project Related Factors			
9. Hardware Developed Concurrently	No		Yes
10. Development Computer Size in K-Bytes of Memory	0-256	257-1024	>1024
11. Stable Requirements Specification	No		Yes
12. Modern Programming Practice Usage	0-25%	26-75%	76-100%
13. Personnel Experience	Low	Medium	High

It was discovered that the first three resource constraints were highly correlated and that the combination of resource constraints, given in Item 4, resulted in significantly lower productivity than any one constraint alone.

On comparing these factors with those identified by the Walston-Felix study, we see first that there are far fewer factors identified in this study. For those factors that appeared in both studies, the effect on productivity was the same except for Items 6 and 7. The data of Walston and Felix showed both client participation and experience to be associated with lower productivity, while the ITT data arrived at the opposite conclusion. Further study is apparently needed to clarify the effect of these factors. The conclusion of this part of the study based on univariate analysis was that productivity is affected by the interactions among many factors, and that no single factor by itself could ensure high productivity.

The second part of the study applied *multivariate analysis* to the performance factors discussed in order to determine how much of the variation in productivity could be accounted for by various combinations of these factors. They first applied multiple regression to the product-related factors to obtain a coefficient of multiple determination (r^2), and then added in the project-related factors to see how much this coefficient would change. The results are given in Table 5.8.

Table 5.8   The Effect of Certain Factors Affecting Productivity in an ITT Study

Factors	Variation in Productivity Explained
Complexity and Resource Constraints	16%
Client Interface Experience and Participation	12%
Total Product-related Factors	28%
MPP Usage and Development Computer Size	24%
Personnel Experience	4%
Concurrent Hardware Development and	
Stability of Specifications	9%
Total Project-related Factors	37%
All Performance Factors	65%

The figures show that project-related factors, which can to some degree be controlled by management, account for about 37% of the variance in productivity. They also show that some 35% of the variation is unexplained by all of the performance factors. The explanation for the unexplained portion may be due to the omission of certain factors, to random data errors, or even to the use of a linear model. In any case, it would be extremely difficult to design a model that would be capable of explaining much more than 65% of the variance in productivity.

The conclusions of this study follow:

(1) Management practices can have a substantial impact on improving productivity.

(2) No one factor, no matter how well controlled, is sufficient to guarantee improved productivity. However, one poorly controlled factor can easily lead to poor productivity.

(3) Continuing quantitative studies of the factors affecting productivity or software quality are needed.

(4) Productivity increases will come about only if management implements an integrated, sustained program incorporating many practices and techniques that address the entire life-cycle process.

In evaluating this study, we note first that, while the size of a product is identified as a significant factor, the authors supply no data for its effect on productivity, and second that this study shows that the number of significant factors required to produce a reasonable productivity model can actually be reduced to a relatively small number — perhaps as few as 7 or 8 in all.

5.7 Productivity Ranges in the COCOMO Model

In 1981, Boehm [BOEH81] developed a model for software cost estimation that he calls COCOMO (COnstructive COst MOdel).[2] In the model, he delineates 15 software *factors* (alternatively called *attributes* or *cost drivers*) which he believes have significant impact on productivity and costs. This is a substantial reduction from the 29 considered by Walston and Felix. Boehm focuses on the effect of each software factor on development effort, but this effect is directly applicable to productivity.

Boehm's model focuses on 15 attributes, which are grouped into 4 categories as follows (taken from [BOEH81]):

---

2. This model will be discussed in more detail in Chapter 6.

(1) Product Attributes

      RELY Required Software Reliability

      DATA Data Base Size

      CPLX Product Complexity

(2) Computer Attributes

      TIME Execution Time Constraint

      STOR Main Storage Constraint

      VIRT Virtual Machine Volatility

      TURN Computer Turnaround Time

(3) Personnel Attributes

      ACAP Analyst Capability

      AEXP Applications Experience

      PCAP Programmer Capability

      VEXP Virtual Machine Experience

      LEXP Programming Language Experience

(4) Project Attributes

      MODP Modern Programming Practices

      TOOL Use of Software Tools

      SCED Required Development Schedule

On comparing these with the Walston-Felix model, we see that the reduction in the number of attributes was achieved partially by combining some attributes that appear to be highly correlated, and partially by omitting some. Some of the major factors omitted by Boehm are type of application, language level, management quality, customer interface complexity, amount of documentation, security and privacy restrictions. Some justification for these omissions are given in [BOEH81]. Moreover, while Walston and Felix use multilinear regression to delineate the most significant attributes, Boehm uses a more heuristic approach combined with a study of other models. Of course, Boehm was using a different data base, which might also account for the differences in the final attributes selected. The Boehm data base consists of 63 projects developed over a period ranging from 1964 to 1979. Like the Walston and Felix data base, the projects are extremely heterogeneous with sizes ranging from 2,000 to 966,000 lines of code, with productivities ranging from 20 to 1250 LOC/PM, and written in some 7 different languages.

Boehm also uses a heuristic approach to determine the effect of each attribute on effort. He quantifies this effect by first assigning ratings to each attribute on a five- or six-point scale (Very Low, Low, Nominal, High, Very High, Extra High), and then assigning numerical values to each rating. For each attribute, the ratings are defined as carefully as possible. The ratings definitions for a few of the attributes are given in Table 5.9.

Table 5.9   Sample Software Cost Driver Ratings (COCOMO)

Ratings	RELY (nature of loss)	AEXP (experience)	STOR (% of available storage)
Very Low	Slight inconvenience	≤4 mos.	–
Low	Easily recoverable loss	1 yr.	–
Nominal	Moderate loss	3 yrs.	≤50
High	High financial loss	6 yrs.	70
Very High	Risk to human life	12 yrs.	85
Extra High	–	–	95

The numerical values assigned to each cost driver for each rating, as given in [BOEH81], are reproduced in Table 5.10. The last column of Table 5.10 contains the productivity range for each attribute. This range is obtained by dividing the largest multiplier for a given attribute by the smallest multiplier. CPLX—"product complexity" — appears to have the largest effect on productivity. This implies that, for a product with a "low" complexity rating, productivity may be as much as 236% greater than on a product with "high" complexity rating. The next most significant factors appear to be "analyst capability" and "programmer capability," which together can result in a productivity gain of over 400%. From a management point of view, this table of productivity ranges is very important since it indicates where the greatest productivity gains are possible. Of course, some of the factors can be controlled or influenced by management while others cannot. Such factors as "required reliability," "product complexity," and "execution time constraint" are not under management control. However, most of the other factors can be controlled to some extent by project managers, and these factors point the way to systematic productivity improvement.

Table 5.10   Cost Driver Effort Multipliers and Productivity Range

| Cost Driver | Ratings | | | | | | Productivity Range |
	Very Low	Low	Nominal	High	Very High	Extra High	
Product Attributes							
RELY	.75	.88	1.00	1.15	1.40		1.87
DATA		.94	1.00	1.08	1.16		1.24
CPLX	.70	.85	1.00	1.15	1.30	1.65	2.36
Computer Attributes							
TIME			1.00	1.11	1.30	1.66	1.66
STOR			1.00	1.06	1.21	1.56	1.56
VIRT		.87	1.00	1.15	1.30		1.49
TURN		.877	1.00	1.07	1.15		1.32
Personnel attributes							
ACAP	1.46	1.19	1.00	.86	.71		2.06
AEXP	1.29	1.13	1.00	.91	.82		1.57
PCAP	1.42	1.17	1.00	.86	.70		2.03
VEXP	1.21	1.10	1.00	.90			1.34
LEXP	1.14	1.07	1.00	.95			1.20
Project attributes							
MODP	1.24	1.10	1.00	.91	.82		1.51
TOOL	1.24	1.10	1.00	.91	.83		1.49
SCED	1.23	1.08	1.00	1.04	1.10		1.23

On comparing the Walston and Felix productivity factors in Table 5.5 with the COCOMO productivity factors in Table 5.10, we can make the following observations:

(1) The COCOMO Model has fewer attributes; thus this model should be easier to manage.

(2) The attributes in the COCOMO Model appear to be more independent of each other.

(3) The COCOMO Model is much more precise and provides greater gradation for the effect of each attribute.

Overall, it appears that the COCOMO model would be much more useful to management provided that we can establish some confidence on the multipliers provided in Table 5.10. It is important to understand that the multipliers in the COCOMO Model were obtained by a combination of expert judgment and calibration using the projects in the available data base. It is highly unlikely that the same procedure applied to a different data base would yield the same or even similar values for the multipliers, especially when we consider the large number of these multipliers, and the interactions and trade-offs implicit in them. We must therefore view the apparent preciseness of the COCOMO Model with some skepticism until it can be corroborated by independent researchers.

5.8 The Effect of Team Size on Productivity

Several studies have indicated that individual productivity decreases as the size of the implementation team increases. For example, the Harr data given in Table 5.3 supports this. Brooks [BROO75], based on his own work with OS/360, also confirms this phenomenon — citing the following as the major reasons for a drop in productivity as team size increases:

(1) As the team size increases, there is greater need to coordinate the activities of the group, thus increasing overhead at the expense of code production.

(2) As members are added to a team, the new members must acquaint themselves with the overall project design and with previously completed work before they can begin to contribute to the project.

While the Boeing Model [BLAC77] and others contain team size as an explicit software development attribute, it is surprising that neither the Walston-Felix study nor Boehm's COCOMO Model directly identify team size as a significant factor in productivity assessment. Undoubtedly, its effect is included indirectly in other factors that may be closely correlated with team size. For example, project size is usually considered a significant factor which is highly correlated with team size.

We have at our disposal a data base of 187 projects from several different sources, which we have described in Section 3.6.6. These projects are written in a variety of languages and span the entire spectrum of complexity types from scientific applications to real-time control. In order to see the relationship between average personnel level and productivity, we have produced a kind of histogram. The data is contained in Table 5.11 and plotted in Figure 5.2.

In Table 5.11, the column $\bar{P}$ indicates the average personnel level computed as $\bar{P} = E/T$, where T is the duration of the project in months and E is the reported effort in person-months. The frequency column indicates the number of projects that correspond to the indicated average personnel level. We have chosen the $\bar{P}$ ranges partially to ensure that the frequency count in each cell is large enough to yield a meaningful productivity average.

Table 5.11 (or Figure 5.2) shows that average productivity drops almost exponentially as the average team size grows. This trend can be modeled by a

Table 5.11   Productivity versus Personnel Level

$\bar{P}$ Range	Range Midpoint (Personnel)	Frequency	Average Productivity(L)
0 - 1	0.5	10	1077
1 - 2	1.5	20	733
2 - 3	2.5	15	476
3 - 4	3.5	14	439
4 - 6	5.0	23	360
6 - 8	7.0	22	310
8 - 10	9.0	8	279
10 - 15	12.5	14	192
15 - 20	17.5	11	240
20 - 30	25.0	15	149
30 - 40	35.0	9	119
40 - 50	45.0	9	143
50 - 100	75.0	10	151
> 100	100.0	7	72

power formula of the form

$$L = a\bar{P}^b$$

If we take the midpoint of the $\bar{P}$ ranges as the independent variable, a least squares fit of $\bar{P}$ to the productivity L produces the result

$$\hat{L} = 777\bar{P}^{-0.5}$$

with a standard error estimate of 0.07 in the log-log plane. Figure 5.3 shows the original data in Figure 5.2 and the function to approximate it plotted using circles. Actually some 80% of the predicted values fall within one standard error range. The accuracy of this model is further confirmed by the following statistical measures of L versus $\hat{L}$:

RANGE OF X AXIS: 0 100
RANGE OF Y AXIS: 0 1100

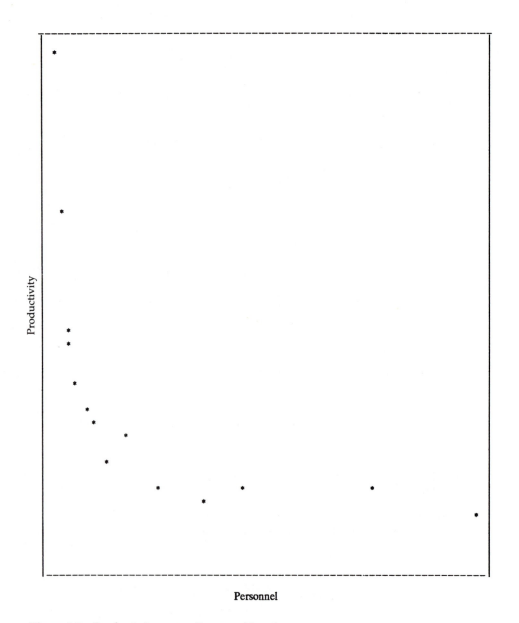

Figure 5.2   Productivity versus Personnel Level.

$$\overline{MRE} = 0.11$$

$$PRED(0.25) = 0.93$$

If we consider the heterogeneity of the projects in our data base, this model performs exceptionally well.

We now proceed to derive a more theoretical model of productivity as a function of average team size. This model is based on the observation first popularized by Brooks [BROO75] that, as the team size grows, the number of human communication paths will also tend to grow in order to provide for proper coordination among program modules. The organization and size of the team will affect the number of communication paths. If, for example, the project is organized in such a way that member of a team of size P must coordinate their activities with every other member of the team, then the number of communication paths will be $P(P-1)/2$. However, if each member of the team is allowed to communicate only with a single supervisor, then there will be only $(P-1)$ communication paths. Between these two extremes (one of which is $O(P)$ and the other $O(P^2)$), management can select organizations that lead to communication paths of length $O(P^\beta)$, $1 \leq \beta \leq 2$.

For example, if we can partition the team and the work into k equal-sized groups to allow full communication within each group, but only one communication path per group with the project supervisor, then the total number of communication paths $C(P)$ will be

$$C(P) = \frac{k}{2} \times \frac{P}{k} \left[\frac{P}{k} - 1 \right] + k \qquad (5.6)$$

Table 5.12 shows how the number of paths changes, as k changes assuming $P=12$. The column β is obtained by solving the equation

$$P^\beta = C(P) \qquad (5.7)$$

We see that β ranges from $\beta_{min} = 1.00$ indicating minimal interaction, to $\beta_{max} = 1.69$ for maximal interaction when $P=12$. As P increases, the value of β will approach 2 for maximal interaction.

Project managers will certainly try to avoid maximal interaction conditions; ideally, they will strive for minimal interaction partitions. However, in practice, they will have to settle for something less than the ideal: for a value of β somewhere in the middle of β_{min} and β_{max}. Therefore, it is reasonable to expect that there is some value of β such that P^β correctly reflects the amount of communication allowed.

Let us assume that on average each member of a team of size P can produce L lines of code per month. Let us further assume that each communication path results in a net loss of l lines of code per month. Then each programmer will on average produce

$$\bar{L} = L - l(P-1)^\gamma \qquad (5.8)$$

RANGE OF X AXIS: 0 100
RANGE OF Y AXIS: 0 1100

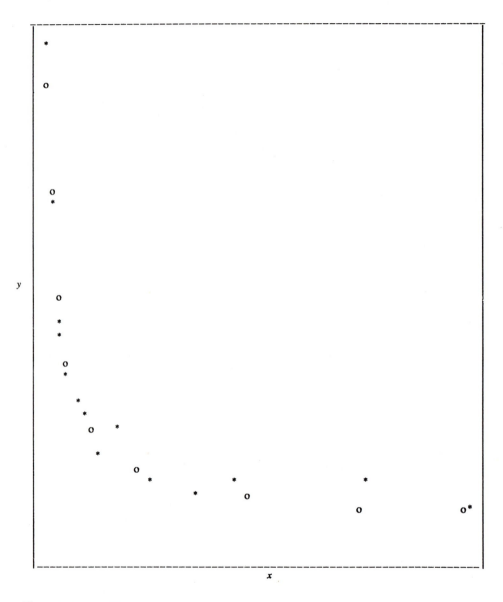

Figure 5.3 $y = 777\,x^{-0.5}$.

Table 5.12 Communication Paths as a Function of Partitions

k	C(P)	β
1	67	1.69
2	32	1.39
3	21	1.23
4	16	1.12
6	12	1.00
12	12	1.00

lines of code per month, where $0 < \gamma \le 1$. The exponent γ indicates the number of communication paths for a single programmer; $\gamma = 1$ implies that this member of the team communicates with every other member. Then the total monthly productivity of this group of size P will be

$$L_{group} = P\bar{L} = P(L - l(P-1)^{\gamma}) \tag{5.9}$$

Equation (5.9) tells us that the total monthly output will rise at first as P rises but will eventually reach a peak and then decrease. We can find this optimal value of P by differentiating Equation (5.9) to get

$$\frac{dL_{group}}{dP} = L - l(P-1)^{\gamma} - l\,\gamma P(P-1)^{\gamma-1} = 0 \tag{5.10}$$

and then solving this equation for P. The solution of Equation (5.10) can be simplified to

$$(P-1)^{\gamma}\left[1 + \frac{\gamma P}{P-1}\right] = \frac{L}{l}. \tag{5.11}$$

Thus given L, l, and γ, we can solve Equation (5.11) to obtain the optimum group size P_{opt}, Equation (5.8) to obtain the average individual productivity $\bar{L}$, and Equation (5.9) to obtain the optimum team productivity. For example, if $\gamma = 1$ if maximal interaction is required among all team members, and if $L = 300$, and $l = 30$ (implying a 10% loss in lines of code per month due to each interaction), then $\bar{L}$ and L_{group} vary with P as indicated in Table 5.13. The starred line in Table 5.13 corresponds to the optimal team size obtained by solving Equation (5.9) with $\gamma = 1$, $L = 300$, $l = 30$. Thus increasing the group size beyond $P = 5.5$ programmers will *decrease* total group productivity.

Table 5.13 $\bar{L}$ and L_{group} as Functions of P ($\gamma = 1, L = 300, l = 30$)

P	$\bar{L}$	L_{group}
1	300	300
2	270	540
3	240	720
4	210	840
5	180	900
5.5*	165*	908*
6	150	900
7	120	840

*Optimal team size

Table 5.14 P_{opt}, $\bar{L}$, and optimal L_{group} for $L = 300, l = 30$

γ	P_{opt}	$\bar{L}$	Optimal L_{group}
1.00	5.5	165	908
0.75	10.6	136	1446
0.60	21.5	116	2500
0.50	45.0	101	4545

The entries in Table 5.14 show how P_{opt}, $\bar{L}$, and optimal L_{group} vary as a function of γ. When $\gamma = 1$ — that is, when full interaction among all team members is allowed — the optimum team size is 5.5 programmers, the average productivity per programmer is 165 lines of code per month, and the maximum group productivity is 908 lines of code. As γ decreases — that is as the number of communication paths decreases — the optimum team size and the total group productivity both increase, even though the individual productivity decreases.

Equations $(5.8)-(5.10)$ may be thought of as a productivity model. They contain three essential parameters L, l, and γ. The parameter L, an individual's productivity, can be estimated from examining a database of small single-person projects that are of the same type of complexity. The parameter γ is a function of the team organization and the degree of interaction required and allowed. In practice, both l and γ can be determined by a least squares analysis based on a database of projects for which the average equivalent full time staff P, the total effort E in person-months, and the project size S_s in lines of code are known. Then we can compute

$$\bar{L} = S_s/E$$

and from Equation (5.8)

$$L - \bar{L} = l(P-1)^\gamma \qquad (5.12)$$

A nonlinear least squares analysis can now be used to find l and γ. Parameter values so found should reflect the average degree of interaction γ and the monthly loss l in lines of code for each interaction for the environment from which the database of projects was obtained. The model in Equation (5.12) requires that $L - \bar{L}$ be positive.

In Table 5.15, we have listed a database of completed projects for which the effort E in person-months, the adjusted size S in thousands of lines of code, the team size P, and the project duration T are known.

To illustrate how the model in Equation (5.12) can be used, we proceed heuristically to estimate the constants L, l, and γ for projects in this NASA Database (see Section 3.6.6). We have no way of knowing how much interaction was required on these projects but, if we assume an average degree of interaction, we can set $\gamma = .5$. After we have chosen γ, then a trial-and-error process produces the "best-fit" constants $L = 580$ and $l = 58$. Hence, we arrive at the model

$$\bar{L} = L - (P-1)^\gamma = 580 - 58(P-1)^{0.5} \qquad (5.13)$$

When applied to the NASA Database, this model produces the results given in Table 5.16. The measures of how good the fit is — namely, $\overline{MRE} = 0.25$ and $PRED(0.25) = 0.53$ — are reasonably accurate considering the large range of actual productivities (from 375 to 1000). The constants in Equation (5.13) are not necessarily the best possible constants, but they are "almost best" for the given database. Actually it would be hard to improve on the performance of this model if we assume that the model parameters are constant for all projects. Since productivity also varies with factors other than team size, it is surprising that this model performs as well as it does. A more realistic version of the model in Equation (5.12) might take the form

$$\bar{L}_c = L_c - l_c(P-1)^{\gamma_c}$$

Table 5.15   NASA/Goddard Development Data

Project	S_e	T	E	P	L
1	90.16	15.77	125.48	7.96	719
2	46.21	19.97	104.00	5.21	444
3	46.46	13.17	85.61	6.50	543
4	54.53	12.47	98.37	7.89	554
5	31.14	8.70	36.69	4.22	849
6	12.75	14.33	20.51	1.43	622
7	10.51	14.33	11.19	0.78	939
8	21.51	14.33	30.86	2.15	697
9	3.06	14.33	7.54	0.53	406
10	4.23	6.93	9.77	1.41	433
11	7.83	14.33	7.93	0.55	987
12	2.05	14.33	5.37	0.37	382
13	4.98	4.13	9.10	2.20	547
14	78.58	17.40	106.97	6.15	735
15	9.74	15.57	16.94	1.09	575
16	12.46	8.33	25.91	3.11	481
17	49.47	20.40	139.51	6.84	355
18	48.97	19.03	132.90	6.98	368
19	12.11	16.33	33.30	2.04	364

where the model parameters are now considered functions of program complexity, where complexity is defined in an appropriate manner. We shall not pursue this generalization here, but we will consider the application of this improved model to effort estimation in Chapter 6.

Table 5.16   Actual versus Predicted Productivity for NASA Data

Project	E	L	$\hat{L}$	RE
1	125.48	719	426	.41
2	104.00	444	460	-.04
3	85.61	543	443	.18
4	98.37	554	427	.23
5	36.69	849	475	.44
6	20.51	622	541	.13
7	11.19	939	580	.38
8	30.86	697	517	.26
9	7.54	406	580	-.43
10	9.77	433	542	-.25
11	7.93	987	580	.41
12	5.37	382	580	-.52
13	9.10	547	516	.06
14	106.97	735	448	.39
15	16.94	575	562	.02
16	25.91	481	495	-.03
17	139.51	355	439	-.24
18	132.90	368	438	-.19
19	33.30	364	520	-.43

$\overline{RE}$ = .04
MRE = .25
$PRED\,(.50)$ = 18/19 = .95
$PRED\,(.25)$ = 10/19 = .53

The model in Equation (5.12) can be used by managers for *crude preliminary* estimates of project effort and duration. Let us suppose that, using an historical database, we arrive at the parameter values given in Equation (5.13). A new project is to be undertaken whose estimated size in lines of code is S_s = 100,000 and a team of 6 programmers is available for the project. Then from Equation (5.13), we have

$$\bar{L} = 580 - 58(5)^{0.5} = 450 \text{ LOC/programmer-month}$$

$$L_{group} = 6 \cdot \bar{L} = 2701 \text{ LOC/team-month}$$

$$T = \frac{100,000}{L_{group}} = 37 \text{ months (duration)}$$

$$E = P \times T = 222 \text{ programmer-months of effort}$$

We wish to emphasize again that this model can be expected to give reasonable results only if the assumptions made are satisfied, and only if the programming environment is similar to that from which the NASA data was collected.

5.9 The Effect of Project Size on Productivity

It is commonly assumed that, for new program development, productivity decreases with program size. For example, Jones [JONE79] presents the data in Table 5.17.

Table 5.17   Apparent Productivity Ranges by Size of Program

Program Size	Minimum PM/K	Median PM/K	Maximum PM/K
Superlarge (over 512K)	4	14	28
Large (64 - 512K)	2	6	16
Medium (16 - 64K)	1	4	8
Low-Medium (2-16K)	0.8	2.5	5
Small (below 2K)	0.5	1.5	3

Table 5.18   Productivity by Size for Median Programs

Size Range (K)	Median Point	Median PM/K	Median L
> 512	512	14	71
64 - 512	288	6	167
16 - 64	40	4	250
2 - 16	9	2.5	400
0 - 2	2	1.5	667

The data is admittedly rough and is drawn from a variety of published sources. The unit of measure in Table 5.17 is person-months of effort per thousand lines of Basic Assembly Language (BAL) source code (PM/KLOC). There are tremendous variances in this table both between the size ranges and within each size range. This variance is understandable from our previous discussion of the various factors other than size that affect effort and productivity. Still, from this data, the conclusion that in general effort per thousand lines of code increases exponentially with program size is inescapable. We can recast the data in Table 5.17 to Table 5.18, which gives the productivity in lines of assembly code per person-month of effort versus size. Again, we see that productivity drops exponentially as the size of the program grows. A least squares power fit of productivity versus the median size point produces the formula

$$L = 887 S^{-0.354} \tag{5.14}$$

with a standard error estimate of 0.117 in the log-log planes, which confirms the exponential nature of the drop in productivity as a function of size exhibited in Table 5.18. Furthermore, the correlation between productivity and size is a fairly strong $r = -0.79$.

Indeed the smooth exponential drop in productivity exhibited in Table 5.18 and the model in Equation (5.14) gives us some cause for concern. It is simply too smooth to represent real-world projects, even when allowance is made for the variations in the data in Table 5.17 and for the small number of data points. In an attempt to confirm the productivity-size relationship, we have made a statistical study of the 187 projects in our combined databases. The raw data is contained in Table 5.19 and plotted in Figure 5.4.

Column 1 of this table indicates the size ranges in thousands of lines of code. The ranges are selected where possible so as to yield frequency counts large enough to make average parameter values meaningful. We have also computed the correlation coefficients between size and $\bar{P}$, $\bar{E}$, and $\bar{L}$. As expected and as the correlation coefficients indicate, both average personnel size and effort increase with size. However, it is surprising that productivity does not show a strong decreasing trend as the program size grows. This observation is confirmed by the weak inverse correlation $r(S,\bar{L}) = -0.43$. Thus, our data fails to confirm the data in Table 5.17 as supplied by Jones, and certainly casts doubt on the exponential decrease in productivity exhibited by Equation (5.14). A least squares power fit of productivity to the midpoint of each size range in Table 5.19 produces the model

$$L = 377 S^{-.05} \tag{5.15}$$

On comparing Equation (5.15) with Equation (5.14), especially the exponent of S, we see that there is a substantial difference in how productivity varies as a function of S. Equation (5.15), unlike Equation (5.14), tells us that program size has only a minor effect on productivity.

Since productivity does vary significantly from one project to another, Equation (5.15) implies that factors other than size can be expected to be much more significant, especially for small projects where individual capabilities may be dominating. In any case, additional databases should be examined to see if the productivity-program size relationship can be confirmed.

Table 5.19   Program Size versus Personnel Level, Effort, Productivity

Size Range (in Table) (S)	Range Midpoint	Frequency	Average Personnel Size $\bar{P}$	Average Effort $\bar{E}$	Average Productivity $\bar{L}$
0 - 2	1	3	1.9	1.7	200
2 - 4	3	10	2.5	27.0	216
4 - 6	5	9	2.5	16.4	402
6 - 8	7	11	4.3	45.7	533
8 - 12	10	11	3.8	48.8	343
12 - 14	13	11	4.9	60.1	272
14 - 18	16	13	5.7	79.8	537
18 - 24	21	12	9.0	97.6	354
24 - 30	27	13	9.1	153.3	454
30 - 36	33	12	7.7	201.3	404
36 - 46	41	11	16.1	323.7	224
46 - 55	51	13	18.4	377.1	488
55 - 75	65	11	14.3	330.1	656
75 - 100	88	10	22.0	451.4	287
100 - 140	120	12	31.0	726.3	297
140 - 240	190	11	60.7	1229.6	174
240 - 350	295	9	65.9	3453.0	183
> - 350	500	5	122.2	5336.6	199
Correlation with S			.99	.98	-.43

RANGE OF X AXIS: 1 500
RANGE OF Y AXIS: 174 656

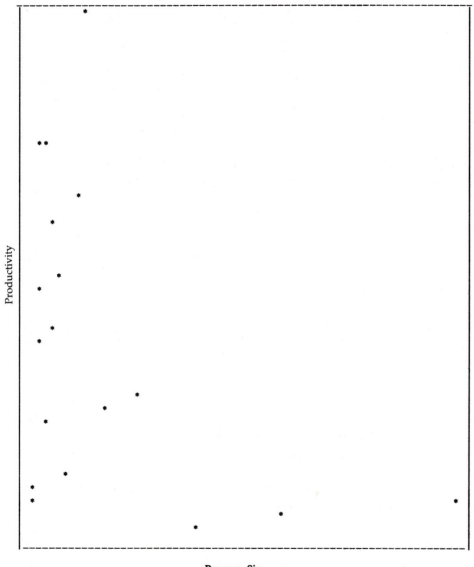

Program Size

Figure 5.4   Productivity versus program size.

5.10 Summary and Conclusions

We have found that the common measure of productivity in KLOC/PM can easily be misinterpreted or misused. The range of values for KLOC/PM for historical project data is simply too large to assume that this is a valid universal measure. Unfortunately, the measure is still used for lack of a better one.

Given the definition of productivity in Equation (5.1), studies have shown that some of the major factors affecting productivity are those related to customer interface requirements and personnel qualifications. In other words, productivity is people-oriented, which is not surprising. It is also difficult to improve poor productivity.

It is generally true that larger projects, which require larger teams of programmers, are associated with lower average productivity. This decrease may be due to the higher complexity of the problem or the higher overhead involved with larger teams. It is this fact that inhibits the direct application of the results from micro-level studies to macro-level projects.

Exercises

1. Discuss the strengths and weaknesses of the definition of productivity given in Equation (5.2). What would be an appropriate definition if automatic code generators are used?

2. Identify the three most important factors affecting productivity according to Table 5.5. Can they be assessed objectively? Are they independent from each other? Justify your answer.

3. What is the range of the productivity index given by Equation (5.3)? Show the possible maximum and minimum values for I.

4. One of the deductions based on an analysis of Walston and Felix data is that structured programming improves productivity, and that the gain is larger for large complex projects (Section 5.5). Outline the design of a controlled experiment to verify or refute this claim.

5. Discuss the difference in the results of productivity studies described in Sections 5.4 and 5.6. Can the difference be attributed to the definitions of productivity? Justify your answer.

6. Identify the three most important factors affecting productivity according to Table 5.10. Can they be assessed objectively? Are they independent from each other? Justify your answer.

7. Compare the factors identified in Problem 2 with those identified in Problem 6.

8. Using the data in Table 5.11 obtain the power fit $(L = a\bar{P}^b)$ by using least-squares for productivity as a function of the average team size.

9. Compute Table 5.13 if $\gamma = 0.9$, $l = 40$, and $L = 300$. (This is a hard problem requiring some skills not taught in this book.)

10. Compute Table 5.14 if $L = 400$ and $l = 50$. (This is a hard problem requiring some skills not taught in this book.)

6 Macro-models for Effort Estimation

The serious magical endeavor and the serious scientific endeavor are twins: one was sickly and died, the other strong and throve.
   C. S. Lewis, *The Abolition of Man*, 1947.

6.1 Introduction

A critical problem faced by all software project managers is that of accurate effort and cost estimation. This is obviously true for all projects subject to competitive bidding. If the estimated bid cost is too high compared to other bids, the contract will be lost, assuming that all other factors are equal. However, a winning bid that is too low may result in a loss to the organization. Accurate estimation is, therefore, critical to all projects of this type.

Even if the proposed project does not involve competitive bidding and the project is only for internal use in an organization, realistic cost estimation is still very important. A decision by management whether to proceed with a project may very well be based on the project leader's estimated cost, even though other factors may be taken into account. The credibility of the project manager is also at stake, especially if that person consistently underestimates software costs. Even decisions as to whether a project should be done in-house or contracted out are likely to be affected by cost and effort estimates.

Unfortunately, the critical need for accurate effort estimation models and the lack of progress in scientific approaches to this problem make many magical approaches appear strong and thriving. It is therefore important to understand the basis of all proposed models in this area, to select those that are strong in both theoretical foundations and empirical support, and to improve on them so that the models that are products of magical endeavors can be put in their proper place.

The first step in making effort and cost estimation into a scientific endeavor is to define a proper metric as discussed in Section 2.7.2. To summarize, although effort and cost are closely related, cost is not necessarily a simple function of effort. Indeed, effort is usually measured in months of the technical staff required to complete a project. Technical staff will normally include programmers, analysts, project leaders, and management directly associated with the project. A cost model must convert the technical effort estimate into a dollar cost figure, usually by computing an average salary per unit time of the technical staff involved and multiplying this average salary by the estimated effort required. It is common to use a *burdened average salary* in carrying out this computation, which might include fringe benefits and other types of overhead.

Burdened cost models must take into account many factors that are primarily environment-dependent, and are therefore not easily transportable from one organization to another. Many organizations have developed in-house cost estimation models. Of particular note are models developed by TRW [WOLV74] and Boeing [BLAC77]. In this chapter, we will be primarily concerned with effort and cost estimation models that are appropriate for *software project development*. Project development will be meant to include life-cycle phases from product design, detailed design, programming/coding, system integration, and installation or delivery. Therefore, these models exclude the requirements analysis and specification phases, as well as post-delivery maintenance. There is some hope that effort and cost models so restricted can be developed that are transportable from one organization to another.

As mentioned in Section 3.5, a large number of effort and cost models have been proposed in recent years. (For example, see [MOHA81], Section 29.7 of [BOEH81], or [BOEH84]). Unfortunately, these models generally yield substantially different estimates of cost or effort for a given project. Furthermore, these differences are too great to inspire much confidence in their general usefulness, and the formulation of some of these models involves techniques that appear magical. In [MOHA81], Mohanty compared 13 cost models using a hypothetical software system, which consisted of some 36,000 executable machine-language instructions. Insofar as possible, all of the data supplied about the system was the same for all models, including a burdened cost per person-year of $50,000. The estimated costs of the various models ranged from a low of $362,500 to a high of $2,766,667 — nearly an order of magnitude difference.

In this chapter, we will review and, wherever possible, critically evaluate a number of cost and effort models. We are actually more interested in the methodology than in the specific models. Hence, we will group models, insofar as possible, into categories depending on the method used in deriving the model. We shall use four such categories:

(1) Historical — Experiential Models

(2) Statistically-Based Models

(3) Theoretically-Based Models

(4) Composite Models

Before we discuss specific models, it is useful to develop criteria for judging the goodness of a model. The following are some of the *subjective* criteria used:

Validity — Does the model give reasonably close estimates at least on the validating database? Are measures of confidence given for the estimates? Is the model applicable to the project under consideration?

Objectivity — Are the estimates based on measurements and data that are algorithmically obtained? Do they depend on subjective factors that can vary significantly with different human estimators?

Ease of Use — Is the data needed for the model easy to obtain? Is too much data needed? Does the effort necessary to gather the needed data require an unacceptable amount of overhead? Is the information needed available early in the life cycle?

Robustness — Does just a small change in one or more input parameters lead to a relatively-greater change in the model estimate?

Transportability — Is the model so dependent on local data that it cannot be used in a different environment?

In Section 3.5, we discussed several *objective criteria* that can be used to compare the performance of models in general. The measures discussed were the coefficient of multiple determination (R^2), the relative error (RE), the mean relative error ($\overline{RE}$), the mean magnitude of the relative error ($\overline{MRE}$), prediction at level l ($PRED(l)$) and the relative root mean square error ($\overline{RMS}$). All of these are used when there is sufficient data for their computation. It is also possible to speak of *acceptable performance* of a model using some of these measures. We will say somewhat arbitrarily that a model is acceptable if it consistently produces predicted values that satisfy one or all of the following criteria:

$$\overline{MRE} \leq 0.25 \tag{6.1a}$$

$$PRED(0.25) \geq 0.75 \tag{6.1b}$$

$$\overline{RMS} \leq 0.25 \tag{6.1c}$$

Unfortunately, the three primary measures — $\overline{MRE}$, $PRED(l)$, and $\overline{RMS}$ — are often not in agreement for a set of projects because one or two may be unacceptable while one or two are acceptable. One model that we have tested on the databases described in Section 3.6 led to the measures shown in Table 3.13, which is reproduced as Table 6.1. As discussed in Section 3.5.6, it appears that the $\overline{RMS}$ measure is generally more conservative than the $\overline{MRE}$ measure. When the data set contains projects that are "heterogeneous" — of widely differing complexity and size — the simultaneous satisfaction of the two following measures is probably more reasonable:

$$\overline{MRE} \leq 0.25 \ \text{and} \ PRED(0.25) \geq 0.75 \tag{6.2}$$

Note that Equation (6.2) does not constitute an industry standard. But, as discussed in Section 3.5.6, we have chosen this criterion for acceptable performance and shall base decisions on it in the remainder of this chapter.

Table 6.1   A Comparison of Measures of Goodness

Data Set	No. Projects	$\overline{MRE}$	PRED (.25)	$\overline{RMS}$
1	23	.16	.78	.34*
2	28	.19	.75	.51*
3	15	.16	.80	.30*
4	19	.11	1.00	.13
5	17	.14	1.00	.20
6	33	.27*	.64*	.46*
7	40	.24	.73*	.95*
8	12	.28*	.83	.12

* Measure is "not acceptable."

6.2 Historical — Experiential Models

Most of the cost estimation methods commonly used today undoubtedly fall into the category of experimental models. In its crudest form, one or more local experts are asked to make judgments about the effort required, either for the total project or for modules into which the project has been divided. In doing so, the experts rely on their own experience with similar projects or modules, on intuition, and possibly on historically maintained information about completed projects. If more than one expert is involved, then a simple or weighted average of their estimates is taken as a "best" starting estimate. This is, of course, a subjective procedure that is highly dependent on the competence and objectivity of the estimators. Clearly such a procedure runs the risk of overlooking some especially difficult subtasks, which may be unique to the current project. On the other hand, an expert can incorporate into his estimate unique strengths or weaknesses of the local organization that would be difficult for a general purpose estimator, which is likely to be based on average organizational characteristics.

The expert judgment and analogy methods just described can be applied at either the overall system level or at the system-component level. These are commonly referred to as *top-down estimating* (overall system) or *bottom-up estimating* (system components). Top-down estimating focuses on the system level and has the advantage that the cost of system level functions — such as integration, documentation, and management — will more likely be taken into consideration. In bottom-up estimating, the system is broken down into modules or components. An estimate is then made for each component. The estimates are added to obtain an overall estimate after allowing for proper component integration. Bottom-up estimating has the apparent advantage that components are generally examined at a more detailed level, implying that a better estimate should follow. On the other hand, bottom-up estimating may overlook the effort required for system integration and testing. While all effort estimation techniques can theoretically be applied either as top-down or bottom-up procedures, some lend themselves more naturally to one of these procedures.

Table 6.2   An Example of the Software Cost Matrix

	Difficulty	OE	OM	OH	NE	NM	NH
	Type	1	2	3	4	5	6
1	Control	21	27	30	33	40	49
2	I/O	17	24	27	28	35	43
3	Pre/post Processor	16	23	26	28	34	42
4	Algorithm	15	20	22	25	30	35
5	Data Management	24	31	35	37	46	57
6	Time Critical	75	75	75	75	75	75

Of the historically based models that have been described in the literature, the TRW Wolverton model [WOLV74], is probably the best known. It derives the system development cost from a Software Cost matrix. An example is shown in Table 6.2. The elements of the matrix are costs per line of code (necessarily dated), which depend on software type and software difficulty. The first step in the process is to identify the types of all modules within the proposed system. Six types are proposed: Control, Input/Output, Pre/Post-Processor, Algorithm, Data Management, and Time Critical. The second step is to estimate the complexity or difficulty of the module based on a six-point scale. The scale proposed in the Wolverton model consists of old-easy (OE), old-medium (OM), old-hard (OH), new-easy (NE), new-medium (NM), and new-hard (NH). If we let C represent the cost matrix, the elements C_{ij} of C are given in dollars per line of code. These costs are derived from historically maintained data from completed projects. (This is an example of "calibration," discussed in Section 1.5.) The third step in the process is to estimate the size of each module in lines of code. If k is a module with an estimated $S_s(k)$ lines of code, and if this module is of type $i(k)$ and difficulty $j(k)$, then the cost of developing module k is

$$C(k) = S_s(k) \, C_{i(k),j(k)} \qquad (6.3)$$

The overall system cost will then be obtained by summing the cost over all modules:

$$\text{System Cost} = \sum_{\text{all modules}} C(k) \qquad (6.4)$$

While this approach does introduce a measure of objectivity, there remains a great deal of subjectivity in the entire process. Furthermore, the cost matrix must be continuously updated to reflect current costs. In addition, the influence of several other factors on cost is not adequately taken into account. For example, personnel capabilities and the use of modern programming practices do not appear to affect the cost estimates produced by this model. We could, of course, enlarge the size of the matrix C by including additional attributes that affect cost, but that would make the problem of calibration of the matrix entries much more difficult.

6.3 Statistically Based Methods

Regression analysis is often used to determine the relationship between programming effort and other parameters (see Sec. 3.2.). A large number of models, both linear and nonlinear, have been proposed for effort estimation. We will describe some of these models beginning with the linear case.

6.3.1 Linear Statistical Models

If we identify E as some unit of effort such as person-months, then a general linear model will have the form

$$E = c_0 + \sum_{i=1}^{n} c_i \, x_i \qquad (6.5)$$

where the x_i are software attributes or factors that are believed to affect software development effort. The x_i are sometimes called *cost-driver attributes*.
We have already indicated that there are literally hundreds of factors that may
affect productivity and hence effort. However, many of these factors are probably insignificant and can therefore be ignored. Other factors are strongly correlated and can be combined into a single factor, thus reducing the number of factors that need to be considered in the model (see Section 3.4.4 on factor analysis). Different models vary in the factors that they include. One of the earliest
studies of linear models was conducted at Systems Development Corporation
(SDC) in the mid-1960s [NELS66]. In this study, 104 attributes were identified
initially. Using a database of 169 projects, an attempt was made to determine
the coefficients using the least squares technique. Different combinations of
attributes were investigated, eventually resulting in a regression model based on
14 attributes and leading to the formula

$$\hat{E} = -33.63 + 9.15\, x_1 + 10.73\, x_2 + 0.51\, x_3 + 0.46\, x_4 + 0.40\, x_5$$
$$+ 7.28\, x_6 - 21.45\, x_7 + 13.5\, x_8 + 12.35\, x_9 + 58.82\, x_{10} \qquad (6.6)$$
$$+ 30.61\, x_{11} + 29.55\, x_{12} + 0.54\, x_{13} - 25.20\, x_{14}$$

where $\hat{E}$ is effort in person months. The attributes x_i and their possible values
are given in Table 6.3.

The SDC model has some major shortcomings, the most serious of which is
that, even when applied to its own validating database, the discrepancies
between projected and actual effort were quite large. In addition, the size of the
project does not enter directly as one of the factors affecting effort, even though
almost all other models assume that effort increases with program size. It is
only indirectly considered in terms of the number of subprograms (x_5).

Farr and Zagorski [FARR65] have also derived some linear models for effort
estimation. They give several equations depending upon *a priori* complexity
classification. One of their regression equations takes the form

$$\hat{E} = -188 + 2.86\, x_1 + 2.3\, x_2 + 33\, x_3 - 17\, x_4 + 10\, x_5 + x_6 \qquad (6.7)$$

where $\hat{E}$ is effort in person months. The attributes x_i and their possible values
are given in Table 6.4. In Equation (6.7), the large negative constant term will
almost surely result in negative effort estimates for small- or medium-sized projects. Furthermore, the $-17x_4$ term will certainly lead to effort underestimates
when used with programmers with a lot (say 10 years) of experience. These are
natural consequences of regression and good examples of why individual coefficients should not be interpreted independent of the other terms in the equation.

In general, linear models have not proven to be satisfactory for effort estimation. One possible explanation for this is that effort is a highly nonlinear
function of a large number of variables, and this nonlinearity cannot be adequately captured in a linear model. Furthermore, the application of a regression
model to projects outside the range of data from which it was derived is ill-

Table 6.3   Attributes in SCD Study

	Attribute	Scale or Value
x_1	Lack of Requirements	0-2
x_2	Stability of Design	0-3
x_3	Percent Math Instructions	Actual percent
x_4	Percent I/O Instructions	Actual percent
x_5	Number of Subprograms	Actual number
x_6	Programming Language	0-1
x_7	Business Application	0-1
x_8	Stand-alone program	0-1
x_9	First Program on Computer	0-1
x_{10}	Concurrent Hardware Development	0-1
x_{11}	Random Access Device Used	0-1
x_{12}	Different Host, Target Hardware	0-1
x_{13}	Number of Personnel Trips	Actual number
x_{14}	Developed by Military Organization	0-1

advised: a regression model derived from single-person projects should not be applied to team projects (and vice versa).

6.3.2 Nonlinear Statistical Models

Most of the nonlinear models that have been studied can be expressed in the form

$$E = (a + bS^c)\, m(X) \tag{6.8}$$

where S is the estimated size of the project measured in thousands of lines of code; a, b, and c, are constants usually derived by regression analysis; and $m(X)$ is an adjustment multiplier that depends on one or more cost-driver attributes denoted by the vector X. In some cases, a, b, and c may also be functions of one or more cost drivers. Since $m(X)$ can also be a complicated

Table 6.4   Attributes in Farr-Zagorski Model

	Attribute	Scale or Value
x_1	Number of instructions	In thousands
x_2	Number of miles traveled	In thousands
x_3	Number of document types delivered	Actual number
x_4	Systems programmer experience	Years
x_5	Number of display consoles	Actual number
x_6	Percentage of new instructions	Decimal equivalent

nonlinear function of several variables, Equation (6.8) is too complex to lend itself readily to standard regression analysis techniques. Instead, it is more customary to derive a base-line or nominal estimator (usually based on least squares) of the form

$$E_{nom} = a + b\,S^c$$

and then to adjust this nominal effort with the adjustment factor $m(X)$. Some typical nominal estimators that have been reported in the literature are

$$\hat{E} = 5.2\,S^{0.91} \qquad \text{(Walston-Felix [WALS77])} \qquad (6.9a)$$
$$\hat{E} = 5.5 + 0.73\,S^{1.16} \qquad \text{(Bailey-Basili [BAIL81])} \qquad (6.9b)$$
$$\hat{E} = 3.2\,S^{1.05} \qquad \text{(Boehm-Mode 1 [BOEH81])} \qquad (6.9c)$$
$$\hat{E} = 3.0\,S^{1.12} \qquad \text{(Boehm-Mode 2 [BOEH81])} \qquad (6.9d)$$
$$\hat{E} = 2.8\,S^{1.20} \qquad \text{(Boehm-Mode 3 [BOEH81])} \qquad (6.9e)$$
$$\hat{E} = 5.288\,S^{1.047}\ (\text{for } S \geq 10) \qquad \text{(Doty [HERD77])} \qquad (6.9f)$$

As these models imply, the primary factor affecting software cost estimation is assumed to be the size of the project, which is normally measured as lines of code in thousands. However, when comparing models, we must be careful that the definitions of size are compatible. The main problem is whether comment lines are included in S. The Boehm and Doty models do not consider comment lines. In the Walston-Felix model in Equation (6.9a), however, S does include comments that constitute up to 50% of the total lines of code. In addition, as discussed in Section 2.2.4, when a program contains both new code and old or adapted code, S must be adjusted to take this factor into account. Unfortunately, there is no general agreement about how to do this. Bailey and Basili, for instance, define S as the sum of the new code plus 20% of all old code, including comment lines. However, Boehm uses a much more complicated formula that takes into account the percentage of design, code, and integration changes required to adapt the old code, excluding comment lines. Similarly, we must (in comparing models) be aware of just what effort is being estimated: that is, E may represent only the effort in coding or (at the other extreme) could be the total analysis, design, coding, and testing effort.

6.3.3 Results of the Walston-Felix Study

Equation (6.9a) is derived in the standard way by assuming a relation of the form

$$E = b\,S^c \tag{6.10}$$

Taking logarithms of both sides, we obtain

$$\log E = \log b + c \log S \tag{6.11}$$

Setting $Y = \log E$, $B = \log b$, and $X = \log S$, we obtain the linear relationship

$$Y = B + cX \tag{6.12}$$

Given a database of projects for which effort in person-months and size in lines of code are available, we can now obtain by linear least squares the best values of B and c in Equation (6.12). Finally, we return to the form in Equation (6.11) using anti-logs (the exponential function) and the defining relationships for Y and X (see Section 3.4.4).

Note that of all of the size-based estimators given in Equation (6.9), only the Walston-Felix estimator in Equation (6.9a) has an exponent less than one. A model with exponent less than one provides economies of scale, while a model with exponent greater than one suggests diseconomies of scale. In software production, we can produce arguments that support both views. On large projects, for example, a manager can afford to invest in special-purpose productivity aids, such as test tools and program library aids, that tend to reduce unit cost. In addition, large organizations that are usually associated with large projects can afford both specialization of labor and more capable analyst and programmers; both of these should result in improved productivity. These factors tend to suggest economies of scale. However, as we saw in Section 5.6, large team sizes usually result in lower productivity since relatively more effort will be required for systems testing and integration, and for resolving interface issues. Whether these competing effects result in overall economies or diseconomies of scale depends on the programming environment and perhaps on the projects in a particular database. Most studies appear to support the diseconomies of scale theory.

The Walston-Felix estimator in Equation (6.9a) is not especially good even when applied to its own validating database. Measures of the accuracy of this estimator are not given in the original paper and the data for the validating database of 60 projects is not available. However, Belady and Lehman [BELA76] published data on 33 projects, listed as Set B in Table B.2, which is apparently a subset of the Walston-Felix database. When Equation (6.9a) is applied to this set, the measures of accuracy are

$$\overline{MRE} = 0.48$$

$$PRED(0.25) = 0.30$$

$$\overline{RMS} = 2.3$$

These poor results may be partly due to the great variety of the projects in the database where the actual productivities range from 30 LOC/PM to 500 LOC/PM with a median productivity of 274 LOC/PM. It suggests that estimators based on size alone cannot be expected to produce good predictions.

A second important objective of this study was to identify those variables that appeared to affect productivity most significantly, and to propose a methodology that would help to account for the observed disparity between predicted and actual effort based on size alone. This methodology is described in detail in Section 5.4. According to this methodology, the project leader produces a productivity index I from estimates of the extent to which 29 identified productivity factors are expected to apply to a new project (see Section 5.4). From Equation (5.5), an estimate of the expected productivity can then be found together with a standard error range. Finally, by using the estimated size S_s and productivity L, we can obtain an effort estimate from the formula

$$E = S_s/L \tag{6.13}$$

where L denotes productivity in LOC/PM. In effect this methodology proposes a different way to obtain an effort estimate. Note that size does not appear explicitly in arriving at the productivity estimate, even though it is known to have an important influence on productivity. As discussed in Section 5.4, this methodology has some severe theoretical limitations and, since neither details of the database nor actual model constants are given, it is also of limited practical significance.

6.3.4 Results of the Bailey-Basili Study

Bailey and Basili were interested in deriving a methodology for effort estimation that could be used at a specific location [BAIL81]. Their contention was that the constants in any effort estimator were very dependent on the environment and personnel at a given installation, and that an estimator validated on a local database would more nearly reflect the local environment. They used as a database a set of 18 projects developed at the NASA Goddard Space Flight Center.[1] These projects were fairly homogeneous — mostly scientific type and mostly written in FORTRAN.

Equation (6.9b) gives the best fit to their database. This equation is of the form

$$E = a + b \, S^c \qquad (6.14)$$

The constant a is interpreted as initial preparation time required to understand the design before programming begins. In the authors' attempt to obtain the constants a, b, and c by least squares analysis, the usual method of transforming the data by taking logarithms first is not effective. Instead, they attempt to calibrate the model by minimizing the "standard error of estimate" expressed as a ratio; they minimize

$$\text{Standard error estimate} = \sum_{i=1}^{N} \left[1 - \frac{a + b \, S_i^c}{E_i} \right]^2$$

Of course, this requires the use of nonlinear least squares regression.

For the best estimator in Equation (6.9b), which we reproduce here

$$\hat{E} = 3.5 + 0.73 \, S^{1.16} \qquad (6.15)$$

they obtain a standard error of estimate of 1.25. This standard error of estimate is a multiplicative factor. Hence, any estimate obtained from Equation (6.15) must be multiplied by 1.25 and divided by 1.25 to obtain the upper and lower bounds, respectively, of the range for one standard error. Equation (6.15) turns out to be remarkably good when applied to the 18 projects in the validating database. For example, as many as 14 (78%) of the predicted efforts fall within 25% of their actual values (that is, $PRED(0.25) = 0.78$), and the mean magnitude of relative error is only 18% ($\overline{MRE} = 0.18$).

Bailey and Basili also suggest a methodology for attempting to account for the differences between Equation (6.15), which is based on size only, and the actual effort. Actually their methodology attempts to adjust for the error ratios defined by

$$ER_{adj} = \begin{cases} R - 1 & \text{if } R > 1 \\ 1 - \dfrac{1}{R} & \text{if } R < 1 \end{cases} \qquad (6.16)$$

where $R = E/\hat{E}$, the ratio between actual (E) and predicted ($\hat{E}$) values. Note that $ER_{adj} = 0$ implies perfect prediction, $ER_{adj} > 0$ implies underprediction, and $ER_{adj} < 0$ implies overprediction. The technique uses known attributes to

---

1. This set of data appears in [BAIL81], but it is *not* a proper subset of the 19 projects given in Table 5.15.

estimate the error ratios.   After an estimate of the error ratios has been obtained, we can improve the estimated effort from the formulas

$$\hat{E}_{adj} = (1 + ER_{adj})\,\hat{E}, \qquad R > 1$$

$$\hat{E}_{adj} = \frac{\hat{E}}{|(1 + ER_{adj})|}, \qquad R < 1$$

Although we can isolate many significant attributes, Bailey and Basili point out that relative to the number of points in their database only a small number of attributes can be used in a statistical sense.   Hence, they combine significant attributes into three categories.   These are as follows:

Total Methodology Attribute (9 subattributes) — This attribute includes tree charts, top-down design, formal documentation, chief programmer teams, formal test plans, formal training, design formalisms, code reading, and unit development folders.

Cumulative Complexity Attribute (7 subattributes) — This attribute includes customer interface complexity, application complexity, program flow complexity, internal communication complexity, database complexity, external communication complexity, and customer-initiated program design changes.

Cumulative Experience Attribute (5 subattributes) — This attribute includes programmer qualifications, programmer machine experience, programmer language experience, programmer application experience, and team experience.

For each group attribute, a score is obtained by assigning to each subattribute in the group a score of 0 to 5 depending on the extent to which that subattribute was judged by project leaders to be present.   The Methodology group had a maximum score of 45 (since there were 9 subattributes in that group), the Cumulative Complexity group had a maximum score of 35, and the Cumulative Experience group had a maximum score of 25.

The methodology then consists of using multilinear least squares regression to fit the equation

$$ER_{adj} = a^*METH + b^*CPLX + c^*EXP + d \tag{6.17}$$

where *METH*, *CPLX*, and *EXP* are Methodology, Complexity, and Experience scores respectively, and are estimated by project personnel for each project; and where ER_{adj} is computed from Equation (6.16).   The error ratios obtained from Equation (6.17) can then be used to obtain an adjusted effort, which in theory should be closer to the actual effort.

A number of other techniques can be used to account for the effect of software attributes other than size.   The COCOMO models, described later, introduce a multiplier for each attribute. The nominal effort multiplied by this value leads to an adjusted effort estimate. Another technique based on least squares can be described as follows: Let V_i represent the ith attribute. Assign to each attribute a score from 0 to 5, as in [BAIL81]. Let ΔE be defined by

$$\Delta E = E - \hat{E}$$

Then using multilinear regression, we can find for a given database of projects the best least squares coefficients of the form

$$\Delta E = \alpha_0^* + \sum_{i=1}^{N} \alpha_i^* V_i \qquad (6.18)$$

For prediction purposes we first obtain $\hat{E}$ from the base-line equation (6.15) based on an estimate of size S. We then score each attribute that is believed to affect productivity, substitute in Equation (6.18) to obtain ΔE, and compute the adjusted effort using

$$\hat{E}_{adj} = \hat{E} + \Delta E$$

The methodology proposed by Bailey and Basili is worth further exploration. It seems to work well on the validating database but, as has been pointed out, this database is fairly homogeneous and does not exhibit the variability encountered in more typical data collections. Furthermore, the method does not indicate in general either how many attributes to include, or which ones are most likely to explain the differences in productivity among different projects. Finally, this methodology rules out a universal effort estimator in favor of locally derived estimators.

6.4 Theoretically Based Models

A number of recent models are based on theories of how the human mind functions during the programming process and on mathematical laws that the software development process is assumed to follow. We call such models *theoretically based*. We shall describe these three such models in this section:

(1) The Putnam Resource Allocation Model

(2) The Jensen Model

(3) The Software Science Effort Model

6.4.1 Putnam's Resource Allocation Model

The basic assumption of this model is that manpower utilization during program development follows a Rayleigh-type curve [PUTN78, PUTN84a]. A Rayleigh curve, pictured in Figure 6.1, is modeled by the differential equation

$$\dot{y} = 2\,Kat\,e^{-at^2} \tag{6.19}$$

where $\dot{y}$ is the manpower utilization rate in appropriate units, t is elapsed time, a is a parameter that affects the shape of the curve, and K is the area under the curve in the interval $[0, \infty)$. Integrating Equation (6.19) over the interval $[0, t]$, we obtain

$$y(t) = K\,(1 - e^{-at^2}) \tag{6.20}$$

where $y(t)$ is the cumulative manpower used up to time t.

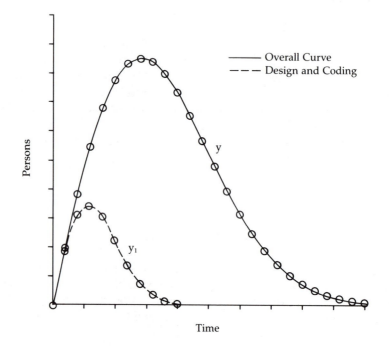

Figure 6.1   The Rayleigh manpower loading curve.

In particular, $y(\infty) = K$, which is the total life-cycle effort from the start of the project through maintenance. If we set the parameter

$$a = 1/(2\,T^2)$$

then T is the point at which the manpower utilization rate $\dot{y}$ is a maximum. Thus, the point T on the time scale should correspond very closely to the total project development time. If we substitute T for t in Equation (6.20), we can obtain an estimate of the development effort:

$$E = y(T) = .3945K. \qquad (6.21)$$

Actually if we divide the life cycle of a project into phases, then each phase can be modeled by a curve of the form given in Figure 6.1. In Figure 6.1, $\dot{y}_1(t)$ represents manpower loading during design and coding. The overall life-cycle curve for manpower utilization then becomes a composite sum of all the individual phase manpower curves.

In the Putnam theory, the *difficulty* metric

$$D = \frac{K}{T^2} \qquad (6.22)$$

plays a major role in determining software development effort. After studying a large number (about 50) of Army-developed software projects, Putnam observed that for systems that were relatively easy to develop, D tended to be small; while for systems that were relatively hard to develop, D tended to be large.[2] This led him to hypothesize that there must be a relationship between D and productivity of the form

$$L = c_1 D^\beta \qquad (6.23)$$

Average productivity L was previously defined as

$$L = \frac{S_s}{E} \qquad (6.24)$$

where S_s is lines of code produced and $E = y(T)$ is cumulative manpower used from $t = 0$ to $t = T$.

By using a nonlinear regression analysis applied to several Army projects, he found that Equation (6.23) becomes

$$L = c_1 D^{-2/3} \qquad (6.25)$$

for some constant c_1, which is not of immediate interest.

Substituting into Equation (6.24), we arrive at the software equation

$$S_s = L \cdot y(T) = c_1 \cdot D^{-\frac{2}{3}} \cdot (.3945K)$$

Using Equation (6.22), we find that

---

2. "Easy" here is related to high productivity rates.

$$S_s = C \left[\frac{K}{T^2} \right]^{-2/3} \cdot K = C \, K^{1/3} \, T^{4/3} \tag{6.26}$$

Putnam calls the constant C a *technology factor*. It reflects the effect on productivity of numerous factors such as hardware constraints, program complexity, personnel experience levels, and the programming environment. Putnam has proposed using a discrete spectrum of 20 values for C ranging from 610 to 57,314 (assuming that K is measured in programmer-years and T in years) depending on an assessment of the technology factor level that applies to the project under consideration. The constant C may also be determined from historical project data.

In order to calibrate Equation (6.26) to an historical project for which S_s, K, and T are known, Putnam suggests first solving Equation (6.26) for C to get

$$C = \frac{S_s}{K^{1/3} T^{4/3}} \tag{6.27}$$

He then searches his table of 20 discrete C-values for the one nearest C — say, $\hat{C}$. We can then solve the equation

$$\hat{K} = \frac{S_s^3}{\hat{C}^3 T^4}$$

to obtain a predicted effort $\hat{K}$. Of course, we would then expect the actual effort K to be close to the predicted effort $\hat{K}$ since $\hat{C}$ was close to C. For predictive purposes, what is needed is a precise algorithm for assessing the technology level and, hence, a value for $\hat{C}$.

Putnam has incorporated his approach to cost estimation into a software product called SLIM (Software LIfe-cycle Methodology).[3] This model embodies some relationships that deviate strongly from other models. An example of this is the trade-off relationship between total life-cycle effort K (which leads to development effort E from Equation (6.21)) and the development time T. On solving Equation (6.26) for K, we obtain

$$K = \frac{S_s^3}{C^3 T^4} = \frac{1}{T^4} \left[\frac{S_s}{C} \right]^3 \tag{6.28}$$

For a software product of a given size and fixed development environment, Equation (6.28) implies that the effort K varies inversely as the *fourth* power of the development time. For instance, if we take the constant C to be 5,000 and if we estimate the size of the project $S_s = 500,000$ LOC, then

---

3. Note that SLIM consists of many estimation aids, in addition to the equations given in this section. Other parts of SLIM are proprietary.

$$K = \frac{1}{T^4} (100)^3$$

Table 6.5 shows how the required effort in programmer-years changes as the development time measured in years changes. Thus, reducing the development time from 5 years to 4 years would increase the total effort and the cost by a factor of 2.4; reducing it to 3 years would increase them by a factor of 7.7. The unusually severe penalty imposed by reducing the development time is not greatly subscribed to by other researchers (although it is well-known that compressing development schedules leads to greater total effort). For example, Boehm estimates that a compression of the development schedule by 20% to 25%, may increase total effort by a more nominal 23% [BOEH81]. Boehm also claims that a compression of more than 25% is not feasible.

Table 6.5   Life Cycle Manpower versus Development Time

T (years)	K (programmer-years)
5.0	1600
4.0	3906
3.5	6664
3.0	12346

Putnam attempted to offer support for his use of T^4 in Equation (6.28) after examining 750 software systems [PUTN84c]. With 251 of them, it was shown that in Equation (6.28) is an acceptable model of the relationship among K, S_s, and T. However, C *was* computed using Equation (6.27); it was not the result of some independent assessment of the technology level. Therefore, the data from the 251 systems given in [PUTN84c] may be said to offer only marginal support for the "fourth power" law. Furthermore, there was no evidence offered that the same relationship holds for the other 499 systems.

The Putnam theory is based on Equation (6.26), the relationship in Equation (6.25) between productivity and difficulty D, and on the constraint

$$\frac{K}{T^3} = \alpha \tag{6.29}$$

which is essentially the magnitude of the gradient of D. The theory asserts that the constant α takes on discrete values corresponding to the difficulty of the system to be developed. For a system consisting of all new code and high complexity, the value of α would be about 7.3, while for a relatively easy system with a large amount of reused code, the value of α would be about 27.

Actually, the Putnam Model incorporates six discrete values for α ranging from 7.3 to 89.0. Equation (6.29) thus imposes a constraint on development time and the total effort. If this constraint is seriously violated, the implication is that it may not be possible to complete the project at all. In particular, if we solve Equation (6.29) for T, we get

$$T = \left[\frac{K}{\alpha} \right]^{1/3} \tag{6.30}$$

Recalling that development effort E is approximately $0.4K$ (at least for large systems) and expressing K and T in months, Equation (6.30) yields the following equation for the development time (in months):

$$T = \frac{12}{(4.8\alpha)^{1/3}} \cdot E^{1/3} = c\, E^{1/3} \tag{6.31}$$

Equation (6.31) gives the minimum development time required to complete a project as a function of the effort. This equation agrees in form with equations proposed by Walston and Felix [WALS77] and Boehm [BOEH81] For example, if $\alpha = 27$, then the development time given by Equation (6.31) becomes

$$T = 2.4E^{1/3}$$

while the Walston-Felix development time obtained by least squares is

$$T = 2.5E^{0.35}$$

and that obtained by Boehm for organic mode projects is

$$T = 2.5E^{0.38}$$

The implication of Equation (6.31) is that the development time T cannot be reduced much from that given by the equation without jeopardizing the entire project.

The Putnam Model also produces a minimum-time solution as follows. Let us assume that, from the project characteristics, we can select a technology constant C and a gradient constant α, and that an estimate of the size S_s is available. Then from Equations (6.26) and (6.29), we obtain the equations

$$K^{\frac{1}{3}} T_{\min}^{\frac{4}{3}} = \frac{S_s}{C} \tag{6.32}$$

$$\frac{K}{T_{\min}^3} = \alpha \tag{6.33}$$

These two equations can be solved simultaneously for $T_{\min}$ and for K, which is designated the minimum-time solution. For example if $S_s = 500{,}000$, $C = 5000$, and $\alpha = 14.7$, then the solution of Equations (6.32) and (6.33) is

T_{min} = 4.9 years

$K(T_{min})$ = 1731.9 person−years

Of course, stretching out the development time will reduce the effort substantially.

As originally proposed in [PUTN78], the technology factor C was a function of the environment. In a recent correspondence [PUTN84b], Putnam suggests that C should also vary with the size of the project. Thus, in attempting to calibrate the value of C to historically derived data, he would replace K by E/β, where E is development effort and β is a size-adjusting factor, whose value ranges from 0.16 for programs of size less than 18,000 lines of code to 0.39 for programs of size greater than 75,000 lines of code.

The Putnam theory was originally validated using a collection of Army projects dating back to 1973. He has refined it using data from several hundred additional projects. Our own investigation of the Putnam models leads to the following comments on their usefulness:

(1) They work reasonably well on very large systems, but seriously overestimate effort on medium- or small-size systems.

(2) They appear to seriously exaggerate the effect of schedule compression on development effort.

(3) The model relies heavily on the size and development schedule attributes, while downplaying all other attributes. The constant C in Equation (6.26) must be used to reflect all other attributes including complexity, use of modern programming practices, and personnel ability.

(4) To use this method, the user must supply a Technology Factor Level (*TF* from 0 to 22) from which a value for C is obtained. The effort estimates are quite sensitive to the choice of *TF*. A difference of 1 in the choice of *TF* might easily result in a difference of 100% or more in the effort estimates.

(5) Independent validation of productivity as a function of D of the form in Equation (6.25) on databases available to us have failed to confirm this relationship. Specifically, a least squares power fit of productivity to difficulty of the form

$$L = cD^{\beta}$$

when applied to our 6 sets of projects produced the results given in Table 6.6. We note that none of the β values in Table 6.6 are close to Putnam's proposed value of $\beta = -2/3$, except possibly for Set E. The straight average value $\beta_{avg} = -0.275$ and the weighted average value $\beta'_{avg} = -0.259$ are also substantially different from Putnam's β value.

Table 6.6   Productivity versus Difficulty

Set	No. of Projects	β
A	63	-.380
B	33	-.054
C	40	-.171
D	19	-.012
E	17	-.711
F	15	-.412

Finally, we should point out that some managers consider the Rayleigh curve as an inappropriate model for manpower buildup, especially at the beginning and at the end of the life cycle. Instead of starting from zero, most projects begin with a finite non-zero manpower level and, during maintenance, instead of tailing off to zero, a more appropriate model would diminish to a constant but non-zero level. An alternative curve called the *sech²-curve* has been proposed but has not yet received much attention [PARR80].

Equation (6.26) when rewritten in development effort units E of person-months and in development time of T months can be expressed as

$$E = C \frac{S^3}{T^4} \qquad (6.34)$$

where S is lines of code in thousands and C is a technology constant.

As already noted, Putnam suggests that C should be estimated on a project-by-project basis by estimating the various factors that are incorporated in C. For our databases, we are given only E, S, and T. The additional information needed to estimate C is not available. A reasonable way to obtain an estimate of C is to apply least squares regression to the projects in a given collection. Since the projects in a given collection were all developed at the same installation during the same time period, a value of $\hat{C}$ obtained by least squares should approximately reflect the environment in which they were developed. It is true that a least squares-derived $\hat{C}$ cannot reflect some of the factors that affect the technology level — for example, the inherent complexity of each project. However, it is the best that we can do with the information available to us. Moreover, while we do not expect superb results from this least-squares-derived model, we do expect the estimates of effort to be reasonable approximations of the actual effort.

Table 6.7   Performance of Putnam Model

Set	No. Projects	$\overline{MRE}$	PRED (.25)
A	63	1.04	.06
B	33	.88	.06
C	40	.83	.05
D	19	.78	.05
E	17	.78	.24
F	15	.97	.13

We have applied Equation (6.34) to several databases (see Section 3.6.6 for some characteristics of these databases). The results are given in Table 6.7. The results show uniformly poor performance for this model regardless of the measure of accuracy used. Independent investigations such as [WING82] seem to substantiate this poor performance.

6.4.2 Jensen's Model

Jensen [JENS84] has recently proposed a model that is very similar to Putnam's Model. However, it attempts to soften the effect of schedule compression on effort. Jensen proposed using the software equation

$$S_s = C_{te}TK^{1/2} \tag{6.35}$$

in place of Equation (6.26), where Jensen, as in the Putnam model, calls C_{te} the *effective technology constant*. However, Jensen proposed to arrive at C_{te} in a somewhat different manner than Putnam. He computes

$$C_{te} = C_{tb}\prod_{i=1}^{13} f_i$$

where C_{tb} is the basic technology constant and f_i is a measure of the ith environmental adjustment factor. The environmental adjustment factors are similar to those used by Boehm [BOEH81] and described in Section 5.7. They take into account the product, personnel, and computer factors that affect effort. Jensen's model also includes the minimum time constraint relation, as given in Equation (6.29). While we cannot test the procedure for determining the effective technology constant C_{te}, we can test Jensen's model on our databases as we did the Putnam model. First, we solve Equation (6.35) for K to obtain

$$K = \frac{S_s^2}{C_{te}^2 T^2}$$

Expressing K, which is life-cycle effort, in terms of development effort E and using S (thousands of lines of code) instead of S_s, we arrive at the effort equation

$$E = c \frac{S^2}{T^2} \tag{6.36}$$

which corresponds to Equation (6.34). The constant c incorporates the effective technology constant as well as scale modifications. Again for our database, where environmental factors are not given, we can attempt to obtain c using a least squares technique. This procedure should result in a value of c^* for each data base, which reflects the average basic technology constant for the developing organization. Using Equation (6.36) with c^*, we can then predict effort and obtain measures of accuracy for this model. The results are given in Table 6.8. The performance is slightly better than that of the Putnam model, but is still very poor.

Table 6.8   Performance of Jensen Model

Set	No. Projects	$\overline{MRE}$	PRED (.25)
A	63	1.01	0.10
B	33	0.76	0.06
C	40	.76	0.10
D	19	0.63	0.21
E	17	.70	0.24
F	15	0.80	0.33

6.4.3   The Software Science Effort Macro Model

The Software Science basic and composite metrics were defined in Chapter 2. In Section 4.3.1 and those that follow, the time equation (4.1) was introduced and its application to small one-person projects was discussed. In this chapter, we are interested in applying, if possible, the Software Science time estimator to large programs. As originally derived, the time equation was assumed to hold under the following conditions:

(1) A complete unambiguous statement of the algorithm to be implemented is available.

(2) The programmer is fluent in the language employed.

(3) The programmer works alone on the program.

(4) The programmer uses a high degree of concentration.

(5) The effort measured includes the time required to study the algorithm specifications, the time to design and implement the algorithm, and the time to test the implementation for reasonable errors.

For a large project involving a team of programmers, some of these conditions will obviously be violated. Nevertheless, we try to modify the effort/time equations so as to apply them to large projects. Another objective in this section is to recast the effort equation (2.33) in a form more suitable for *a priori* effort estimation.

Most effort estimators use program size as the primary attribute for *a priori* estimation. The Software Science E estimator can be adapted to use size in the following way. Let us assume that the operators and operands are equal so that $\eta_1 = \eta_2 = \eta/2$. Furthermore, we assume that the totality of operators and operands are equal so that $N_1 = N_2 = N/2$. Then starting with

$$E = \frac{\eta_1}{2} \cdot \frac{N_2}{\eta_2} \cdot N \log_2 \eta$$

we obtain

$$E = \frac{1}{4} N^2 \log_2 \eta \qquad (6.37)$$

Equation (6.37) can be used for *a priori* effort estimation if the size of a project S_s in LOC can be estimated. The steps involved in doing so follow:

Step 1 — Compute

$$N = k \times S_s \qquad (6.38)$$

where k is a constant that for each language gives the average number of operands and operators per line of code. Examples are $k \approx 7$ for FORTRAN, and $k \approx 5$ for PL/S [SMIT80].

Step 2 — Solve the equation

$$N = \eta \log_2 \frac{\eta}{2} \tag{6.39}$$

for the vocabulary η. This can be done by an iterative process such as the secant method.[4]

Step 3 — Compute $\log \eta$ and then use (6.37) to find E.

The assumptions used to arrive at Equation (6.37) are seldom exactly met in practice so that we must view the effort estimator with considerable skepticism. The net result of these assumptions is that the estimator generally tends to over-estimate actual effort. This fact, together with our desire to obtain an even simpler formula for E as a function of size, has led us to approximate $\log_2 \eta$ by N^α, in which case Equation (6.38) becomes

$$E \approx \frac{1}{4} N^{2+\alpha} \tag{6.40}$$

To find a value for α, we have constructed Table 6.9, which contains the vocabulary η within a reasonable range and the corresponding values of $\log_2 \eta$, N, and α.

Table 6.9   Values of α in $N^\alpha = \log_2 \eta$

η	$\log_2 \eta$	$N = \eta \log \eta/2$	α
64	6	320	.31
128	7	768	.29
256	8	1792	.28
512	9	4096	.26
1024	10	9216	.25

This range of vocabulary sizes can accommodate most reasonably sized modules. The values of α can be seen to change very little within this range. If we take the median value of $\alpha = 0.28$, then Equation (6.40) becomes

$$E \approx \frac{1}{4} N^{2.28} \tag{6.41}$$

---

4. See, for example, *Elementary Numerical Analysis,* by Conte, S. D. and C. de Boor. New York: McGraw-Hill, 1981.

If we set $N = k \times S_s$, then we obtain an expression for E directly as a function of program size in LOC:

$$E \approx \frac{1}{4} k^{2.28} \cdot S_s^{2.28} = c \cdot S_s^{2.28}$$

Most of the effort estimators discussed so far have exponents of size much smaller than 2.28. The very large exponent of N in Equation (6.41) suggests that E will *over-estimate* effort if applied directly on large projects. However, applying E in this manner would violate a primary condition of the Software Science theory — namely that the theory applies to small, one-person programming tasks. The proper use of the Software Science E estimator on large projects (whichever form is used) requires first subdividing the project into modules of reasonable size, then applying the E estimator to each module, and finally adding the module estimators to get the overall project estimate. It is always true that if the basic estimator is of the form $E = a \, S^b$, $b > 1$ and if we divide a project P into m modules M_i of length S_i so that $\sum_{i=1}^{m} S_i = S$, then[5]

$$\sum_{i=1}^{m} E(M_i) < E(P)$$

For example, we now consider the use of Equation (6.37) as an effort estimator and apply it to a program P of Software Science length $N = 10,000$. We divide this program into m equal modules, each of size N/m. The total effort will then be m times the effort required to write one module of size N/m. The results for different values of m are given in Table 6.10.

Table 6.10 Variations in Total Effort with Module Size $\left[\frac{N}{m}\right]$ where $N = 10,000$

m	N/m	$E(N/m)$	$E(P) = m \, E(N/m)$	$E(M)$ in PM
5	2000	8,622,911	43,114,555	4.3
10	1000	1,828,403	18,284,029	1.8
20	500	406,778	8,135,560	.81
25	400	249,942	6,248,550	.62
40	250	89,500	3,580,000	.36
50	200	54,920	2,746,000	.27

---

5. A similar discussion appeared in Section 4.3.2.

The third and fourth columns give effort in elementary mental discriminations. These can be converted into person-months by dividing by 10,000,000.[6] It is evident that the total effort drops dramatically as the number of modules increases. If the program being considered was written in FORTRAN, then $N = 10,000$ corresponds to a program with approximately 1333 lines of code. On a qualitative basis, $m = 50$ gives an obviously low effort estimate of 0.27 PM, while $m = 5$ gives a rather high estimate of 4.3 PM. This leaves open the question of deciding what the most appropriate module size should be. We will discuss this question later, but we should point out now that, when a program is modularized, additional effort will be required for intermodule coordination so that the total effort will be greater than that indicated in Table 6.10.

The theory of Software Science initially captured the imaginations of many researchers since it proposed what appeared to be a sound theoretical basis for understanding the human mental processes involved in programming. As mentioned in Section 2.6, subsequent research [COUL83] has cast considerable doubt on the psychological assumptions underlying the theory. Furthermore, the weight of empirical evidence that initially seemed to support the theory at least for small projects tends to dispute the validity of Software Science E as an effort estimator on more realistic projects.

6.5   A Composite Model — COCOMO

Composite models incorporate a combination of analytic equations, statistical data fitting (either with linear or non-linear models), and expert judgment. Putnam's resource allocation model [PUTN78, PUTN84a], although based on the Rayleigh curve, is in effect a composite model. Another such composite model is the RCA PRICE S model [FREI79]. PRICE S uses project size, type, and complexity as primary attributes to produce a top-down estimate of the cost of system functions for each phase of the project. The best known of all composite models is COCOMO (COnstructive COst MOdel) [BOEH81, BOEH84], which is our focus in this section.

COCOMO is the most complete and thoroughly documented of all models for effort estimation. It provides specific formulas for estimating the development time schedule, overall development effort, effort breakdown by phase and activity, and maintenance effort.

There are three levels of COCOMO: Basic, Intermediate, and Detailed.

---

6. $10{,}000{,}000 \approx 18 \dfrac{\text{e.m.d.}}{\text{second}} \times 60 \dfrac{\text{second}}{\text{minute}} \times 60 \dfrac{\text{minute}}{\text{hour}} \times 40 \dfrac{\text{hour}}{\text{week}} \times 4 \dfrac{\text{week}}{\text{month}}$

The development effort estimation equations are of the form

$$E = a_i \, S^{b_i} \, m(X) \tag{6.42}$$

where S is source lines of code in thousands excluding comments and $m(X)$ is a composite multiplier that depends on 15 cost driver attributes. The principal cost driver in Equation (6.42) is, thus, program size. Three development modes are identified by Boehm and the constant a_i changes with the mode and level, whereas the constant b_i changes only with the mode. These modes and the values of a_i and b_i for the Basic and Intermediate levels are shown in Table 6.11.

Table 6.11 COCOMO Parameters

	Basic		Intermediate	
Mode	a_i	b_i	a_i	b_i
Organic	2.4	1.05	3.2	1.05
Semidetached	3.0	1.12	3.0	1.12
Embedded	3.6	1.20	2.8	1.20

Projects of the *organic mode* are characterized by being relatively small in size, requiring little innovation, having relaxed delivery requirements, and being developed in a stable in-house environment. Projects of the *embedded mode* are characterized by being relatively large, needing to operate within tight constraints, and having a high degree of hardware and customer interface complexity, rigid requirements, and greater need for innovation. Projects of the *semidetached* mode fall somewhere in between the organic and embedded modes.

In Basic COCOMO, $m(x) = 1$ for each cost driver x; in Intermediate COCOMO, they are assigned various values. The 15 recommended cost driver attributes are grouped into four categories as described in Section 5.7.

Complete definitions of each cost driver are given in [BOEH81]. After defining each driver attribute, ratings are assigned to each cost driver on a five- or six-point scale from Very Low to Very High or to Extra High, depending on the degree to which that attribute applies to a given project. A numerical value is then assigned to each rating for each attribute.

Multipliers for the three cost drivers RELY, MODP, and SCED, for example, are given in Table 6.12 (see Section 5.7 for the definitions). The factor $m(X)$ in Equation (6.42) is simply the product of all 15 cost driver multipliers. Of course, $m(X)=1$ if all cost drivers are given a nominal rating. The productivity range figure is obtained by taking the ratio of the highest multiplier to the lowest multiplier for each attribute.

Table 6.12   Example Cost Drivers in COCOMO

Rating	RELY	MODP	SCED
Very Low	.75	1.24	1.23
Low	.88	1.10	1.08
Nominal	1.00	1.00	1.00
High	1.15	.91	1.04
Very High	1.40	.82	1.10
Productivity Range	1.87	1.51	1.23
|high-low|	0.65	0.42	0.23

On the surface, the use of Equation (6.42) for project-effort estimation appears simple enough. After a thorough requirements analysis, the project is assigned to one of the three modes, the size S of the project is estimated, and a nominal effort estimate is obtained using the equation

$$E_{nom} = a_i \, S^{b_i}$$

for the appropriate values of a_i and b_i. From the problem requirements, and a knowledge of the programming team and the programming environment, each of the cost driver attributes is given a rating. Numerical values are assigned to each cost driver from the table of multiplier values given in [BOEH81] and [BOEH84]. The product of these multipliers then yields the effort adjustment factor $m(X)$ and the adjusted estimated effort is then computed from Equation (6.42). While the procedure is fairly straightforward, we can expect considerable variation in practice because both the size of the project and the attribute ratings (the result of a subjective process) will vary considerably from one analyst to another.

In addition to development effort estimates, COCOMO also provides equations for nominal development time in months, as well as a breakdown of effort by life-cycle phase and activity. For example, the development schedule equations, which also vary by mode are

$$T = 2.5 \, E^{0.38} \text{ (Organic Mode)}$$

$$T = 2.5 \, E^{0.35} \text{ (Semidetached Mode)}$$ (6.43)

$$T = 2.5 \, E^{0.32} \text{ (Embedded Mode)}$$

The schedule equations generally agree in form with similar equations obtained by Walston and Felix [WALS77], and Putnam [PUTN78].

6.5.1   Validation of the COCOMO Model

The COCOMO equations were derived from a database of 63 projects, which were completed over a period of 15 years from 1964 to 1979 primarily at TRW Systems, Inc. The projects were written in several different languages, including assembly language, FORTRAN, COBOL, PL/1, and Jovial. The projects vary in size from about 2,000 to about 1,000,000 lines of code (excluding comments), and they vary in type from business and scientific applications to systems, control, and supervisory types. Productivity in lines of code per person-month ranged from a low of 28 to a high of 1250. Cost driver attribute ratings were assigned to each project using expert judgment based on a Delphi-type technique [BOEH81].[7] These ratings are subject to considerable error, especially when applied to projects completed many years ago, for which complete documentation must not have been available.

The equations derived in COCOMO were not obtained directly from a least squares regression method. Instead the author used a combination of experience, results of other cost estimation models, the subjective opinion of experienced software managers, and trial-and-error to arrive at initial model parameters based on a subset of the entire database. These initial parameter values were further refined, "tuned," and calibrated using additional projects from the database.

The performance of COCOMO on its own validating database is shown in Table 6.13. Basic COCOMO does not perform well even when applied to its own database. Intermediate (1) does much better, while Intermediate (2) gives excellent results. In addition to the 15 cost drivers described earlier, Intermediate (2) introduces another cost driver called RVOL (Requirements Volatility). This measures the changes in problem requirements after programming has begun. This cost driver multiplier has values ranging from 0.91 to 1.62. Based on these measures of accuracy, we can conclude that Intermediate COCOMO yields excellent results, at least when applied to its own validating database. This is especially true when we consider the extreme ranges of productivity evidenced in this database.

---

7. In a Delphi technique several people prepare estimates independently and are then told how their estimates compare to those of the others. Next, they are allowed to alter their estimates. This leads to an iterative technique in which many of the estimates finally converge to a narrower range from which a single value may be chosen.

Table 6.13   Performance of COCOMO on Its Own Database

Model	$\overline{MRE}$	PRED (.20)	PRED (.25)
Basic COCOMO	.60	.25	.27
Intermediate (1)	.22	.52	.63
Intermediate (2)	.19	.67	.76

6.5.2 Evaluation of the COCOMO Model

Any model, regardless of how it is derived, should be tested on an independent database. To our knowledge, there have been no published reports on the performance of COCOMO as applied to independent databases. A major problem in attempting to do so is that the information needed to use COCOMO is seldom available in published data. Intermediate COCOMO requires, as we have seen, a collection of 15 or 16 parameters in addition to the size. Furthermore, the mode parameter has 3 choices and each of the 16 attribute parameters has a choice of 4 to 6 ratings. The large number of parameter choices provides the model with great flexibility and range, but at the same time with great volatility. From the numerical values for cost driver attributes provided in [BOEH81], for example, we can calculate that max $m(X) = 72$ while min $m(X) = 0.088$; if we assign to each cost driver its maximum possible value, the adjusted multiplier will be 72. Thus, if for a given project $E_{nom} = 100$ PM, the model could predict an estimated effort of as much as 7200 PM or as low as 8.8 PM. The maximum estimated effort is more than 800 times the minimum estimated effort![8] The extreme range of possible estimates is both a strength and a weakness of the model. We might also consider the presence of 16 parameters a practical weakness as well — requiring the manager to supply a large amount of information in order to obtain an effort estimate.

In [MOHA81], Mohanty applied 13 different cost estimation models to a hypothetical project of size 36,000 lines of code and obtained cost estimates ranging from \$362,500 to \$2,766,667. If we assume that the project falls in the semidetached mode, Intermediate COCOMO gives the nominal effort

$$E_{nom} = 3.0 \ (36)^{1.12} = 166 \ PM$$

---

8. The range is from 117 to 0.081 if RVOL is included. The ratio is then 1447 to 1, compared with 800 to 1 if RVOL is not included.

and using a cost per person-month of ($50,000/12), we obtain an estimated nominal cost of $691,781. This fits comfortably in the middle of the range obtained by Mohanty. Not enough information is given to determine most of the cost driver attribute ratings but, recalling the 800:1 ratio discussed earlier, it is evident that this nominal estimate could easily fall outside of the Mohanty range depending on cost driver values.

This discussion leads us to a first major criticism of COCOMO. The model involves *too many* parameters that must be estimated. A simpler yet perhaps equally useful model could be constructed based on 3 or 4 parameters by combining some of the attributes into a single cost driver. For example, the essence of personnel experience could be captured in a single overall personnel attribute cost driver. The loss of precision in using one cost driver in place of 5 can probably be kept well within the accuracy inherent in the model itself. Furthermore, it is likely that some of the cost drivers are highly correlated in practice, if not in theory. Further possible combined attributes might be the development mode and the attribute CPLX, and the attributes TOOL and MODP (see Section 5.7 for the definitions).

A second major criticism concerns the way in which the cost driver values are obtained. The author admits that all constants in his models were obtained *empirically*, which implies that they were tuned to give good results on his database. It is an open question whether the same constants will do equally well on another database. If the parameters must be tuned to fit different environments, then the model loses a great deal of its attraction as a universal effort estimator. These remarks apply particularly to the multipliers assigned to the different cost driver ratings. The multipliers assigned to the RELY attribute, for example, are 0.75, 0.88, 1.00, 1.15, and 1.40. It is hard to believe that the precision of two significant digits is meaningful considering all of the other possible errors in models of this type. For example, estimating the size alone is subject to errors of 50% or more (see Section 4.3.8), and errors of this magnitude will swamp any minor changes in the multipliers. Furthermore, the tradeoffs among multiplier assignments are so complex that someone else using a different database would almost surely come up with an entirely different set of multiplier values.

6.5.3 Results of Basic COCOMO Applied to Other Databases

As already noted, it is impossible to test Intermediate COCOMO on other databases because the detailed information about the 16 cost driver ratings is simply not available. We may be able to test Basic COCOMO, however, since this level requires knowledge only of the size of the project and the mode. In our database, the size is given, although mode information is not. It is reasonable to expect a correlation between mode and observed project productivity, an available quantity. A reasonable way to determine the mode of a project based on observed productivity is given in Table 6.14, where *L* means productivity.

The use of productivity to determine a mode can only be applied to historical data collections. It cannot be used in predictive models.

Table 6.14   Mode versus Productivity

Mode	Productivity Range
Organic	$L > 350$ LOC/PM
Semi-detached	$100 < L \leq 350$ LOC/PM
Embedded	$L \leq 100$ LOC/PM

Using Table 6.14, we can now apply Basic COCOMO to any database for which the size S, the actual effort E, and the productivity L are given. The performances of Basic COCOMO on its own database (Set A) and other databases are given in Table 6.15. The results in Table 6.15 show that the correspondence between mode and productivity given in Table 6.14 is favorable to Basic COCOMO since it produces somewhat better results than Boehm's own mode classification scheme.

Table 6.15   Performance of Basic COCOMO

Set	No. Projects	$\overline{MRE}$	$PRED$ (.25)
A	63	.48	.27
B	33	.30	.55
C	40	.45	.43
D	19	.61	.32
E	17	2.12	.18
F	15	.22	.67

We see that the model performs extremely poorly on Set E and reasonably well only on Sets B and F. While there may be explanations for poor performance (such as some of the databases include comment lines in the line of code count, while others do not), nevertheless these results demonstrate how difficult it is to apply this model successfully in the absence of much more detailed information.

6.5.4 A Modification of COCOMO Parameters

As already noted, the COCOMO parameters were obtained by a process of calibration using the projects in its own database. The parameter values are not necessarily the "best possible" since they are not derived from a formal mathematical process. Indeed, if we look at the model parameters for Intermediate COCOMO given in Table 6.11, we note that the scalar coefficients a_i decrease as the mode complexity increases. This behavior seems counterintuitive, and suggests that systematic changes in the model parameters might lead to better performance. We present here an example of a modified set of formulas, discovered through a process of calibration, which does perform better than the original COCOMO formulas. These are

$$E = 2.6 \; S^{1.08} \; m(X) \quad \text{(Organic Mode)}$$

$$E = 2.9 \; S^{1.12} \; m(X) \quad \text{(Semidetached Mode)}$$

$$E = 2.9 \; S^{1.20} \; m(X) \quad \text{(Embedded Mode)}$$

where $m(X)$ represents the same multiplier used in Intermediate (2).

The performance of these modified formulas on the COCOMO database yields $PRED(0.25) = 50/63 = 0.79$ and $\overline{MRE} = 0.19$, which is a slight improvement over the Intermediate (2) model presented in Table 6.13 ($PRED(0.25) = 48/63 = 0.76$ and $\overline{MRE} = 0.19$). It may be possible to find another set of parameters that performs even better, although any expectation of significant improvement is unrealistic.

6.6 A Composite Model — SOFTCOST

A number of organizations that have attempted to use existing software cost estimation models have generally found them individually to be unsatisfactory. Some models seemed to lack adaptability to different environments or to a broad range of application areas. Other models emphasized particular productivity factors, while neglecting the effect of others. Thus, different models have different strengths and weaknesses. It appears to make sense to produce a composite model that incorporates the best features of the best-known models. This was the stated goal of research initiated at Jet Propulsion Laboratory under the direction of R. C. Tausworthe. They produced a model that was later implemented as a program called SOFTCOST [TAUS81]. The SOFTCOST model utilizes 7 factors from the GRC model [CARR79] and the 29 factors from the Walston-Felix study [WALS77]. In addition, a modified Rayleigh-Putnam model is used to check on the feasibility of resource estimates and resource allocation.

The model contains 68 parameters relating to productivity, duration, staffing level, documentation, and computer resources. The SOFTCOST program is interactive and can deduce these parameter values from some 47 questions asked of the user.

Output of the program consists of development effort and duration broken down into a standard Work Breakdown Structure, together with variances in each estimate. In addition, it produces estimates of the staffing level, pages of documentation as a function of size, and CPU requirements as a function of size.

The SOFTCOST model assumes a linear relationship between size and effort:

$$E = S/P_1 \tag{6.44}$$

where S is defined as total equivalent lines of executable code in thousands and P_1 is the average productivity rate in KLOC/PM. Thus, given a program of estimated size S, this model focuses on estimating the average productivity rate P_1 using various technology and environmental factors. The model makes the assumption that the productivity rate P_1 for projects of the same size may vary by as much as 50:1.

The productivity rate has the form

$$P_1 = P_0 A_1 A_2 \tag{6.45}$$

where P_0 is a constant, A_1 is a multiplicative factor that incorporates 6 factors judged by the GRC Model to be significant [CARR79], and A_2 incorporates the 29 factors judged by the Walston-Felix model to be significant [WALS77].

The productivity adjustment factors taken from the GRC model include the following:

   (1)   A language adjustment factor, A_{lang}

   (2)   A timing-critical adjustment factor, A_{t-crit}

   (3)   A capacity-critical adjustment factor, A_{c-crit}

   (4)   A difficulty (complexity) adjustment factor, A_{diff}

   (5)   A requirements and design stability adjustment factor, A_{stable}

   (6)   An experience adjustment factor, A_{exp}

These are combined to produce the A_1 factor by the formula

$$A_1 = [(1 + A_{lang} + A_{t-crit} + A_{c-crit})A_{diff}A_{stable}A_{exp}]^w \tag{6.46}$$

The exponent w is chosen so as to produce a 50:1 spread in the productivity rate P_1. Explicit formulas are also given for computing each of the A measures required in Equation (6.46).

The second productivity adjustment factor A_2 in Equation (6.45) is derived from the factors in the Walston-Felix study and takes the form

$$A_2 = \exp \left[w \sum_{i=1}^{N} x_i \log \frac{P_{hi(i)}}{P_{lo(i)}} \right] \tag{6.47}$$

where $P_{hi(i)}/P_{lo(i)}$ is the ratio of productivities derived in the Walston-Felix study for the ith factor and x_i takes on the values 1, 0, or -1.

The model requires a total of 68 parameter values. The program SOFTCOST arrives at these parameters through answers supplied by the user to a series of questions. Tausworthe admits that the accuracy of the model is at present unknown. Apparently, it has not yet been applied to any significant database for which sufficiently detailed information is available.

The SOFTCOST Model differs by comparison with the COCOMO Model for the following reasons:

(1) SOFTCOST has not been tested on any significant database as COCOMO has. A user can, therefore, have very little confidence in the accuracy of the model.

(2) SOFTCOST is unnecessarily complicated. Not only does it require a total of 68 parameter values, but the parameter values are used in different ways to determine productivity adjustment factors. By contrast, COCOMO requires about 17 parameter values and all of them are treated in essentially the same way.

(3) The SOFTCOST approach of taking the union of adjustment factors from different models is very unsatisfying. Many of the factors from the GRC model must be highly correlated with similar factors from the Walston-Felix model. Introducing redundancy in these adjustment factors does not guarantee performance improvement.

(4) SOFTCOST assumes a linear relationship between effort and size; COCOMO assumes a nonlinear relationship.

(5) SOFTCOST is designed to accommodate productivities that vary by a factor of 50:1; COCOMO appears capable of permitting variations of up to 800:1.

The SOFTCOST Model has been implemented to run on the HP3000. It is currently undergoing additional testing and calibration, and it is hoped that it will become a useful tool for project managers.

6.7 Effect of Team Size on Effort — The COPMO Model

In this section we consider a new model known as COPMO, that includes metrics concerning project size and programming team size. This work has led to a general effort model with potential for explaining, and even predicting, the cost of software development. Furthermore, a set of models based on COPMO might be useful when specific information is known about the complexity of the software to be developed.

6.7.1 The Interchangeability of Personnel and Time

Many project managers facing a tight development schedule have discovered that schedules do *not* shrink in proportion to the number of programmers assigned to the project. As the manager of the colossal OS/360 project, Brooks proposed the following popular law based on his experience [BROO75]:

> *Adding manpower to a late software project makes it later.*

The intuitive argument supporting the law is that, when tasks are partitioned among several programmers, the effort associated with the coordination of the programmers must be taken into account. This additional effort may include programmer training so that new members may be assimilated into the existing team, and the necessary communication between team members so that the parts they create individually may function as an integral unit later. As discussed in Section 5.8, if a team of P programmers is considered as a graph of P vertices, the number of communication paths between programmers range from $O(P)$ for a tree-structured team organization, to $O(P^2)$ for an organization where each programmer is expected to coordinate with each other programmer on the team. Two examples showing the impact of this additional effort on the interchangeability of personnel and time is shown in Figure 6.2. The lower curve corresponds to a "perfectly partitionable task" requiring no communication among programmers. For example, if such a task required 18 months for one programmer to complete, then 9 and 6 months would be required for 2 and 3 programmers, respectively. The total effort in any case is 18 PM. The upper curve corresponds to a "task with complex interrelationships." Even though some reduction of time is possible as programmers are added, adding more of them beyond a certain point would make the coordination effort a dominating factor, and would require more total effort *and* more time. Therefore, it is important to recognize this effect so that project managers will not attempt the impossible

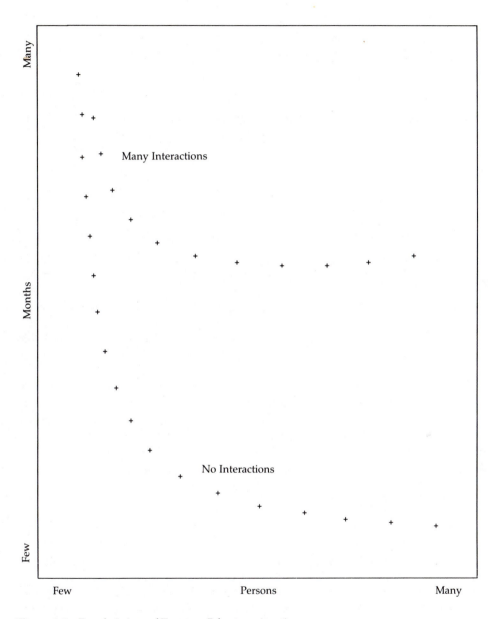

Figure 6.2 Brooks' view of T versus P for two situations.

and incur unnecessary costs. However, the pragmatic use of this law is limited due to its *qualitative* nature.

One quantification of this law is provided by Putnam's model (Section 6.4.1). Since the number of programmers on the project varies with time as shown in Figure 6.1, we can only refer to the *average* personnel level defined as

$$\bar{P} = E / T \tag{6.48}$$

The software equation as expressed in Equation (6.34) can be used to relate the tradeoff between personnel and time *quantitatively* as

$$\bar{P} = C \frac{S^3}{T^5} \tag{6.49}$$

or

$$T = C^{1/5} \frac{S^{3/5}}{\bar{P}^{1/5}} \tag{6.50}$$

Figure 6.3 shows the basic behavior of Equation (6.50) when S is fixed, with the lower curve the same as that for the perfectly partitionable tasks shown in Figure 6.2. Although it appears that the development schedule can be arbitrarily compressed at a tremendous cost, the difficulty constraint in Equation (6.29) stops the decrease at a certain point. (The constraint curve is shown as small circles in Figure 6.3.) Thus, this model fails to support the observed relationship between time and people for complex tasks, shown as the upper curve in Figure 6.2.

Intermediate COCOMO (Section 5.7 and 6.5) addresses the schedule compression issue through the cost driver SCED. Its values depend on the amount of compression (or expansion), defined as $T/\hat{T}$, where T is the actual development duration and $\hat{T}$ is the nominal duration. The SCED values and $T / \hat{T}$ are given in Table 6.16.

If we factor out SCED from Equation (6.42), then $E = E' \times \text{SCED}$, where E' is the effort estimate excluding the SCED multiplier. Since $E = T \times \bar{P}$, Equation (6.42) becomes

$$T = \frac{E' \times \text{SCED}}{\bar{P}} \tag{6.51}$$

The curve represented by the circles in Figure 6.4 shows the basic behavior when E' is fixed; that is, S and all multipliers except SCED are fixed. Again, the lower curve is the same as that for the perfectly partitionable tasks shown in Figure 6.2. The scale is changed so that the differences can be seen more clearly. Like Putnam's model, Intermediate COCOMO does not support the behavior of complex tasks, shown as the upper curve of Figure 6.2.

In the search of an analytic model that supports the behavior of both curves quantitatively, Thebaut [THEB83] developed a unique model that incorporates average team size (denoted by $\bar{P}$) and program size in thousands of lines of code (denoted by S). Hereafter, we will refer to this model as *COPMO*

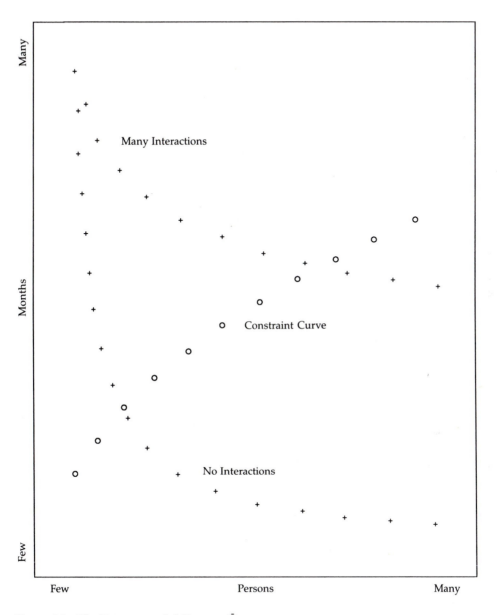

Figure 6.3 The Putnam model: T versus $\bar{P}$.

(COoperative Programming MOdel). This effort model is of the additive non-linear type

Table 6.16   The Cost Driver SCED in COCOMO

SCED Value	$T/\hat{T}$
(impossible)	< 0.75
1.23	0.75
1.08	0.85
1.00	1.00
1.04	1.30
1.10	≥ 1.60

$$E = E_p(S) + E_c(\bar{P}) \tag{6.52}$$

where E is the overall effort, $E_p(S)$ is the effort required by one or more persons working independently on modules requiring no interaction with other modules, and $E_c(\bar{P})$ is the effort required to coordinate the development process with other programmers on the team. The average full-time equivalent team size is $\bar{P}$. In practice, if the total effort E in person-months and the duration of a project T in months are known, then $\bar{P}$ is computed using Equation (6.48). For $E_p(S)$, the model assumes the form

$$E_p(S) = a + b\,S$$

and, for $E_c(\bar{P})$, a model of the form

$$E_c(\bar{P}) = c\,\bar{P}^d$$

Thus, the model can be expressed as

$$E = a + b\,S + c\,\bar{P}^d \tag{6.53}$$

This four-parameter, additive, nonlinear model does not lend itself readily to direct least squares analysis. Instead, Thebaut proposes a two-stage least squares process. In the first stage, he determines the parameters a and b in $\hat{E}_p(S)$ by using only those projects from the database for which $\bar{P} \approx 1$. With a and b fixed, he now proceeds to a second stage where he uses least squares to determine c and d by fitting

$$E - \hat{E}_p(S) = c\,\bar{P}^d \tag{6.54}$$

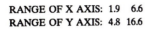

RANGE OF X AXIS: 1.9   6.6
RANGE OF Y AXIS: 4.8   16.6

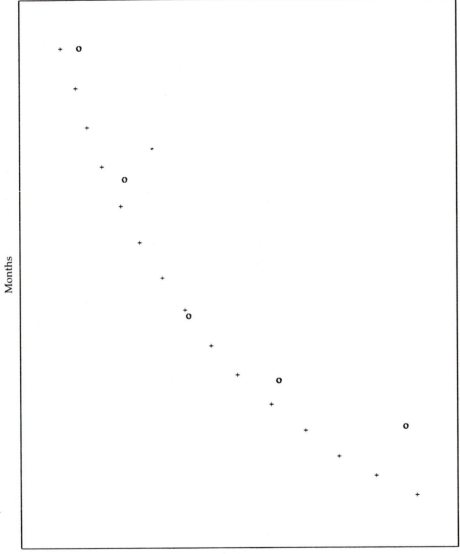

Figure 6.4   Intermediate COCOMO: T versus $\bar{P}$.

to all projects for which $\bar{P} \geq 2$. In effect, the model assumes that $\hat{E}_p(S)$ will *underestimate* actual effort as the team size grows, and that the additive term $c\,\bar{P}^d$ can be used to compensate for this underestimate. Note that $\hat{E}_p(S)$ is a minimum effort estimator for a project of size S. If a project of size S requires less than $\hat{E}_p(S)$ effort, it will not be possible to adjust this model to reflect that situation.

The model can be rewritten as

$$E = \begin{cases} a + bS, & \bar{P} \leq 1 \\ a + bS + c\bar{P}^d, & \bar{P} > 1 \end{cases} \qquad (6.55)$$

Note that COPMO is not continuous when $\bar{P} \approx 1$. This model is not intended to be used for small projects with team sizes of nearly 1.

Table 6.17   Parameters in the COPMO Model

Set	No. Projects	a	b	c	d	$\overline{MRE}$	PRED (.25)
A	63	3.42	1.31	2.59	1.60	.43	.41
B	33	3.42	1.31	1.54	1.71	.43	.39
C	40	3.42	1.31	*.**	1.34	.57	.38
D	19	4.75	0.53	3.02	1.60	.23	.63
E	17	3.09	0.26	6.74	1.59	.26	.61
F	15	3.42	1.31	8.19	1.22	.28	.47

*The value of parameter C is omitted at the request of the source supplying that set.

Applying the procedure described earlier based on the model in Equation (6.55) to several databases to calibrate the model, the best-fit parameter values given in Table 6.17 are obtained. Table 6.17 also includes some measures of accuracy of the model, as applied to the entire database. Sets B, C, and F do not contain enough projects with $\bar{P} \approx 1$; hence, the values for Set A are also used for these sets since all 4 data sets come from similar environments. The value of parameter c for Set C is omitted at the request of the source supplying that set. Overall, COPMO performs reasonably well on these data sets, although it is clearly unacceptable based on our accuracy criteria ($\overline{MRE} \leq 0.25$ and $PRED(0.25) \geq 0.75$). On Set A, the COCOMO database, it does much better than Basic COCOMO, which is a model of similar complexity since it uses both the size and the mode information.

The parameters derived from Set A are used to plot Figure 6.5 for a hypothetical project with $S = 10$. Note that the upper curve is similar to the

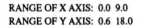

RANGE OF X AXIS: 0.0 9.0
RANGE OF Y AXIS: 0.6 18.0

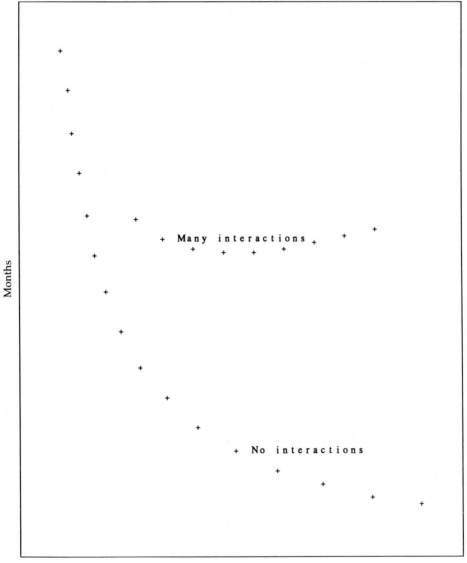

Figure 6.5   COPMO: T versus $\bar{P}$ using parameters derived from Set A.

corresponding curve of Figure 6.2, showing that the third term of Equation (6.53) could become dominant under certain circumstances. The lower curve still reflects a perfectly partitionable task as shown in Figure 6.2. It can be modeled by COPMO when the third term of Equation (6.53) is small compared to the other two.

It is instructive to examine the model parameters in greater detail. First we note that the value of a is small, compared to the actual effort on the large projects. It would not be unreasonable, in fact, to set $a = 0$. Also note that the weighted value of d is 1.53 indicating that team size does indeed have a significant impact on effort. The parameter d (from our previous discussion of a productivity model) may be interpreted as the order of the number of communication paths. The constant c, which ranges from 1.54 to 8.19, may be interpreted as the strength of each communication path.

While this model appears to perform relatively well based on our measures of accuracy, it has several limitations, especially when used for predictive purposes. These limitations follow:

(1) The model parameters are derived by least squares, which minimizes the sum of squares of the errors in the estimates, but does not necessarily minimize the two primary measures $PRED(l)$ and $\overline{MRE}$.

(2) The model parameters differ significantly from one database to another, reflecting in effect the environment in which the projects were produced. Moreover, adding or deleting projects even from the same environment will often change the parameter values significantly. It would be useful to have a set of universal parameter values that are environment-independent.

(3) Regression-derived parameters must reflect the average characteristics of the projects in the database — hence, they cannot reflect the characteristics of projects of widely differing complexity. To improve performance, the model parameters must in some manner reflect the complexity of a project and cannot be constant over all projects.

(4) For predictive purposes, the model requires estimates of the size of the project and the average personnel level $\bar{P}$. Unfortunately, $\bar{P}$ is generally not known at the beginning of a project. It would be useful to replace $\bar{P}$ by a more tractable variable.

6.7.2 The Generalized COPMO Model

To remove some of the limitations of COPMO discussed earlier, it is interesting to investigate a generalized model of the form

$$E = a_i + b_i S + c_i \bar{P}^{d_i} \tag{6.56}$$

where i is used to denote an effort complexity class EC_i. (The definition of these effort complexity classes will be discussed later.) We assume that these complexity classes are ordered so that EC_i is of lower complexity than EC_{i+1} and that it is possible to assign a project into one of these classes. Hence, it is reasonable to expect that all of the model parameters increase as i increases, or at least that they do not decrease. In this model, there are 4 parameters that must be determined so as to maximize $PRED(l)$ for a given complexity class. To determine these parameters, we rely not on least squares but on a process of calibration that assumes that we have several projects that have been correctly assigned to their corresponding complexity class.

Thus, we have a four-dimensional space of parameter values to search. This space can be reduced with little loss in generality by looking at the least squares generated parameters. The constant a was usually small in relation to reported effort; hence, we arbitrarily set $a_i = 0$ for all i. The weighted average value of d was 1.53. For simplicity, we arbitrarily set

$$d_i = 1.5$$

and note that the effect of the term $c_i \bar{P}^{d_i}$ can still be determined since c_i can be adjusted. The model in Equation (6.48) can now be written as

$$E = b_i S + c_i \bar{P}^{1.5} \tag{6.57}$$

which still contains sufficient flexibility for our purposes. The problem is now reduced to the following:

> *Given projects where the size S, actual effort E, and the average personnel $\bar{P}$ are known and given that the projects fall into complexity class EC_i, find the coefficients b_i and c_i that will maximize PRED(l) for these projects.*

The values of b_i and c_i are found by a process of calibration if a sufficiently large number of projects falling into class EC_i are known. The critical question is, how do we assign a given project to a complexity class? This will depend on an estimate of many factors that are known to affect productivity and, hence, effort. One way to determine a complexity class (if we are given a historical database of projects) is on the basis of reported productivity. Productivity is inversely proportional to our effort complexity classes. For projects of the same size, those projects with lower productivity will require greater effort. One straightforward way to assign effort complexity classes based on observed productivities L is given by the assignment algorithm

$$EC_i := i \text{ if } 100\,i < L \leq 100(i+1), \text{ for } i = 0, 1, \cdots \tag{6.58}$$

If the effective maximum productivity is 1000 LOC/PM, then Equation (6.58) would produce 10 complexity classes. However, more sophisticated assignment algorithms involving unequally spaced productivity intervals may be more effective, depending on the databases used for calibration.

Table 6.18   Complexity Classes and Calibrated b and c Values

Productivity Range	Complexity Class	b_i	c_i
0-85	1	4.7	3.6
86-200	2	3.0	2.0
201-300	3	2.4	1.5
301-400	4	2.2	1.2
401-500	5	1.8	1.0
501-600	6	1.6	0.9
601-700	7	1.2	0.8
701-900	8	1.1	0.7
901-1000	9	0.9	0.5
1001-	10	0.7	0.4

In Table 6.18, we give one such assignment algorithm with calibrated values for b_i and c_i, which appears to give excellent results for the databases available to us. Most of the projects in the databases have maximum productivity less than 1000. However, Set E has 8 projects with productivities greater than 1000 and one as high as 3300, undoubtedly due to a high percentage of reused code. In Table 6.19, we present the performance of the model in Equation (6.57) on the databases discussed in Section 3.6. The overall value of $PRED(0.25)$ is 0.76 while the weighted value of $\overline{MRE}$ is 0.21. If we consider the great heterogeneity of the projects in these databases, the performance of this model must be considered exceptionally good. These good results are largely due to the fact that we have based our effort complexity classes on observed productivity. If the model is to be used for *predictive purposes*, we must have some way to decide complexity classes that does not use observed productivity.

The determination of complexity classes could be based on various software attributes that are believed to affect productivity. There are many schemes for accomplishing this. Models such as Walston-Felix [WALS77], COCOMO

Table 6.19   Performance of Generalized COPMO

Set	No. Projects	PRED (.25)	$\overline{MRE}$
A	63	.78	.19
B	33	.64	.27
C	40	.65	.26
D	19	1.00	.09
E	17	.82	.23
F	15	.73	.17

Overall Performance

$PRED(.25) = 140/187 = .75$

$\overline{MRE} = .21$

Table 6.20   Complexity classes based on $m(X)$ and Calibrated Values of b_i, c_i, and the Performance of COPMO

$m(X)$ range	Complexity Class	Number of projects	b_i	c_i
0 - .66	4	14	1.1	1.0
.67 - 1.20	3	24	2.0	2.0
1.21 - 2.20	2	6	3.0	2.5
2.21 - ∞	1	19	5.0	3.5

Performance on COCOMO Database

$PRED(.25) = .78$

$\overline{MRE} = .25$

[BOEH81], Boeing [BLAC77], RCA-PRICE S [FREI79], and others all use somewhat different schemes. Rather than developing one of our own, we have chosen to use the scheme proposed by Boehm for his COCOMO model. This choice has the advantage that it is readily available in Boehm's book and, most importantly, that his scheme has been calibrated to a set of projects whose detailed characteristics have been published. The effect of the 16 software attributes on effort is effectively captured in the multiplier $m(X)$, which is the product of 16 cost drivers described earlier. For the 63 projects in the COCOMO database, $m(X)$ ranges from 0.25 to 7.62 when 16 cost drivers are included, and from 0.25 to 5.50 when only the first 15 cost drivers are included. We can base our effort complexity classes on the values of $m(X)$. We would like to use as small a number of complexity classes as possible in order to ease the burden of assigning a project into a particular class. Table 6.20 presents one partition of $m(X)$ into 4 complexity classes assuming 16 cost drivers and the corresponding calibrated b_i and c_i values. We cannot test the performance of our model on the databases in Appendix B, except for the COCOMO database, because we do not have the detailed information required to compute $m(X)$. The performance of our model on the COCOMO database is as follows:

$$PRED(0.25) = 0.78, \quad \overline{MRE} = 0.25$$

This model performs slightly better than Intermediate COCOMO, and clearly demonstrates that it is capable of producing acceptable predictions.

6.7.3 The Use of COPMO for Effort Prediction

To use COPMO for predictive purposes, we need, in addition to an estimate of the size S, an estimate of the average personnel level $\bar{P}$. Since $\bar{P}$ is generally not known before a project starts, and is often a sought-after output from a model, we now propose a method for eliminating $\bar{P}$ as an input parameter. Our general model has the form

$$E = a + b\,S + c\,\bar{P}^d \tag{6.59}$$

Using the definition $\bar{P} = \dfrac{E}{T}$, where T is project duration in months, and rearranging Equation (6.59), it becomes

$$E - \frac{c\,E^d}{T^d} = a + b\,S \tag{6.60}$$

$$f(E) = E - c\,\frac{E^d}{T^d} - a - b\,S \tag{6.61}$$

Now the variable T is usually much more tractable than $\bar{P}$. For many projects, T is specified by the customer and does not vary greatly. If we specify the duration T and estimate the size S, then Equation (6.61) is a nonlinear equation for the effort E. It can be solved readily by a Newton iteration method [CONT81] for fixed S, or even by a simple bisection method. A good initial approximation to E is given by

$$E_0 = a + b S$$

The Newton iteration then becomes

$$E_{n+1} = E_n - \frac{f(E_n)}{f'(E_n)}$$

where

$$f'(E_n) = 1 - \frac{c \, d \, E^{d-1}}{T^d}$$

Actually it can be shown that there is a value of T called T_{min}, below which Equation (6.61) will not have a solution. Thus, the theory produces a minimum duration and implies that the project cannot be completed in time $T < T_{min}$, regardless of how many persons are assigned to the project. To take a specific example, suppose we have a project with $S = 200$. From our model, we get the parameter values $a = 0$, $b = 4.6$, $c = 2.3$, and $d = 1.5$. Table 6.21 gives the results of solving Equation (6.61) for various values of T. We see that as T increases beyond its minimum, both the average personnel level and the estimated effort decrease. This type of analysis can be useful to managers who can make decisions based on the tradeoffs involved between duration and effort.

Table 6.21   Effort versus Duration for $S = 200$

T	$\bar{P}$	$\hat{E}$
<32	(No solution)	
33	61.5	2028
34	53.6	1823
35	48.4	1695
36	44.6	1604
37	41.5	1534

Note that the effort predicted by the theory drops quickly as T increases beyond T_{min}. For example, Table 6.21 shows that the effort decreases by 205 PM as T increases from 33 months to 34 months. However, a further increase in the duration to 35 months, reduces the effort by only 128 PM. Increasing the duration by 4 months reduces effort by about one fourth. In practice, it appears that a good choice of project duration should be about 10% greater than T_{min}.

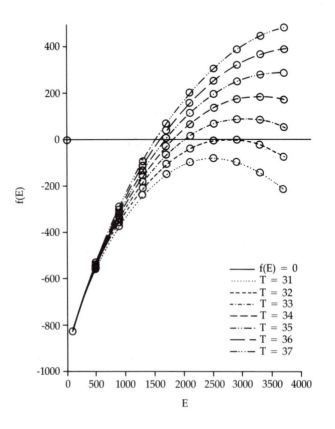

Figure 6.6   The COPMO equation as a function of E.

Figure 6.6 gives a graphical representation of the curves for $f(E)$ as a function of E, with T fixed. The solutions of Equations (6.61) are the points at which these curves intersect the E-axis. In particular, the curve corresponding to T_{min} is the curve tangent to the E-axis. At this tangent point, we must have both $f(E) = 0$ and $f'(E) = 0$.

The existence of a minimum duration makes it possible for us to simplify our effort model further so that project size becomes the only parameter that must be estimated. Because of its importance, we derive here a formula for T_{min}, the corresponding effort $E(T_{min})$, and the average personnel size $\bar{P}(T_{min})$. Referring again to Figure 6.6, we see that when $T = T_{min}$, we must have both $f(E) = 0$ and $f'(E) = 0$. Hence, we have from Equation (6.61)

$$f(E) = E - c\frac{E^d}{T^d} - a - bS$$

Keeping in mind that S is a constant in this relationship, we differentiate to obtain

$$f'(E) = 1 - \frac{cdE^{d-1}}{T^d}$$

On setting $f'(E) = 0$ and solving for T, we obtain

$$T = (cd)^{1/d} E^{\frac{d-1}{d}} \tag{6.62}$$

Then substituting back into $f(E) = 0$, we get

$$E - \frac{c}{cd} \cdot \frac{E^d}{E^{d-1}} = a + bS$$

$$E(1 - 1/d) = a + bS$$

or

$$E(T_{\min}) = \frac{a + bS}{(1 - 1/d)} \tag{6.63}$$

This is the effort required if the project is completed in time $T_{\min}$. Note that $E(T_{\min})$ is actually the maximum effort within the range of permissible times.

Substituting back into Equation (6.62), we obtain

$$T_{\min} = (cd)^{1/d} \left[\frac{a + bS}{(1 - 1/d)} \right]^{\frac{d-1}{d}}$$

which simplifies to

$$T_{\min} = cd \left[\frac{a + bS}{c(d - 1)} \right]^{\frac{d-1}{d}} \tag{6.64}$$

Finally, we can obtain the average personnel level at $T_{\min}$ from the equation

$$\bar{P}(T_{\min}) = \frac{E(T_{\min})}{T_{\min}}$$

Note that $T_{\min}$ is a function of a, b, c, d, and S, while $E(T_{\min})$ is a function of a, b, d, and S but not of c. Thus, by changing the parameter c, we can change the minimum time without changing the effort at $T_{\min}$.

Returning to the example in Table 6.21 with $S = 200$, $a = 0$, $b = 4.6$, $c = 2.3$, and $d = 1.5$, we compute

$$T_{min} = (2.3)(1.5) \left[\frac{920}{(2.3)(.5)} \right]^{1/3} = 32 \text{ months}$$

In practice, generalized COPMO can be used in the following way. Given the problem requirements and specifications, and the characteristics of the implementing team and the programming environment, an estimate of the project size S, as well as its complexity class EC_i, is determined. This is undoubtedly the hardest part. After this is done, the model parameter values are fixed and we can solve Equation (6.64) for T_{min}. Next, we choose some duration time $T_j > T_{min}$ and solve Equation (6.61) for the corresponding required effort E_j and the average personnel level $\bar{P}_j$. Depending on customer cost and schedule, management is now in a position to select one of the sets $(T_j, E_j, \bar{P}_j)$ that appears to be most feasible. We should hasten to point out, however, that a great deal of research remains to be done to establish the validity and usefulness of this model.

6.7.4 Effort Complexity Classes and the Calibration Procedure

As already noted, generalized COPMO relies heavily on our ability to determine a project's effort complexity class EC_i. In this section, we suggest some possible methods for assigning a project into such a class.

The first method is based on observed productivity and is useful primarily for data fitting as opposed to prediction. One partitioning scheme based on observed productivity is presented in Table 6.18, where values of b_i and c_i corresponding to the effort complexity class EC_i are given. While not directly useful in prediction, this method does provide a reasonable starting range for values b_i and c_i of the model parameters.

A second method that we have already discussed is to use the product of the 15 cost driver multipliers from COCOMO, which we have designated as $m(X)$. For the COCOMO database, $m(X)$ ranges from 0.25 to 5.50. A possible — though by no means unique — partition of this range is given in Table 6.20. This partition of $m(X)$ into 4 complexity classes is clearly influenced by the projects in this particular database. In arriving at the 4 class partitions, we were motivated by two objectives:

(1) Selecting a partition and corresponding model parameters so that the model gave good performance characteristics on the COCOMO database.

(2) Making it relatively easy for a project manager to assign a new project into one of these classes.

The latter objective is best met by having as small a set of classes as possible. We can perhaps improve the performance of COPMO on the COCOMO database by increasing the number of partitions. Our experience with productivity-based complexity classes suggests that a minimum of 7 or 8 partitions will be necessary to allow for observed differences in effort for similarly sized projects.

Table 6.22 Partitions of $m(X)$ into 7 complexity classes using the COCOMO Database

Complexity Class	$m(x)$ Range	b_i	c_i	Mean Productivity
1	$m > 3.75$	4.7	3.6	31
2	$2.75 < m \leq 3.75$	4.3	2.8	63
3	$1.70 < m \leq 2.75$	4.0	2.8	95
4	$1.25 < m \leq 1.70$	2.6	2.0	144
5	$.75 < m \leq 1.25$	1.9	1.5	235
6	$.50 < m \leq 0.75$	1.8	1.5	329
7	$0 < m \leq 0.5$	1.1	.7	712

Performance on COCOMO Database

$PRED(.25) = .78$

$\overline{MRE} = .21$

For example, another partition of $m(X)$ into 7 complexity classes, with appropriate calibrated values for b_i and c_i, is given in Table 6.22. This partitioning is based on the use of 15 cost drivers with the range of $m(X)$ being from 0.25 to 5.50. The performance of this partitioning ($PRED(0.25) = 0.76$, $\overline{MRE} = 0.24$) is about as good as the previous partitioning into 4 classes (see Table 6.20). The productivity column gives the average productivity of all projects in a given class, and the trend is exactly what we would expect.

It is also interesting to compare the range of the b and c values using the two methods discussed earlier for obtaining these parameters. This comparison is given in Table 6.23. The ranges based on productivity classes are taken from Table 6.18. If we consider that the parameter values were arrived at independently and that the databases are different, the ranges are remarkably close. The lower limit of the ranges for both b and c values using the first method is accounted for by the fact that the 187 projects contain some with much higher productivities than those in the COCOMO database.

A major weakness of discrete partitioning schemes such as this concerns the treatment of projects that fall near the boundary of the partitions. In effect, there is a discontinuity at these boundaries. Thus, a relatively small change in

Table 6.23   Comparison of COPMO Model Parameters

Method	No. of Projects	Range of b Values	Range of c Values
Productivity Classes	187	$0.7 \leq b \leq 4.7$	$0.4 \leq c \leq 3.6$
Cost Driver Classes	63	$1.1 \leq b \leq 4.7$	$0.7 \leq c \leq 3.6$

the classification of the project may lead to a relatively large change in the model parameters and in the predicted effort. We could avoid this problem by fitting a continuous curve to the discrete model parameters. Since the parameters b_i and c_i are more or less uniformly decreasing functions of the effort complexity classes, we can obtain a reasonable fit by exponential formulas of the type

$$b(z) = \alpha_1 e^{\beta_1 z}$$

$$c(z) = \alpha_2 e^{\beta_2 z}$$

where z is some measure of the complexity level.

For example, if we choose z_i to be the midpoint of the $m(X)$ range in the complexity classes of Table 6.22, then a least squares exponential fit to the b and c data in Table 6.22 yields the equations

$$\hat{b} = 1.4207 \, e^{.31339Z}$$

$$\hat{c} = 1.0496 \, e^{.30845Z}$$

This formula can be used in place of the table values to find appropriate b and c values that correspond to an estimated $m(X)$ value. However, we do not advocate the use of continuous curves for parameter determination in this model. One reason is its performance is much poorer than the discrete parameter model. Another reason is the use of continuous curves suggests a level of precision far beyond the capability of this or any other effort estimation model. In addition, all the available evidence suggests that effort is not only a nonlinear function but also probably a discontinuous function of many variables.

After we have decided on a method for producing our effort complexity classes, the next step is to find the best values of the model parameters b_i and c_i. For this purpose, we assume that we have a database of projects that have already been assigned into each of our complexity classes. A least squares fit of the projects in each complexity class will produce initial parameter values — such as $\hat{b}_i$ and $\hat{c}_i$. While these values will minimize the sum of the square of the deviations between actual and predicted effort, they will not in general optimize either of our preferred measures $PRED(l)$ and $\overline{MRE}$. In addition, there will often be too few projects in a given class, thus casting doubt on least squares derived parameters. The performance of our model based on our preferred measures can always be improved by using a calibration procedure, such as by adjusting the parameter values in a systematic way until the best possible performance is achieved. Further improvement will be possible by changing the effort complexity class ranges and redetermining the optimum b and c values.

6.8 Summary and Conclusions

In this chapter, we have discussed and attempted to evaluate several models for software effort estimation. Those models differ significantly in their ease of use, completeness, availability, amount and type of information required, and performance characteristics.

COCOMO [BOEH81] stands out as the most complete, most readily available, and the easiest method to use. Other models that are comprehensive in scope and readily accessible are Putnam's SLIM Model and the RCA PRICE-S Model, both of which are being marketed as proprietary products.

We have shown that it is difficult to compare the performance of those models on independent databases because the information required is not always available. A primary impediment to good research in this area is a lack of quality databases of software projects. Nevertheless, we have attempted to compare the performance of these models on sets of projects for which some information is available using as our primary measures of accuracy $\overline{MRE} \leq 0.25$ and $PRED(0.25) \geq 0.75$. In most cases, none of the models seem capable of achieving this level of accuracy on independent databases, although some were able to achieve good accuracy on their own database of projects.

We have also proposed a new model — COPMO and its generalizations — which appears capable of achieving consistent performance on all the databases that we have examined. It appears to be a very promising approach because of its simplicity, ease of use, and reasonable performance characteristics. However, more research is needed to determine appropriate complexity classes and the corresponding model parameters.

Research on software effort estimation and software metrics in general are on-going functions of the Software Metrics Research Group at Purdue University. Through several industrial contacts, we are continuously adding project data to our collection. While we are a long way from reliable and accurate effort estimators, our recent research results are sufficiently promising that we can look forward with some confidence to much-improved models.

It should be clear that much work remains to be completed in order to obtain a general model of the software development process, to estimate size and effort better, and to allow managers to control this activity more effectively. It seems sensible to combine the best features of several existing models (such as Jensen's, COCOMO, COPMO), as well as any future models that seem promising into one comprehensive, composite model. Other sciences have been able to do this. For example, in physics, there are not several models describing the path and velocity of a falling object. There may have been several originally, but if so they have been combined into one by repeated testing and observation. In a similar manner, further experimentation, gathering and evaluating more university and industrial data, and combining and enhancing models will be necessary for computer scientists to progress to metrics, measurements, and models that will allow us to explain and control the software development process more accurately.

Exercises

1. There are both subjective and objective criteria to judge the appropriateness of cost estimation models. Explain why that objective criteria *alone* are not enough.

2. What are the differences between top-down and bottom-up estimating? Discuss their advantages and disadvantages.

3. Give three factors that are *not* considered in the TRW Wolverton model, but are considered to be important factors affecting productivity in Chapter 5.

4. Discuss the strengths and weaknesses of cost models that are based solely on linear regression.

5. The exponent term in the Walston-Felix model is less than one, while the exponent term in other similar models is greater than one. Discuss the implications of this difference.

6. The parameters of the Bailey-Basili model are obtained by minimizing the sum of the squared error of the estimates (*Err*). Would you expect the results to be significantly different if we obtain the parameters by minimizing the sum of the squared errors, as in linear regression?

7. What is the implication of the constant term a in Equation (6.14) in the Bailey-Basili model?

8. In the Bailey-Basili model, the maximum scores of effort-adjusted factors for *METH*, *CPLX*, and *EXP* are 45, 35, and 25, respectively. Does this imply

that *METH* is more important than *CPLX*, which in turn is more important than *EXP*?

9. What is the difference between the two approaches for adjusting effort given in Equations (6.16) and (6.18)? Discuss the assumptions of each approach. Which approach is better? Justify your answer.

10. According to the Putnam model, show that the development effort is about 40% of the lifetime effort (Equation (6.21)).

11. Assuming the Putnam model, and given $S_s = 100,000$, $C = 5000$, and $\alpha = 15$, compute T_{min} and $K(T_{min})$.

12. What is meant by *mode* in Boehm's COCOMO? Give one example of a software product for each mode.

13. Basic COCOMO and Intermediate COCOMO use different sets of parameters for the nominal effort. Explain the difference.

14. For a program of 100 KLOC, estimate the effort and duration for each of the three modes using Basic COCOMO.

15. COPMO assumes that the communication overhead depends only on the personnel level. Therefore, E_c for a five-person team to develop a 10 KLOC program is the same as E_c for a five-person team to develop a 100 KLOC program. Is this reasonable? Justify your answer.

16. Generalized COPMO is based on the criterion of maximizing *PRED(l)*. If we use the criterion of minimizing the sum-squared errors, do you expect to obtain significantly different results? Justify your answer.

17. Compute Table 6.21 for $d = 1.1$, assuming the other parameters are not changed.

18. Consider Equation (6.61) as a function of T rather than E and find the minimum of T by taking the derivative of Equation (6.61) with respect to E. Do you expect to get the same results as (6.62)?

19. For the example given in Table 6.21, compute T_{min}, $E(T_{min})$, and $\bar{P}_{min}$, assuming $d = 1.0$ and the other parameters are not changed.

20. For the example given in Table 6.21, compute T_{min}, $E(T_{min})$, and $\bar{P}_{min}$, assuming $d = 2.0$ and the other parameters are not changed.

21. Derive Equations (6.62), (6.63), and (6.64).

7 Defect Models

If there are two or more ways to do something, and one of those ways can *result in a catastrophe, then someone* will *do it.*

Capt. Edward A. Murphy, Jr., USAF, 1949. Reported in *Science* 4, 1 (January/February 1983): 78.

7.1 Introduction

The statement quoted here, made after the discovery of improperly installed sensors as the cause of the failure of a dangerous and expensive rocket-sled experiment, was the basis of the popular Murphy's law: "If something can go wrong, it will." This recognition of human frailty in assembling complicated systems has led to so-called *structured designs* that make it either impossible or much more difficult to install subassemblies incorrectly. Examples are the bulges on auto head-lamps that must be fitted into the corresponding bracket notches, and the odd shapes of multi-wire cable connectors for computer peripherals that can only be placed into the appropriate receptacles in the proper way. These designs definitely enhance the reliability of hardware systems.

Unfortunately, the analogy does not carry over to programming — the human assembly of computer instructions to produce complicated software systems. Methodologies such as structured design, design reviews and code walkthroughs, and conventions for module interfaces are attempts to reduce the probability of human error. But, it is almost impossible to enforce earlier software design decisions in the same way as using physical constraints to enforce hardware design decisions. As a matter of fact, "adapting" a library module to a particular system by "patching over" parts of it is a practice often encouraged and rewarded (see Section 2.2.4). It should not be surprising that, since there are practically an *infinite* number of ways to do something and *many* of those ways can result in a catastrophe, there *are* defects in most software systems. However, it should be surprising under these circumstances that software products *can* be as reliable as they sometimes are.

As discussed in Section 2.8, since it is not yet possible for programmers to produce error-free code consistently, a significant amount of effort is often allocated to the testing phase of the software life cycle. Strategies such as white- and black-box testing, bottom-up and top-down testing, and others have been proposed and adopted. (For definitions and discussions of these testing strategies, see [MYER79], [BEIZ84], [DUNN84].) An *a priori* knowledge of the error-proneness of the software modules being tested could make the testing process more efficient: for example, more effort or resources could be allocated to the parts of software that are more likely to contain defects. In addition, testing managers often do not feel that the software is adequately tested when the scheduled delivery date approaches. A delay in the delivery may cost the company a significant amount of money per day in penalties or lost revenues, yet a premature release may cost the company more money in making fixes in the field or in damages to its reputation. An accurate knowledge of the number of defects that remain in the software can make the decision on the release date more rational.

This chapter describes two types of models that assess some quality aspects of software modules. A *static* model uses software metrics to estimate the number of defects in the software. A *dynamic* model uses the past defect discovery rate to estimate this rate for the future. We believe that, as more accurate models of defects (static or dynamic) are developed, the testing process can become more systematic and less dependent upon intuition or luck.

7.2 Static Models of Defects

A *static* model of software defects assumes the general model form of Equation (1.9), which is reproduced here:

$$y = f(x_1, x_2, \cdots, x_n) \tag{7.1}$$

The *dependent* variable y is normally a defect metric as discussed in Section 2.8, such as the number of defects found during a particular phase of the life cycle, or the number of program changes made during that phase. The *independent* variables $x_1, x_2, \cdots, x_n$ can be either product- or process-related. The model is *static* in the sense that it estimates the dependent variable based on the current values of the independent variables, ignoring, for example, the rate of change of any metric over time. Naturally, a reasonable predictive model for a certain defect count depends only on metrics that can be measured *before* the defect count itself can be measured. For example, a predictive model of post-release defects (d_2) based on product metrics is reasonable, since all of the product metrics can be objectively measured before the product is released to customers. On the other hand, a model of the number of defects found during the testing phase (d_1) cannot use the number of post-release defects (d_2) as an independent variable, even though both data may be available at some later date when the analysis is made. We are most interested in reasonable models whose independent variables can be measured much earlier than the dependent variable, since such models have the potential of being used to guide the testing and maintenance processes.

The defect counts used in the models discussed in this section may be either the number of "defects found" or the number of "changes," as discussed in Section 2.8. The former metric is used when the analysis is done at the "product level" — defects are measured for completed programs or systems. The latter metric is often used when the analysis is done at the "module level." When both metrics are available, the latter count is at least as large as the former since a defect may require changes in more than one module. It is important to note the phase in which the defect count is measured and the definition used ("defects found" or "changes") in the following subsections.

7.2.1 Akiyama's Study

One of the first studies of the relationship between defects and product metrics examined data from a software product developed at Fujitsu, Ltd. of Japan and was published by Akiyama in 1971 [AKIY71]. The product analyzed was a system called SAMPLE, which was implemented in FASP assembly language on the Fujitsu FACOM 230−60. The system apparently had ten modules,[1] one of which was considered unusual in its structure and excluded from later analysis.[2] The metrics used in the analyses included the program size in *steps* or lines of code (S_s) and the count of decisions (DE). The number of subroutine calls J was also recorded for each module. A composite metric C, called the *nature* of a program, was defined as the sum of DE and J. An argument similar to that discussed in Section 2.4.1 was used to suggest that C was related to the complexity of debugging the module. Actually, $C = v(G)$ if each subroutine is called only once. The dependent variable, the total number of bugs found, included all of the defects found during the testing phase (d_1) and those found during the two months after release (d_2). It is appropriate to represent the dependent variable *total defects* by d_{tot} (which equals $d_1 + d_2$). Table 7.1 shows the data given by Akiyama and the performance of the linear regression models based on S_s, DE, J, and C. The parameters for the models are the following:

$$\hat{d}_{tot} = 4.86 + 0.018\,S_s$$

$$\hat{d}_{tot} = -1.14 + 0.2\,DE$$

$$\hat{d}_{tot} = 6.9 + 0.27\,J$$

$$\hat{d}_{tot} = -0.88 + 0.12\,C$$

---

1. Table 1 of [AKIY71] listed only seven modules, but Table 2 provided data for nine modules without explanation. Data for ten distinct modules were given in the two tables.

2. The module was responsible for table initialization and contained many literal strings for messages. Such modules often have low counts of DE and high counts of $VARS$ or η_2, relative to their size. It is inappropriate to include such data in analyses that involve metrics on program size, decision count, and unique variable count.

All correlations reported in the table are significant at the 0.01 level.

Table 7.1   Prediction of d_{tot} (total defects) using Akiyama's Data

Module	d_{tot}	S_s	DE	J	C = DE + J
MA	102	4032	372	283	655
MB	18	1329	215	44	259
MC	93	5453	552	362	914
MD	26	1674	111	130	241
ME	71	2051	315	197	512
MF	37	2513	217	186	403
MG	16	699	104	32	136
MH	50	3792	233	110	343
MX	80	3412	416	230	646
Sum	493	24955	2535	1574	4109
$\overline{RE}$		-.13	-.13	-.07	-.08
$\overline{MRE}$		.31	.29	.24	.21
PRED (.25)		.44	.78	.67	.78
Correlation		.83	.89	.91	.92
Rank Corr.		.90	.93	.93	.95

Akiyama's data shows that linear models of several simple metrics provide reasonable estimates for the total number of defects. Most metrics discussed in Chapter 2 were not considered since they were not known to Akiyama at the time of this study. As a result, his analysis was not as thorough as some other analyses discussed in later subsections. Nevertheless, his data remains valuable and was used by several researchers later ([HALS77], [OTTE79], and even [GAFF84]). However, we must be careful to note that the data was collected in 1971 and earlier. Analyzing Akiyama's data to develop models for today's programming environments may no longer be a valid approach (see Section 3.2.3).

7.2.2 Motley and Brooks' Study

Motley and Brooks of IBM's Federal Systems Division were commissioned in 1976 by the Rome Air Development Center to develop multilinear regression models for program defects [MOTL77]. Two large Department of Defense command and control software projects totaling nearly 300 KLOC were studied. The first project called *sample S* contained 534 program modules with a combined size of more than 181 KLOC of CENTRAN, which was a high-level language. The second project called *sample T* contained 249 program modules with a combined size of over 115 KLOC of JOVIAL. The large amounts of code required the use of automatic code analyzers to collect metric data. These analyzers were apparently developed by the individual teams for other purposes — leading to the collection of different metrics. In addition to the error data that was collected during the testing phase (d_1), the analyzer for sample S provided counts of 53 variables, and the analyzer for sample T provided counts of 15 variables. Several items collected were related to S_s (X1 in S and TS in T), *VARS* (X39 in S), and *DE* (X14, X15, X18, and X41 in S; and LL, IF, and LS in T). Examples of others that were collected but not discussed in Chapter 2 were, for example, the number of comment statements (X5 in S and COM in T), the number of variables that were referenced but not defined within the program (X37 in S), the number of source instructions in all "second level" DO loops (X49 in S), and the number of data handling statements (DATA in T). Motley and Brooks made no attempt to equate or compare the two sets of metrics. Rather, each sample was thoroughly and independently analyzed using linear regression techniques. Even though no comparative study was made, the results are valuable since either sample was much larger than those used in other similar studies.

The multi-linear model used assumed the form of Equation (3.20), which is reproduced here:

$$\hat{d}_1 = b_0 + b_1 x_1 + \cdots + b_n x_n \tag{7.2}$$

Motley and Brooks discovered that many of the metrics collected were linearly related to each other. They used factor analysis (described in Section 3.4.4) to remove some of them from consideration. A standard procedure[3] from a commercial statistics package was then used to select the independent variables from the metrics that remained and to determine the coefficients $(b_0, b_1, \cdots, b_n)$, so that the resulting formula provided the highest coefficient of multiple determination R^2 (see Sections 3.4.4 and 3.5.1). The procedure started by including the independent variable having the highest correlation with the dependent variable. More variables that increased R^2 were included until the value approaches its expected maximum. Variables that had minimal effect on R^2 were then eliminated from the model.

---

3. This is similar to a stepwise multilinear regression technique available in many statistical packages.

The brute-force application of multilinear regression often leads to results that cannot be reasonably interpreted (cf. Section 6.3.1). For example, the best 10-variable function for a project in sample S is given below:

$$\hat{d}_1 = -0.465 \ X4 + 0.762 \ X5 + 0.544 \ X8 - 0.176 \ X17 - 0.386 \ X23$$

$$+ \ 0.600 \ X28 + 0.436 \ X37 - 0.386 \ X42 - 0.374 \ X51 + 0.602 \ X53$$

Table 7.2 lists the definitions of the variables involved. The R^2 for this model is 0.895, which is significant at the 0.001 level.

Although the model performs well according to the R^2 criterion (only 10% of the observed variance in d_1 is not accounted for), its interpretation may be difficult. All variables except X17 are positively correlated with d_1 individually. The many negative coefficients in the regression model are merely artifacts, as many of the variables are correlated with each other (see Section 3.4.4). Furthermore, the +0.762 coefficient for X5 suggests that the *use* of comments leads to defects — hardly a defensible conclusion. In addition, the specific references to the fourth- and sixth-level DO loops (X51 and X53), while leaving out the other intervening levels, do not inspire confidence in the model.

Motley and Brooks applied this analysis to 3 subsets of sample S and 8 subsets of sample T. They were generally able to obtain regression models with R^2 around 0.5 when 5 independent variables were involved, and around 0.6 when 10 independent variables were involved (sample S only). However, the variables selected by the statistical package varied from one model to another. For example, only 2 variables (X4 and X37) were consistently chosen for the 10-variable models for sample S. Thus, they were unable to arrive at a "universal" model for defect estimation using multilinear regression.

It is reasonable to ask which metric is the *best single-variable* predictor of program defects. For subsets of sample S, the metric X37 (number of variables referenced but not defined) appeared best in three out of five analyses. It was the second best in the other two. For subsets of sample T, the metric DATA (number of data handling statements) appeared best in three out of six analyses. Although it is generally true that larger programs have more defects, metrics of program size (X1 in S and TS in T) were not the best single-variable predictors in either sample.

This study of program defects is probably the most thorough study ever made with the largest volume of data. The results are typical of those studies using regression analysis — the "goodness of fit" may be reasonable (in terms of R^2), but the potential use as a predictive model is very limited. The number of metrics involved that have not been used by anyone else (such as X53) makes comparisons with other studies difficult. Nevertheless, the results suggest that we cannot depend on regression analysis alone to obtain a model of program defects that can be used to guide the testing process.

Table 7.2   Some Variables used in the Study by Motley and Brooks

Variable	Definition
X4	Number of USING instructions which establish data structure interface
X5	Number of COMMENT statements
X8	Number of unconditional branch instructions
X17	Number of instructions performing scale/round operations
X23	Number of times address variables are referenced
X28	Number of times fixed-point variables are referenced
X37	Number of variables which were referenced but not defined within the program
X42	Number of non-nested DO loops
X51	Number of source instructions in all fourth-level DO loops
X53	Number of source instructions in all sixth-level (and beyond) DO loops

7.2.3 Studies by Halstead and Ottenstein

The models of defects discussed in Sections 7.2.1 and 7.2.2 are models derived through data-fitting. Although such models may fit the data well, their interpretation may be difficult. A model with some theoretical basis *and* with support by empirically collected data is preferred to a model driven by data only (see Section 1.3.4). Both Halstead and Ottenstein attempted to create such models by extending the theory of Software Science ([HALS77], [OTTE79]).

As discussed in Section 2.6, Software Science suggests that the programming process is a selection process: a program is constructed by selecting (with replacement) tokens from a set of unique operators and unique operands. Halstead considered the Software Science V metric to be a measure of the number of *mental comparisons* needed to write a program of length N. Halstead and Ottenstein hypothesized that the total number of defects for a program with volume V could be represented as

$$\hat{d}_{tot} = \frac{V}{3000} \tag{7.3}$$

The constant 3000 in Equation (7.3) was defined as the "mean number of elementary mental discriminations between potential errors in programming." It was not obtained through regression analysis, but was derived from other assumptions related to the potential volume V^*, the program level L, and the language level λ. However, similar to many other derivations in the Software Science model, the derivation of Equation (7.3) also appears tenuous and will not be presented here.

When Equation (7.3) was proposed, no published data on defects included the basic parameters of Software Science η_1, η_2, N_1, and N_2, which were needed in order to compute V directly. When only the size in LOC (S_s) was given for a program, early researchers used the following procedure to obtain V (see also Section 6.4.3):

(1) Compute $N = c\, S_s$, where c is an appropriate constant for the language in question.

(2) Assuming $\eta_1 = \eta_2 = \eta/2$, use the length equation (2.26) $N = \eta \log_2(\eta/2)$ to compute η. An iterative procedure was used.

(3) Compute $V = N \log_2 \eta$.

The model in Equation (7.3) was shown to work well for the data published by Akiyama and others ([HALS77], [OTTE79], [LIPO82]), but was disputed by other studies that will be described later.

As mentioned in Section 2.2.2, the metrics S_s, N, and V are linearly related, and appear to be equally valid as measures of program size. Since the procedure given earlier depends only on S_s, we would expect the performance of Equation (7.3) to be similar to that of a linear regression model based on a size metric. Table 7.3 shows the analysis of two commercial products for which complete Software Science metrics and defects are available. The products are described in more detail later in Section 7.2.5. There are 19 data points in Product A and 108 data points in Product B1. The correlations are significant at the 0.01 level for both cases. Due to the proprietary nature of the data involved, we have chosen not to show the linear regression models derived for these products. However, we notice that the constant c in

Table 7.3   Performance of Several Linear Models of Defects

Product A	*N*	*V*	*V* /3000
$\overline{RE}$	-.08	.02	.31
$\overline{MRE}$	.55	.53	.53
PRED (.25)	.37	.42	.21
Correlation	.73	.75	.75
Rank Corr.	.81	.80	.80
Product B1	*N*	*V*	*V* /3000
$\overline{RE}$	.19	.31	.36
$\overline{MRE}$	.51	.55	.55
PRED (.25)	.23	.24	.21
Correlation	.84	.85	.85
Rank Corr.	.79	.80	.80

$$\hat{d}_{tot} = \frac{V}{c}$$

for both products are remarkably close to the hypothesized 3000. One of them differs from 3000 by only 8%.

Variations of Equation (7.3) have been proposed by Lipow who used a series function of S_s to approximate V [LIPO82], and by Gaffney who claimed that V increases as $S_s^{4/3}$ [GAFF84]. Since both variations were still based on program size only, no significant improvement was found beyond the basic model in Equation (7.3).

7.2.4   Potier's Study

Models that estimate the number of defects share a common problem: the data collected to validate the models may not be precise and accurate. As discussed in Section 2.8.2, a low count of defects discovered during the Testing phase (d_1) for a software module may be the result of either good design and coding, *or* bad testing. A program may have a high count of defects after release (d_2) if the latter case is true. It appears that the total number of defects $(d_{tot} = d_1 + d_2)$ is a better target for static models such as Equation (7.1). However, even in the case of bad testing, the module may still have a low d_2 count if it is seldom referenced during field applications. Therefore, we do not expect any model to estimate the number of defects with great accuracy. On the other hand, models that effectively *discriminate* between modules with a high probability of defects and those without may be of great value. Such a model can be used to direct more testing resources to the modules that are determined to be more likely to have defects, with the hope that the defects can be found and corrected before product release. The actual count of defects may not be relevant. Note that such an approach is not a meaningful one if most of the modules have defects (or if most have none).

Potier *et al.* studied the error data of a family of compilers for the purpose of identifying the metrics that can be used to discriminate between modules with defects and modules with no defects [POTI82]. The compiler was written in a real-time language called LTR. It had 11 subsystems called *compiling units*, with a total of about 62 KLOC. It was divided into 1106 procedures, 606 of which were without errors. Since the defect data included both the testing and maintenance phases that spanned nearly 10 years, it was amazing that more than half of the procedures were defect-free. Nevertheless, the analysis of the distribution of these defects produced results comparable to those published in [MOTL77] and [LIPO79].

The metrics considered in [POTI82] included the basic Software Science metrics discussed in Sections 2.2.2, 2.6.2, 2.6.3, and 2.6.4; the cyclomatic complexity discussed in Section 2.4.1; and the paths and reachability metrics discussed in Section 2.4.2. Since many of these metrics were related to program length N, a set of *normalized* metrics[4] was defined by dividing individual metrics by N. The approach was to compute the mean values of the complexity metrics for the set of procedures that had errors *and* for the set of procedures that did not. The "discriminant effect" of a metric was defined as the ratio of these mean metric values. For example, the 606 defect-free procedures had mean value $\bar{\eta} = 27.43$, while the remaining 500 modules with defects had $\bar{\eta} = 69.69$. The discriminant effect of $\bar{\eta}$ was thus $69.69/27.43 = 2.54$. A number between these two mean values may be used to decide whether a procedure will have defects. For example, if we use $\eta = 39$ as the threshold value, 485 out of 618 procedures with $\eta < 39$ were defect-free, and 367 out of 488 procedures with $\eta > 39$ had defects.[5] A technique called *non-parametric discriminant analysis* can be used to select a set of metrics and their threshold values to produce a decision tree. Such a decision tree is shown in Figure 7.1. The metrics R_N and R'_N are related to reachability, and $v(G)_N$ and $v(G)'_N$ are related to

---

4. More on normalizing (i.e., removing the effect of size) will appear in Section 7.2.6.

5. That is, 75% of the modules were classified correctly.

the cyclomatic complexity. They are normalized by division by N. Each of the leaf nodes is labeled by a pair (a,b), where a is the number of procedures without errors and b is the number of procedures with errors.

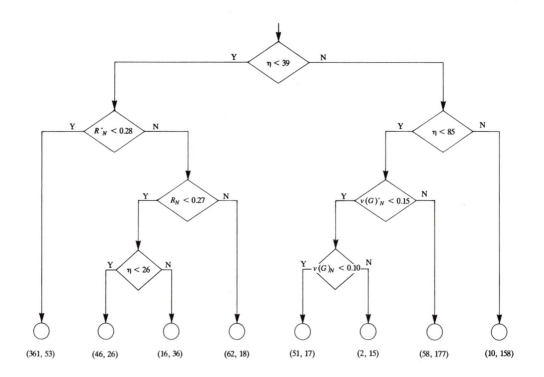

Figure 7.1   An example of a decision tree to identify error-prone modules.

Figure 7.1 illustrates that it is very difficult to find threshold values that correctly discriminate error-free and error-prone procedures. Furthermore, the threshold values probably will change from one application to another. However, it is encouraging to see that the metric most effective for discrimination at the first level is η ($= \eta_1 + \eta_2$), which has the potential for being available *early* in the development process. We shall discuss this feature further in the next section.

7.2.5 Shen's Study

Successful producers of commercial software have learned two important principles regarding software defects:

(1) It is extremely important to deliver defect-free software to customers.

(2) Should there be defects, the cost of correcting them can increase enormously with the time to discovery.

Consequently, a technique that facilitates the *early* detection of the majority of software defects should be very useful. One approach is to identify those software components that are believed to have the highest concentration of defects *early* so that more testing and correcting resources can be directed to them. The earlier these components are known, the less costly it is to remove the defects. Therefore, it is of interest to study the metrics that are available during the development phases to see if any metric (or a combination of some) can be used to guide the testing process.

The products studied by Shen *et al.* were developed at IBM's Santa Teresa Laboratory and released during the period between 1980 and 1983 [SHEN85]. Product A is a software metrics counting tool written primarily in Pascal and designed for the internal use of various development organizations within IBM. Product B is a compiler written primarily in PL/S (a system derivative of PL/1) and released in three successive versions (B1, B2, and B3). Product C is a database system written primarily in assembly language.

Programs were composed of separately compilable subprograms called *modules*; typically, each module supports one or more system functions. Each module was classified as one of the following types:

BASE modules — unchanged modules from a previous release of the same product

MODIFIED modules — changed modules from a previous release of the same product

NEW modules — modules that did not exist in a previous release of the same product

The size and principal language of the products considered are given in Table 7.4. The column labeled "KTSI" shows the total number of source instructions (excluding comments) in thousands of lines of code. The column labeled "KCSI" shows the number of NEW or MODIFIED lines in thousands. Note that the KTSI and KCSI entries are the same for the two newly developed products A and B1.

The number of program changes were recorded as defect data during the testing and maintenance phases. (These are denoted by d_1 and d_2 in the following discussion.) All the metrics related to Software Science and the number of decisions (DE) were available for analysis. If we divide the development

Table 7.4   Summary of Products Used in Shen's Study

Product	Modules	KTSI	KCSI	Language
A	25	7	7	Pascal
B1	253	86	86	PL/S
B2	253	89	3	PL/S
B3	258	94	5	PL/S
C	639	326	60	Assembly

process into design, coding, and testing phases, the available metrics at the end of each phase are as follows:

End of Design — η_1, η_2, and *DE*.   The metric η_1 was assumed to be available since metric studies on PL/S and Pascal show that η_1 increases very slowly with program size when the programming language used discourages the use of GOTO statements ([FITS80], [WANG84]).   The metrics η_2 and *DE* were assumed to be available since a design methodology that promotes the early definition of program data and logic structures was rigorously applied.   In this study, the actual values at the end of coding were used to approximate the values that could be available at this time (but had not actually been recorded).[6]

End of Coding — All software metrics that are derivable from the source code are available at this time.   The Software Science related metrics and the logic structure metric *DE* were used in this study.

End of Testing — At this point, in addition to the information already available, test results (d_1) for each module are known and were used in the study.

The authors were interested in regression models that could be used to predict the total number of defects (d_{tot}) at the end of all phases.   In addition, since most modules did not have any defects after product release ($d_2 = 0$), and those that did typically had only one or two, a binary dependent variable $P[d_2 > 0]$ whose value is *zero* if the module has no post-release defects (and *one* otherwise) was also of interest.   A regression-derived estimator for $P[d_2 > 0]$ has

---

6. Wang has shown that under certain controlled conditions the values of some data structure metrics (η_2, *VARS*) change little from the end of design to the end of coding phases (see Section 4.4).

a potentially useful interpretation — it represents the *expected probability* that a particular module will contain one or more defects after release. An "all possible regressions" search procedure was used to identify the "best" set of one, two, and three independent variables from the pool of variables available at the end of each phase.[7] The coefficient of multiple determination, R^2, was used to select the best regression model in each case.

Table 7.5 Best Predictors at the End of Design Phase and the End of Coding Phase

Product	d_{tot}	$P[d_2 > 0]$	Subset
A	η_2	η_2	
B1	DE	η_2	1
B2	η_2	η_2	2
B3	η_2	DE	2
C	DE	η_2	3
C	η_1	η_2	4

1. NEW modules, excluding table initialization modules.

2. MODIFIED modules, excluding table initialization modules.

3. NEW assembly language modules.

4. MODIFIED assembly language modules.

The metrics found to be the best single predictors of d_{tot} and $P[d_2>0]$ at the end of the design phase are shown in Table 7.5. Modules that were mainly responsible for table initializations were eliminated, as in Akiyama's study. The number of unique operands (η_2) was found to be the best single predictor overall. For the subsets for which DE was the best predictor, the difference in performance between η_2 and DE was small: it was found not to be significant at the 0.01 level.[8]

At the end of the coding phase, it was surprising to find that the best predictors shown in Table 7.5 remain the best predictors, even though many more metrics are now available. This finding is consistent with Akiyama's results,

---

7. This "exhaustive" procedure is different from the "heuristic" used by the statistics package in Motley and Brooks' study (Section 7.2.2), which had a much larger pool of variables to choose from.

8. A test of significance based on Fisher's z' Transformation was used (see [NETE74], pp. 404–407).

where DE was found to be a good predictor (Section 7.2.1). It lends some support to the finding by Motley and Brooks that the number of undefined variables and the number of unconditional jumps were identified as the best single-variable predictors (Section 7.2.2). The first of these measures is a subset of η_2, while the second is related to DE. However, it differs with the finding by Halstead and Ottenstein, who considered V to be the best predictor.

At the end of the testing phase, d_1 can be added to the set of available independent variables. Only $P[d_2>0]$ is considered as a dependent variable since d_1 accounts for 60% to 90% of the variance observed in d_{tot}. The best single-variable predictors are shown in Table 7.6. Values of R^2 were higher for η_2 than for d_1 in four of six cases. However, the differences were generally small (amounting to around ten percent or less of the observed variance in $P[d_2>0]$), and were found not to be significant.

Table 7.6   Best Metrics at the End of Testing Phase

Product	$P[d_2>0]$	Subset
A	η_2	
B1	η_2	1
B2	η_2	2
B3	d_1	2
C	d_1	3
C	η_2	4

1. NEW modules, excluding table initialization modules.

2. MODIFIED modules, excluding table initialization modules.

3. NEW assembly language modules.

4. MODIFIED assembly language modules.

Product B1 was chosen for a more detailed analysis because of its large size, homogeneity in language and module types, and completeness in error data. The evaluation of the regression model[9] $\hat{d}_{tot} = b_0 + b_1\eta_2$ produces $R^2 = 0.74$, $PRED(0.25) = 0.43$, and $\overline{MRE} = 0.47$. Inclusion of additional

---

9. The constants b_0 and b_1 are omitted at IBM's request.

metrics in the model does not improve performance appreciably. The model $\hat{P}[d_2 > 0] = c_0 + c_1\eta_2$ can be evaluated differently. If we classify modules with $\hat{P}[d_2 > 0] \geq 0.5$ as high risk, and those with $\hat{P}[d_2 > 0] < 0.5$ as low risk, 75% of the modules in B1 were classified correctly using the model.[10] Note that these values reflect the goodness-of-fit of these models with the data used to develop them, and are probably higher than would be expected if the models were applied to new data.

The performance of the models using other metrics is worse than that of the model using η_2 as the independent variable, although in some cases the difference is minor. The issue of how soon these metrics can be accurately estimated becomes quite important. Since η_2 may be useful in identifying *at an early stage* those modules most likely to contain errors, it may be used to target certain modules for early or additional testing, in order to increase the efficiency of the defect removal process. The idea of relating software errors to some metrics that can be obtained at an early stage of development has also been explored by Troy and Zweben in a study of a medium-sized project [TROY81] (see also Section 2.9).

7.2.6 Removing the Effect of Module Size

If there is one finding with regards to program defects with which all studies agree, it is "larger modules have more defects." Correlation analyses of published data show that a linear relationship between defects and size is significant at the 0.01 level (for example, $r = 0.83$ for Akiyama's data, 0.81 for Shen's Product A, 0.84 for Shen's Product B1). Halstead's model hypothesizes a perfect correlation between defects and V, a metric of program size. Thus, it is not unreasonable to consider a *normalized* metric for program quality, called *defect density*, defined as in

$$\text{defect density} = \frac{\text{number of defects in module}}{\text{module size}} \tag{7.4}$$

(See also Section 2.8.1.) It is hoped that after the size component is extracted (by division), the resultant density metric will be independent of module size and will serve as a useful measure for the module's quality. Using a similar argument, many metrics that are linearly related to module size can also be normalized before analysis ([AKIY71], [MOTL77], [POTI82]).

An interesting phenomenon was observed by several researchers independently — larger modules seem to have lower defect densities ([MOTL77], [BASI84]). Since larger modules are generally more complex, a lower defect density is rather unexpected. Motley and Brooks suggested that, in their case, longer programs were less thoroughly tested.[11] In addition to this possibility,

---

10. This result is comparable to that found in Potier's study.

11. Recall that they used d_1, defects uncovered during the testing phase, as the dependent variable.

Basili and Perricone also suggested that there may have been a large number of interface errors that were distributed evenly across all modules, thus biasing the measurement against the smaller modules. Furthermore, larger modules might have been coded with more care than smaller modules because of their size. These explanations are attempts to support the intuition that defect density should be independent of module size, even though such independence has not been observed.

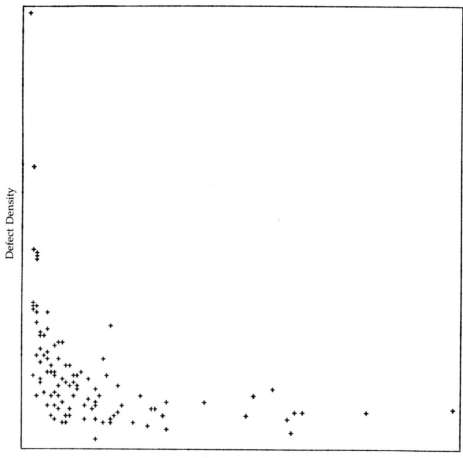

Figure 7.2   Defect Density (d_{tot}/N) versus Module Size (N) for Product B1.

The plot of d_{tot}/N versus N for Product B1 in [SHEN85] is shown in Figure 7.2. Again, we observe the trend that there is a higher defect density in smaller modules. Whatever the reasons, the finding that $b_0 + b_1N$ is a better model for d_{tot} than is b_1N is consistent with this result. If

$$d_{tot} \approx b_0 + b_1N$$

then the defect density becomes

$$\frac{d_{tot}}{N} \approx \frac{b_0}{N} + b_1$$

Thus, as N increases, $\dfrac{d_{tot}}{N}$ decreases asymptotically to b_1, as suggested in Figure 7.2. Further analysis of the data showed that the minimum size beyond which error density could reasonably be considered unrelated to module size was $N = 2500$, or approximately 500 lines of code. Only 24 (out of 108) modules were this large or larger. Analysis of products B2 and C produced similar results.

The existence of interface errors (suggested by Basili and Perricone) could explain why $b_0 > 0$ in the regression model. Our analysis leads to the conclusion that error density is generally a poor size-normalized index of program quality. Its use in comparing the quality of programs without regard to related factors, such as complexity and size, is ill-advised. Similarly, normalizing other metrics by division by a size metric should be examined carefully. Even if the metric in question is linearly correlated with the size metric, such normalization is meaningful only if the constant term (b_0) in the regression model is approximately zero.

Feuer and Fowlkes used a somewhat different approach in extracting the size component [FEUE79]. They retained the defect density metric as the dependent variable. Since most metrics were found to relate to program size in a study of 197 PL/1 programs, they proposed the following procedure to remove the effect of the size component for any metric M:

(1) Find constants b_0 and b_1 so that $\hat{M} = b_0 + b_1S$ is the regression model for M where S is lines of code in thousands.

(2) Compute $M_R = M - \hat{M}$ as the "residual" M. This is presumed to be the component of the metric that is unrelated to S.

The relationship between L_R (Halstead's residual L metric) and defect density (for groups of programs) is shown in Figure 7.3. The interpretation is that for two programs of the same size, the one with lower level L measure (higher difficulty D measure) is expected to have higher density of defects. A comparable study using Product B1 of Section 7.2.5 is shown in Figure 7.4. In this case, the trend observed by Feuer and Fowlkes is *not* evident at all.

A detailed study of the data shows that a linear model relating the N metric and the L metric is not appropriate. In fact, Figure 7.5 is a plot of the level metric L and the program length N for Product B1. We have found that this relationship is best represented by the "power" curve:

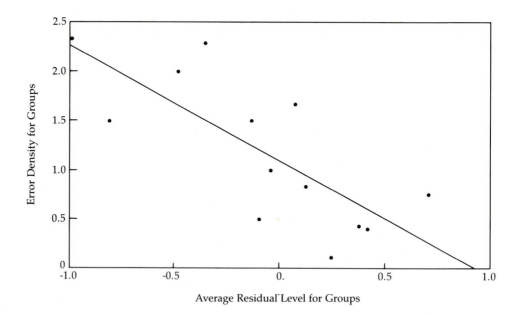

Figure 7.3   Defect (Error) Density versus Residual Level. © 1979 IEEE.

$$L = 1.72 N^{-.66}$$

Thus, we cannot say that the residual level L_R is a size-normalized metric. If we include the problem inherent in the defect density metric, it is not surprising that we cannot detect a relationship when defect density is plotted against L_R. Although extracting the size component using residuals may be a meaningful approach under certain circumstances, its widespread use without careful testing for appropriateness is unwarranted.

7.3   Dynamic Models of Defects

A *dynamic* model of software defects includes the component of time, which is the interval between successive detections of defects. This interval is considered a random variable with cumulative distribution $F(\tau)$ and probability density function $f(\tau)$. As discussed in Section 2.8.3, the *reliability* of the software system is defined in Equation (2.37), which is reproduced here:

RANGE OF X AXIS: -1.64987465e-02 1.394950
RANGE OF Y AXIS: 4.78468900e-04 4.166666

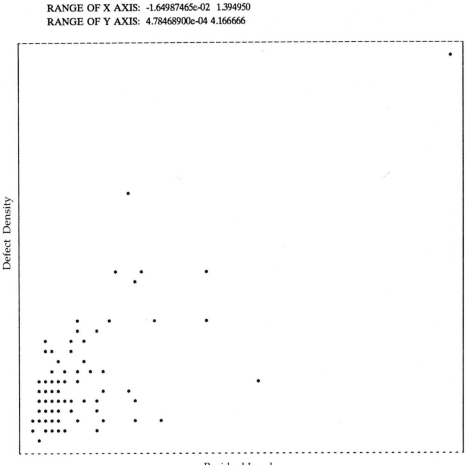

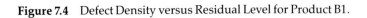

Residual Level

Figure 7.4 Defect Density versus Residual Level for Product B1.

$$R(\tau) = 1 - F(\tau) \qquad\qquad (7.5)$$

The *mean time to failure* (MTTF) is derived from Equations (2.44) and (2.45):

$$\text{MTTF} = \int_0^\infty \tau f(\tau)d\tau = \int_0^\infty R(\tau)d\tau \qquad\qquad (7.6)$$

Another measure of interest is the *hazard rate* $h(\tau)$, which is the probability that the software fails during the interval $(\tau, \tau+d\tau]$ given that it has not failed before τ. This is defined in Equation (2.39) and reproduced here:

RANGE OF X AXIS: 48 12863
RANGE OF Y AXIS: 2.30675078e-03 1.72727273

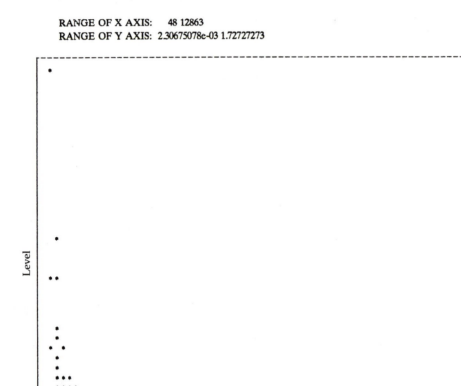

Figure 7.5   Level versus Program Length N for Product B1.

$$h(\tau) = \frac{f(\tau)}{1 - F(\tau)} \qquad (7.7)$$

If the hazard rate is known instead of the distribution function, the reliability can be computed using Equation (2.42).

$$R(\tau) = e^{-\int_0^\tau h(x)dx} \qquad (7.8)$$

Equation (7.6) can then be used to compute MTTF.

Most dynamic models that have been proposed consider the software system as a "black box"; the reliability (and MTTF) is estimated without regard to the complexity of the program. An excellent survey of these models has been published recently by Ramamoorthy and Bastani [RAMA82]. Many of them are called *reliability growth models.* The general assumption is that all defects detected during the development and testing phases are corrected, and the correction process does not introduce new defects. This ideal process allows the reliability to increase. The cost of testing and fixing may then be balanced against the increase in reliability to produce a software system with minimal cost, while meeting reliability objectives. Several other models do not consider the correction of defects after detection. They assume the software is being tested for the purpose of estimating its reliability. These models may be used to show that the software possesses high reliability, without having to prove its correctness using analytical methods. All models include some constraint on the distribution of defects ($F(\tau)$ or $f(\tau)$) or the hazard rate ($h(\tau)$). We shall discuss one such model in detail as an example.

7.3.1 The Musa Model

One of the reliability growth models was proposed by Musa in 1975 and later revised in 1980 [MUSA80]. It may be based either on execution time (software is in use continuously) or calendar time (software may not be in use continuously due to other resource limitations). We shall discuss the execution time model first, which makes the following assumptions:

Random inputs — Test input sets should be selected randomly from the complete set of input sets anticipated in actual operation. This should be true for any time interval during the testing process, even if it is small. This assumption may be valid at the beginning of the testing phase, since any set of initial test cases may be considered to be a random sample of all test cases. It may not be valid later on if some elaborate testing strategies are used, which exercise certain error-prone modules more or which test boundary values of loops.

Complete observation — All software failures are observed. This may not be easy when the output of the test is not a numerical value, but a sequence of events for a real-time system.

Independence — Failure intervals are independent of each other. This is a basic assumption in order to use the derivations that lead to the reliability measure. This is not unreasonable; even if a programmer makes several errors that are related, their discovery using random inputs may still be an independent random process.

Exponential distribution — The distribution function assumes the form $F(\tau) = 1 - e^{-\lambda\tau}$ and the density function assumes the form $f(\tau) = \lambda e^{-\lambda\tau}$.

Equation (7.7) then reduces the hazard rate to a constant (λ) during the interval between failures. This assumption greatly simplifies the analysis and has been used extensively in many related research areas.

Hazard rate — The hazard rate is proportional to the number of defects remaining in the system. If we let $d_{tot} = d_1 + d_2$ be the total number of defects and $d_1(t)$ be the number of defects detected so far, then

$$h(t) = \lambda(t) = c(d_{tot} - d_1(t)) \tag{7.9}$$

Note that the hazard rate is fixed during an interval between failures, but is a decreasing function of the execution time t.

The rate of defect detection — The rate is proportional to the hazard rate:

$$\frac{dd_1(t)}{dt} = bh(t) \tag{7.10}$$

Although $h(t)$ is actually a step function of t since one or more defects are corrected at each failure, it may be viewed as a continuous function if the failure intervals are small. This assumption is essential to make the analysis simple.

Equations (7.9) and (7.10) may be combined to obtain the following differential equation:

$$\frac{dd_1(t)}{dt} + bcd_1(t) = bcd_{tot} \tag{7.11}$$

Since $d_1(t) = 0$ at $t = 0$, the solution of Equation (7.11) is

$$d_1(t) = d_{tot}(1 - e^{-bct}) \tag{7.12}$$

From Equation (7.9), we have

$$h(t) = cd_{tot}e^{-bct} \tag{7.13}$$

The exponential distribution assumption also simplifies the computation of the mean time to failure MTTF. Using the first equality of Equation (7.6), we have

$$\begin{aligned}
\text{MTTF} &= \int_0^\infty \tau f(\tau)d\tau \\
&= \int_0^\infty \lambda \tau e^{-\lambda \tau}d\tau \\
&= \frac{1}{\lambda}
\end{aligned} \tag{7.14}$$

Using Equations (7.13) and (7.14), and noting that MTTF is actually a function of the execution time t, we have

$$\text{MTTF}(t) = \frac{1}{h(t)} = \frac{1}{cd_{tot}}e^{bct} \tag{7.15}$$

Note that the MTTF grows during the Testing phase as t increases.

The parameters of Equation (7.15) must be estimated using some other methods in order to use this model. Musa suggested that the Akiyama model (Section 7.2.1) be used to estimate d_{tot} as a linear function of program size. In fact, a dynamic model cannot be accurate unless it incorporates an accurate *static* model that produces d_{tot}. The parameters b and c are to be determined by observing the defect history of a "similar" program. Musa claimed that data taken for 16 software systems indicated that the model, characterized by Equation (7.12), was followed "quite well." He gave an example, which is reproduced in Figure 7.6. Note that the vertical axis has been transformed so that the model's estimates given by Equation (7.12) appear as a straight line. The defects were detected faster than that predicted by the model earlier in the testing phase, but slower later. The model was also more accurate later in the testing phase.

As discussed in Section 2.8.2, testing of commercial software normally proceeds as follows: the detection of defects by an independent test group, the transmission of defect reports to the development team for correction, the actual defect correction, and the subsequent transmission back to the test group. Depending on the resource limitations, the software may not be actively tested while waiting for the correction to take place. Therefore, it is necessary to convert the execution time t in the model to the calendar time t'. With a number of additional assumptions, Musa was able to derive the conversion factor as a function of d_{tot}, the number of personnel available to fix the defects, the average resource expenditure per defect correction, and several other process-related constants. The factor may be adjusted to be more or less than one, for example, by decreasing or increasing the personnel. (See also [MUSA80].)

7.3.2 Other Dynamic Models

The Musa model, the Jelinski-Moranda linear de-eutrophication model [JELI72], the Shooman model [SHOO82], and the Schick-Wolverton model [SCHI78] all share the first four assumptions of Section 7.3.1. They can be generalized and can be called the "general Poisson model" ([ANGU80], [RAMA82]). The hazard rate is of the form

$$h_j = (d_{tot} - M_j)\phi \tag{7.16}$$

where M_j is the number of defects corrected *before* the jth failure and *after* the $(j-1)^{th}$ failure. In the Musa model, $M_j = d_1(t)$ and $\phi = c$. All of the Poisson models have the simple property that MTTF $= \dfrac{1}{h_j}$.

Ramamoorthy and Bastani discussed other reliability models in [RAMA82]. Some modify Assumption 4 in Section 7.3.1 so that $h(t)$ decreases during the period between failures. Others allow new defects to be introduced during the correction process. Variations in the assumptions lead to variations in the

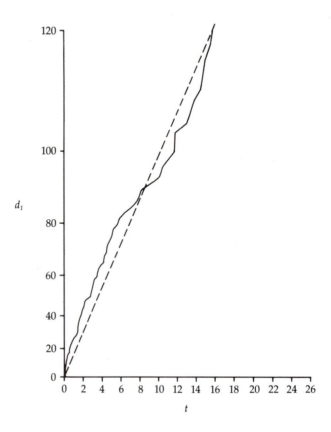

Figure 7.6   The defects discovered (d_1) as a function of testing time (t).

derivations of the reliability measure R and the mean time to failure measure MTTF. The lack of reliable data makes the validation of any of these models difficult. It appears that future research concerning these defect models will not lead to significant results unless the data collection process is much improved, as suggested in Chapter 2.

7.4 Summary and Conclusions

Since there appear to be no error-free software development techniques in use (or on the horizon), the testing phase cannot be eliminated. Any technique to identify error-prone modules that may require more testing should be very useful. Because of the uncertainties involved in defect detection, models that accurately estimate the total number of defects are difficult to formulate and validate. It may not even be necessary — knowing a module will almost certainly have errors in it is enough to guide the testing process. Studies described in [POTI82] and [SHEN85] addressed this need. They provide methods to set threshold values for certain metrics so that modules with measurements higher than the threshold are more likely to have errors than others. If the threshold values can be determined for a wide range of programs, then they may be included in programming conventions so that programs with measurements that exceed the threshold values receive extra attention. There should also be some theoretical basis for the particular values chosen. More studies are certainly needed.

Static models, rather than dynamic ones, can be used to determine threshold levels. Before more supporting evidence becomes available, dynamic models of software reliability (or MTTF) are primarily of academic interest. However, the recording of defects and their times of discovery is still very valuable. The data on the discovery times may be combined with other product and process metrics to construct "hybrid" models that assess the reliability of the software during various phases of its life cycle.

Exercises

1. Discuss the possible differences between product-level defect counts and module-level defect counts.

2. State the condition(s) when the C metric used in Akiyama's study is equivalent to McCabe's $v(G)$ metric.

3. Which of the variables listed in Table 7.2 are likely to be highly correlated with each other? Which of these variables would probably be grouped together through factor analysis? (See Section 3.4.4.) Justify your answer.

4. Discuss the problems of using multilinear regression models, especially the problems associated with Motley and Brooks' study.

5. Use the procedure given in Section 7.2.3 to determine the V metric from Akiyama's data given in Table 7.1. Use a c value of 3. Test the model in

Equation (7.3) with the results. Compare the performance of this model with those results shown in Table 7.1.

6.   Generate a decision tree similar to that shown in Figure 7.1 for the data given in Table 7.1. The modules MC, MD, and MF had no post-release errors [AKIY71]. Which metric (and threshold value) would you use as the first-level discriminant? What is the percentage of modules that are classified correctly? (This is a hard problem requiring some creative thinking.)

7.   Describe a design methodology that, when applied rigorously, can provide good estimates for η_2 and DE at the end of the design phase.

8.   Why do smaller modules usually have higher defect density than larger ones? Does this imply that larger modules are of higher quality than smaller ones?

9.   Show that $f(\tau) = h(\tau) \times R(\tau)$.

10. What is the difference between the τ given in Assumption 4 and the t given in Assumption 5 of Section 7.3.1?

11. What is the physical meaning of b as given in Equation (7.10)?

12. Most dynamic models assume that a defect is fixed immediately after it is detected. Which assumptions, if any, of Section 7.3.1 depend on this requirement? Why?

13. The Schick-Wolverton model assumes $h(t) = c(d_{tot} - d_1(t))t = \lambda(t) \times t$. Compute the MTTF for this model. (This is a hard problem requiring some skills not taught in this book.)

14. Musa's model assumes no new defects are introduced during error correction. Suppose one defect is introduced for every five error corrections. Modify Equation (7.10) to incorporate this assumption.

The Future
of Software Engineering
Metrics and Models

8

The tar pit of software engineering will continue to be sticky for a long time to come. ... The management of this complex craft will demand our best use of new languages and systems, our best adaptation of proven engineering management methods, liberal doses of common sense, and a God-given humility to recognize our fallibility and limitations.

Frederick P. Brooks, Jr., Epilogue in *The Mythical Man-Month*, Addison-Wesley, Reading, MA (1975).

8.1 Introduction

The goal of software engineering can be summarized as follows:

> *To produce higher quality software at lower cost.*

In this book, we have emphasized the fundamental role of measurement as we seek to understand programming productivity and program quality. The goal of software engineering cannot be achieved without objective measurement of software phenomena. We have discussed several metrics. We found it useful to differentiate between *process* metrics, which are attributes of the development process, and *product* metrics, which are attributes of the resulting software product. We also suggested that the proper use of statistics and experimentation is essential in assessing the effects of languages, methodologies, and systems. Advances in the study of metrics and measurements may make the tar pit of software engineering less sticky.

We also stated that metrics can be combined with hypotheses to produce *models* of software behavior. There are many potential practical benefits and uses of metrics and models, which include:

- The ability to describe quantitatively the current state of software parameters, such as software quality, resources expended, and productivity.

- The ability to predict software parameters, such as system cost, delivery time, and reliability.

- The ability to express requirements quantitatively both as goals and as acceptance criteria.

- The ability to quantify trade-offs that can be used by management in allocating resources.

- The ability to monitor progress, to anticipate problems, and to provide feedback to software personnel about potential problems.

However, it is fair to say that the technology is a long way from realizing these potential benefits. There has been significant progress in the development of metrics and models in recent years. However, a great deal of research is still required to refine and validate existing models, and to develop new and better ones. The validation of proposed metrics and models is an especially pressing need. In most cases, metrics have been proposed by individual researchers based on limited amounts of data or on small-scale experiments. The validity of these metrics needs to be confirmed by independent researchers using additional data or experiments from (or resembling) real-world conditions. Unfortunately, the value system in the research world gives very little credit to researchers who conduct confirmatory studies as opposed to "original" research. Nevertheless, validation studies should be encouraged. Indeed, the very process of attempting to validate a given metric or model frequently reveals new underlying relationships and leads to new hypotheses which can be further explored. We particularly note the progress that has been made in software cost and productivity models. As a result of recent studies, we now have a much better knowledge of the primary factors that affect cost and a much more precise estimate of how much effect each factor can have on cost. With this information, managers are in a better position not only to estimate the cost of software, but also to improve productivity and, thus, to control cost. Although much remains to be done, progress has been made.

A major impediment to research concerning software is the general lack of good industrial data. The DoD STARS-SEI initiative recognizes this problem and suggests some steps to correct it. We need a concerted effort to collect a common core of data from a large number of software projects accompanied by precise definitions of the software parameters and metrics of interest. It is proposed that SEI will assume a leadership role in identifying and defining a common set of software parameters, in collecting this information in a software database, and in disseminating this database to interested researchers and institutions. Only with such a database can we hope to develop and validate metrics and models that can be confidently used by practitioners.

We recognize that it is impossible to persuade industrial sources to place their raw data in the public domain due to marketing consequences, such as a competitor learning the productivity rate of a certain company. However, this data should still be made available to *researchers* for model development and evaluation. The purpose of models is the description of trends and relationships, rather than the identification of actual data values. Steps can be taken in the publication of such results so that the proprietary nature of the information is protected.

The identification and validation of good metrics and models will not by itself result in improved software development on the national level. We must also facilitate their widespread use among managers and programmers. It is undoubtedly true that little use is made today of software models and metrics, even when some confidence in these has been established. The STARS program envisions three activities to encourage their use:

Developing Measurement Tools — Software tools that automatically collect data for appropriate metrics need to be developed. These tools should be unobtrusive and efficient so that they result in only minimal distraction to software personnel. The availability of tools will also ensure consistency across different organizations and projects.

Disseminating Information about Metrics — A systematic attempt to disseminate information about measurement should be undertaken. Guidelines on data collection, the availability and usage of tools, results validating various metrics, and interpretation of these results should be made easily available.

Developing Training Programs and Clinics — Training programs have been used effectively to disseminate information and to educate potential users. Training programs and clinics can also serve to obtain feedback from users about their experiences in using the guidelines and about problems that arise from incorporating a measurement program.

8.2 Quantitative Assessment of Software Engineering Techniques

In this book, we have discussed the factors that seem to affect programming productivity and program quality in both the micro- and macro-level cases. In some macro-level cases, we have discussed how much effect a given factor can have on productivity. Improvements in productivity by factors of from 2 to 10 are believed achievable over a period of perhaps 10 years. These improvements can be achieved by better managing those factors that are controllable. We know that some factors that affect productivity are not controllable. These include the inherent problem complexity and required reliability. Those that can be controlled include the use of modern programming practices, tool availability, improved programming environments, personnel capability and experience, use of higher level languages, and reduced requirements volatility.

It is generally conceded that significant productivity improvement is not easily achievable. Indeed, it appears that a systematic effort by management over a long time period will be required. In addition, renewed effort to assess quantitatively the effect of each factor on productivity will be required. If we do not know how much effect a factor has on productivity, then it will be impossible to know how much we can improve productivity by improving or controlling that factor. At the current time, our knowledge of these effects is very meager.

Table 8.1   Estimated DoD Software Initiative Impact on Software Productivity

| | DoD Average Effort Multipliers | | |
Cost Driver	1976	1983	1993
Use of Software Tools	1.05	1.02	0.85
Use of Modern Programming Practice	0.98	0.95	0.85
Programming Language Experience	1.03	1.02	0.98
Software Environment Experience	1.05	1.03	0.95
Computer Execution Time Constraint	1.25	1.18	1.11
Computer Storage Constraint	1.22	1.15	1.06
Computer Turnaround Time	1.03	1.01	0.90
Reduced Requirement Volatility	1.17	1.15	1.00
Retool Avoidance	1.06	1.06	1.00
Software Reuse	0.93	0.90	0.50
Relative Effort	2.01	1.54	0.36
Productivity Gain		1.30	4.34

A major attempt to assess (quantitatively) potential productivity improvement is outlined in a paper by Druffel [DRUF82]. The primary assumption is that the cost drivers in the COCOMO model are indeed significant and that the cost driver multipliers correctly assess their effect on development effort. The result of this study is given in Table 8.1. The 1976 and 1983 columns contain the estimated relative effect of each factor on nominal effort, while the 1993 column contains the projected effect if management attempts to control the indicated factor. Thus, the relative effort multiplier for 1993 of 0.36 compared to the relative multiplier of 1.54 for 1983 is seen to result in a productivity gain of 4.34 over this 10-year span. The projected productivity gains due to each of the cost driver factors is about 10% except for the Software Reuse factor, which is projected to yield a gain in productivity of 45%. The extent to which these gains are achievable is very difficult to assess, especially when they are applied to the entire software industry.

There is some consensus that the factor that is capable of yielding significant productivity gains is that of software reuse. Historically, reusable code has been most successful in the scientific applications area where substantial libraries of subroutines are available. Its use in other application areas, such as real time systems and operating systems, has been much less successful. Success in these latter areas will depend on our ability to identify, produce, and catalog a set of "standard" software modules that have wide ranging applicability. In addition, flexible interfaces must be provided, as well as a convenient unifying language that will allow easy access to modules. It is likely that these libraries of standard modules will, at least initially, be somewhat application dependent. It is generally agreed that truly significant productivity gains can only be achieved through software reuse.

8.3 A New Software Development Paradigm

A more revolutionary approach to software development is advocated by Balzer, Cheatham, and Green [BALZ83]. They begin by observing that maintenance accounts for some 80% of total life-cycle effort and that, because maintenance is performed on the source code which has already been optimized by skilled programmers, system maintainers have difficulty in understanding and enhancing that software. They suggest an automation-based software paradigm in which maintenance is performed on the specification of the software, rather than on the code implementation as is the current custom. They believe that this approach will eliminate the difficulties that arise from complexities in the code artificially introduced by programmers. When enhancements in a product are called for, they would change the specification and then reimplement the code. To be successful, the implementation process would have to be fast, reliable, and inexpensive. They believe that automated implementation support tools either already exist or can be readily constructed for this purpose. While the authors claim that this software paradigm is capable of producing orders of magnitude improvement in productivity and quality, at this time, the development of this approach is still in its infancy.

It has long been a belief of the artificial intelligence (AI) research community that some AI techniques can be successfully applied to automatic programming. A recent paper by Frenkel surveys research efforts in this area and tries to provide a perspective on the progress that can be expected [FREN85]. The goal is to develop an "expert" system to generate a design and high-level language instructions from a complete specification of a user's requirements. This is in the same spirit as developing a compiler to generate machine code from a high-level language. A typical expert system consists of a *knowledge base*, which contains facts and rules that capture the reasoning of human experts in a given problem domain, and an *inference machine*, which is capable of deriving new facts from the knowledge base. When applied to software development, we can envision a series of "knowledge-based software assistants" for each of several phases of the software life cycle, including project management, requirements analysis, implementation, validation and testing, and maintenance. One objective of an Expert Maintainer's Assistant Program, for example, would be to help the software maintainer to modify an existing program. The human maintainer decides what changes to make and initiates them, but the Maintainer's Assistant identifies all parts of the system that are affected by these changes and updates them consistently.

Whether such expert systems can be successfully applied to software development and whether they can help improve programming productivity by orders of magnitude are not yet known. Such systems themselves take years to develop and may consume a huge amount of computer resources. It is doubtful that expert systems for automatic program generation will be successfully developed in the near future that will have a significant impact on productivity. It is reasonable, however, to expect that some restricted forms of these may be available soon to assist programmers in certain life-cycle phases.

8.4 A Last Word — Looking Forward

As we complete this book in 1986, the future of software engineering metrics and models appears unclear. There is no question that the software development industry is in desperate need of better means of estimating costs and completion times, of controlling the development process, and of eliminating costly errors. Many project managers, team leaders, systems analysts, and programmers have developed their own intuitive techniques for dealing with the difficult world in which they operate. Many of these techniques are adequate, but most provide far less precise estimates and control than are desired.

There is a small, but dedicated, cadre of scientists in universities, research organizations, and industry trying to find solutions to software development problems. Most of these researchers are basing their techniques on metrics and models. But much research is frustrated by lack of accurate data, the inherent variability of any process involving human beings, and unrealistic expectations of the concerned community.

It is our hope that this book serves the following purposes:

(1) To state as clearly as possible the software "problem"

(2) To acquaint readers with the software engineering metrics and models that exist

(3) To describe enough experimental design and statistical analysis techniques to allow readers to be knowledgeable critics of empirical studies or to consider conducting these themselves

(4) To describe the results and models from a number of so-called "small-scale laboratory experiments"

(5) To describe the results and models from a number of larger studies concerning productivity and effort estimation

(6) To discuss existing defect models and the general problem of determining software quality

We sincerely hope that the reader will be inspired to join in the continuing effort to obtain better means of estimating, measuring, and controlling the software development process. It will only be through a concerted effort of all practitioners and researchers that real progress will be made. If this book provides a better understanding of the state of affairs to those who will help advance the state of the art, then its objective will have been met.

References

[AKIY71]   Akiyama, F. An example of software system debugging. *Information Processing* 71 (1971): 353-379.

[ALBR79]   Albrecht, A. J. Measuring application development productivity. *Proceedings of the Joint SHARE/GUIDE Symposium* (October 1979): 83-92.

[ALBR83]   Albrecht, A. J., and J. E. Gaffney, Jr. Software function, source lines of code, and development effort prediction: a Software Science validation. *IEEE Transactions on Software Engineering* SE-9, 6 (November 1983): 639-647.

[ANGU80]   Angus, J. E., R. E. Schafer, and A. Sukert. Software reliability model validation. *Proceedings of the Annual Reliability and Maintainability Symposium* (January 1980): 191-199.

[BAIL81]   Bailey, J. W., and V. R. Basili. A meta-model for software development resource expenditures. *Proceedings of the Fifth International Conference on Software Engineering* (1981): 107-116.

[BAIL82]   Bailey, J. W. Personal correspondence with S. Thebaut (April 1982).

[BAKE72]   Baker, F. T. Chief programmer team management of production programming. *IBM Systems Journal* 11, 1 (1972): 56-73.

[BAKE80]   Baker, A. L., and S. H. Zweben. A comparison of measures of control flow complexity. *IEEE Transactions on Software Engineering* SE-6, 6 (November 1980): 506-512.

[BALZ83]   Balzer, R., T. E. Cheatham, and C. Green. Software technology in the 1990s: using a new paradigm. *IEEE Computer* 16, 3 (March 1983): 39-45.

[BARL75]   Barlow, R. E., and F. Proschan. *Statistical Theory of Reliability and Life Testing.* New York: Holt, Rinehart and Winston, 1975.

[BASI75]   Basili, V. R., and A. J. Turner. Iterative enhancement: a practical technique for software development. *IEEE Transactions on Software Engineering* SE-1, 4 (December 1975): 390-396.

[BASI77]   Basili, V. R., M. V. Zelkowitz, F. E. McGarry, R. W. Reiter, Jr., W. F. Truszkowski, and D. L. Weiss. The Software Engineering Laboratory. *Rep. SEL-77-001,* Software Engineering Laboratory, NASA/Goddard Space Flight Center, Greenbelt, MD (May 1977).

[BASI79]   Basili, V. R., and R. W. Reiter. An investigation of human factors in software development. *IEEE Computer* 12, 12 (December 1979): 21-38.

[BASI81]   Basili, V. R., and T. Phillips. Evaluating and comparing the software metrics in the Software Engineering Laboratory. *Performance Evaluation Review* (ACM SIGMETRICS) 10 (March 1981): 95-106.

[BASI83]   Basili, V. R., R. W. Selby, Jr., and T.-Y. Phillips. Metric analysis and data validation across FORTRAN projects. *IEEE Transactions on Software Engineering* SE-9, 6 (November 1983): 652-663.

[BASI84]   Basili, V. R., and B. T. Perricone. Software errors and complexity: an empirical investigation. *Communications of the ACM* 27, 1 (January 1984): 42-52.

[BEAN84]   Beane, J., N. Giddings, and J. Silverman. Quantifying software designs. *Proceedings of the Seventh International Conference on Software Engineering* (1984): 314-322.

[BELA76]   Belady, L. A., and M. M. Lehman. A model of large program development. *IBM Systems Journal* 15, 3 (1976): 225-252.

[BELA79]   Belady, L. A., and M. M. Lehman. The characteristics of large systems. In *Research Directions in Software Technology*, edited by P. Wegner, 106-138. Cambridge, MA: MIT Press, 1979.

[BEIZ84]   Beizer, B. *Software System Testing and Quality Assurance*. New York: Van Nostrand Reinhold, 1984.

[BELL74]   Bell, D. E., and J. E. Sullivan. Further investigation into the complexity of software. *MITRE Technical Report 2874-2* (June 1974).

[BERS84]   Bersoff, E. H. Elements of software configuration management. *IEEE Transactions on Software Engineering* SE-10, 1 (January 1984): 79-87.

[BLAC77]   Black, R. K. D., R. P. Curnow, R. Katz, and M. D. Gray. BCS software production data. *RADC-TR-77-116*, Boeing Computer Services (1977): NTIS No. AD-A039852.

[BOEH73]   Boehm, B. W. Software and its impact: a quantitative assessment. *Datamation* (May 1973): 48-59.

[BOEH76]   Boehm, B. W., J. R. Brown and M. Lipow. Quantitative evaluation of software quality. *Proceedings of the Second International Conference on Software Engineering* (1976): 592-605.

[BOEH81]   Boehm, B. W. *Software Engineering Economics*. Englewood Cliffs, NJ: Prentice-Hall, 1981.

[BOEH83a] Boehm, B. W. The hardware/software cost ratio: is it a myth? *IEEE Computer* 16, 3 (March 1983): 78-80.

[BOEH83b] Boehm, B. W., and T. A. Standish. Software technology in the 1990s: using an evolutionary paradigm. *IEEE Computer* 16, 11 (November 1983): 30-37.

[BOEH84]   Boehm, B. W. Software engineering economics. *IEEE Transactions on Software Engineering* SE-10, 1 (January 1984): 4-21.

[BROO75]   Brooks, F. P. *The Mythical Man-Month*. Reading MA: Addison-Wesley, 1975.

[BROO80]   Brooke, J. B., and K. D. Duncan. An experimental study of flowcharts as an aid to identification of procedural faults. *Ergonomics* 23 (1980): 387-399.

[BROO81]   Brooks, W. D. Software technology payoff − some statistical evidence. *The Journal of Systems and Software* 2 (1981): 3-9.

[CAMP63] Campbell, D. T., and J. C. Stanley. *Experimental and Quasi-Experimental Designs for Research.* Chicago: Rand McNally and Co., 1963.

[CARB68] Carbonell, J. R., J. I. Elkind, and R. S. Nickerson. On the psychological importance of time in a time-sharing system. *Human Factors* 10 (1968): 135-142.

[CARR79] Carriere, W. M., and R. Thibodeau. Development of a logistics software cost estimating technique for foreign military sales. *GRC Report CR-3-839* (June 1979).

[CHRI81] Christensen, K., G. P. Fitsos, and C. P. Smith. A perspective on Software Science. *IBM Systems Journal* 20, 4 (1981): 372-387.

[COME81] Comer, D. Principles of program design induced from experience with small public programs. *IEEE Transactions on Software Engineering* SE-7, 2 (March 1981): 169-174.

[CONT81] Conte, S. D. The Software Science language level metric. *CSD-TR-373,* Purdue University (September 1981).

[CONT82] Conte, S. D., V. Y. Shen, and K. Dickey. On the effect of different counting rules for control flow operators on Software Science metrics in FORTRAN. *Performance Evaluation Review (ACM SIGMETRICS)* 11, 2 (1982): 118-126.

[COOK82] Cook, M. L. Software metrics: an introduction and annotated bibliography. *Software Engineering Notes (ACM SIGSOFT)* 7, 2 (April 1982): 41-60.

[COUL83] Coulter, N. S. Software Science and cognitive psychology. *IEEE Transactions on Software Engineering* SE-9, 2 (March 1983): 166-171.

[CURT79a] Curtis, B., S. B. Sheppard, P. Milliman, M. A. Borst, and T. Love. Measuring the psychological complexity of software maintenance tasks with the Halstead and McCabe metrics. *IEEE Transactions on Software Engineering* SE-5, 2 (March 1979): 96-104.

[CURT79b] Curtis, B., S. B. Sheppard, and P. Milliman. Third time charm: stronger prediction of programmer performance by software complexity metrics. *Proceedings of the Fourth International Conference on Software Engineering* (1979): 356-360.

[CURT80] Curtis, B. Measurement and experimentation in software engineering. *Proceedings of the IEEE* 68, 9 (September 1980): 1144-1147.

[DECK82] Decker, W. J., and W. A. Taylor. FORTRAN static source code analyzer program (SAP) user's guide (Revision 1). *Rep. SEL-78-102,* Software Engineering Laboratory, NASA/Goddard Space Flight Center, Greenbelt, MD (May 1982).

[DIJK68] Dijkstra, E. W. Go to statements considered harmful. *Communications of the ACM* 11, 3 (March 1968): 147-148.

[DIJK72] Dijkstra, E. W., O. J. Dahl, and C. A. R. Hoare. *Structured Programming.* New York: Academic Press, 1972.

[DRUF82] Druffel, L. E. *Strategy for a DoD Software Initiative*. Washington, DC: CSS DUSD(RAT), 1982. Also in [BOEH83b].

[DUNH83] Dunham, J. R., and E. Kruesi. The measurement task area. *IEEE Computer* 16, 11 (November 1983): 47-54.

[DUNN84] Dunn, R. H. *Software Defect Removal*. New York: McGraw-Hill, 1984.

[DUNS79] Dunsmore, H. E., and J. D. Gannon. Data referencing: an empirical investigation. *IEEE Computer* 12, 12 (December 1979): 50-59. Also in *Human Factors in Software Development*, edited by Bill Curtis, 170-179. Silver Spring, MD: Computer Society Press, 1981.

[DUNS80] Dunsmore, H. E., and J. D. Gannon. Analysis of the effects of programming factors on programming effort. *The Journal of Systems and Software* 1, 2 (1980): 141-153. Also in *Tutorial on Models and Metrics for Software Management and Engineering*. edited by V. R. Basili, 93-105. New York: IEEE Catalog No. EHO-167-7, Computer Society Press, 1980.

[DUNS85] Dunsmore, H. E. The effect of comments, mnemonic names, and modularity: some university experiment results. *Proceedings of Second Symposium on Empirical Foundations of Information and Software Sciences*, (1985).

[ELSH76] Elshoff, J. L. An analysis of some commercial PL/1 programs. *IEEE Transactions on Software Engineering* SE-2, 2 (June 1976): 113-120.

[ELSH77] Elshoff, J. L. The influence of structured programming on PL/I program profiles. *IEEE Transactions on Software Engineering* SE-3, 5 (September 1977): 364-368.

[ELSH78] Elshoff, J. L. An investigation into the effect of the counting method used on Software Science measurements. *ACM SIGPLAN Notices* 13, 2 (February 1978): 30-45.

[FARR65] Farr, L., and H. J. Zagorski. Quantitative analysis of programming cost factors: a progress report. In *ICC Symposium Proceedings on Economics of Automatic Data Processing*, edited by A. B. Frielind. Amsterdam: North-Holland, 1965.

[FELL68] Feller, W. *An Introduction to Probability Theory and Its Applications*. 3rd ed. John Wiley & Sons, New York: 1968.

[FEUE79] Feuer, A. R., and E. B. Fowlkes. Some results from an empirical study of computer software. *Proceedings of the Fourth International Conference on Software Engineering* (1979): 351-355.

[FITS80] Fitsos, G. P. Vocabulary effects in Software Science. *Proceedings of COMSAC 80*, (1980): 751-756.

[FREI79] Freiman, F. R. and R. E. Park. PRICE software model - version 3: an overview. *Proceedings of the IEEE-PINY Workshop on Quantitative Software Models* (October 1979): 32-41.

[FREN84]   Frenkel, K. A.   Toward automating the software development cycle.   *Communications of the ACM* 28, 6 (June 1985): 578-589.

[GAFF84]   Gaffney, J. E.   Estimating the number of faults in code.   *IEEE Transactions on Software Engineering* SE-10, 4 (July 1984): 459-464.

[GILL78]   Gill, J. L.   *Design and Analysis of Experiments, Vol. 2.*   Ames, IA: The Iowa State University Press, 1978.

[GORD79]   Gordon, R. D.   Measuring improvements in program clarity.   *IEEE Transactions on Software Engineering* SE-5, 2 (March 1979): 79-90.

[GOUL74]   Gould, J. D., and P. Drongowski.   An exploratory study of computer program debugging.   *Human Factors* 16, 3 (1974): 258-277.

[GREE77]   Green, T. R. G.   Conditional program statements and their comprehensibility to professional programmers.   *Journal of Occupational Psychology,* 50 (1977): 93-109.

[GREM84]   Gremillion, L. L.   Determinants of program repair maintenance requirements.   *Communications of the ACM* 27, 8 (August 1984): 826-832.

[HALE84]   Haley, A., and S. Zweben.   Development and application of a white box approach to integration testing.   *Journal of Systems and Software* 4, 4 (November 1984): 309-315.

[HALL84]   Hall, N. R., and S. Preiser.   Combined network complexity measures,   *IBM Journal of Research and Development* (January 1984): 15-27.

[HALS77]   Halstead, M. H.   *Elements of Software Science.*   New York: Elsevier North-Holland, 1977.

[HANS78]   Hansen, W. J.   Measurement of program complexity by the pair (cyclomatic number, operator count).   *ACM SIGPLAN Notices* 13, 3 (March 1978): 29-33.

[HARR69]   Harr, J.   Programming experience for the no. 1 electronic switching system.   *Proceedings of the AFIPS Spring Joint Computer Conference* (1969).

[HENR81]   Henry, S., and D. Kafura.   Software structure metrics based on information flow.   *IEEE Transactions on Software Engineering* SE-7, 5 (September 1981): 510-518.

[HERD77]   Herd, J. R., J. N. Postak, W. E. Russell, and K. R. Stewart.   Software cost estimation study — study results.   Final Technical Report.   *RADC-TR-77-220,* Doty Associates, Inc., Rockville, MD (June 1977).

[HOLL73]   Hollander, M., and D. A. Wolfe.   *Nonparametric Statistical Methods.*   New York: John Wiley & Sons, 1973.

[IMSL82]   *The International Mathematics and Statistics Library Reference Manual.*   Houston, TX: IMSL Inc., 1982.

[JELI72]   Jelinski, Z., and P. Moranda.   Software reliability research.   In *Statistical Computer Performance Evaluation,* edited by W. Freiberger, 465-484.   New York: Academic Press, 1972.

[JENS84]   Jensen, R. W. A comparison of the Jensen and COCOMO schedule and cost estimation models. *Proceedings of International Society of Parametric Analysis* (1984), 96-106.

[JOHN83]   Johnson, M. S., ed. *Proceedings of the ACM SIGSOFT/SIGPLAN Symposium on High-Level Debugging, ACM Software Engineering Notes 8, 4* (August 1983).

[JONE79]   Jones, T. C. The limits of productivity. *Proceedings of the Joint SHARE/GUIDE/IBM Symposium* (October 1979): 77-82.

[JONE81]   Jones, T. C., ed. *Tutorial on Programming Productivity.* IEEE Catalog No. EHO 186-7, Computer Society, Los Angeles, CA (1981).

[KEMP52]   Kempthorne, O. *The Design and Analysis of Experiments.* New York: John Wiley & Sons, 1952.

[KERN74]   Kernighan, B. W., and P. J. Planger. Programming style: examples and counter examples. *ACM Computing Surveys* 6, 4 (December 1974): 303-319.

[KERN78]   Kernighan, B. W. and P. J. Plauger. *The Elements of Programming Style.* New York: McGraw-Hill, 1978.

[KNUT73]   Knuth, D. E. *The Art of Computer Programming, Vol. 3: Searching and Sorting.* Reading, MA: Addison Wesley, 1973.

[LAWR82]   Lawrence, M. J. An examination of evolution dynamics. *Proceedings of the Sixth International Conference on Software Engineering* (September 1982): 188-196.

[LIPO79]   Lipow, M. Prediction of software failures. *The Journal of Systems and Software* (1979): 71-75.

[LIPO82]   Lipow, M. Number of faults per line of code. *IEEE Transactions on Software Engineering* SE-8, 4 (July 1982): 437-439.

[LOHS84]   Lohse, J. B., and S. H. Zweben. Experimental evaluation of software design principles: an investigation into the effect of module coupling on system and modifiability. *Journal of Systems and Software* 4 (1984): 301-308.

[MART83]   Martin, E. W. Strategy for a DoD software initiative. *IEEE Computer* 16, 3 (March 1983): 52-59.

[MCCA76]   McCabe, T. J. A complexity measure. *IEEE Transactions on Software Engineering* SE-2, 4 (December 1976): 308-320.

[MILL81]   Miller, E., and W. E. Howden, eds. *Tutorial on Software Testing and Validation Techniques.* 2nd ed. IEEE Catalog No. EHO 180-0, Los Alamitos, CA: Computer Society Press (1981).

[MILL83]   Mills, H. D. *Software Productivity.* Boston: Little, Brown and Co., 1983.

[MOHA81]   Mohanty, S. N. Software cost estimation: present and future. *Software Practice and Experience* 11 (1981): 103-121.

[MOTL77] Motley, R. W., and W. D. Brooks. Statistical prediction of programming errors. *RADC-TR-77-175,* Rome Air Development Center, Griffiss AFB, NY (May 1977).

[MUSA80] Musa, J. D. Software reliability measurement. *The Journal of Systems and Software* 1, and 2 (1980): 223-241.

[MYER77] Myers, G. J. An extension to the cyclomatic measure of program complexity. *SIGPLAN Notices* 12, 10 (October 1977): 61-64.

[MYER79] Myers, G. J. *The Art of Software Testing.* New York: John Wiley & Sons, 1979.

[NELS66] Nelson, E. A. Management handbook for the estimation of computer programming costs. *AD-A648750,* Systems Development Corporation (October 31, 1966).

[NETE74] Neter, J. and W. Wasserman. *Applied Linear Statistical Models.* Homewood, IL: Irwin, 1974.

[NIE75] Nie, N. H., D. H. Bend, and C. H. Hull. *SPSS: Statistical Package for the Social Sciences.* 2nd Ed. New York: McGraw Hill, 1975.

[OGLE83] Oglesby, C. E., and J. E. Urban. The human resources task area. *IEEE Computer* 16, 11 (November 1983): 65-70.

[OTTE79] Ottenstein, L. M. Quantitative estimates of debugging requirements. *IEEE Transactions on Software Engineering* SE-5, 5 (September 1979): 504-514.

[OVIE80] Oviedo, E. I. Control flow, data flow, and program complexity. *Proceedings of the IEEE Computer Software and Applications Conference* (November 1980): 146-152.

[PADE81] Padegs, A. System/360 and beyond. *IBM J. Research and Development* 25, 5 (September 1981): 337-390.

[PARR80] Parr, F. N. An alternative to the Rayleigh curve model for software development effort. *IEEE Transactions on Software Engineering* SE-6, 3 (May 1980): 291-296.

[PAUL83] Paulsen, L. R., G. P. Fitsos, and V. Y. Shen. A metric for the identification of error-prone software modules. *TR 03.228,* IBM Santa Teresa Laboratory, San Jose, CA (June 1983).

[POTI82] Potier, D., J. L. Albin, R. Ferreol, and A. Bilodeau. Experiments with computer software complexity and reliability. *Proceedings of the Sixth International Conference on Software Engineering* (1982): 94-103.

[PUTN78] Putnam, L. H. A general empirical solution to the macro software sizing and estimating problem. *IEEE Transactions on Software Engineering* SE-4, 4 (July 1978): 345-361.

[PUTN84a] Putnam, L. H., D. T. Putnam, and L. P. Thayer. A tool for planning software projects. *The Journal of Systems and Software,* 5 (January 1984): 147-154.

[PUTN84b] Putnam, L. H. Personal correspondence (April 1984).

[PUTN84c] Putnam, L. H., and D. T. Putnam. A data verification of the software fourth power trade-off law. *Proceedings of the International Society of Parametric Analysis* 3, 1 (May 1984): 443-471.

[RADC82] Rome Air Development Center (RADC). Quality Metrics Study. *RADC-TR-80-109.* Rome, NY (1982).

[RAMA82] Ramamoorthy, C. V. and F. B. Bastani. Software reliability — status and perspectives. *IEEE Transactions on Software Engineering* SE-8, 4 (July 1982): 354-371.

[REMU80] Remus, H. Planning and measuring program implementation. *Proceedings of the Symposium on Software Engineering Environments*, Lahnstein, Germany (Gesellschaft fuer Mathematick und Datenverarbeitung), North Holland, (1980): 267-279.

[SACK68] Sackman, H., W. J. Erikson, and E. E. Grant. Exploratory experimental studies comparing online and offline programming performance. *Communications of the ACM* 11, 1 (January 1968): 3-11.

[SCHE70] Schein, E. *Organizational Psychology.* 2nd Ed. Englewood Cliffs, NJ: Prentice-Hall, 1970.

[SCHI78] Schick, G. J. and R. W. Wolverton. An analysis of competing software reliability models. *IEEE Transactions on Software Engineering* SE-4, 2 (March 1978): 104-120.

[SCHN79] Schneidewind, N. F., and H. Hoffmann. An experiment in software error data collection and analysis. *IEEE Transactions on Software Engineering* SE-5, 3 (May 1979): 276-286.

[SHEN80] Shen, V. Y., and H. E. Dunsmore. A Software Science analysis of COBOL programs. *CSD-TR-348*, Department of Computer Science, Purdue University (August 1980).

[SHEN83] Shen, V. Y., S. D. Conte, and H. E. Dunsmore. Software Science revisited: a critical analysis of the theory and its empirical support. *IEEE Transactions on Software Engineering* SE-9, 2 (March 1983): 155-165.

[SHEN85] Shen, V. Y., T. J. Yu, S. M. Thebaut, and L. R. Paulsen. Identifying error-prone software — an empirical study. *IEEE Transactions on Software Engineering* SE-11, 4 (April 1985): 317-324.

[SHEP78] Sheppard, S. B., M. A. Borst, B. Curtis, and T. Love. Predicting programmers' ability to modify software. *TR 78-388100-3*, General Electric Company (May 1978).

[SHNE77] Shneiderman, B., R. Mayer, D. McKay, and P. Heller. Experimental investigations of the utility of detailed flowcharts in programming. *Communications of the ACM* 20, 6 (June 1977): 373-381.

[SHNE84] Shneiderman, B. Response time and display rate in human performance with computers. *ACM Computing Surveys* 16, 3 (September 1984): 265-285.

[SHOO83]   Shooman, M. L. *Software Engineering.* New York: McGraw-Hill, 1983.

[SIEG56]   Siegel, S. *Nonparametric Statistics for the Behavioral Science.* McGraw-Hill Publishing Co., NY (1956).

[SIME73]   Sime, M. E., T. R. G. Green, and D. J. Guest. Psychological evaluation of two conditional constructions used in computer languages. *International Journal of Man-Machine Studies* 5, 1 (January 1973): 105-113.

[SMIT80]   Smith, C. P. A Software Science analysis of programming size. *Proceedings of the ACM National Computer Conference* (October 1980): 179-185.

[STRO67]   Stroud, J. M. The fine structure of psychological time. *Annuals of New York Academy of Science* 138, 2 (1967): 623-631.

[SZUL81]   Szulewski, P., P. Bucher, S. DeWolf, and M. Whiteworth. The measurement of Software Science parameters in software designs. *Performance Evaluation Review (ACM SIGMETRICS)* 10, 1 (1981): 89-94.

[TAUS81]   Tausworthe, R. C. Deep space network software cost estimation model. *Publication 81-7,* Jet Propulsion Laboratory, Pasadena, CA (1981).

[THAD84]   Thadhani, A. J. Factors affecting productivity during application development. *IBM Systems Journal* 23 (1984): 19-35.

[THEB83]   Thebaut, S. M. *The Saturation Effect in Large-Scale Software Development: its Impact and Control.* Ph.D. Thesis, Department of Computer Science, Purdue University, West Lafayette, IN (May 1983).

[THEB84]   Thebaut, S. M., and V. Y. Shen. An analytic resource model for large-scale software development. *Information Processing and Management* 20, 1-2 (1984): 293-315.

[TROY81]   Troy, D. A., and S. H. Zweben. Measuring the quality of structured designs. *The Journal of Systems and Software* 2 (June 1981): 113-120.

[TURN80]   Turner, J. The structure of modular programs. *Communication of the ACM* 23, 5 (May 1980): 272-277.

[VOSB84]   Vosburgh, J. *et al* Productivity factors and programming environments. *Proceedings of the Seventh International Conference on Software Engineering* (1984): 143-152.

[WALS77]   Walston, C. E., and C. P. Felix. A method of programming measurement and estimation. *IBM System Journal* 16, 1 (1977): 54-73.

[WANG84]   Wang, A. S. *The Estimation of Software Size and Effort: an Approach based on the Evolution of Software Metrics.* Ph.D. Thesis, Department of Computer Science, Purdue University (August 1984).

[WEGN80]   Wegner, P. *Programming with Ada: an introduction by measures of graduated examples.* Englewood Cliffs, NJ: Prentice-Hall, 1980.

[WEIN70]   Weinberg, G. M. *PL/1 Programming: A Manual of Style.* New York: McGraw-Hill, 1970.

[WEIS74] Weissman, L. Psychological complexity of computer programs: an experimental methodology. *ACM SIGPLAN Notices* 9, 6 (June 1974): 25-36.

[WILS72] Wilson, R. I. *Introduction to Graph Theory.* New York: Academic Press, 1972.

[WING82] Wingfield, C. G. USACSC experience with SLIM. *Report IAWAR 360-5,* U.S. Army Institute for Research in Management Information and Computer Science, Atlanta, GA (1982).

[WIRT76] Wirth, N. *Algorithms + Data Structures = Programs.* Englewood Cliffs, NJ: Prentice-Hall, 1976.

[WOLV74] Wolverton, R. W. The cost of developing large-scale software. *IEEE Transactions on Computers* C-23, 6 (1974): 615-636.

[WOOD79] Woodward, M. R., M. A. Hennell, and D. Hedley. A measure of control flow complexity in program text. *IEEE Transactions on Software Engineering* SE-5, 1 (January 1979): 45-50.

[WOOD80] Woodfield, S. N. *Enhanced Effort Estimation by Extending Basic Programming Models to Include Modularity Factors.* Ph.D. Thesis, Department of Computer Science, Purdue University (December 1980).

[WOOD81a]
Woodfield, S. N., H. E. Dunsmore, and V. Y. Shen. The effect of modularization and comments on program comprehension. *Proceedings of Fifth International Conference on Software Engineering,* (March 1981): 215-223.

[WOOD81b]
Woodfield, S. N., V. Y. Shen, and H. E. Dunsmore. A study of several metrics for programming effort. *The Journal of Systems and Software* 2, 2 (December 1981): 97-103.

[YOUR79] Yourdon, E., and L. Constantine. *Structured Design.* Englewood Cliffs, NJ: Prentice-Hall, 1979.

[YU84] Yu, T. J., and B. A. Nejmeh. Software metrics data collection. *CSD-TR-421,* Department of Computer Science, Purdue University, West Lafayette, IN (October 1984).

[YU85] Yu, T. J. *The Static and Dynamic Models of Software Defects and Reliability.* Ph.D. Thesis, Department of Computer Science, Purdue University, West Lafayette, IN (December 1985).

[ZELK78] Zelkowitz, M. V. Perspectives on software engineering. *ACM Computing Surveys* 10, 2 (1978): 197-216.

[ZOLN81] Zolnowski, J. C., and D. B. Simmons. Taking the measure of program complexity. *Proceedings of the National Computer Conference* (1981): 329-336.

Appendix A

Table A.1 Critical Values for Two-tailed t-distribution

df	.50	.20	.10	.05	.02	.01
1	1.0000	3.0777	6.3138	12.7062	31.8207	63.6574
2	0.8165	1.8856	2.9200	4.3027	6.9646	9.9248
3	0.7649	1.6377	2.3534	3.1824	4.5407	5.8409
4	0.7407	1.5332	2.1318	2.7764	3.7469	4.6041
5	0.7267	1.4759	2.0150	2.5706	3.3649	4.0322
6	0.7176	1.4398	1.9432	2.4469	3.1427	3.7074
7	0.7111	1.4149	1.8946	2.3646	2.9980	3.4995
8	0.7064	1.3968	1.8595	2.3060	2.8965	3.3554
9	0.7027	1.3830	1.8331	2.2622	2.8214	3.2498
10	0.6998	1.3722	1.8125	2.2281	2.7638	3.1693
11	0.6974	1.3634	1.7959	2.2010	2.7181	3.1058
12	0.6955	1.3562	1.7823	2.1788	2.6810	3.0545
13	0.6938	1.3502	1.7709	2.1604	2.6503	3.0123
14	0.6924	1.3450	1.7613	2.1448	2.6245	2.9768
15	0.6912	1.3406	1.7531	2.1315	2.6025	2.9467
16	0.6901	1.3368	1.7459	2.1199	2.5835	2.9208
17	0.6892	1.3334	1.7396	2.1098	2.5669	2.8982
18	0.6884	1.3304	1.7341	2.1009	2.5524	2.8784
19	0.6876	1.3277	1.7291	2.0930	2.5395	2.8609
20	0.6870	1.3253	1.7247	2.0860	2.5280	2.8453
21	0.6864	1.3232	1.7207	2.0796	2.5177	2.8314
22	0.6858	1.3212	1.7171	2.0739	2.5083	2.8188
23	0.6853	1.3195	1.7139	2.0687	2.4999	2.8073
24	0.6848	1.3178	1.7109	2.0639	2.4922	2.7969
25	0.6844	1.3163	1.7081	2.0595	2.4851	2.7874
26	0.6840	1.3150	1.7056	2.0555	2.4786	2.7787
27	0.6837	1.3137	1.7033	2.0518	2.4727	2.7707
28	0.6834	1.3125	1.7011	2.0484	2.4671	2.7633
29	0.6830	1.3114	1.6991	2.0452	2.4620	2.7564
30	0.6828	1.3104	1.6973	2.0423	2.4573	2.7500
31	0.6825	1.3095	1.6955	2.0395	2.4528	2.7440
32	0.6822	1.3086	1.6939	2.0369	2.4487	2.7385
33	0.6820	1.3077	1.6924	2.0345	2.4448	2.7333
34	0.6818	1.3070	1.6909	2.0322	2.4411	2.7284
35	0.6816	1.3062	1.6896	2.0301	2.4377	2.7238
36	0.6814	1.3055	1.6883	2.0281	2.4345	2.7195
37	0.6812	1.3049	1.6871	2.0262	2.4314	2.7154
38	0.6810	1.3042	1.6860	2.0244	2.4286	2.7116
39	0.6808	1.3036	1.6849	2.0227	2.4258	2.7079
40	0.6807	1.3031	1.6839	2.0211	2.4233	2.7045
41	0.6805	1.3025	1.6829	2.0195	2.4208	2.7012
42	0.6804	1.3020	1.6820	2.0181	2.4185	2.6981
43	0.6802	1.3016	1.6811	2.0167	2.4163	2.6951
44	0.6801	1.3011	1.6802	2.0154	2.4141	2.6923
45	0.6800	1.3006	1.6794	2.0141	2.4121	2.6896

Adapted from Handbook of Statistical Tables, by Owen, D.B., Reading, MA: Addison/Wesley, 1962.

df	.25	.10	.05	.025	.01	.005
1	1.323	2.706	3.841	5.024	6.635	7.879
2	2.773	4.605	5.991	7.378	9.210	10.597
3	4.108	6.251	7.815	9.348	11.345	12.838
4	5.385	7.779	9.488	11.143	13.277	14.860
5	6.626	9.236	11.071	12.833	15.086	16.750
6	7.841	10.645	12.592	14.449	16.812	18.548
7	9.037	12.017	14.067	16.013	18.475	20.278
8	10.219	13.362	15.507	17.535	20.090	21.955
9	11.389	14.684	16.919	19.023	21.666	23.589
10	12.549	15.987	18.307	20.483	23.209	25.188
11	13.701	17.275	19.675	21.920	24.725	26.757
12	14.845	18.549	21.026	23.337	26.217	28.299
13	15.984	19.812	22.362	24.736	27.688	29.819
14	17.117	21.064	23.685	26.119	29.141	31.319
15	18.245	22.307	24.996	27.488	30.578	32.801
16	19.369	23.542	26.296	28.845	32.000	34.267
17	20.489	24.769	27.587	30.191	33.409	35.718
18	21.605	25.989	28.869	31.526	34.805	37.156
19	22.718	27.204	30.144	32.852	36.191	38.582
20	23.828	28.412	31.410	34.170	37.566	39.997
21	24.935	29.615	32.671	35.479	38.932	41.401
22	26.039	30.813	33.924	36.781	40.289	42.796
23	27.141	32.007	35.172	38.076	41.638	44.181
24	28.241	33.196	36.415	39.364	42.980	45.559
25	29.339	34.382	37.652	40.646	44.314	46.928
26	30.435	35.563	38.885	41.923	45.642	48.290
27	31.528	36.741	40.113	43.194	46.963	49.645
28	32.620	37.916	41.337	44.461	48.278	50.993
29	33.711	39.087	42.557	45.722	49.588	52.336
30	34.800	40.256	43.773	46.979	50.892	53.672
31	35.887	41.422	44.985	48.232	52.191	55.003
32	36.973	42.585	46.194	49.480	53.486	56.328
33	38.058	43.745	47.400	50.725	54.776	57.648
34	39.141	44.903	48.602	51.966	56.061	58.964
35	40.223	46.059	49.802	53.203	57.342	60.275
36	41.304	47.212	50.998	54.437	58.619	61.581
37	42.383	48.363	52.192	55.668	59.892	62.883
38	43.462	49.513	53.384	56.896	61.162	64.181
39	44.539	50.660	54.572	58.120	62.428	65.476
40	45.616	51.805	55.758	59.342	63.691	66.766
41	46.692	52.949	56.942	60.561	64.950	68.053
42	47.766	54.090	58.124	61.777	66.206	69.336
43	48.840	55.230	59.304	62.990	67.459	70.616
44	49.913	56.369	60.481	64.201	68.710	71.893
45	50.985	57.505	61.656	65.410	69.957	73.166

Table A.2   Critical Values for the Mann-Whitney
Two Sample Statistic

n1	n2	.002	.01	.02	.05	.10	.20
3	2	-	-	-	-	-	0
	3	-	-	-	-	0	1
4	2	-	-	-	-	-	0
	3	-	-	-	-	0	1
	4	-	-	-	0	1	3
5	2	-	-	-	-	0	1
	3	-	-	-	0	1	2
	4	-	-	0	1	2	4
	5	-	0	1	2	4	5
6	2	-	-	-	-	0	1
6	3	-	-	-	1	2	3
	4	-	0	1	2	3	5
	5	-	1	2	3	5	7
	6	-	2	3	5	7	9
7	2	-	-	-	-	0	1
7	3	-	-	0	1	2	4
	4	-	0	1	3	4	6
	5	-	1	3	5	6	8
	6	0	3	4	6	8	11
	7	1	4	6	8	11	13
8	2	-	-	-	0	1	2
	3	-	-	0	2	3	5
	4	-	1	2	4	5	7
	5	0	2	4	6	8	10
	6	1	4	6	8	10	13
8	7	2	6	7	10	13	16
	8	4	7	9	13	15	19
9	1	-	-	-	-	-	0
	2	-	-	-	0	1	2
	3	-	0	1	2	4	5
9	4	-	1	3	4	6	9
	5	1	3	5	7	9	12
	6	2	5	7	10	12	15
	7	3	7	9	12	15	18
	8	5	9	11	15	18	22
9	9	7	11	14	17	21	25
10	1	-	-	-	-	-	0
	2	-	-	-	0	1	3
	3	-	0	1	3	4	6
	4	0	2	3	5	7	10

Adapted from Handbook of Statistical Tables, by Owen, D.B., Reading, MA:
Addison/Wesley, 1962.

n1	n2	.002	.01	.02	.05	.10	.20
10	5	1	4	6	8	11	13
	6	3	6	8	11	14	17
	7	5	9	11	14	17	21
	8	6	11	13	17	20	24
	9	8	13	16	20	24	28
10	10	10	16	19	23	27	32
11	1	-	-	-	-	-	0
	2	-	-	-	0	1	3
	3	-	0	1	3	5	7
	4	0	2	4	6	8	11
11	5	2	5	7	9	12	15
	6	4	7	9	13	16	19
	7	6	10	12	16	19	23
	8	8	13	15	19	23	27
	9	10	16	18	23	27	31
11	10	12	18	22	26	31	36
	11	15	21	25	30	34	40
12	1	-	-	-	-	-	0
	2	-	-	-	1	2	4
	3	-	1	2	4	5	8
12	4	0	3	5	7	9	12
	5	2	6	8	11	13	17
	6	4	9	11	14	17	21
	7	7	12	14	18	21	26
	8	9	15	17	22	26	30
12	9	12	18	21	26	30	35
	10	14	21	24	29	34	39
	11	17	24	28	33	38	44
	12	20	27	31	37	42	49
13	1	-	-	-	-	-	0
13	2	-	-	0	1	2	4
	3	-	1	2	4	6	9
	4	1	3	5	8	10	13
	5	3	7	9	12	15	18
	6	5	10	12	16	19	23
13	7	8	13	16	20	24	28
	8	11	17	20	24	28	33
	9	14	20	23	28	33	38
	10	17	24	27	33	37	43
	11	20	27	31	37	42	48

(continued)

n1	n2	.002	.01	.02	.05	.10	.20
13	12	23	31	35	41	47	53
	13	26	34	39	45	51	58
14	1	-	-	-	-	-	0
	2	-	-	0	1	3	4
	3	-	1	2	5	7	10
14	4	1	4	6	9	11	15
	5	3	7	10	13	16	20
	6	6	11	13	17	21	25
	7	9	15	17	22	26	31
	8	12	18	22	26	31	36
14	9	15	22	26	31	36	41
	10	19	26	30	36	41	47
	11	22	30	34	40	46	52
	12	25	34	38	45	51	58
	13	29	38	43	50	56	63
14	14	32	42	47	55	61	69
15	1	-	-	-	-	-	0
	2	-	-	0	1	3	5
	3	-	2	3	5	7	10
	4	1	5	7	10	12	16
15	5	4	8	11	14	18	22
	6	7	12	15	19	23	27
	7	10	16	19	24	28	33
	8	14	20	24	29	33	39
	9	17	24	28	34	39	45
15	10	21	29	33	39	44	51
	11	24	33	37	44	50	57
	12	28	37	42	49	55	63
	13	32	42	47	54	61	68
	14	36	46	51	59	66	74
15	15	40	51	56	64	72	80
16	1	-	-	-	-	-	0
	2	-	-	0	1	3	5
	3	-	2	3	6	8	11
	4	2	5	7	11	14	17
16	5	5	9	12	15	19	23
	6	8	13	16	21	25	29
	7	11	18	21	26	30	36
	8	15	22	26	31	36	42
	9	19	27	31	37	42	48

n1	n2	.002	.01	.02	.05	.10	.20
16	10	23	31	36	42	48	54
	11	27	36	41	47	54	61
	12	31	41	46	53	60	67
	13	35	45	51	59	65	74
	14	39	50	56	64	71	80
16	15	43	55	61	70	77	86
	16	48	60	66	75	83	93
17	1	-	-	-	-	-	0
	2	-	-	0	2	3	6
	3	0	2	4	6	9	12
17	4	2	6	8	11	15	18
	5	5	10	13	17	20	25
	6	9	15	18	22	26	31
	7	13	19	23	28	33	38
	8	17	24	28	34	39	45
17	9	21	29	33	39	45	52
	10	25	34	38	45	51	58
	11	29	39	44	51	57	65
	12	34	44	49	57	64	72
	13	38	49	55	63	70	79
17	14	43	54	60	69	77	85
	15	47	60	66	75	83	92
	16	52	65	71	81	89	99
	17	57	70	77	87	96	106
18	1	-	-	-	-	-	0
	2	-	-	0	2	4	6
	3	0	2	4	7	9	13
	4	3	6	9	12	16	20
	5	6	11	14	18	22	27
	6	10	16	19	24	28	34
18	7	14	21	24	30	35	41
	8	18	26	30	36	41	48
	9	23	31	36	42	48	55
	10	27	37	41	48	55	62
	11	32	42	47	55	61	69
18	12	37	47	53	61	68	77
	13	42	53	59	67	75	84
	14	46	58	65	74	82	91
	15	51	64	70	80	88	98
	16	56	70	76	86	95	106

(continued)

n1	n2	.002	.01	.02	.05	.10	.20
18	17	61	75	82	93	102	113
	18	66	81	88	99	109	120
19	1	-	-	-	-	0	1
	2	-	0	1	2	4	7
	3	0	3	4	7	10	14
19	4	3	7	9	13	17	21
	5	7	12	15	19	23	28
	6	11	17	20	25	30	36
	7	15	22	26	32	37	43
	8	20	28	32	38	44	51
19	9	25	33	38	45	51	58
	10	29	39	44	52	58	66
	11	34	45	50	58	65	73
	12	40	51	56	65	72	81
	13	45	57	63	72	80	89
19	14	50	63	69	78	87	97
	15	55	69	75	85	94	104
	16	60	74	82	92	101	112
	17	66	81	88	99	109	120
	18	71	87	94	106	116	128
19	19	77	93	101	113	123	135
20	1	-	-	-	-	0	1
	2	-	0	1	2	4	7
	3	0	3	5	8	11	15
	4	3	8	10	14	18	22
20	5	7	13	16	20	25	30
	6	12	18	22	27	32	38
	7	16	24	28	34	39	46
	8	21	30	34	41	47	54
	9	26	36	40	48	54	62
20	10	32	42	47	55	62	70
	11	37	48	53	62	69	78
	12	42	54	60	69	77	86
	13	48	60	67	76	84	94
	14	54	67	73	83	92	102
20	15	59	73	80	90	100	110
	16	65	79	87	98	107	119
	17	70	86	93	105	115	127
	18	76	92	100	112	123	135
	19	82	99	107	119	130	143
	20	88	105	114	127	138	151

Table A.3   Critical Values for the Product Moment
Correlation Coefficient

n	.20	.10	.05	.02	.01
3	0.9511	0.9877	0.9969	0.9995	0.9999
4	0.8000	0.9000	0.9500	0.9800	0.9900
5	0.6870	0.8054	0.8783	0.9343	0.9587
6	0.6084	0.7293	0.8114	0.8822	0.9172
7	0.5509	0.6694	0.7545	0.8329	0.8745
8	0.5067	0.6215	0.7067	0.7887	0.8343
9	0.4716	0.5822	0.6664	0.7498	0.7977
10	0.4428	0.5493	0.6319	0.7155	0.7646
11	0.4187	0.5214	0.6021	0.6851	0.7348
12	0.3981	0.4973	0.5760	0.6581	0.7079
13	0.3802	0.4762	0.5529	0.6339	0.6835
14	0.3646	0.4575	0.5324	0.6120	0.6614
15	0.3507	0.4409	0.5140	0.5923	0.6411
16	0.3383	0.4259	0.4973	0.5742	0.6226
17	0.3271	0.4124	0.4822	0.5577	0.6055
18	0.3170	0.4000	0.4683	0.5426	0.5897
19	0.3077	0.3887	0.4555	0.5285	0.5751
20	0.2992	0.3783	0.4438	0.5155	0.5614
21	0.2914	0.3687	0.4329	0.5034	0.5487
22	0.2841	0.3598	0.4227	0.4921	0.5368
23	0.2774	0.3515	0.4132	0.4815	0.5256
24	0.2711	0.3438	0.4044	0.4716	0.5151
25	0.2653	0.3365	0.3961	0.4622	0.5052
30	0.2407	0.3061	0.3610	0.4226	0.4629
35	0.2220	0.2826	0.3338	0.3916	0.4296
40	0.2070	0.2638	0.3120	0.3665	0.4026
45	0.1947	0.2483	0.2940	0.3457	0.3801
50	0.1843	0.2353	0.2787	0.3281	0.3610
60	0.1678	0.2144	0.2542	0.2997	0.3301
70	0.1550	0.1982	0.2352	0.2776	0.3060
80	0.1448	0.1852	0.2199	0.2597	0.2864
90	0.1364	0.1745	0.2072	0.2449	0.2702
100	0.1292	0.1654	0.1966	0.2324	0.2565

Adapted from Handbook of Statistical Tables, by Owen, D.B., Reading, MA:
Addison/Wesley, 1962.

Table A.4   Critical Values for the Spearman Rank
Correlation Coefficient

n	.20	.10	.05	.02	.002
4	.8000	.8000			
5	.7000	.8000	.9000	.9000	
6	.6000	.7714	.8286	.8857	.9429
7	.5357	.6786	.7450	.8571	.8929
8	.5000	.6190	.7143	.8095	.8571
9	.4667	.5833	.6833	.7667	.8167
10	.4424	.5515	.6364	.7333	.7818
11	.4182	.5273	.6091	.7000	.7455
12	.3986	.4965	.5804	.6713	.7273
13	.3791	.4780	.5549	.6429	.6978
14	.3626	.4593	.5341	.6220	.6747
15	.3500	.4429	.5179	.6000	.6536
16	.3382	.4265	.5000	.5824	.6324
17	.3260	.4118	.4853	.5637	.6152
18	.3148	.3994	.4716	.5480	.5975
19	.3070	.3895	.4579	.5333	.5825
20	.2977	.3789	.4451	.5203	.5684
21	.2909	.3688	.4351	.5078	.5545
22	.2829	.3597	.4241	.4963	.5426
23	.2767	.3518	.4150	.4852	.5306
24	.2704	.3435	.4061	.4748	.5200
25	.2646	.3362	.3977	.4654	.5100
26	.2588	.3299	.3894	.4564	.5002
27	.2540	.3236	.3822	.4481	.4915
28	.2490	.3175	.3749	.4401	.4828
29	.2443	.3113	.3685	.4320	.4744
30	.2400	.3059	.3620	.4251	.4665

Table A.5   Critical Values for the Chi Square Distribution

df	.995	.99	.975	.95	.90	.75
1	-	-	0.001	0.004	0.016	0.102
2	0.010	0.020	0.051	0.103	0.211	0.575
3	0.072	0.115	0.216	0.352	0.584	1.213
4	0.207	0.297	0.484	0.711	1.064	1.923
5	0.412	0.554	0.831	1.145	1.610	2.675
6	0.676	0.872	1.237	1.635	2.204	3.455
7	0.989	1.239	1.690	2.167	2.833	4.255
8	1.344	1.646	2.180	2.733	3.490	5.071
9	1.735	2.088	2.700	3.325	4.168	5.899
10	2.156	2.558	3.247	3.940	4.865	6.737
11	2.603	3.053	3.816	4.575	5.578	7.584
12	3.074	3.571	4.404	5.226	6.304	8.438
13	3.565	4.107	5.009	5.892	7.042	9.299
14	4.075	4.660	5.629	6.571	7.790	10.165
15	4.601	5.229	6.262	7.261	8.547	11.037
16	5.142	5.812	6.908	7.962	9.312	11.912
17	5.697	6.408	7.564	8.672	10.085	12.792
18	6.265	7.015	8.231	9.390	10.865	13.675
19	6.844	7.633	8.907	10.117	11.651	14.562
20	7.434	8.260	9.591	10.851	12.443	15.452
21	8.034	8.897	10.283	11.591	13.240	16.344
22	8.643	9.542	10.982	12.338	14.042	17.240
23	9.260	10.196	11.689	13.091	14.848	18.137
24	9.886	10.856	12.401	13.848	15.659	19.037
25	10.520	11.524	13.120	14.611	16.473	19.939
26	11.160	12.198	13.844	15.379	17.292	20.843
27	11.808	12.879	14.573	16.151	18.114	21.749
28	12.461	13.565	15.308	16.928	18.939	22.657
29	13.121	14.257	16.047	17.708	19.768	23.567
30	13.787	14.954	16.791	18.493	20.599	24.478
31	14.458	15.655	17.539	19.281	21.434	25.390
32	15.134	16.362	18.291	20.072	22.271	26.304
33	15.815	17.074	19.047	20.867	23.110	27.219
34	16.501	17.789	19.806	21.664	23.952	28.136
35	17.192	18.509	20.569	22.465	24.797	29.054
36	17.887	19.233	21.336	23.269	25.643	29.973
37	18.586	19.960	22.106	24.075	26.492	30.893
38	19.289	20.691	22.878	24.884	27.343	31.815
39	19.996	21.426	23.654	25.695	28.196	32.737
40	20.707	22.164	24.433	26.509	29.051	33.660
41	21.421	22.906	25.215	27.326	29.907	34.585
42	22.138	23.650	25.999	28.144	30.765	35.510
43	22.859	24.398	26.785	28.965	31.625	36.436
44	23.584	25.148	27.575	29.787	32.487	37.363
45	24.311	25.901	28.366	30.612	33.350	38.291

Adapted from Handbook of Statistical Tables, by Owen, D.B., Reading, MA:
Addison/Wesley, 1962

Appendix B

Table B.1 Commercial Data Used in This Book

Set	No. of Projects	Source
A	63	Boehm's book [BOEH81]
B	33	Belady-Lehman [BELA79]
C	40	Industry (anonymous)
D	19	NASA/Goddard [BAIL81]
E	17	Yourdon 78-80 Survey
F	15	U.S. Army [WING82]

Table B.2   Set B· The Belady-Lehman Data [BELA79]

No.	S (KLOC)	T (months)	E (PM)
1	30.000	12	77
2	11.164	8	51
3	17.052	9	46
4	140.000	31	462
5	47.377	13	241
6	229.000	36	1665
7	401.099	24	1022
8	712.362	28	2176
9	58.540	28	723
10	80.990	12	527
11	94.000	42	673
12	18.775	32	199
13	14.390	17	227
14	35.057	19	71
15	11.122	8	43
16	6.092	8	47
17	5.342	4	14
18	12.000	8	60
19	19.000	10	50
20	25.271	12	169
21	20.000	14	106
22	12.000	9	57
23	7.000	9	195
24	13.545	17	112
25	14.779	7	67
26	30.000	68	1107
27	69.200	35	852
28	486.834	67	11758
29	220.999	61	2440
30	128.330	10	673
31	32.026	36	136
32	15.363	7	37
33	4.747	3	10

Table B.3   Set D: The NASA/Goddard Data [BAIL81]

No.	S_n (KLOC)	S_{tot} (KLOC)	S_e (KLOC)	T (months)	E (PM)
1	84.729	111.868	90.157	15.8	125.5
2	43.955	55.237	46.211	20.0	104.0
3	45.345	50.911	46.458	13.2	85.6
4	49.316	75.393	54.531	12.5	98.4
5	20.075	75.420	31.144	8.7	36.7
6	12.227	14.863	12.754	14.3	20.5
7	9.568	14.282	10.511	14.3	11.2
8	18.680	32.822	21.508	14.3	30.9
9	2.451	5.497	3.060	14.3	7.5
10	4.160	4.525	4.233	6.9	9.8
11	7.350	9.727	7.825	14.3	7.9
12	2.052	2.052	2.052	14.3	5.4
13	4.921	5.204	4.978	4.1	9.1
14	76.883	85.369	78.580	17.4	107.0
15	9.627	10.172	9.736	15.6	16.9
16	11.878	14.765	12.455	8.3	25.9
17	45.004	67.325	49.468	20.4	139.5
18	44.644	66.266	48.968	19.0	132.9
19	10.822	17.271	12.112	16.3	33.3

Table B.4   Set E: The Yourdon 78-80 Survey Data

No.	S (KLOC)	T (months)	E (PM)
1	40.00	35.20	81.8
2	70.00	24.10	142.0
3	132.20	32.00	116.4
4	23.00	16.40	21.6
5	34.50	16.40	130.2
6	14.00	15.10	29.7
7	25.00	16.90	61.6
8	52.10	16.00	21.9
9	7.10	11.30	20.5
10	25.90	16.00	13.4
11	16.30	14.10	14.2
12	17.40	11.60	11.9
13	33.90	12.30	39.9
14	55.80	27.00	16.9
15	21.00	12.40	23.7
16	7.58	9.97	6.1
17	8.78	19.00	28.6

Table B.5   Set F: The U.S. Army Data [WING82]

No.	S (KLOC)	T (months)	E (PM)
1	85.0	35	1176
2	450.0	34	5112
3	341.0	40	4992
4	163.0	18	1908
5	200.0	24	2124
6	80.0	24	288
7	200.0	24	2064
8	126.5	17	1248
9	250.0	38	576
10	75.0	12	336
11	85.0	12	240
12	49.8	30	852
13	324.0	24	1680
14	173.5	33	444
15	100.0	34	588

Illustration Credits

Figure 5.1   Copyright 1977, International Business Machines Corporation. Re-rendered with permission from C. E. Walston and C. P. Felix, "A method of programming measurement and estimation," *IBM Systems Journal* 16, 1 (1977.)

Figure 7.3   Copyright 1979, Institute of Electrical and Electronics Engineers. Re-rendered with permission from A. R. Feuer and E. B. Fowlkes, "Some results from an empirical study of computer software," *Proceedings of the Fourth International Conference on Software Engineering* (1979.)

Index

As Benjamin/Cummings accelerates its exciting publishing venture in the Computer Science and Information Systems, we'd like to offer you the opportunity to learn about our new titles in advance. **If you'd like to be placed on our mailing list** to receive pre-publication notices about our expanding Computer Science and Information Systems list, just fill out this card **completely** and return it to us, postage paid. Thank you.

NAME_____

STREET ADDRESS_____

CITY_____STATE_____ZIP_____

BUSINESS_____

ASSOCIATION AFFILIATION:_____

_____

TELEPHONE (_____) _____

AREAS OF INTEREST:

41 ☐ Operating Systems (Please specify)_____

_____

42 ☐ Programming Languages (Please specify)_____

_____

43 ☐ Systems Languages (Please specify)_____

_____

44 ☐ Artificial Intelligence
45 ☐ Computer Graphics
46 ☐ Software Documentation
47 ☐ Systems Analysis and Design
48 ☐ Systems Architecture
49 ☐ Data Communications
50 ☐ Software Engineering
51 ☐ Microcomputer Literacy

52 ☐ Other (Please specify)_____

_____

☐ I am writing.
   Area:_____

BUSINESS REPLY CARD
FIRST CLASS PERMIT NO. 450   MENLO PARK, CA 94025

Postage will be paid by Addressee:

Product Manager

**The Benjamin/Cummings
Publishing Company, Inc.®**

2727 Sand Hill Road
Menlo Park, California 94025

Notation used in this Book

α	Significance level
β	Stroud number
C	Communication paths (Thebaut)
C	Cost matrix (Wolverton)
C	Technology factor (Putnam)
$\hat{C}$	Estimated technology factor
C_{bt}	Basic technology constant
C_R	Complexity
C_{te}	Effective technology constant
CF	Control flow complexity
CM	Coding modification
CMH	Cumulative number of modules
CSR	Component Status Report
CYC	Cyclomatic Complexity
D	Difficulty metric (Putnam, $D = K/T^2$)
D	Difficulty metric (Halstead, $D = \dfrac{\eta_1}{2} \times \dfrac{N_2}{\eta_2}$)
df	Degrees of freedom
DF	Data flow complexity
DE	Decision count
DM	Design modification
e	Edges
E	Actual development effort in programmer months
$\hat{E}$	Predicted (estimated) development effort
E_P	Programming effort
E_C	Coordinating effort
EC_i	Effort complexity class
H_0	Null hypothesis
H_i	High level characteristic
I	Productivity index
I^*	Projected productivity index
IM	Integration modification
K	Total life cycle effort (Putnam)
$\hat{K}$	Predicted (estimated) total life cycle effort
λ	Number of predicates
L	Program level (Halstead)
L	Productivity in LOC/programmer-month
L_{group}	Group productivity
LV	Live variables
m_i	Number of primitive characteristics
M_R	System size
$m(X)$	Cost driver multipliers
MH_R	Number of modules changed
MRE	Magnitude of the relative error ($|RE|$)
$\overline{MRE}$	Mean magnitude of the relative error
η_1	Number of unique operators